D0848814

MODERN DRAMA AND GERMAN CLASSICISM

MODERN DRAMA AND GERMAN CLASSICISM

Renaissance from Lessing to Brecht

Benjamin Bennett

CORNELL UNIVERSITY PRESS

Ithaca and London

Cornell University Press gratefully acknowledges a grant from the Andrew
W. Mellon Foundation that aided in bringing this book to publication.

First published 1979 by Cornell University Press.
Published in the United Kingdom by Cornell University Press Ltd.,
2–4 Brook Street, London W1Y 1AA.

International Standard Book Number 0-8014-1189-0
Library of Congress Catalog Card Number 79-14644

Printed in the United States of America

This book is dedicated to two dead men, emeritissimi, at a stroke, of faculties both known and undiscovered, the one a Renaissance penguin, the other human in his parts, but an ancient charlatan for it. That they appear thus redisguised on this page (though not from any who knew them) corresponds to their neither having left, in writing, anything remotely recognizable as himself. I take this to have been free choice, guided not by a contempt for historical immortality, but by an understanding of it.

Acknowledgments

The writing of this book was made possible by a Summer Stipend from the National Endowment for the Humanities, a Fellowship from the American Council of Learned Societies, and a Sesquicentennial Associateship from the Center for Advanced Studies at the University of Virginia. For advice and criticism I am grateful to Ruth K. Angress, A. James Arnold, Stephen L. Baehr, Lilian Hoverland, Marilyn Johns, Wm. A. Little, Margareta Mattsson, David H. Miles, Frank G. Ryder, and Walter H. Sokel, as well as to the editors and consultants at Cornell University Press. If graduate students find the book useful, thanks will be due in part to criticisms of the manuscript by the students in my drama-and-theory seminar, Thomas M. Heine, Michael W. Jennings, Alan C. Leidner, Michael M. Morton, and Steven C. Pippin. For assistance in preparing the typescript I am indebted to Joyce Garver and Lorraine Indermill. I am also indebted to members of my family, but in ways I will not attempt to define. English translations used below are my own unless otherwise noted, and the abbreviations in the footnotes are those of the Modern Language Association.

For permission to use copyrighted material I am grateful to the following: Familiari Pirandello–Rome to quote from *Opere di Luigi Pirandello*, 4th edition—Mondadori Editore; Hermann Luchterhand Verlag to quote from Adam Müller, *Kritische, ästhetische und philosophische Schriften* (1967); Suhrkamp Verlag and also Random House, Inc., and Eyre Methuen Ltd, to quote, and use my own translations from, Bertolt Brecht, *Gesammelte Werke,* "Werkausgabe" (1967), copyright in the original © 1967 Suhrkamp Verlag, copyright in the translation © Stefan S. Brecht 1979; The Society of Authors on behalf of the Bernard Shaw Estate to quote from Bernard Shaw, *Collected Plays with Their Prefaces* (1970–1974); Verlag Ullstein GmbH to quote from Gerhart Hauptmann, *Sämtliche Werke,* Centenar-Ausgabe (1962), © Verlag Ullstein GmbH 1962; Walter de Gruyter & Co. to quote from the critical edition of Nietzsche's *Werke,* ed. Colli and Montinari; and the Lessing Society, to use parts of my article "Reason, Error and the Shape of History," which appeared in *The Lessing Yearbook,* 9 (1977).

Benjamin Bennett

Charlottesville, Virginia

Contents

Abbreviations

DT	Dantons Tod (Büchner)
DVLG	Deutsche Vierteljahrsschrift für Literaturwissenschaft und Geistesgeschichte
ECS	Eighteenth-Century Studies
Eg.	Egmont (Goethe)
ELWIU	Essays in Literature (Western Illinois University)
GL&L	German Life & Letters
GQ	The German Quarterly
GRM	Germanisch-romanische Monatsschrift
HD	Hamburgische Dramaturgie (Lessing)
JDSG	Jahrbuch der deutschen Schillergesellschaft
JEGP	Journal of English and Germanic Philology
KO	Kleines Organon für das Theater (Brecht)
L	Laokoon (Lessing)
NA	Schillers Werke, National-Ausgabe (Weimar, 1943–)
NRF	Nouvelle Revue Française
PMLA	Publications of the Modern Language Association
SA	Schillers Sämtliche Werke, Säkular-Ausgabe, 16 vols. (Stuttgart and Berlin, 1904)
WA	Goethes Werke, "Weimarer Ausgabe," 143 vols. (Weimar, 1887–1918)
WW	Wirkendes Wort

MODERN DRAMA AND
GERMAN CLASSICISM

Introduction

The discussion of "movements," as applied to German literature of the eighteenth and nineteenth centuries, has produced much disagreement, for which there are obvious reasons. The concept of a movement by nature fails to account for the uniqueness of any particular work. When a critic becomes excited about the work or author he is submerged in, therefore, part of his excitement, part of the feeling that his text has afforded him a glimpse of the true and universal, tends to relieve itself as resentment against the coolness of the literary historian who appears merely to classify—say, *Faust* as a "Romantic drama," or Stifter as a "Biedermeier" figure. Thus a typically unresolvable scholarly dispute about definitions is born. If we consider, in addition, that the historical discussion of German literature from the late eighteenth century on involves not only the difficult idea of Romanticism but also an idea of "Classicism" based mainly on a selection from the work of only two authors, Goethe and Schiller, then we need look no further for sources of terminological discomfort.

There is, however, at least one other important reason for this discomfort. The terms customarily used to describe movements in German literature of the last two centuries do not give an adequate sense for the development of *drama*. The *Sturm und Drang*—despite its name—is quite well defined. It has an acknowledged canon of works, all written within a relatively short time; many of the authors were in contact with one another; and the defining characteristics of the movement, including certain features of dramatic form, appear to be both intentional and artistically essential where they occur in practice. Even the transition from *Sturm und Drang* to "Classicism," in Goethe's and Schiller's apparent repudiation of tendencies in their own earlier writings, can be located quite exactly as a historical phenomenon, and involves a fairly clear development in dramatic form.

But here we begin to experience difficulty. How shall we define Classical German drama without reducing the canon to so small a number of works that the idea of a movement becomes inappropriate? Or shall we look not for works but merely for a collection of disembodied "Classical" characteristics in works which as wholes do not deserve the name? And how shall we learn anything from the distinction between Classical and Romantic, when the very idea of Romanticism (at least in most treatments of it) tends to focus not upon drama, but upon the inwardly expansive form of lyric poetry and the outwardly expansive form of the novel? "The Romantic movement, as a whole," says Raymond Williams, "produced one line of great drama, from *Faust* to *Peer Gynt* and beyond."[1] But even supposing that the obvious connection between these two works constitutes a "line," and even if we add the ungeometrical scribble represented by the Romantically ironic dramas of Tieck, Brentano, and Grabbe, still, once we have set these over against the tight circle of unquestionably Classical German dramas, where does this leave Heinrich von Kleist, not to mention certain important works of Goethe and Schiller themselves? Shall we be content to identify the Classical and Romantic "elements" in Kleist's plays—thus suggesting, whether we say so or not, that these plays lack their own artistic coherence?

And then, when we come to the distinction, or transition, between Romanticism and realism, our problems only increase, for "realistic drama" is at best a shaky concept. The theater, even when both text and stage are constructed with a view to maximum verisimilitude, will always remain a temple of artifice; what we encounter there is always an unashamed visionary intensification of reality. The reality in narrative, the believable physicalness and psychological coherence of the fiction, is imaginary, evoked inside our mind by the words we read; and although the imaginary is different from the real, it is not necessarily opposed to it. Memory, for example, is a form of imagination, and the imaginary objects of memory are presumably the continuation of real experiences, the mental reverberations of real objects; therefore it does not occur to us to conclude that an object is not real merely because it is imaginary. In a performed drama, however, the physicalness and psychological unfolding of the fiction are not imaginary but actual (i.e. exactly located by my senses, say fifty feet southwest of where I am sitting in the theater), yet at the same time artificial; and the concept of the artificial, unlike that of the imaginary, does imply a certain opposition to the real. The imaginary object, at least potentially, is a natural continuation or reverberation of the real (like memory, hence the appropriateness of the "epic preterite"), whereas the artificial object, if it resembles reality, is a deliberate counterfeit.

It seems to me, in fact, that the concept of realism, as it has developed in literary thought, is not directly applicable to drama, but belongs primarily to the study of narrative. Even if the choice of subject (avoiding fantasy and allegory) and the choice of conventions (avoiding elevated style) contribute to our sense of a work's realism, what ultimately makes the work realistic is the perceived authorial attitude. We distinguish a realistic novel from an ironic or tendentious or sentimental novel by perceiving that the author is not toying with his material or enraptured by it or using it to make a point, but rather maintains a constant and sober, yet unobtrusive, distance from it.[2] And this sort of perception we can not have with respect to a drama. The dramatist can be present in his work—he can express opinions, for example—but he cannot be present in exactly the same way as can the realistic novelist. The fiction of a novel is realized as an image in the reader's mind and so exists on the same plane as the words that evoke it; the words and the image are continuous with each other, and since we know that the words have an author, it follows that we have the sense of a governing authorial presence even in the nonverbal trappings which our own mind contributes to the fictional vision. What we "see" mentally while reading a novel is determined, strictly speaking, by our own idea of reality, but it also depends on the author's words; it can be shattered or altered or radically recolored by a mere phrase, and we receive the impression of realism when the author nevertheless remains unobtrusive. The situation in a theater, where we actually see and hear the fiction, is fundamentally different, however; the interplay of word and world and imagination does not arise in the same way, and the concept of "realism" can be applied only to the work's content.

It is a mistake, for example, to consider late nineteenth-century dramatic "naturalism" as a development of the movement of narrative realism. Realism is an essential characteristic of the works by which it is exemplified; whereas naturalism, at least in drama, is a superficial characteristic, a convenient name that has stuck but does not say anything important about any work of quality. Hauptmann could be doggedly naturalistic and uninhibitedly visionary by turns, but this shifting does not show special versatility on his part. What it shows, rather, is that consistent naturalistic style was a device he used or discarded according to the deeper requirements of the individual case, in much the same way that Goethe uses verse for *Tasso* and prose for *Egmont*. To say that *Tasso* is in verse, or that *Rose Bernd* does not violate naturalistic conventions, is to make an obvious statement, which then needs to be used as evidence for a more penetrating interpretation. To say, on the other hand, that *Der Nachsommer* is a realistic novel is to make a problematic statement which itself needs to be penetrated and explored with reference to the text.

In any event, we can be fairly certain not only about the fact, but also about the reason for the fact that German drama, from Lessing and the *Sturm und Drang* through much of the nineteenth century, shows a certain incommensurability with the usual terminology of literary movements. German drama, during this period, is the only major European drama. Most critics would not be upset by Raymond Williams' assertion, with reference to England, that "the period from 1750 to 1850 is the most barren in our dramatic history, if it is work of any lasting value we are looking for";[3] and while a French critic might perhaps not express himself so drastically, still he could not point to a succession of names like Lessing, Goethe, Schiller, Kleist, Büchner, Grillparzer, Hebbel. The customary historical terminology is for the most part pan-European, whereas the specific tradition we are concerned with is uniquely German. Hence the incongruence.

What I propose, therefore, is that we speak of a *dramatic movement* in Germany from Lessing to Nietzsche, up to the point where European drama as a whole begins its modern resurgence. German dramas and dramatic theories, from Lessing on, have far

more in common with one another than they have severally with
the various literary movements to which they are normally assigned. This epoch of German drama is thus a true movement; its
cohesiveness arises from deep common intellectual concerns.
And it is truly a dramatic movement; its intellectual concerns are
inextricably entwined with technical questions concerning drama
as a genre.

I will also call this movement a "Renaissance" and defend the
designation in several ways.[4] I will argue that German drama from
Lessing to Nietzsche, and on at least to Brecht, represents a
genuine birth, that it may be seen as the nucleus of the development of modern European drama as a whole. Of practically no
European literature could it be said that the few decades around
1900 are "barren" of drama; and while the interplay of traditions
that brings about this general re-emergence of the genre is quite
complex, it can be shown that the German movement from the few
decades around 1800 plays an extremely important part. I will
argue further that the German movement is a re-birth, that it is a
revival of dramatic form, not a revolution, that it arises from the
confrontation not with new questions but with essential questions
of the genre. Actually, I think it is possible to show a continuous
intellectual tradition from Elizabethan poetics to the dramatic
theory and practice of the eighteenth-century German Renaissance; the Germans were not merely hero-worshiping Shake-
spearasters, but rather their feeling of affinity with Shakespeare
was derived from a profound sense of their own historical situation. I do not attempt to carry out this particular argument in the
present work, but at least a few deep parallels between German
Classical and Elizabethan dramatic thought will suggest themselves as we go on. And I hope, finally, to justify the use of the
word "Renaissance" by showing, in several detailed interpretations, that the major works of the German dramatic movement are
among the most brilliantly conceived and executed in the history
of European drama. Thus it seems to me appropriate to retain the
German critical term "Classical," which I use in an expanded
sense, to refer to figures as early as Lessing and as late as Büchner.

I do not claim to advance a new dramatic theory, but I do hope
to pull together the theoretical and the historical into a single
cohesive view of modern drama. The idea of an inherent irony in
dramatic form, which occurs frequently below, has been explored,

for example, by Robert Sharpe and Bert O. States, and what I call
the paradox of detachment and involvement has been treated in
some detail by John Gassner and J. L. Styan; but none of these
writers gives any attention to the significance of German Classical
drama (in the broadened sense of the word "Classical") with respect to the ideas he develops. Indeed, to judge from two of the
very best works in English on the nature and background of
modern drama, Eric Bentley's *Playwright as Thinker* and Francis
Fergusson's *Idea of a Theater*, one would suppose that Richard
Wagner's is the most significant German achievement in the field;
and German critics, like Peter Szondi, tend to operate with rigid
categories which deny them the broader view necessary to appreciate the Europeanness of their own tradition. Exceptions are Karl S.
Guthke's two books on tragicomedy, which do give a sense for the
importance of German drama and thought in the genesis of a modern
theater. But Guthke's focus on a special dramatic type leads him
away from what seem to me the most crucial conclusions.[5]

In general, despite the continuing health of comparative literature as a discipline, despite the occasional coming into vogue of
such authors as Nietzsche, and despite the patient efforts of a
number of important English and American scholars in the field
of Romanticism, the Germans have still never really been given
their due. It is significant, for example, that not once in the text of
Northrop Frye's *Anatomy of Criticism* does the word "Lessing"
appear. I do not mean to say that Frye is ignorant of Lessing, or
that his work could have been substantially improved by reference to Lessing. My point is that the word "Lessing," for an author
and reader who recognize Lessing as their intellectual ancestor,
constitutes an extremely useful shorthand allusion to certain un-
surpassedly profound observations on the theory of genres and
the nature of drama. That Frye does not avail himself of this shorthand is symptomatic that Lessing is not ordinarily recognized as
an intellectual ancestor except by Germans. Toward correcting
this state of affairs I hope to make some contribution. Once again, I
will argue that German literature, in at least one crucial area and
at one crucial point in history, plays a leading role in the development of European literary forms, that the German dramatic
movement is not an isolated occurrence but rather the stirring of a
true Renaissance. We tend, with some justification, to see our own
century as a time of endless variety in opinion and spirit, in in-

tellectual directions and artistic forms; and this variety can be interpreted either negatively, as confusion, "the centre cannot hold," or positively, as a sign of irrepressible vitality. Yet, at least in one major area of literature, there is a center that can hold, a single powerful tradition that can be regarded as generating, or at least representing and ordering, phenomena that otherwise refuse to be grasped except one by one.

1 *Prinz Friedrich von Homburg:*
Theory in Practice

It will be useful to develop a sense for the main characteristics of the German dramatic movement before proceeding to
the historical argument that such a movement exists. Therefore
we shall begin with the interpretation of one central work which
has an exceptionally clear dramaturgical substructure, Kleist's
Prinz Friedrich von Homburg.

1

Despite the absence of any detailed theoretical essays among his
writings, Kleist does have a well-developed theory of drama,[1] and
this theory is most clearly expressed in *Prinz Friedrich.* Such
incorporation of theory into dramatic practice ought not to be
surprising, for it is quite common in the history of Western drama.
When Oedipus asks, at the beginning of the *Colonus,* "What
men's city have we come to?" the implied answer, "Athens,"
applies both to the fiction and to the real location where the play
is being performed; thus Sophocles reminds the Athenians of his
audience that they, like the Athenians in the play, will be called
upon to make a religious and philosophical decision concerning
history's greatest outrage against nature. Or we think of Euripides'
Bacchae, which Nietzsche in my opinion interprets quite correctly as a warning about certain forces inherent in the very form
of tragedy. Or we think, obviously, of the players in *Hamlet,* or of
the "Vorspiel auf dem Theater" in *Faust,* or of Camille's speech in

Dantons Tod or the "Bude" in *Woyzeck,* or of Pirandello.[2] In any event, Kleist could easily have gotten the idea of writing a drama about drama from Adam Müller, who says, "If the criticism of poetry cannot itself be a poem, then it must at least give the impression that it has tried to be one."[3] In *Prinz Friedrich,* as we shall see, Kleist actually attempts to make a "poem" out of dramatic criticism and theory.

This theoretical tendency is already present in the first scene, where the Elector, in taking the wreath and winding his chain around it, *stages a poetic vision for the Prince.* By symbols the Elector expresses the idea that heroic energy or individual freedom (the wreath) must somehow undergo a synthesis with law (the chain) and that this synthesis cannot be achieved once and for all but must remain in the distance as an object of endless desire and striving; this last is why he hands the symbol to Natalie (object of desire) and retreats with her from the eager Prince. He thus creates a symbolic dream which the Prince then misinterprets, yet still somehow fulfills.

Crucial here is the parallel between the symbolic vision presented by the Elector to the Prince and the symbolic vision presented by the play to the audience. The Elector's intended meaning, in the dream he stages, is clearly part of the meaning of the play—the idea of an eternally striven-for synthesis of free heroic energy with respect for established law. As the play progresses, therefore, we become more and more aware that the opening scene had presented us with a picture of our own situation as recipients of a symbolic vision in the theater, and Kleist thus obliges us to think about the relation of play to audience; he sets the stage for the unfolding of a theory of drama. Possibly this intention is hinted at in the word "Rampe," which occurs no less than eleven times in stage directions as well as three times in the Prince's description of his "dream" (so that the audience hears it), and which means not only "ramp" but also "footlights."[4]

Again this idea of creating *on* the stage a symbolic image *of* the stage could easily have come to Kleist from Adam Müller, who was a great admirer of irony in drama and in particular of Tieck's *Der gestiefelte Kater.* Kleist is a good deal subtler than Tieck, but Müller could still almost be talking about *Prinz Friedrich* when he says, "the poet sets up a miniature stage on the real stage and places before it a miniature audience, into whose mouths he puts the typically false and limited artistic judgments of the larger audience."[5] Even the last part of this quotation applies to Kleist's play; we shall see that the Prince's faulty interpretation of his vision in the garden is meant to reveal to us a limitation in our own relation to the work of art.

2

The many subtle psychological interpretations of *Prinz Friedrich* have given rise to a solid scholarly tradition which culminates in the challenging arguments of John Ellis.[6] But the self-generating power of this tradition has also exaggerated the psychological factors and is largely to blame for critics' having in general overlooked the central dramaturgical notions about which the play is constructed.

Prinz Friedrich is psychologically subtle but not psychologically obscure; the intentions and motives of the characters are not quite so mysterious as they have been made out to be. For example, the Elector never really entertains the notion of marrying Natalie to the Swede. In the first place, he has not said a word to Natalie herself; otherwise she would surely at least hint at her awareness of the situation when she pleads for the Prince's life, especially when she makes a point of renouncing her own informal betrothal to him (1083, 1085). And that the Elector would seriously consider disposing arbitrarily of her future without even informing her (indeed, it is not at all clear that he has the legal right to do this)[7] is inconceivable unless we resolutely disbelieve every word he says about his feelings toward her.

In the second place, when Natalie describes the Prince's abject plea for his life, the Elector is genuinely shocked, "im äussersten Erstaunen" (preceding 1156). When he then hits upon his plan about what to write to the Prince, therefore, he clearly hopes the Prince will answer nobly, but he does not *know* the Prince will do this. Perhaps the Prince does regard the court's judgment as unjust; perhaps he will accept the offer in the letter. The Elector is aware, moreover, that the Prince and Natalie are in love (921–22, 1790). Hence, if he were really thinking of marrying Natalie to the Swede, sending her to the Prince with his letter ("So kann er, für sein Leben, gleich dir danken" [1198]) would be gratuitously cruel; he would be throwing the young lovers together for a moment of happiness, in order to destroy that happiness immediately by packing the girl off to Sweden. It is much more reasonable to conclude that he is toying with Count Horn, stringing him along with no intention of accepting his proposal. This of course raises the question of why he should play such a game, rather than summarily dismiss the count—a question I shall deal with later.

Another and more important question of intent, however, must be disposed of first, the question whether the Elector ever intends to allow the Prince to be executed. Again, I think the answer is no. When the Elector declares his intention to prosecute whoever had led the cavalry (715–22, 735–38), he is acting on the assumption that this was not the Prince (of which "fact" he quickly reassures himself by asking a question he has obviously asked earlier, "Der Prinz von Homburg hat sie nicht geführt?" [722]); and when the Prince himself then steps forth in perfect health and announces that he did lead the cavalry, the Elector cannot instantly rescind the declaration he has just made, for this would be far too blatant a display of favoritism.

In any case, two pieces of evidence show that the Elector never intends to carry out the sentence. First, when he carefully frames the wording of his letter, he is hoping that the Prince will reject his offer; and again, therefore, since he knows that Natalie is in love with the Prince, it would be exceptionally cruel of him to send her with the letter (thus forcing her to witness the Prince's hoped-for decision) if he did not intend to give the affair a happy ending. He has, as I shall note below, an obvious reason for keeping the Prince and Natalie in suspense; he does not intend merely to bludgeon them emotionally before sending them off, respectively, to death and despair.

There is, however, a stronger piece of evidence. When Kottwitz arrives in the city unsummoned, the Elector, after considering the possibility of drastic measures, decides instead to act in "the Brandenburgian manner" (1419) and simply persuade him to return to his station. But as Politzer points out, this is not the Brandenburgian manner[8]—at least not in the terms of this text. When a Brandenburgian subordinate, even with good intentions, disobeys a direct order (as the Prince had), he is liable to court-martial and execution; why, then, is the Elector suddenly so lenient? It cannot be argued (despite 1610–12) that the Elector's feelings will not allow him to prosecute dear old Kottwitz, since earlier, feelings or no, he had condemned Kottwitz to death! When he declares that he will execute the leader of the cavalry, he assumes the Prince has been *hors de combat,* and it follows that he intends to execute Kottwitz, whom in his written orders (276–77) he has explicitly named second in command.

There can thus be only one reason for his mild attitude toward Kottwitz in Act V: he knows perfectly well that he is going to pardon the Prince; to prosecute Kottwitz, at the same time and for a similar violation, would be grossly unfair. It is important, moreover, that the Elector's monologue occurs before he receives the Prince's letter, for this shows that the Prince's decision to accept his death sentence plays no role in the Elector's decision to pardon him.[9] The Elector has never intended to carry out the sentence, and this is why he cannot afford just now to be strict with Kottwitz.

3

And yet, what are the Elector's principal motives and values? We have understood something about what he does not intend, but what are his positive goals? We can best start from Ellis' strong comment on "the Elector's ineptness in assigning roles in the battle"; "the matter," says Ellis, "is not simply that the best use of the Prince is conspicuously avoided: he is actually placed in a role [as the one who must wait rather than act] in which he can be expected to do very badly. The Elector's planning shows more than mere inefficiency; he is downright negligent" (p. 33). How can the Elector, who claims to value the upholding of law above all else, deliberately create a situation in which his orders are likely to be disobeyed? How, if he claims that victory at Fehrbellin is a victory "on which no less depends than my throne and realm" (352), can he knowingly assign his subordinate commanders in such a way that the plan of battle is bound to be disrupted?

Ellis' answers to these questions are ingenious but textually unverifiable, because they depend on the analysis of "a deeper level of his [the Elector's] mind" (p. 34). In my opinion deep psychological analysis is not necessary. The trouble with Ellis (as with many other critics) is that he is willing to doubt practically everything that appears on the surface of the play, but still accepts the Elector's assertion that he attaches more importance to the authority of law than to anything else (733–34, 1567–68). Ellis shows that there are serious inconsistencies between what the Elector says and what he does, but before attributing these to unconscious drives we must be sure that we have a full understanding of the Elector's conscious motives, motives he may have a conscious reason for not talking about.

Of course the Elector has an interest in upholding the law, but is this his principal conscious aim in what he does? At least within the action of the play one object is clearly more important to him than either law or today's victory, and that is the education of the Prince. This aim should be clear from the first scene, where the Elector's actions are by no means the "joke" (83, 1717–18) he himself later calls them. On the contrary, he carefully creates an educational symbol and attempts to implant it in the Prince's unconscious, thus unguarded, mind. He does this, moreover, in the full knowledge that he is taking a risk thereby—"Bei Gott! Ich muss doch sehn, wie weit ers treibt!" (64)—but the education of the Prince is so crucially important to him that he is willing to take this risk even with only a few hours remaining before an important battle, in which everything will depend on the clearheadedness of his officers. The idea (suggested strongly by the "school" metaphor [1822]) that the Elector is deliberately educating the Prince, has of course been advanced often enough, but the Elector's reason for attaching such importance to this has never been adequately discussed.[10] At first glance there appears to be a conflict of motives, between the Elector's educational goal and his duty to the "sacred" fatherland (1120–21); but in fact there is no real conflict, and the idea of such a conflict is based on a misunderstanding of the Elector's political thought. Given his official position, the Elector must profess publicly a strict insistence upon law; in truth, however, his idea of the state is a good deal more flexible than he admits, and (for reasons we shall return to) it not only allows but requires him to be concerned primarily with the Prince's education.

The Prince, at any rate, apparently needs to be educated. His courage and tactical flair are unquestioned, but he must learn discipline and a respect for larger strategic and political considerations. The need for combining heroic energy with respect for law and for the state is what gives the Elector his idea for the chain-and-wreath symbol, and is also the reason for the "ineptness" of his battle plan. Because the education of the Prince is more important than winning the battle, the Elector deliberately places the Prince in a position calculated to teach self-discipline. Then later, after inadvertently sentencing the Prince to death, the Elector recognizes that the death sentence might have the educational effect he had failed to achieve by his earlier stratagem. Therefore he delays the pardon. We can now also understand why he is so astonished and perturbed when Natalie tells him of the Prince's abject pleading. In the first place, he had expected the Prince, whose courage he knows, to rise to the occasion and accept the sentence. When he asks Natalie, "Are those cousin Homburg's thoughts as well?" (1142), he expects that this question will defeat all her arguments, in the same way that he later overcomes Kottwitz by saying, "and to end the dispute I call upon another advocate of my own position, the Prince of Homburg!" (1612–14). Now with Natalie, as later in Act V, he is calling the Prince as a witness for the prosecution, fully confident that the Prince will act as such a witness, and this is one reason Natalie's answer shocks him as it does.

But in the second place, the Elector also has not given any serious thought to whether the death sentence against the Prince is fully justified. Since he does not intend to carry out the sentence anyway, he thinks of it mainly as an educational, not a legal, measure. In order to function educationally, however, the sentence must be just, and when Natalie tells of the Prince's pleading, the Elector suddenly realizes that he has not sufficiently considered this aspect of the situation. Hence his extreme perturbation. Perhaps the sentence is not just. Perhaps there are circumstances he has overlooked. Perhaps he has been torturing the Prince and Natalie for no good purpose.

Let me remark that I do not mean simply to revive the so-called "education theory" of the play. I will not argue that the Elector *succeeds* in educating the Prince; my point is that he *wishes* to educate the Prince, and that this concern is uppermost in his mind when the play opens.

4

We have already postponed a number of important questions— why the Elector is so interested in educating the Prince, why he stalls Count Horn, what his true political opinions are—but in order to answer them fully we shall have to postpone them a bit longer still, and take up first the question of the play's allusions to other dramas.

When he sees the Prince making a wreath, the Elector is at first dumbfounded, but then says, "I'll bet I know what this young fool has on his mind" (54–55). Hohenzollern immediately answers, "Tomorrow's battle of course!" (56), but the Elector shows by his ensuing actions that he considers Hohenzollern at best only partly right; for he now takes the wreath from the Prince, winds his chain about it, and hands it *to Natalie.* The creation of the wreath-and-chain symbol can be understood as an expression of the Elector's general educational intent, but the handing of the wreath to Natalie has further significance; when the Elector says he is willing to wager that he understands the Prince's feelings, he means that he knows the Prince is in love with Natalie. Furthermore, by handing the wreath to her, he indicates that he will approve her marriage with the Prince, but only after the Prince has accepted fully the meaning of the wreath-and-chain. The Elector is attempting to impress on the Prince's mind the image of Natalie as a prize to be won by the achievement of that synthesis for which she now holds the symbol. The Prince's behavior, however, as later in his reaction to the death sentence, is not what it should be. He is not chastened; he is only inflamed, and the Elector is forced to retire somewhat more precipitously than he had planned. But even now he does not forget the message he has been attempting to communicate, for his last words—"We'll see each other again, if you please, on the battlefield! Prizes like this are not won in a dream!" (75–76)—though in tone a reprimand, contain in substance a promise. "In a dream" the Prince cannot achieve his desires, but in reality, by implication, he can, provided he learns the lesson of self-discipline that the Elector has built into the battle plan. Indeed, the Elector makes a special point of reminding him of this later (348).

For our purposes, however, the action involving the Elector, the Prince, and Natalie is especially interesting because of the comparison it suggests to Schiller's *Wallenstein.*[11] In both *Wallenstein* and *Prinz Friedrich,* the motif of the old leader's desire to arrange a politically advantageous marriage for his "daughter" occurs, but in Kleist's play this desire turns out not to exist. The Elector is a kind of enlightened Wallenstein. Whereas Wallenstein is blind to the love between his protegé and his daughter, and thwarts it unfeelingly, the Elector, from the beginning, is sensitive and sympathetic to what is going on, and he seeks only to ennoble the young people's relationship. Thus the Schillerian catastrophe is averted; it is the "hypochondriac" Kleist, curiously enough, who here practices "avoidance of tragedy."

This is of course not the only allusion to Schiller in *Prinz Friedrich*. Richard Samuel, in his notes to the play, mentions Schiller twenty-three times, and at that there are a number of references or echoes he has missed. But most of the references to Schiller suggest a contrast or an overturning of the original. With regard to the obvious allusion to Schiller's poem "Der Kampf mit dem Drachen," for example, Samuel remarks that the Prince's attitude at the end is not "humility in control of itself" but the opposite, a resurgent pride and self-respect.[12] Or we think of the scene where Natalie writes the marching orders for Kottwitz but orders Count Reuss not to use the document until she directs him to. This is meant to remind us of Queen Elizabeth's handling of Mary Stuart's death warrant in Schiller. But whereas Schiller's Elizabeth uses the device of a signed but not specifically reconfirmed document to avoid responsibility for an act within her legal power, Natalie does the opposite; she assumes responsibility for a daring and humane act that is beyond her legal power. Or we think of the encounter between the Prince and Natalie in Act V, scene viii, which reminds us for a second of Karl Moor's final encounter with Amalia in *Die Räuber*; Natalie's only wish now is "to love him" (1802) in spite of everything, but the Prince, having decided for death, shouts "Away!" In all these cases a Schillerian catastrophe, or a scene of anguished renunciation, is transmuted into an action culminating in joyful resolution.

Nor is it only with Schiller that Kleist undertakes this sort of transmutation. Sigurd Burckhardt has shown that *Prinz Friedrich* includes an attempt to overturn Goethe's *Egmont*,[13] and there is a similar attempt, even clearer and more direct, with regard to *Tasso*. Of course the crowning with a laurel wreath by a beloved lady reminds us of *Tasso*, but so does the Prince's posturing in Act II, scene v. Whereas Tasso is a poet who is confused by attempting to think of himself as a hero, the Prince is a "young hero" (1053) who tries to act like a poet—in the three stiltedly tragic speeches (1022–36, 1039–52, 1062–68) in which he imagines his own retirement to a rustic life, advises Natalie to enter a nunnery, and then envisions her as a winged angel. In fact the Prince's evocation of rustic life (1030–36) echoes quite strongly the speech in which Tasso desires to become a castle-caretaker (*Tasso*, ll. 3198–3211). And the ruler in *Tasso*, like the ruler in *Prinz Friedrich*, is obliged to inflict upon his protegé a punishment which the protegé takes more seriously than the ruler had expected.

But the strongest connection between *Tasso* and *Prinz Friedrich* is still the laurel wreath, and here the overturning of *Tasso* becomes clearest. Whereas Alfons, blind to the emotional significance of his action, insists that the crowning be carried out, the Elector, who is fully aware of the emotional situation, carefully avoids this. True, the Prince succeeds in snatching a trophy for himself anyway, and the emotional consequences are not all that different from the consequences of Tasso's crowning. But still, unlike Alfons, the Elector is aware of the psychological realities of the case, and a catastrophe is avoided. The reconciled ending of *Prinz Friedrich* thus shows the Elector to be a more enlightened and more effectual governor than either Alfons or Wallenstein, and the allusions to Goethe and Schiller thus dovetail with the suggestions above concerning the Elector's knowledge and intentions.

Especially important, however, is the technique Kleist employs here, the technique of alluding to and overturning specific motifs from existing dramatic literature. *Prinz Friedrich*, again, is psychologically subtle and interesting, but not psychologically obscure; it employs psychology but is not about psychology. It is, rather, *a drama about drama*, and its true principal intention, its center of gravity, is thus indicated by its critical allusiveness as well as by the ironic structure of play-within-play.

5

The Elector's political thinking is best approached by way of the question of what is wrong with the Brandenburgian polity and army, what internal problems the Elector is faced with. In his very fine treatment of the characters Golz and Dörfling, Ellis points out that Golz is presented as "too timid to speak up" (p. 44) to either Kottwitz or the Prince. Golz is entrusted with transmitting an important message to Kottwitz (340–43), and strictly speaking he carries out his duty (390–99); but he does not do enough. He "relies ... on the mere fulfillment of an order, without questioning whether the spirit of the order requires something more" (p. 44). So also Dörfling, who "knows of great weaknesses in the Elector's battle plan, but does not mention them to the Elector [346–47] ... Obviously afraid of disputing with the Elector, he accepts the Elector's personal style of managing battles" (p. 45). Both Golz and Dörfling, at crucial and conspicuous points in the play, are afraid to say anything that might displease their superiors—and this is a symptom of what is really rotten in the state of Brandenburg: not too little discipline and subordination, but rather too much. The play stresses not the need for law as a corrective to energy but rather the need for energy and initiative as correctives to excessively literal reliance on law. By far the longest single speech, thirty-nine lines (1570–1608), is Kottwitz's argument about the uselessness of strict legalistic subordination, where he concludes by asserting that he himself would have acted as the Prince had, even if it had meant being executed. (These words are especially striking because the Elector *has* condemned Kottwitz to death earlier.) And it is only reasonable to suppose that this conspicuously long speech, at a moment of high climax, expresses an essential part of the play's meaning. Moreover, Natalie's twenty-line speech making a similar argument (1122–41) is exceeded in length only by the Prince's narration of his dream (172–91) and Sparren's telling of the Froben story (655–77).

This idea—of the insufficiency of law and the need for energy and free initiative in a state or army—is not merely the play's main political burden, but it also represents the Elector's own thinking. The Elector cannot express himself verbally in this vein for two simple reasons. In the first place, his position prohibits it. If the ruler or general, the man who embodies the law, states out loud that he does not consider the law absolutely holy, the result among his subordinates will be carelessness and eventually chaos. In the second place, one cannot foster energy and initiative by advocating them in words; these qualities, by definition, must originate in the person who possesses them. If one orders a subordinate to act with energy and initiative, the result will be a self-consciously stilted energy, a misplaced initiative, again eventually chaos. And Kleist of course well knew the dangers of excessive consciousness.

The Elector therefore cannot express himself verbally, but he does express himself unambiguously in his otherwise unaccountable actions. The reason for his overriding interest in the Prince's education, for example, now becomes clear. The Prince is a young man in whom the qualities of energy and initiative are abundant; this man must therefore be trained as a true leader for the army, in order that the rest may profit from his fiery example. There is a fine ambiguity in Dörfling's worried plea to the Elector: "You know that every army loves its hero. But don't let this energy-suffusing spark become a devouring holocaust" (1460–62). What he means is that the Elector should ward off the possibility of a mutiny in the Prince's favor. But his words can also be read as an expression of exactly what the Elector, from the beginning, has been attempting to do: to mold the Prince into a true leader, to temper his boundless youthful energy but not to curb it, so that it may function as a life-giving spark rather than a destructive blaze.

There is some question about whether the Elector's education of the Prince can be said to have succeeded; but the success of his education of his army, or at least of his officer corps, his success-ful use of the Prince as a vital spark, seems quite clear. At the beginning of the play the officers are all timidly pedantic in carry-ing out their orders; even old Kottwitz is careful to disclaim re-sponsibility (496) before following the Prince into battle. But at the end of the play, without committing any actual insubordina-tion, the officers are willing to stick their necks out quite a bit in disputing with their commander-in-chief. Count Reuss, for exam-ple, knows perfectly well that Natalie is not transmitting the Elec-tor's orders; he would have to be a moron not to know this after she gives him the orders but tells him to delay their execution. Dörfling, who had earlier concealed all possible unpleasantness from the Elector, is still not exactly courageous; but in his concern for the Elector's welfare, he does paint as black a picture as possi-ble of what is going on in the city. And Kottwitz and Hohenzol-lern then mount direct frontal assaults on the Elector's intellectual position. This is the kind of officer corps the elector wants—men who respect him and the law, but without violating their own feelings and energetic self-respect in the process. "My heart is of their party" (1442), says the Elector when he hears that the of-ficers are meeting to seek the Prince's pardon, and he means this in more ways than one.

Hohenzollern's case is especially instructive. At the beginning, when he brings the Elector to witness the Prince's dreaming, it is not correct to say that he "regards this only as a curiosity, even a joke" (Ellis, p. 47). On the contrary, he is quite obviously telling tales out of school. His emotional situation is deeply (but not Freudianly) ambivalent. He has genuine affection for the Prince, but at the same time he is disturbed and a bit envious that the Elector has granted so much favor and responsibility to a man whose record as a general is hardly even promising (349–50, 1818–21). Without wishing to harm the Prince, he still wishes to make the Elector aware of a weakness in the military plan, but like Dörfling he is too timid to come out and say what he means.

By the end of the play, however, he has undergone considerable development (perhaps more than the Prince) and is now prepared to assert that the Elector had been at fault in disrupting the battle plan. Furthermore, he is justified in this assertion; the Elector's objection, that Hohenzollern himself had been equally at fault (1714–19), is unfounded. Hohenzollern, believing the Elector to be primarily interested in the battle rather than in the education of the Prince, had assumed that the Elector would simply wake the Prince and reprimand him; he had suggested this in so many words (31). The responsibility for playing the dream-game with the Prince is thus entirely the Elector's, and Hohenzollern is calmly aware (1721–22) that the Elector, despite his vehement counterattack, knows this. Hohenzollern has thus grown in the course of the play, and this kind of growth, the awakening of initiative and of confidence in their convictions, is precisely what the Elector has desired from his officers.

A number of other questions about the play now resolve themselves with no difficulty. The Elector's reason for not dismissing immediately the Swedish Count Horn, for example, is that he does not know until the last act exactly what course he must pursue in negotiations. He has no intention of sacrificing Natalie, but he is still not sure whether to send back a counterproposal or simply (as he eventually does) a renewed challenge; and he cannot be sure of this until he knows the state of his army's morale. Once the Prince's heroic energy and pride have revived, however, and especially now that signs of these qualities are shown by the other officers as well, the Elector need hesitate no longer. He is confident now of victory at the head of a high-spirited army, and his decision is reached as soon as he reads the Prince's letter (1480).

We can now also understand that the essence of the contrast between the Elector and Wallenstein is that the latter, who does sacrifice his daughter, is interested only in political advantage for himself, whereas the former is interested in forming a healthy body politic (where rigidity of law is counteracted by vital energy) for the sake of future generations. Natalie's speech on this subject (1122–41), though directed by her against the Elector, in truth expresses exactly the principles on which the Elector bases his actions—in the same way that Kottwitz's speech against the Elector expresses the Elector's own political goal.

Still more important, however, is that we can now see the way in which the obvious relationship of *Prinz Friedrich* to *Measure for Measure*[14] is also in essence an overturning, though not so negatively critical as that of *Wallenstein* or *Tasso*. The trouble in Shakespeare's fictional Vienna is that the state's "strict statutes" (*M.f.M.* I.iii.19) have not been enforced, "And liberty plucks justice by the nose" (I.iii.29); therefore Duke Vicentio delegates his power to "the strict deputy" (I.ii.186) Angelo, who can be expected to insist on the letter of the law. The situation in *Prinz Friedrich* is an exact reversal of this. Observance of the law has become too strict in Brandenburg, and the Elector therefore vests great power and responsibility in the Prince (setting him before Kottwitz as Angelo is set before Escalus) in order that vital energy and initiative may reassert themselves. Moreover, the Elector is not only seeking to improve the state but also testing the Prince, just as the Duke is testing Angelo. That there is some sort of close relationship with *Measure for Measure* is clear from the Prince's fear-of-death scene (III.v; cf. *M.f.M.*, III.i.48–151) as well as from other verbal and thematic parallels; that this relationship is likely to include an overturning or reversal is suggested by Kleist's treatment of *Tasso* and *Wallenstein;* and the particular reversal intended ought to be clear from the basic contrast between the Elector's situation as head of an overdisciplined state (with the pedantic subordination of Hohenzollern, Golz, Dörfling) and the Duke's as head of an underdisciplined state. The Duke and the Elector are both faced with essentially the same problem, how to enforce a respect for law without stifling all free human flexibility; but they have erred in different directions, and just as the Duke cannot be strict without appearing a tyrant, so the Elector cannot openly advocate free initiative without appearing ineffectual. Therefore they must make devious use of their subordinates, Angelo and the Prince.

If this idea of the Elector's aims seems still unverifiable, because he does not say directly what he means, then there is yet another confirming pattern in the play's structure, besides the Shakespeare parallel, which can serve as evidence: a pattern of characters' speaking against their own true wishes—"for I can speak / Against the thing I say" (*M.f.M.* II.iv.59–60)—which involves not only the Elector but the Prince and Natalie as well. First, when the Prince begs the Electress and Natalie for his life, it is clear, at least beginning with the "Get thee to a nunnery" speech (1039–52), that he is posturing; after he has poured out his feelings to the Electress, the imagery of his speeches suddenly becomes very elaborate, and we recognize that he is now only assuming a tragic pose—as is also suggested by the echo of *Tasso*. Nor is it hard to see the reason for this change. When the Prince turns from the Electress to Natalie, from his "mother" to his bride, he naturally begins to feel more like a man, less like a little boy (cf. 1010–15), and he begins to recognize that he does not want to demean himself by begging. Although he continues to plead, the resurgence of dignity in him is already under way (as is also shown by the short monologue of Act IV, scene iii, 1286–96), and his pleading becomes stilted because he is pleading against his own true wishes.

Then, when Natalie comes to him in prison, it is important that she has already forged the marching orders, for this shows (as does her reaction at the end of the interview [1386–90]) that she is in truth hoping for the heroic reply she receives, even though she pleads earnestly and energetically against it. Thus, again, the Elector's difficult situation, the necessity that he argue strongly against his own true aims, fits into a larger artistic pattern. This argument is not a logical demonstration, but it is a type of reasoning without which literary criticism would get nowhere, the argument that a particular reading, though not strictly verifiable, produces a more comprehensive and satisfying idea of the work's wholeness. I shall attempt below, by essentially the same method, to defend my reading of the Elector's motives yet further.

6

But does this reading not in a sense weaken the play? If the Elector, from the very beginning, is as enlightened as I have made him out, then it follows that he does not undergo any significant development in the course of the action, that his conflict with the Prince does not change him, and where then is the dramatic purpose of this conflict? Let me begin by saying that I think the idea of character development is generally overemphasized, especially in German dramatic criticism. Characters can grow within their dramas (Hohenzollern appears to), but that they should do so is neither necessary nor always desirable. Especially in the case of the Prince it ought to be clear that neither the Elector nor Natalie nor the army nor the audience wishes any real development to take place. "I desire only that he exist" (1087), says Natalie, and these words come close to expressing the Elector's attitude as well. The Elector needs the Prince *as he is* at the head of the army, as a vital spark of energy and initiative to inspire others. At most the Elector wishes to get him somewhat under control, to make a true leader of him and so harness his burgeoning youthful energy. But perhaps even this is too much to ask. After the pardon is announced, Kottwitz assures the Elector, "You yourself could be standing at the brink of destruction, and without a direct order the Prince would not budge to save you" (1826–28). This little speech is an obvious *reductio ad absurdum* of the whole idea of "educating" a hero in the first place, for the achievement of any real control over the Prince would destroy precisely those qualities that make him valuable. The Elector, it appears, will simply have to accept the Prince as he is.

At any rate, apart from anyone's wishes, the Prince does not change in the course of the play. Indeed, there is an exact parallel between his illegal victory over the Swedes and his sublime victory over the specter of mortality. The two lines (528) which he first overruns on his charge correspond to the two battles he has already fought, in which he has not achieved victory but has still managed to acquire the respect and love of the army. Then, however, he is pinned down by the murderous fire from a Swedish fortification (530), and at this point he and his riders look up to see the man on a white horse whom they take for the Elector (537–41). This moment corresponds, in the larger action of the play, to the check suffered by the Prince when his third battle turns out to be a crime for which the Elector sentences him to die. It is significant, moreover, that the man on the white horse is not the Elector, for this circumstance corresponds to the fact that the figure of the Elector, as it later hovers over the Prince in the valley of death, is also essentially an illusion, the fact that it is not the Elector's true intent to carry out the death sentence.

Then, however, the Elector is apparently destroyed, which rouses the Prince to make his final successful attack (550–53). In the larger action of the play, this moment corresponds to the point where the Elector (in conversation with Natalie) becomes uncertain about the equity of his sentence against the Prince; he is no longer as it were borne aloft on the steed of unquestioned justice, and now, by placing the Prince's fate in his own hands, he removes his own commanding person from the picture, as he had in the battle by changing horses. As in the battle, the brilliant, overpowering figure of the Elector now no longer stands above the Prince; the Prince is now suddenly free, under no external authority, and as in the battle (though with different emotions) he rouses himself, overcomes his check and successfully storms death, the ultimate enemy. He never shows any sign of regret or contrition for his violation of law; he has not in this sense learned anything at all. His victory at the end of the play is a resurgence of exactly the same impulsive energy by which he had illegally won the battle against the Swedes.

Thus there is no special reason to look for personal development in the Elector either. Like the Prince, in fact, the Elector is the same at the end of the play as at the beginning, shaken but ultimately confirmed in his basic nature and purposes. I do not mean by this that he is a symbol of changeless divinity—any more than the Prince is—or that he possesses infallible wisdom.[15] He does have very sound and sensible political attitudes, conducive to the future health of his country. He is (hardly by accident) what Adam Müller would call a "dramatic" statesman, as opposed to a "monologic" or a "dialogic" statesman (p. 173). He is not at heart excessively rigorous (i.e. monologic) about adherence to law, but he is also intelligent enough to recognize that his true opinions, if expressed in detail, would produce a disordered or dialogic situation; he wishes to use the Prince's energy as a vital spark, but he knows that he must also use his own position and authority to keep that spark from becoming a destructive blaze.

And yet, for all his good sense, he is still only a man. He has, at the beginning of the play, quite a reasonable plan for testing and educating the Prince, by ordering him to watch the battle rather than participate, thus forcing him to exercise self-control. But in his overintentness upon his goal (comparable to the Prince's overeagerness) he makes two serious mistakes. First, when he is

shown the Prince in the garden, he thinks he sees an opportunity
for reinforcing his educational scheme by working on the pupil's
unconscious mind; but the result is to inflame the Prince beyond
all possibility of control, so that the original plan cannot work any
longer—although the Elector does not realize this until Hohenzollern's important explanation later (1622–1722). The Prince, once
he learns that the glove belongs to Natalie, knows that the
"dream" had been reality! He knows that *in actuality* the Elector
had symbolically promised him Natalie as the victor's prize;
hence the confidence with which he assumes that the Elector,
now apparently dead, would have blessed their union (609–11).
This is the danger which the Elector most fears and which forces
him to be silent about his true intentions—the danger that if he
expresses his "mildness" (1111) too clearly (as he does inadvertently with the Prince), his subordinates will take their discipline
lightly and chaos will ensue. The Prince's insubordination is thus
not only the Elector's fault, but it is a fault the Elector has himself
long been wary of. Hence also the Prince's outrageous optimism
when he is first imprisoned, and then his collapse into utter despair. He has not only dreamt of the Elector's true intentions, he
has seen the Elector express them and he knows he has seen this;
therefore the Elector's apparent complete turn-about comes as an
enormous shock.

And after inadvertently sentencing the Prince to die, when the
Elector thinks he sees an opportunity to make up the educational
ground that has apparently been lost on the battlefield, he lets the
sentence stand as long as possible; but again he is mistaken. The
Prince is not chastened by his imprisonment but bewildered, because of what he knows from the evidence of his own eyes and
Natalie's glove. When he finally pulls himself out of despair, this
act is not submission to the law but proud self-assertion. "Er
handle, wie er darf," he says almost contemptuously of the Elector; "Mir ziemts hier zu verfahren, wie ich soll!" (1374–75), "Let
him exercise his rights; I shall do the right thing!"

And yet, although the Elector's two crucial mistakes disrupt his
original plan for educating the Prince, still he appears in the end
to have achieved his ultimate aim, the revitalization of his army
and state. Again, therefore, our reading is supported by a simple
unifying structure in the work. Just as the Prince sets out to win
his fortune (including Natalie) in the most direct way, then makes

a mistake that apparently dashes his hopes, but in the end finds himself very close to his goal, so also the Elector makes a mistake that eventually seems to profit him more than the successful completion of his original plan would have. This—not only in the fictional action but also in the meaning for an audience—is the play's *master pattern* (and bears a fairly clear relation to the pattern of characters' speaking against their own true wishes). Even Natalie's role exhibits this master pattern, provided we agree that it is out of character for her to cause a lengthy interruption in an important council of war for the sake of a glove. It is clear, in Act I, scene v, that she has seen the glove where the Prince is carrying it conspicuously, and wishes (by making the commotion she does) to communicate to him that it is hers, in order that he know better where he stands and how she feels, rather than be prey to confusing "dreams." In her solicitude for the Prince, then, she compounds the Elector's mistake with one of her own (since the Prince's knowledge that the dream had been reality confuses him more than the dream itself had), and again this mistake eventually has the effect of bringing her nearer her goal.

7

There is still an important difficulty in this reading, for the problem of an overdisciplined state, with its too rigid legal structure and its need of revitalizing heroic energy, is not chosen at random. In the humiliated Germany of the Napoleonic period it is a real and pressing problem for Kleist, and had already become something of a traditional problem in German literature—in Hölderlin's view of the bookish but inactive Germans, for example, or Karl Moor's disgust "at this inkslinging age." It is, moreover, a general philosophical problem, which Kleist treats in "Über das Marionettentheater," where it occurs as the problem of the revitalization of the human race: our unavoidable self-conscious condition tends to stultify our existence and rob us of our natural grace and activity: we *know* ourselves, but this knowledge divides us internally, so that we are no longer fully at one with ourselves; and the especially frustrating aspect of this problem is that a clear conscious grasp of it only aggravates it. Cassirer characterizes Kleist's reaction to Fichte as follows: "Fichte's system was intended, in the radical sense, as a philosophy of action, but for precisely this reason it appeared to supplant action by philosophy; it appeared to make the reflection about action into a source and precondition of action itself."[16] How shall we find our way back to a life of genuine activity when mere thinking about this goal only drives us further away? This is the problem that faces the Elector in a state where strict adherence to principles and rules has become an unbreakable habit that poisons individual initiative at its source. The problems of the state of Brandenburg are a symbol for the problem of the revitalization or reactivation of the human race, and it is essentially this problem which the Elector deals with by declining to express his true intentions—by attempting, that is, to avoid contributing to the insidiously self-perpetuating and self-potentiating fabric of human self-consciousness—and by placing his subordinates, *without their knowledge*, in a situation where energy and initiative, coupled with self-discipline, are likely to arise spontaneously, inspired in others by the example of the Prince.

Herein, however, lies the difficulty in our reading. If the problems of Brandenburg are equivalent to the problem of the human race, then Kleist is attempting to educate his audience in the same way that the Elector educates his army. And yet the Elector's true purposes, hence by analogy the author's true purposes, are known to the audience. Has the author failed in his purpose, then, since he has only managed to involve those who understand his meaning more deeply in the complexities of self-consciousness? We recognize that the play teaches a "philosophy of action," but our recognition of this, as Cassirer suggests, subordinates activity to reflection.

This philosophical and political problem, from the late eighteenth century on in Germany, had come to be associated especially with drama. That the Germans as a people, by contrast with the English or the French, lacked national identity and social cohesion, was widely recognized and deplored, but one of the most conspicuous reactions to this state of affairs was the constantly renewed movement to form a national theater. The idea of political or legal unification was not prominent in the intellectual atmosphere. Such men as J. E. Schlegel and Lessing, Herder, Schiller, Goethe (in *Wilhelm Meisters theatralische Sendung*), and later the Romantics hoped for an upsurge of national feeling and style, a unification by creative energy, not by restrictive precept or principle. The problem in Germany was thus seen more or

less as Kleist sees the problem in his historical-fictional Brandenburg, and a fairly obvious approach to this problem was through
the theater, for the theater is a communal institution, a kind of
social cement, which binds people together not by restricting them
but by relaxing, exciting, and uplifting them. When Schiller argues
that the true function of art is to awaken free moral initiative in the
individual, and when at the same time he comes back repeatedly
to the idea of the theater as a communal and community-forming
force,[17] he is working out in theory the basic considerations which
had generated the national-theater movement in Germany—and
which also underlie the maneuvering of Kleist's Elector, who hopes
for a rebirth of free initiative in such a way as to strengthen rather
than endanger the communal order.

Once we understand the relation between these ideas and drama
or theater, it becomes easier to see the connection between the
Elector's *mistake* and the ironic structure, the play-within-play,
of *Prinz Friedrich*. In particular, the Elector's communication
to the Prince (in the latter's "dream") of more than he intends
to communicate, corresponds to an inherent difficulty in drama.
Within the specific cultural situation of early nineteenth-century
Germany, or within the general situation of humanity corrupted
by its self-consciousness, the natural function of drama, hence the
proper intention of every dramatist, is revitalization of the communal, the awakening of free energy and initiative in such a way
that these tend to create a true community rather than disrupt it.
But every drama is also a work of poetry, in which the author's
intention and the communicated meaning are ideally the same,
and if the dramatic poet communicates to us his intention of revitalizing us, then he has actually only increased our self-
consciousness and so thwarted his own purpose.

Drama, like the Elector, who communicates to the Prince more
than serves his purpose, tends to say too much for its own good.
We recall, moreover, that in the first scene a clear parallel is
drawn between the Prince and the audience—in that both are
presented with deliberately contrived symbolic visions—and we
can now understand that the Prince's confusion in interpreting
his vision is meant to illuminate a general problem about audiences. The audience of a drama always, as it were, snatches a real
glove from the imaginary vision presented it; it always interprets
what it sees and attempts to apply its interpretation to real life.

But in the case of *Prinz Friedrich*—or in the case of any work that attempts to fulfil Kleist's idea of the function of drama, to revitalize human community—this process of application must always lead to confusion. The message of such a play, if we extract and attempt to apply it, must be that free initiative and communal duty are identical, that the "orders" we must follow in preference to all others are those that come from the "heart" (474–75), that it is our duty to act freely; and this is too much of a paradox to provide a sound basis for judgment or activity. If we feel that free initiative is a duty required of us, then we shall become hasty in seeking opportunities for free action, as the Prince is in the battle. This consideration also illuminates the meaning of the Prince's arresting the young officer who attempts to stop him. It has often been remarked that the Prince here reveals a glaring inconsistency in his attitudes; he insists on "the ten Brandenburgian commandments" (487) in the very act of disobeying them. True, but the point of the scene is that the Prince sees no inconsistency between what he is doing and the demands of the state. He has learned (from the "dream" he knows had been real) that freedom and duty, heroic energy and sound political order, the wreath and the chain, are inextricably intertwined, and he has been told that he is to apply this lesson "on the battlefield" (75). That he insists on others' doing their duty is meant to remind us that he has reason to believe he is doing his own.

In Fichtean metaphysics it may be true that freedom and duty are identical, that the world arises ultimately from "productive imagination," that the apparently external pressures on us (e.g. duty) are in truth the expression of our own free being. But in our immediate experience, as we feel them acting upon or through us, freedom and duty are always in tension with one another; their very definitions require this. If it is made clear to us (as the Elector inadvertently makes clear to the Prince) that despite the lack of any measurable merit by which we can be said to have earned it, the highest authority intends nonetheless to grant our fondest wish, whence shall a meaningful sense of duty arise in us? Shall we not feel ourselves too free for our own good, like Goethe's Tasso, who says of the Princess' supposed love that it is better to receive such a gift "pure and undeserved" (*Tasso*, 1182–83) than to earn it by achievement? Immediately after speaking these words, Tasso, like the Prince, involves himself in an unlawful

combat (with Antonio); and of course the Prince, after learning
that the glove is Natalie's, that the dream had been real, also
makes his overweening prayer to "fortune" (358; cf. *Tasso*, 1189).

The Elector's mistake, then, corresponds to a difficulty that appears to be unavoidable in drama, and the Prince's mistake corresponds to what appears an unavoidable confusion in the thinking
of an audience that sees deeply enough into the meaning of the
work—since the work as a whole does after all suggest a synthesis
of energetic freedom and valid communal order. But both the
Elector and the Prince, in spite of their mistakes, eventually find
themselves closer to the realization of their aims. Is this supposed
to be true by analogy of the dramatist and the audience as well?
And if so, then by what ironic process is this master pattern produced in the theater? The Elector's plan to educate the Prince
quite clearly fails; nothing is *learned* in the fictional world but
something still *happens*, and perhaps, by analogy, something is
meant to happen in the real world of the theater, to the audience.
At any rate nothing is learned in the theater, because of the nature
of the play's message; there is no such thing as a teachable "philosophy of action."

8

The Prince, if our reasoning so far is correct, is a kind of projection of the audience—not an *image*, not a typical German
theater-goer of the period, but a larger-than-life *projection*. The
contrived symbolic vision he is presented with is parallel to the
symbolic vision which is the play as a whole; the mistake made by
the Elector, the presenter of this intendedly educational vision,
reveals a difficulty in the form of drama itself, a "mistake" that
every dramatist makes by being a dramatist; and this mistake in
turn necessarily leads the audience into a confusion (our consciousness of the play's meaning endangers that meaning) which
is then projected in the Prince's confused application of the meaning of the garden scene. But once we have come this far, what do
we do? Evidently we must abandon any attempt to apply the
play's meaning; we must abandon what Adam Müller calls our
"monologic interest in the stage" (p. 143), our search for a "practical rule or maxim" (p. 145) as the play's message. The situation
is hopeless; we cannot learn anything from this work. The experience may make a better audience of us, inasmuch as it denies us

the opportunity of trivializing the work "monologically" by deriving a simple doctrine; but it does so at the cost of leaving us, apparently, with no meaning at all.

And yet, even this hopelessness (as it arises in the audience) is projected in the Prince's despair. Just as we are forced to abandon all hope of deriving from the play "a sure way to find and enjoy happiness,"[18] so the Prince must abandon his hopes of possessing Natalie and glory, the two prizes promised him in his vision. The connection here between the Prince and the audience may appear rather tenuous—since the Prince is after all under sentence of death—but the association of ideas in the play is tight enough. In the first scene, a figure of authority approaches a man sleeping in a garden, takes an object from the sleeping man (something rather more significant than a rib) and incorporates it into the figure of a woman; the reference is obvious. But when we leave the Garden of Eden, as the Prince then does, we take two curses with us, our self-consciousness and our mortality, and the two are clearly equivalent. Kleist says as much in "Über das Marionettentheater," where he argues that our self-consciousness alone distinguishes us not only from animals but also from gods. If we were not self-conscious, we would not undergo mortality as an experience; either we would live in the innocence of beasts, or else we would not be mortal.

But self-consciousness, the legacy of Eden, is what makes the audience's situation hopeless. We understand what the play means; we know that ultimately we are free and that our freedom belongs harmoniously in the general order of things, that the chain and the wreath are somehow intertwined. But we also recognize that our consciousness of this truth divides us from ourselves and excludes us from our own unified being, so that we can never realize the perfect union of freedom and order in actual experience. This dissonance in our nature is in turn equivalent to mortality. We cannot revert to the emotionless simplicity of "chasing life in its circle, till at evening it sinks down and dies" (1035–36); our glimpsed knowledge that death ought to have no rights over us only makes us fear it the more abjectly. Thus it is entirely logical that our self-consciousness should be projected in the Prince's fear of death.

Again, this is a projection, not an image. We do not merely see our self-consciousness on the stage—as the audience of *Der ge-*

stiefelte Kater presumably sees itself—but rather we see what our self-consciousness implies; we are faced with the full potential horror of our condition. The mechanism of play-within-play compels us to reflect on our own state; and the recognition that the Prince is a projection of ourselves reminds us that our self-consciousness, intensified by our reflecting on it, tends toward mortal terror. This, for Kleist, is the business of tragedy: to bring about a situation in the theater whereby the spectator is induced to experience in himself the full potential tragicness of the self-conscious human condition. Tragedy provides us not with an escape but with an intensification of our normal self-consciousness, to the point where its tragic implications are revealed. This end is served not only by the specific details of *Prinz Friedrich* but also by the basic artistic process of projection, the projection of the audience's situation onto the stage, which transforms the whole auditorium into a model of the self-observing and agonizingly self-divided mind.

And yet, this theory by no means excludes tragic pleasure. The recognition that our daily existence on its most basic level, our self-consciousness, is an unceasing encounter with the terrifying specter of mortality, must tend to produce in us not despair but rather a kind of pride. It is a recognition of the essential heroism of our daily existence; tragedy enables us to experience the truth that every instant of self-consciousness is potentially a heroic and victorious confrontation with death, for in the theater we freely enjoy the tragic aspect of our condition. And our affirmation and enjoyment of our ultimately terrifying self-conscious condition is what is projected in the Prince's final free decision to undergo his sentence. It is this developing sympathy between what happens in the Prince and what happens in the audience that has prompted commentators to suggest that we actually wish the Prince to die;[19] it is this, not any special quality in the rhetoric or imagery, which lends Act V, scene x—"Nun, o Unsterblichkeit, bist du ganz mein!" (1830) and the few words with Stranz about flowers—its unquestionable beauty.

Now we can understand something about how the play's master pattern, as I have called it, is supposed to be realized on the level of meaning. The play does not and cannot teach us how to be free; what it does, rather, is make us free[20] by leading us to the true seat of our freedom. Once again, the process of understanding the play, if we understand it correctly, is identical with the process of penetrating into our own self-consciousness to the point where its tragic potential is revealed, to the point where the mere act of thinking about ourselves becomes a constant recognition and (in that we still carry out this act) a constant affirmation of the incomprehensible but inexorable sentence of death under which we stand. Self-consciousness is by nature equivalent to a certain basic freedom, inasmuch as without it we could not intend or effect any specific change in ourselves. Now, however, in the theater, we experience self-consciousness as itself the shadow of death, and we therefore experience our freedom as a heroic freedom, which we express merely by existing in man's intolerable condition. Existence itself is now a free heroic act, and freedom in this sense no longer conflicts with law or communal order; it no longer needs to be expressed in some form of rebellion, because it resides in our very being. In fact this sort of freedom tends naturally to strengthen the communal order, for its nature is to affirm and so overcome death, the most outrageously arbitrary of all externally imposed necessities, the absolute necessity in relation to which all particular requirements of law become mere symbols. If mortality itself is a free act, carried out in every instant of self-conscious existence, how shall our freedom be impaired by any legal restriction on what we may do? Thus the play's master pattern appears once again on the level of meaning. The unavoidable failure of the play to circumvent our self-consciousness, its failure to teach effectively the unity of freedom and duty, in the end brings us closer to this unity—by complicating and intensifying our self-consciousness.

This is not a lesson we learn from the play. When the Prince formulates triumphantly what he has "learned," he expresses himself in mere contradictions: "Quiet! It is my inflexible will! Before the army, by my free death, I shall glorify the sacred law of war which I have offended" (1749–51). But a free act, by definition, does not glorify the law; nor does one submit to law by an assertion of "inflexible will." Nor, for that matter, has the Prince triumphed, as he claims, over "defiance" and "arrogance" (1757); his triumph has been over the helpless terror of mortality implied by human self-consciousness, which is in truth "the most ruinous of enemies within us" (1756–57). The Prince's speech is a kind of heroically joyful sophistry. Only a short while earlier he himself had shown considerable arrogance when, in preparing to answer the Elector's letter, he had dismissed the death sentence as morally negligible, as only an arbitrary exercise of power ("Er [der Kurfürst] handle, wie er darf"). But despite his unquenched defiance, what the Prince does, when he declares his triumph verbally, is defend the law, with little logic but with much rhetorical power, and his reason for doing so is the same as the Elector's for doing the same thing throughout the play—that it makes no sense to attempt to express the truth of human freedom, for this truth cannot take the form of an articulable doctrine, there can be no "philosophy of action." In any case, when the Prince heaps his dying benedictions on the Elector (1794–99), he does so not in response to the latter's lawful strictness but in response to an expression of fighting spirit (1784–93).

Again, therefore, we do not learn about freedom, but rather, by affirming and enjoying our own self-consciousness as we sit in the theater, we *are* free, with a freedom we also see projected before us, a freedom that requires no particular action of us but rather resides in our very being. This is the aim of tragedy—to effect a liberation of the audience here and now, in the theater.

9

But *Prinz Friedrich* is not a tragedy. It cannot be a tragedy, for we have known from the start what the Elector's true intentions are. Moreover, the overturning in *Prinz Friedrich* of tragic scenes and motifs from *Egmont*, *Tasso*, *Die Räuber*, *Wallenstein* and *Maria Stuart* suggests strongly that Kleist is in fact attempting something like an anti-tragedy. The Prince's death is made necessary, as the capstone of the tragic structure of the work's relation to its audience; but it is also made impossible. Why does Kleist do this?

We must not underestimate the force with which it is suggested that the Prince's death would be desirable. This suggestion is a main point of the Froben episode, for there is an exact parallel between Froben's fate and the Prince's. Like Froben, the Prince as it were mounts the Elector's horse; he takes law into his own hands by obeying the orders from his heart instead of those from his commander. He does morally what Froben does physically; he usurps the Elector's position; and he even imagines that he, like Froben, is doing his duty thereby. Thus it is especially significant that Froben's catafalque is in evidence when the Prince (in Act II, scene x), merely by walking onto the stage, walks into the arms of death—since the Elector has already pronounced sentence. Like Froben, the Prince, having mounted the Elector's horse, now moves boldly forward into the light (i.e. onto the stage) and, at least *in posse*, is instantly destroyed. All that is needed to complete this parallel satisfyingly is that the Prince actually be executed, and it is no accident that he himself says of Froben, "He has his reward!—If I had ten lives, I could hope to use them no better than that!" (678–79). Like Froben's, the Prince's death would shed glory upon the Elector—not in the sense that it would glorify law, but rather as a shining example of heroic freedom. Thus, again, the Prince ought to die, but he does not. Why is this?

Suppose the Prince were executed. The result, for the audience, would be a climactic image of the heroism of human existence. Our ability to watch and enjoy the Prince's death would be testimony to our own triumph. Adam Müller says: "Actions and incidents accumulate until the hero either triumphs or succumbs. It is better if he falls. To be defeated by circumstances does not demean him, and it is important that the weaker among the spectators be denied the opportunity of idolizing his person, that in the whole audience only the thought of the eternal peace of nature remain, thrown into relief by the spectacle of a truly heroic struggle" (pp. 156–57). If the hero falls, our enjoyment is purer and we achieve an intellectual triumph. In particular, it is necessary for Goethe's *Egmont* to die, because "the spectator or Egmont himself then recognizes that the soul, in order to free itself more powerfully, must submit to the oppression of prison walls, that that passage through the dungeon to the scaffold is a path leading to the highest freedom, to the mind's superiority over world and fate, to the most glorious of feelings, the feeling of victory over death" (Müller, p. 225). The applicability of these thoughts to *Prinz Friedrich* is obvious, and would have been obvious to Kleist.

Kleist, however, is writing not an *Egmont* but an anti-*Egmont*, in which he wishes to avoid the "knowledge" Müller is speaking of ("the spectator . . . recognizes"). Once again, Kleist understands that there is no such thing as knowledge of our "highest freedom," since such knowledge would have to be more than a feeling of "the mind's superiority"; it would have to be a "philosophy of action," an understanding of the absolute unity of freedom and duty or freedom and fate, which is impossible. The Prince's death, as Müller in effect points out, would confirm our feeling of freedom, and this confirmation, this reduction of freedom to a lesson or feeling, must be avoided if we are to retain the experience of *freedom itself,* which is the constant re-overcoming of an abject terror ceaselessly inherent in our self-conscious existence. If our terror is suppressed, if the feeling of mortality that arises from our self-consciousness is superseded by a comfortable feeling of "superiority," then our actual experience of freedom is destroyed. Therefore the play at the end, like the Elector at the beginning, thrusts us "back into Nothingness" (74), back into that realm of utter uncertainty where the experience of freedom is born.[21] In this sense the play does truly come full circle and lead us back to the original garden.

And yet, this withdrawal of tragic confirmation is not carried out arbitrarily; the Prince is not saved by a *deus ex machina.* His pardon, rather, forces us to look back over the work as a whole and recognize that we have known all along what would eventually happen, that the play's tragic tension, out of which our sense of freedom has grown, is nothing but illusion, nothing but our own mental contrivance. "Is it a dream?" says the Prince; and Kottwitz answers, "A dream, what else could it be?" (1856). Our true freedom, our constant overcoming of death, insofar as we are conscious of it or in any way know it, is indeed a mere dream, for such knowing necessarily conflicts with that actual presence of mortal terror upon which freedom depends for its existence. At the end, therefore, the play plunges us back again into the hopeless complications of self-consciousness (hence mortality) and so actually gives us our freedom. To this extent, even the Prince's survival, his continued freedom to live, is a projection of the audience's actual situation, but only insofar as the audience is disturbed by it.

It should now also be clear why Kleist handles the psychology of his characters, especially the Elector, as he does. If the Elector's true interests and motives were made explicit (in monologues, for example), then a sense of tragic tension could not arise in the first place; we would not be able to take the Prince's fear of death at all seriously, and it would therefore not function as a projection of the mortal terror implied by our own self-consciousness. On the other hand, if the Elector's true interests and motives were completely hidden, if it were impossible to deduce what he has in mind, then the indispensable sense, at the end, of a collapse of the play's fabric into mere dream or contrivance, could not happen either. Again, we must recognize at the end of the play not that the tragic has been avoided but rather that it had never been anything more than mere illusion in the first place. The tragic aspect of the play corresponds to our sense of the heroism inherent in our own self-conscious condition, thus to our knowledge of true human freedom, which knowledge cannot really exist. By being denied this knowledge, therefore, or by recognizing that the play's tragic aspect is illusory, we are cast back into that "Nothingness" where our freedom is in truth generated. Again, we must know what the Elector has in mind; but he may not say it.

10

It remains to be shown that the implications of *Prinz Friedrich* constitute a theory of drama rather than merely a general theory of the tragic, and in order to show this it is necessary to show that an actual performance, as opposed to reading, is indispensable to the achievement of Kleist's aim. The spectator, provided he understands the implications of the first scene, is obliged to think about his situation as the recipient of a symbolic vision; in particular he must understand that his consciousness of the vision's meaning prevents him from realizing the envisioned synthesis of freedom and duty. This state of potentiated consciousness (consciousness conscious of its own implications) is then projected and magnified in the Prince's terror of death, and in this magnification it is revealed as a true inner freedom entirely consistent with the strict fulfillment of communal duty, which freedom is now also projected in the Prince's proud reassertion of himself. Then, however, the tragic culmination is denied us; we are forcibly reminded of our knowledge, from the start, that there would be no tragedy. We recognize that our sense of immediate freedom had been our own mental contrivance; and this recognition is in turn reflected within the work's fiction in that we must also recall that the whole plot is the story of the Elector's educational contrivance for the Prince, a contrivance which does not work as planned, but which the Elector still carries through. Again, it is significant that the last scene brings us back to the garden of contrived symbols.

The important point, however, is that this sense of the necessary contrivedness or illusoriness of any supposed knowledge of our true freedom is reflected yet again and underscored by our situation as spectators in the theater. We, in the theater, do not receive valid evidence of the truth, but rather, like the characters in the first and last scenes, we take part in a symbolic ceremony that is deliberately calculated to express a particular idea of the human condition. The theater itself thus symbolically reflects a necessary component of the play's meaning. Our recognition that the idea of freedom which the play has awakened in us, precisely by being an idea, is false or at best unreliable becomes one with our awareness of our actual situation as participants in a consciously contrived ritual.

Yet the symbol itself, the inner fictional coherence of the play, remains untouched. The ironic disillusionment at the end of *Prinz Friedrich* is not the same drastic illusion-breaking that is practiced by Tieck or Grabbe or Frisch. The realistic consistency of the plot is reaffirmed rather more strongly than we might have wished, inasmuch as the Elector's intention of pardoning the Prince had been fully motivated from the outset. The *symbol itself*, in other words (i.e. the entirely credible fabric of cause and effect that is the plot), remains before us in all its power and clarity; only the idea we have derived from it is called into question by the terminal irony. But at the same time, the symbol still symbolizes the idea; indeed, the completed symbol does so with special clarity, in that the Prince, having reasserted his freedom, is now received once more into the communal order. It is as if the play's symbolic revelation of true human freedom were being drawn away from us tantalizingly, as Natalie draws away the symbol at the beginning. In the very act of denying us the tragic or cathartic confirmation of our idea, the play still expresses that idea symbolically.

This type of ironic effect is possible only in drama. In a narrative work (or a play, if we merely read it) the fictional world is created entirely in our imagination; images of this world are evoked in us by the work's language, not presented to us by actors.[22] The symbol as such (the fictional world) and the symbol's meaning exist in the same way, as mental realities. Indeed, symbol and meaning are intertwined in their genesis; in the process of constructing the fictional world in our imagination, we also think about its meaning, so that our interpretive thought and our imaginative construction are each conditioned by the other. If, therefore, by means of an ironic twist, the author calls into question the meaning of his work, he also calls into question the coherence and credibility of the fiction. Kleist avoids this by means of the form of drama (where the symbol is realized physically, independently of our ideas), in order to aim at the only possible valid expression of the idea of true freedom, an expression which retains its symbolic relation to the idea while also, paradoxically, denying the expressibility of the idea *as* an idea.

Or to look at the whole question differently, while it may be true that our appreciation of narrative involves a good deal of contrivance, still there is always an assumed genuineness in the relation between the author and the reader of any book. The author of a novel is attempting to say something, and our first task is to understand it; even if he deliberately calls our attention to the contrivedness of his fiction, he is still presumably making a serious point, perhaps a point about the nature of the novel or the difficulty of communication. But drama is different, for in drama the author and his authority are absent; drama, as we experience it in the theater, is nothing but contrivance, a contrived ritual in which not only the author but even the spectator plays an indispensable part, comparable to the confused but indispensable part played by the Prince in the first scene of *Prinz Friedrich*. When, therefore, by analogy with the Elector's final carrying out of his original contrivance with respect to the Prince, we are obliged to think about the contrivedness of the situation in which we actually find ourselves, it must occur to us that the idea of human freedom we have derived from the play is *our* idea, created by ourselves for ourselves, perhaps shared by the other participants in the ritual, but lacking the authority which (as long as we accept our conventional position as readers) the ideas in a book have. And again the effect of this recognition is twofold. On one hand, the idea of an heroic freedom inherent in every instant of conscious existence is called into question, since the symbolic argument by which it had been impressed upon us is now revealed as a mere contrivance in which we ourselves have knowingly played a part. But on the other hand, this idea, by being now our idea, independent of any external authority, gains a new potential genuineness, as an intimation of what we truly are. As with practically every aspect of the play's meaning, moreover, this ambiguous state of affairs is also projected on the stage. The Elector contrives to teach the Prince about the necessary combination of free

initiative and communal duty, but the Prince, as a result, undergoes the experience of a much more profound freedom than the
Elector had intended, an experience that includes the Elector's
teaching but does not constitute a learning of it; and this incommensurability between what is taught and what is experienced
corresponds to the state generated in the audience by its enforced
attention to the contrivedness of the theatrical situation. We, like
the Prince, learn more than we are taught.

Or yet again, the basic technique of projection by which the
play operates is meant to be analogous to the process of self-
consciousness; we see ourselves in the Prince. Something of this
kind can occur in narrative, by the process we call "identification"; our mental image of a hero and our mental image of ourselves can be made more or less to merge. What is different in
drama, and specifically in the case of the Prince, is the *physical
distance* between the spectator and the actor, which serves as a
powerful symbol for the internal divisiveness of self-consciousness, whereas the relationship between mental images of self and
hero must tend to emphasize the opposite aspect of self-consciousness, as self-completion. The genre of drama, then, is uniquely
well equipped to explore self-consciousness as a *problem*, and
we have argued that precisely this is Kleist's aim in *Prinz Friedrich*. Drama seeks not to soothe our self-consciousness but rather
to exacerbate it, to realize fully its potential as primal curse and
mortal terror, in order that our true freedom, the true heroism
of ordinary existence, be revealed. *Prinz Friedrich* is Kleist's attempt to carry out the doctrine of "Über das Marionettentheater,"
where we read: "Such blunders [the disturbances of natural grace
by self-consciousness] have been unavoidable since we ate of the
Tree of Knowledge. But Paradise is locked and the cherub stands
guard over it; we must travel all the way round the world and
see if we can find some back entrance to it."[23] There is no retreat from self-consciousness. Rather we must press forward in
our self-conscious being, intensify it and realize its last consequences, in the hope of arriving at "infinite consciousness."[24]
Again, this "trip around the world" is suggested in *Prinz Friedrich* quite clearly by the circular return to the garden.

We may thus formulate Kleist's theory of drama, or at least the
theory of drama at which he arrives in *Prinz Friedrich*, as follows.
Drama is an exercise for the spectator in problematic self-con-

sciousness, an attempt to conduct the spectator's self-consciousness "through the infinite"[25] in order that the little community in the theater become the model and seed of a revitalized humanity; and the idea of revitalized humanity, as this is implied by the idea of drama and by the thematic structure of *Prinz Friedrich*, is in turn Kleist's attempt to specify the vague ideal suggested in his puppet-theater essay. The nature of theater as a social institution, moreover, is indispensable to this theory of drama, for if an exercise of self-consciousness like *Prinz Friedrich* were imposed upon the solitary reader—and there is room for doubt that this is possible—the result would be either megalomania or despair. The key idea, once again, in the functioning of such a dramatic exercise, is the idea of the heroism of normal human existence from instant to instant, and this idea is meaningless (at least on the level of immediate experience) unless we *are* in the midst of normal human existence—unless we find ourselves actually among men, rather than in the solitary, abstracted dream-state of the reader of fiction.

Let it be emphasized, finally, that the reason for the complexity of our argument is not any comparable complexity in *Prinz Friedrich* itself, but rather the welter of tentative critical opinions that has gradually grown into a more or less standard view of the play. *Prinz Friedrich* is extremely simple and compact, and the theory of drama embodied in it does not include any specific psychological assumptions concerning the spectator. Only one assumption is necessary, that the spectator will understand fully what the work is meant to convey. If he understands the Elector's true motives and intentions (which are not deeply hidden), plus a few symbolic touches like the Garden of Eden image at the beginning, then he knows the importance of the problem of self-consciousness, since this problem determines the Elector's devious behavior. If, in addition, the spectator understands the connection between the Prince's symbolic "dream" and the form of drama, and deduces from this the allusion to problems of drama in the Elector's and the Prince's mistakes, then the mechanism of projection (the Prince as a projection of the audience) has been set in motion by this understanding alone, with no special psychological condition presupposed, and the exercise in self-consciousness is already under way.

The apparent complexity of *Prinz Friedrich* is only the complicatedness of the ways in which critics have read it, and this complicatedness in turn is the result of one general fault, that critics have read the play as readers (of a symbolic fiction, a quasi-narrative) rather than with constant reference to its proper mode of realization as a theatrical performance. Once we understand that our first task with respect to this text is to work out the theory of drama implied by it, the obscurities disappear, leaving a monumentally simple and powerful work. I do not mean by this that *Prinz Friedrich* lacks profundity, that it does not raise difficult questions. What I have attempted to do, rather, is to show that psychological and philosophical categories are not sufficient to explain the play, that the play's questions assume their full depth only in a dramaturgical context. And this, in turn, I offer as the model of a general procedure for considering the German dramatic movement. An intense concern with the question of drama as a genre, especially in relation to philosophical problems arising from the notion of self-consciousness, is what knits this movement together and constitutes its significance in the development of modern drama as a whole.

2 Lessing and the Problem of Drama

In *Prinz Friedrich von Homburg*, the inherent artificiality of dramatic performance has an indispensable function in generating the poetic meaning; the intellectual or self-conscious component of the audience's attitude, the audience's awareness of its own situation in the theater, is necessary for a full understanding of what the work is meant to convey. This is part of what I have described as Kleist's theory of drama, the idea of drama as a ritual intensification, and ultimately a kind of communal transfiguring, of our self-consciousness. But this theory is historically important not so much in itself as in its reflection of an intense concern, on Kleist's part, with the problem of drama at its most fundamental, a concern not merely with such questions as how a plot should be constructed, what social class the characters should belong to, what emotions should be encouraged in the spectator, but rather with the question of how the generically unique features of a dramatic work—those arising from its realization as performance and from the socio-aesthetic situation in a theater—may be integrated into the deepest level of poetic meaning. This concern with the relation between a dramatic work and the immediate perceptions and self-consciousness of an audience is what gives unity and continuity to the German dramatic movement.

1

What must be shown first of all, therefore, is that the "problem of drama" is genuinely a problem in eighteenth- and early

nineteenth-century Germany, not merely in Kleist. For the purposes of the present work, however, it will not be necessary to
discuss in detail either the genesis of the German dramatic tradition or its broad historical environment. My aim is to show not
where the German tradition comes from but where it is going, to
show that it is a true movement with important consequences in
modern European literature as a whole. If it can be shown that the
problem of drama is central and prominent in a cohesive group
of the most influential works (works from what I shall term the
"Classical" age, Lessing to Büchner), then the question of how
this problem arose need not be treated minutely. It is sufficient to
know that eighteenth-century intellectual Germany was significantly more concerned than her neighbors with questions relating
to drama and the theater, and to understand in general terms the
reasons for this.[1]

I do not mean to deny the importance, whether positive or negative, of the Baroque legacy or the tradition from Italian comedy or
the new bourgeois genres or the Gottschedians or the *Sturm und
Drang,* or of the thought of, say, J. E. Schlegel or Justus Möser or J.
M. R. Lenz. I do not mean to suggest that the German dramatic
movement would have been possible without its historical preparation. But its historical importance, in my opinion, resides in its
transmission to future generations of drama as a special kind of
poetic problem, involving the categories of ritual and fiction,
self-consciousness and illusion; and I shall begin, therefore,
where it seems to me that the problem is first fully developed, in
the works of Lessing.

2

Lessing's *Hamburgische Dramaturgie* is not a systematic
theoretical work, and there is much in it of no interest to the
modern reader. But at the end of no. 79 and the beginning of no.
80, we suddenly find ourselves at a major turning point in European literature.

> A poet can have done much, yet accomplished nothing. It is not
> enough that his work have an effect on us, but rather it must have
> those effects which, by its genre, are proper to it. These it must have
> above all, and if it lacks them, then nothing else can make up the
> lack—especially when the genre is of such importance, and in-
> volves such difficulty and cost, that all the effort and expense were

futile if only those effects were intended which could be provided by an easier and less circumstantial genre. . . .

Why the drudgery of dramatic form? [Wozu die sauere Arbeit der dramatischen Form?] why should I build a theater, stuff men and women into costumes, stuff their memories with roles, invite the whole city to gather? if, with my work and its performance, I intend merely to bring forth the emotional stirrings which could also be brought forth by a good story, read at home in an armchair.[2]

It is the question that must interest us here, not the attempt at an answer which immediately follows: "Dramatic form is the only form by which pity and fear can be aroused; or at least these passions cannot be aroused in as high a degree by any other form." This answer is inadequate, even in its qualified form, even in the light of Lessing's own extensive discussion of Aristotle, for it rests upon psychological assumptions that are unverifiable, assumptions concerning what actually happens inside a spectator's or a reader's breast. If we argue that the aim of tragedy is to excite fear and pity, we are talking mainly about artistic techniques; but if we talk about the *degrees* of fear and pity actually aroused in people under different circumstances, then we are speculating in an area where simple practical experience is bound eventually to prove us wrong.

The question, however, not the answer, is what concerns us, the question of *why there is such a thing as drama in the first place*, at least in modern Europe. Why should we, in an age supposedly characterized, above all, by "the voice of sound reason" (*HD* 1, p. 187), still be willing to bear the considerable trouble and expense required by dramatic performances? What does drama accomplish that can be accomplished by no other art form? If we are merely imitating the Greeks or the Elizabethans or the court of Louis XIV, then our effort is wasted. If having a national theater, for Germans, is merely a matter of prestige, then the artists involved even in a successful national theater will have prostituted themselves. Or if we feel that the time has come to express a new spirit in literature, say the spirit manifest in serious comedy and nonheroic tragedy, shall we not also seek a new form to embody this spirit? Especially in the case of the new "bourgeois" types, with their depiction of common human emotions and their generally sentimental appeal, with their concentration on "private life"[3] rather than on the public deeds of kings and heroes, it is not immediately apparent why the public institution of the theater should be chosen as their vehicle.

Lessing's question is therefore a very important one, but in Europe from, say, 1750 to 1850, this question was not even asked, let alone answered, outside Germany. A negative statement of this type, if insisted upon absolutely, can of course be refuted by a single counter example, which may very well exist. But as far as major writers are concerned, I am fairly sure of my ground. If the general question of why there should be such a thing as drama was asked outside Germany, then at least it did not reverberate; it did not take root and flower as it did in the minds of the Germans. The *Hamburgische Dramaturgie* may not be a complete theory of drama, but like several of Lessing's own plays, it was an important intellectual event in its time; and *Laokoon,* which deals more systematically with the whole question of artistic genres and their raisons d'être, had been even more of an event, at least according to Goethe.[4] My point is that part of what Lessing's works transmit and cause to reverberate in the culture at large is the general question or problem of drama.

Without covering the available material in detail, we can at least visualize the situation in eighteenth- and nineteenth-century Europe by comparing Lessing with Diderot on the one hand and Coleridge on the other, for there is a certain completeness and intensity in Lessing's view of drama which neither of the others possesses. Diderot is minutely aware of the relation between drama and its theater; he deals admirably with the craft and psychology of acting, with stage techniques and their effect, with the psychology of the spectator (given certain assumptions concerning the nature of artistic illusion), and with a number of other questions having to do with the playwright's immediate aim.[5] But he does not inquire into the ultimate purpose of drama, the human or social need that drama alone satisfies, and he does not broach the question of drama's origin. Coleridge, on the other hand, is mainly interested by the last two questions, and in one set of lecture notes, apparently with some assistance from Schelling, he approaches the type of argument I have attempted for *Prinz Friedrich* above: that undergoing dramatic illusion is not merely a kind of dream-experience but also the purified enactment of a conscious process that is ultimately the essence of our humanity and

leads us toward the divine.[6] Coleridge, however, has not Diderot's
sense for the immediacy and mechanics of the theater, and in the
course of his argument on dramatic illusion, he shifts his ground
from drama alone to "the universal principle of the fine arts." He
thinks of drama mainly in terms of existing monuments, especially Shakespeare, and not as a birth in progress, at which the
critic as midwife must concern himself with the messy details; he
thinks of the origin of drama as an event, or several events, in the
past, not as a repeated historical challenge with which each age
must deal as if it were new.

The importance and, at least in this limited comparison, the
uniqueness of Lessing's question thus emerges, for Lessing, without allowing himself to be distracted from the actual business of
the theater, still asks, in the most general terms, why there should
be such a thing as drama. I do not mean that Diderot and Coleridge
are typical of French and British thinking, nor do all non-German
thinkers on drama fall into one of the two classes they represent.
Hazlitt, for example, as it were straddles Lessing's position. He is
deeply concerned with the theatrical, and in the essays "On Actors and Acting" and "On Play-Going and on Some of Our Old
Actors," he works out a profound idea of the theater as an institution tending to generate human brotherhood in society at large.
But his interest here is mainly in questions of social structure and
feeling, not questions of artistic genre; and when, elsewhere, he
proposes a literary-critical discussion of "the dramatic" as opposed to the narrative and the epical, in the lecture "On Shakespeare and Milton," he does not attempt to keep the specifically
theatrical in focus.

While the component elements of Lessing's question, variously
permuted, may be widely present in intellectual Europe of the late
eighteenth and early nineteenth centuries, then, the question itself is not precipitated as a palpable intellectual event except in
Germany. The importance of this fact becomes clear when we
consider what might have happened if England, for instance, had
had one or two Lessings of her own, if such talents as Blake, Keats,
Shelley, and Byron, all of whom experimented with drama, had
breathed an intellectual atmosphere in which the most concrete
theatrical questions and the most abstract questions of dramatic
meaning were firmly bound, not only with each other, but also

with the sense of an urgent need in the "budding literature" of a new national epoch.[7]

3

Without unduly dramatizing the subject matter or overextending our metaphors, we can say that Europe in Lessing's time was intellectually pregnant with a drama of the future, and we can understand the main reasons for this if we begin by recognizing that the bourgeois drama and the more uniquely German *Sturm und Drang* have in common a basic anti-rationalistic tendency. The immediate reason for the eighteenth century's interest in drama (though not an adequate reason in the sense of Lessing's question) was that drama communicates not only by way of the mind, as books do, but also directly, by way of the senses; drama is thus the most powerfully "aesthetic" literary type, to use Baumgarten's rapidly accepted term; it does not flatter or improve the higher level of mental existence so much as it releases a deeper level; in a word (a word repeated ad nauseam in the dramatic theory of the time), drama can make us weep. Drama, therefore, provided it is not merely an imitation and does not insist on following antiquated rules, provided it springs from our own situation like a plant from the earth (to use the metaphor of Herder's Shakespeare essay), a bourgeois drama, therefore, if we are bourgeois, or a drama expressing the German "Denkungsart"[8] if we are Germans, seems to promise a way of rediscovering the natural center of our existence, a way of revitalizing our community and resisting the stagnation that sets in when men believe too complacently in the perfectibility of human society by means of reason alone.

There are two obvious ways in which drama may attempt to release a deeper level of experience in its eighteenth-century bourgeois spectator. The stage may be used either as a mirror or as a bludgeon. Either the spectator is presented with characters basically like himself, "von gleichem Schrot und Korne" (*HD* 75, p. 104)—whose disasters are conceivable in his own existence, so that he may learn to experience his life's dull everydayness as a mere surface, concealing at least the possibility of extreme anguish and even heroism—or else the form and content of the drama jolt him out of his habitual manner of experiencing—things are said and done on the stage that will offend him if possible and confuse him if necessary, so that his truer, more natural self may rise among the shattered fragments of his conventional sensibilities. The two possibilities are a theater of sympathy and a theater of shock, and their manifestations are the bourgeois drama and the drama of *Sturm und Drang*.

For reasons that will appear as we go on, however, I do not agree with many of the claims that have been made for the eighteenth-century theaters of shock and sympathy as predecessors of modern social drama and epic theater. Bourgeois drama and *Sturm und Drang* drama represent only a groping toward drama, the uncertainty of which can be observed in Lessing, who anticipates the *Sturm und Drang* in *Philotas*, pioneers bourgeois theater in *Miss Sara Sampson*, and perhaps tries to combine the two in *Emilia Galotti*, but is never satisfied with either mode.[9] And it is Lessing's struggle with the problem of drama which points the way toward an authentic renewal of the form. The categories of sympathy and shock are not sufficient to produce an achievement on the order of Kleist's *Prinz Friedrich*, for they involve untenable assumptions concerning the spectator's response; they do not address the problem of integrating drama's ritual and fictional aspects with one another. They do not answer Lessing's question.

But if the groping toward drama, via shock and sympathy, is a European phenomenon, why is it that around 1800 only the Germans grope their way into the light? One answer is suggested by a speech in Goethe's *Iphigenie auf Tauris*, where Arkas describes the situation and needs of the Tauridians. Precisely the *lack* of an indigenous dramatic tradition works to the Germans' advantage. To judge from the opening section of the essay *De la poésie dramatique*, Diderot cannot, or does not bother to, conceive of a society without its theater; there are only differences among the types of theater various societies possess; Diderot's aim is to modify an existing tradition, not to found a new one. And in England there is Shakespeare, who, for all the enthusiasm he awakens, inhibits the growth of a self-conscious modern drama by drawing attention to the past and by being too huge a figure for the modern poet to measure himself against. Of course Shakespeare casts a large shadow in Germany as well, but at least the German poet writes a different language and need not compare himself with Shakespeare directly; one could dream of becoming the German Shakespeare,[10] as one obviously could not dream of becoming the English Shakespeare.

German thinkers of the eighteenth century, moreover, felt the lack not only of a dramatic tradition but of a poetic tradition in general, especially by comparison with the neighbors they were most conscious of, France and England. Klopstock, Lessing, Herder, the *Sturm und Drang* poets, Goethe and Schiller, even the early Romantics, all felt in various ways that their task was to create a German literary tradition, and drama was especially important as an object of this feeling because the proudest achievements of France and England were in that field. Gottsched and his disciples had long rubbed Germany's nose in the excellence of French classical drama—many young poets would have considered this exactly the right metaphor—and the tendency to equate national literary excellence with excellence in drama could then only increase with the growing interest in English literature and Shakespeare. The question of drama was thus urgent in Germany as it was nowhere else; hence Germany's special tenacity in the quest for an authentic renewal of dramatic theory and practice.

4

Again, one of the prime examples of this tenacity is Lessing's career. We shall see that drama was an insurmountable intellectual problem for him to the very end, when he made a last brilliant assault on it with *Nathan der Weise*; but let us begin with *Laokoon* and the apparently harmless remark that drama as performance is a "lebendige Mahlerey" (*L* iv, p. 23). We could consider this idea of drama as "living painting" merely an ornamental metaphor if it did not occur in a work that seeks to establish a fundamental opposition between the temporally extended (or moving, "living") verbal arts and the spatially extended arts. Lessing comes dangerously close to suggesting that drama is a counter example to his whole aesthetics, for how shall drama, given its character as poetry, avoid imitating nature in a manner that conflicts with its character as "painting," or vice versa? Or let us consider the statement, "Only that is fruitful which allows free play to the imagination" (*L* iii, p. 19), which apparently means that art ought to stimulate in us a free mental activity that completes the artistically conveyed image and in doing so makes the image more convincing, more continuous with our own mind, than it would have been if the artist had attempted to do all our imaginative work for us. That painting can only suggest action, and poetry only suggest objects, is thus not a disadvantage but an advantage, for we ourselves, in that we supply imaginatively the missing half of the depicted world, are involved in the creative process and so more deeply involved in the illusion; elsewhere Lessing argues specifically that art imitates not things or events in themselves but rather the structure of our experiencing them mentally (HD 70, pp. 82–83). And yet, where does this leave drama, which presents us directly with both the objects and the actions that constitute its fictional world, and in addition even helps us along with "the fixing of our attention" (HD 70, p. 82)? How can drama be "fruitful" in the sense of allowing "free play" to our imagination? In Laokoon it is stated specifically that imagination is necessary in drama, in order to bring about sympathy between ourselves and the character, "somewhat of a commensurate feeling in us" (L iv, p. 23); but the basic need filled by imagination, according to the systematic thought of Laokoon, does not exist in drama. Genius often succeeds where theory despairs, says Lessing (L iv, p. 24), but this profession of faith does not resolve the logical difficulty in his thinking.

At least he seems to be aware of the difficulty, for he picks up the same idea in the Dramaturgie and develops it a bit further:

> The art of acting stands midway between the pictorial arts and poetry. Its highest law, since it is a visible depicting, must be beauty; but as a transitory depicting, it does not always have to give its images that striking repose which characterizes ancient art. It may, indeed it must, from time to time allow itself the extravagance of a Tempesta, the audacity of a Bernini. . . . But it may not sustain these moods too long; it must resolve them, by what follows, into the general mood of propriety; it may never develop its excesses with the strength that is permissible in poetry as such. [HD 5, pp. 204–5]

Lessing seeks to give the impression here that the art of acting is uniquely free, but actually he is imposing special limitations on it, which necessarily imply limitations on the art of the playwright as well, limitations on what he may ask his actors to do. Drama, it appears, may not go too far in the direction of either visual beauty or violent activity; drama is "living painting," but it must avoid living too vigorously or painting too beautifully, and does this not make for an insipid art? Lessing is apparently aware of this danger in *Laokoon,* when he goes out of his way to defend the extremity of Sophocles' *Philoctetes* (*L* iv, pp. 24–33); but in both *Laokoon* and the *Dramaturgie,* Shakespeare's *Richard III* remains a stumbling block, which Lessing can neither condemn outright nor find adequate reasons for defending (*L* xxiii, pp. 141–43; *HD* 73–79). Again, how can drama be sufficiently bold and energetic to achieve tragic penetration, while still restraining itself sufficiently to avoid the potential conflicts inherent in its ambiguous aesthetic nature as "living painting"?

There seems to be a relatively easy way out of this dilemma. Lessing is moving toward the idea of drama as a form in which the artificiality of the medium plays an important expressive role. The extreme combination of moral and physical ugliness in Shakespeare's Richard need no longer trouble us if it is balanced by our awareness of both ourselves and the actor as participants in a ritual, a mere game; propriety (*das Wohlanständige*) is no longer so important if we do not think of the character as a real person by whom we can be repelled. This type of thinking, in fact, was suggested to Lessing quite clearly by the argument on illusion in Moses Mendelssohn's essay "Von der Herrschaft über die Neigungen," and could also have been suggested by Marmontel;[11] both Mendelssohn and Marmontel argue that dramatic illusion must include a certain intellectual detachment, that it must be a state we voluntarily submit to. Even the anonymous author of the early German treatise "Vom bürgerlichen Trauerspiele" is aware that, despite the similarity between spectator and character in bourgeois drama, the emotions felt by the two must remain clearly different because of their different situations;[12] and Lessing himself, in his argument on Aristotle and *Richard III,* makes use of this idea explicitly (*HD* 78, p. 115).

But still, Lessing does not so much refute the idea of self-conscious artificiality in drama as he doggedly resists it. In his letter of 2 February 1757, responding to Mendelssohn's essay, he challenges Mendelssohn's examples, but speaks as if this were a refutation of the basic idea, which it is not. Moreover, he always attempts to limit as strictly as possible the implications of the idea that the spectator's emotions must be different from the character's. In no. 11 of the *Dramaturgie,* in order to be able to argue that the ghost in *Hamlet* does not alienate us intellectually, he goes so

far as to claim that our modern disbelief in ghosts is only a relatively superficial prejudice which the poet can overcome by in-
ducing us to sympathize with a character to whom a ghost appears; Hamlet reacts to the ghost, and "the impression it makes on
him reverberates in us" (p. 230). That Lessing himself is not too
happy with this argument is clear from his appeal at the beginning of it—as at the beginning of the defense of the *Philoctetes* in
Laokoon—to that "genius" which "defies all our philosophy" (p.
228).

Lessing agrees that the feelings of a spectator are different from
those of the character, but he still repeatedly comes back to the
idea that we are somehow swept up in the character's feelings.
This is why he insists upon his dubious definition of *to philan-
thropon* in Aristotle as a "feeling similar to pity" (*HD* 76, p. 108),
as the beginnings of pity, which we can feel even for a villain, but
not yet actually pity itself, which we can feel only for someone
more or less our moral equal.[13] By understanding "the philanthropic" as similar to pity but still clearly distinguished from it,
Lessing restricts pity to our feeling for those with whom we also
sympathize (the German word "Mitleid" is conveniently ambiguous); even if pity, the principal emotion aroused in the audience
viewing a tragedy,[14] is not exactly what the fictional characters
feel, still pity in its restricted sense presupposes our sympathy
or emotional resonance with the characters. Somehow we must
ourselves be transported into the fictional world, at least in our
feelings; and accordingly, when Lessing speaks of illusion, he
is a good deal closer to Diderot than to Mendelssohn in insisting
on the total and involuntary nature of this phenomenon. In the
first number of the *Dramaturgie* he says that the dramatist's job
is "not to describe the passions, but rather to make them originate naturally before the spectator's eyes, with such an illusion of
uninterrupted growth that the spectator must sympathize whether
he will or no" (*HD* 1, p. 185). And this statement is typical of the
work as a whole.[15]

But if Lessing is himself aware of certain difficulties in his idea
of drama, and if his difficulties could be relieved by the idea that
we are meant to be conscious of drama's artificiality, then why
does he resist this idea so stubbornly? The fact that he does resist
it, I think, shows how important to him his basic question is: why
should there be such a thing as drama in the first place? If the

question is asked in this form, it seems absurd to suggest that the purpose of all the paraphernalia and effort by which drama replaces a mere mental image with an actual physical image could be anything but to strengthen the illusion of reality. Moreover, if drama were to insist too much on its artificiality, how could it even begin to interest the spectator, at least the modern spectator for whom a theatrical performance is no longer a religious ceremony?

We might also consider the deeper answers that Lessing suggests to his basic question, the idea, for example, that drama brings about a kind of human brotherhood in the theater, a community of purified and properly directed emotion which is then meant to spill over into real life. Lessing writes to Nicolai in November 1756 that the whole aim of tragedy is to give us practice in feeling "Mitleid" (pity or sympathy), because "*The man most able to pity is the best man,* the readiest in all social virtues, all types of magnanimity"; and the corresponding point about comedy as practice in laughing at the truly laughable is found in no. 29 of the *Dramaturgie.* Or we recall Lessing's argument that the purposefulness and completeness of a drama's plan should "accustom" us to the thought that ultimately there is also a plan behind the apparent confusion of everyday reality (*HD* 79, p. 120), which thought will then enable us to live more confidently and sensibly. Each of these ideas presupposes that we shall sense a basic continuity between our mood in the theater and the real world outside, and how can this happen without a powerful illusion of reality in the theater?

All of this, however, only aggravates the problem of drama for Lessing. Drama must create the strongest possible artistic illusion, yet is prevented by its nature from allowing the free play of the imagination by which illusion is produced most "fruitfully" in our minds. Drama is sufficiently like painting to be subject to painting's limitations, but cannot hope to achieve that ideal repose of beauty for which the painter actually aims; drama is a type of poetry, but may not take full advantage of poetry's freedom in the presentation of evil or ugliness. Furthermore, although Lessing is aware of these problems, he appears to insist upon aggravating them; especially on the subject of artistic illusion, he refuses even to consider the merits and implications of an idea proposed by his closest friend. Is it possible that he is saying less than he knows? Critics have long been willing to consider the possibility of complicated ironies in Lessing's theological writings, ironies that have to do with the distinction—made, let us recall, in Aristotle's *Poetics*[16]—between esoteric and exoteric doctrine. Is there any special reason we should not apply the category of irony to Lessing's poetics as well?

It is at least conceivable that Lessing resists Mendelssohn's idea of illusion not because he judges it to be an invalid idea so much as because he feels it to be a dangerous idea. It is conceivable that Lessing makes a distinction (as Goethe also does) between drama's immediate and ultimate aims, and that he deliberately restricts his theoretical arguments to the immediate. Even if the ultimate aim of drama involves our awareness of its artificiality, still, and for just this reason, a drama must begin by *being* a well-made artifice. If the fiction in *Prinz Friedrich*, for example, were not psychologically cohesive and interesting, then our gradual recognition of the implications of its artificiality would lack significance; it would no longer be a complex, indirect recognition concerning ourselves and the heroic character of our existence, but simply a direct perception of imperfect workmanship on the part of the poet. The effect of a drama, as Lessing says, must be immediately compelling; but if the audience knows in advance that what ultimately counts is their awareness of theatrical artifice, how shall the necessary immediate effect be achieved? Will our anticipatory theoretical knowledge not prevent it? On these grounds it could be argued that the theory of drama's ultimate aims is properly esoteric, not for publication.

Or perhaps there is even one further reason for Lessing's insistence upon making drama as much a problem as possible: namely, the recognition that drama, at least from a practical point of view, always is a problem, for which we must avoid providing apparent theoretical solutions. The trouble with French theater before Diderot, according to Lessing, is its theoretical complacency, which in turn had infected Gottsched and stifled any real talent he might have possessed (*HD* 81). The aesthetic theoretician therefore serves his culture best by offering not solutions to the problems he poses, but rather the problems themselves, in as fruitfully radical a form as possible. Any solution to an aesthetic problem, anything that can be interpreted as a prescriptive rule, is at best highly contingent (again we think of Lessing's insistence on the ability of genius to defy theory) and always artistically deadening. The aes-

thetician must probe his material until he arrives at the deepest
problems possible, endless problems capable of arousing both the
spectator's interest and the poet's creativity. Of course this principle can be applied to every poetic genre, but Lessing, mindful of
the dangers in French prescriptive theory, was especially careful
not to conceal from himself the necessarily problematic quality of
his meditations on drama. And in this he set an important example for his contemporaries and successors in the German dramatic
movement.

Let us look at one further instance of the problematic in Lessing's theory. Maffei's *Merope* is criticized in the *Dramaturgie*
because in one line, and as a mere rhetorical embellishment, a
character speaks the word "theater-stage." This alone, says Lessing, "the mere words 'stage' and 'invented'" (*HD* 42, p. 363), is
sufficient to ruin the illusion by reminding the spectator of his
situation in the theater. And yet, in no. 5, Lessing quotes Hamlet's
advice to the players—surely a much more drastic disturbance of
the illusion than Maffei's—without even a hint of criticism.
Again, where does the necessary compellingness of drama end,
and the unavoidable artificiality begin?

Or we think of the conversation on art in the second and fourth
scenes of *Emilia Galotti*. Ilse Graham has shown that this conversation reflects Lessing's own deepest artistic concerns,[17] and presumably, therefore, it is meant to convey or awaken something of
these concerns in the spectator. But will it then not disrupt the
dramatic illusion entirely, by confronting the spectator simultaneously with both an implied theory of art and an actual example (i.e. the play), thus forcing him into a state of intellectual
detachment? We can conclude this phase of our discussion of
Lessing by taking a closer look at *Emilia*.

5

Emilia Galotti appears, from its genesis, to bear an especially
close relation to its author's abstract aesthetic thinking. Its growth
through several versions from 1758 to 1772 straddles the writing
of both *Laokoon* and the *Hamburgische Dramaturgie*, and the
work itself seems to represent a straddling of the difference between bourgeois drama and the more extreme tendencies beginning to emerge in the *Sturm und Drang*. There are, moreover, a
number of passages in *Laokoon* and the *Dramaturgie* that could

be taken to refer directly to *Emilia,* and in a curiously uncomfortable way. Fred O. Nolte points out, for example, that Odoardo's phrase in Act V, scene viii, "to follow up my deed in the manner of a dull tragedy," violates exactly Lessing's point against Maffei, and that Emilia's surprising confession of seducibility in Act V, scene vii, violates the principle of characterization laid down in no. 9 of the *Dramaturgie.*[18]

But there are even more important difficulties. In no. 82 of the *Dramaturgie,* Lessing ridicules the way in which Corneille stretches Aristotle to accommodate his own plays, and he is especially caustic about Corneille's assertion (in defense of *Polyeucte*) that it is acceptable in tragedy to have a highly virtuous man come to grief at the hands of a man who is not thoroughly wicked but rather shows more weakness than malice. And yet, does this not describe the relation between the Prince and Appiani? Of course there are differences. The killing of Appiani is a dramatically subordinate action, the Prince does not order it specifically, and the Prince's shallow regret afterwards, unlike that of Corneille's villain-from-weakness, is obviously not meant to move us. But the basic pattern, and the causes of what Lessing calls "the gruesome" (p. 134), the Aristotelian *miaron,*[19] are still there. Why does Lessing do this? Does he wish to contrast an un-tragic sub-action with the presumably tragic main action that culminates in Emilia's death? If so, then he is counting on the intellectual alertness of the audience, for on the level of pure emotional response—assuming that Appiani's death is merely appalling and Emilia's tragic—the two actions would interfere with each other.

Or we turn to *Laokoon,* where Lessing, in dealing with Caylus's ideas for paintings based on Homer, asks, "have we become accustomed in paintings, as well as in the theater, to accept the ugliest actress as a ravishing princess if only her prince claims to feel a good warm love for her?" (*L* xxii, p. 134). This suggests the question of Emilia Galotti's beauty and the inescapable fact that an actress does not exist whose appearance could satisfy an audience's expectations after the conversation between the Prince and Conti in Act I, scene iv. The audience at this play will not be prepared to accept Emilia's beauty as given, but rather will experience disillusionment when the actual imperfect actress finally shows herself. Not only from the infatuated Prince do we hear that Emilia's is the most perfect beauty imaginable, but we also receive

a professional opinion on this point from a painter, and in case we
forget that this is a professional opinion, the Prince reminds us,
"Only a painter is really able to judge beauty" (I.iv). The effect,
when even an extremely good-looking actress steps forth as
Emilia, would perhaps not be quite so strong as the effect, say, of
seeing Othello played by a freckled redhead, but it will not be
different in kind.

Is this merely a mistake on Lessing's part? If so, then it is a
mistake which the author of *Laokoon* ought to have been wary of:
"The poet, since he can only show the components of beauty one
after the other, avoids altogether the depiction of physical beauty
as such. He feels that these components, successively ordered,
cannot possibly have the same effect as when they stand next to
each other in space" (L xx, p. 121). And yet, Conti does explicitly
list Emilia's attributes: "This head, this face, this brow, these eyes,
this nose, this mouth, this chin, this neck, this breast, this body,
all this in combination, is from now on my sole standard of
feminine beauty" (I.iv.). If we could count on Emilia to surpass this
description, as painting surpasses poetry in the depiction of physical beauty, everything would be fine. But Emilia is not a painting; she is, for us, a real woman (the actress) who cannot possibly
meet our expectations. By as much as Conti's enumeration falls
short of painting, by so much again must the actress fall short of
Conti's enthusiasm, and the alienating effect is thus, if anything,
redoubled.

If it were not for Lessing's repeated insistence on the in-
violability of dramatic illusion, we would conclude that the intent
in *Emilia* is to make the audience aware of the imperfect artificiality of the stage, to approach the audience intellectually rather than
sensually. Whether or not this can be argued, however, need not
concern us here. It is sufficient to recognize that in *Emilia* the
problem of drama, the problem of balancing or reconciling sensory and intellectual components, becomes especially acute, for
this will enable us to see *Emilia* as a step on the way toward
Lessing's supreme dramatic achievement in *Nathan der Weise*.[20]

For the Lessing of *Emilia*, theory and practice are complicatedly
intertwined. Theory has been developed to a point where the problems of drama become impassable, and these problems (not any
firm, unambiguous principles) then prove a fruitful source of dramatic creativity. We shall have occasion to observe this process

in Goethe as well, and yet again in Schiller; and in fact it is not until Nietzsche that anything like a real theoretical breakthrough occurs. Even Nietzsche's thinking, however, has the practical effect of making drama not easier but harder, more of a problem, if correspondingly more rewarding.

3 *Nathan der Weise:*
Breakthrough in Practice

The trouble with *Emilia* is that the results of Lessing's deepening theoretical awareness of the problem of drama are forced onto a dramatic plan which had not been conceived with such subtleties in mind. But the case of *Nathan der Weise* is different. *Nathan* is also apparently developed from an older plan (letter to Karl Lessing, 11 August 1778), but the immediate occasion of its execution was the Goeze controversy, and Lessing's polemical interest is what gave him the energy for an entirely fresh start. In any event, *Nathan* has proved an endlessly challenging work. Reams have been written on its form, its verbal suggestiveness, and the ins and outs of its logic, morality, philosophy, psychology, theology, and social relevance.[1] But is it significantly subtle as a drama, not merely as a text? Does Lessing even bother to think of it in relation to his own painful struggle with drama's generic problems, or is he using dramatic form only as a roundabout way of preaching—as he himself suggests to Elise Reimarus (6 September 1778)?

1

The bulk of the evidence in this case will have to be taken from the text itself, but in general it is hardly conceivable that Lessing should not have considered carefully the implications of *Nathan* with respect to drama as a genre. In the first place, drama was an unsolved problem for him; it was not an intellectual matter that he could imagine he had successfully disposed of. There were times when he claimed to have put the theater completely out of his mind, especially after his move to Wolfenbüttel (letter to Karl Lessing of 14 November 1771); but during the early years in Wolfenbüttel he also struggled grimly with the problem of writing tragedy, in *Spartacus* and then *Emilia Galotti*.[2] In the second place, the Goeze controversy was not merely a theological dispute concerning the role of the Bible in Christian belief; it was an important public controversy, involving not only the reputations of the contestants but also broad questions of ecclesiastical policy and thus, by extension, the question of how people in general should be encouraged to think. The ultimate goal, for both Lessing and Goeze, was not to score a theological point but rather to exercise a decisive influence on the intellectual life of the nation. Thus Lessing writes to Elise Reimarus that he wishes to use the theater as a pulpit, not merely that he wishes to use a dramatic text as a parable. Hence questions of the effect upon an audience, questions of the theater as theater, could not but have occurred to him.

And in the third place, the generically problematic quality of *Emilia* is manifest primarily in a number of disharmonies between the play and theoretical principles or remarks in *Laokoon* and the *Hamburgische Dramaturgie*. Such disharmonies are also found in *Nathan*. We can probably excuse the Patriarch's explicit reference to the theater[3] on the grounds that Lessing, in his criticism of Maffei, still permits this form of irony in comedy—although laughter, "unser Lachen" (*HD* 42, p. 363), is not what appears to be aimed at in this passage, where the Templar has rashly placed Nathan in danger of his life. But it is not so easy to reconcile the structure of *Nathan* with Lessing's argument (following Diderot) that it is better to avoid surprise for the spectators.[4] The spectator does not have to be surprised at the end of *Nathan*. He has a fair idea that the Templar's resemblance to Assad will turn out not to be a mere coincidence; he learns in Act II, scene vii, that the Templar also resembles someone named "Wolf," whose family name "Filnek," however, is mentioned only inconspicuously (II.vii.612); and in Act IV, scene vii, he learns that Recha is Wolf von Filnek's daughter. But it takes an extremely alert spectator to catch all these hints and put them together while the play is in progress; for practical purposes, the end does come as a surprise.[5]

Yet again, Lessing explicitly concedes Diderot's argument against "contrasting" characters (*HD* 86, p. 151).[6] Characters ought to be in contrast or tension with their situations rather than with each other, for contrasts built into the characters themselves (e.g. the schematic opposition between fathers in Terence's *Adelphi*) are too obviously contrived, whereas well-conceived oppositions between character and situation give the impression of naturalness and so can provide moral instruction in a form directly applicable to our own lives.[7] The characters in *Nathan*, however, while psychologically complex, are arranged in a pattern more obviously contrived than would ordinarily be acceptable outside farce. A Jew, a Christian, and a Mohammedan are the main characters—plus Recha, who is revealed by turns as belonging to each of the three cultures—and they are not contrasted with their situations, but rather the cultural contrasts among them are their situation. This comes very close to being the typical structure of a fable, not a drama; and in case we forget this, at the center of *Nathan* is an actual fable. Fable and drama, however, are genres that Lessing himself had carefully distinguished from one another, not only in the *Dramaturgie* (no. 35) but also in his earlier treatise "Von dem Wesen der Fabel."

Or how does Lessing expect to get away with using blank verse as he does in *Nathan*, especially in view of the discussion of natural language in no. 59 of the *Dramaturgie*? Peter Demetz argues brilliantly, if somewhat bewilderingly, that Lessing deliberately writes bad verse here—verse, in order to reflect and justify the cultural distance between the fiction and the world of the spectator; but bad verse, for the sake of direct accessibility or "familiarity" to the spectator.[8] Too much perfection in form, it seems, would give the spectator a feeling of exclusion from the fictional world. This argument would be merely bewildering, not also brilliant, if it did not explain Lessing's cryptic remark to his brother, on 7 December 1778, concerning the verse in *Nathan*: "If it were much better, it would be that much the worse." But even so, are the Oriental setting and "tone"[9] of the play really a sufficient reason for verse if the verse is going to be shattered by natural language anyway? As in the case of *Emilia*, it appears as if Lessing intended to emphasize the artificiality of his work, here by making natural language itself emerge as an artifice-upon-artifice, as an inappropriate distortion, thus obviously contrived

or artificial, of the already artificial form of verse. In any event, I
have shown that this emphasis on artifice would not involve an
actual contradiction between theory and practice; it would involve simply a relocation of the inescapably problematic boundary between drama's artificial naturalness and its natural or
necessary artificiality.

Can it be argued, finally, that an author's failure to follow his
own dramatic prescriptions shows that he has conceived his play
with a view to its genre? In this case it can. In the first place, given
Lessing's general concern with questions of artistic genre, it is
hard to imagine that he could leave this factor out of account in
planning his own works. In the second place, Lessing regards his
own apparently prescriptive statements not as rigidly valid but as
heuristic; he repeatedly reminds us that genius can defy them.
And in the third place, he makes no attempt to relieve or conceal
the disharmonies between theory and practice; these disharmonies, rather, in both *Emilia* and *Nathan,* are pointed, and
therefore are apparently intended to carry some specific meaning,
at least for the aesthetically sophisticated spectator.

2

One of the most interesting things about *Nathan* is that, despite
the idea of tolerant humanity which informs it, there is also a
special emphasis on the ineradicable barbarity of mankind. Our
attention is drawn especially by the choice offered Nathan at the
end of Act II.[10] Nathan has been gently ironic with Al-Hafi about
the latter's obsession with chess (II.ix.687–92), but Al-Hafi coun-
ters by suddenly becoming very serious. He invites Nathan to join
him in a total philosophical retreat from the world, and surpris-
ingly enough, Nathan takes the invitation seriously:

> Nathan: I thought we would keep that as a last resort, Al-Hafi. And
>   yet, let me think about it. Wait . . .
> Al-Hafi: Think about it? No thinking is needed for this.
> Nathan: Wait at least until I return from the Sultan, until I have
>   taken leave . . . [II.ix.712–17]

There are two possible reasons for Nathan's attitude. First, Al-Hafi
has warned him that he is in danger of being driven slowly into
bankruptcy by Saladin's generosity. And second, he already has a
fairly clear idea of the true family relationships that will be re-

vealed at the end: he knows that Wolf von Filnek, Recha's natural father, had not been a European, and he knows that the Templar resembles both Wolf and Assad. Perhaps Saladin, who has sent for him, also suspects something. In any case, those family relationships are bound to come out soon, and when they do, Nathan will be forced to relinquish his daughter, who means more to him than any possessions. If it turns out, therefore, from his interview with Saladin, that he is going to lose his daughter and his ducats, and if his ducats would be worthless to him without his daughter anyway, why should he not take his leave willingly and simply renounce the whole world?

To be sure, it appears almost immediately that he is constitutionally unable to do this. Al-Hafi vehemently interrupts his plea for time to consider: "By 'thinking about it' you mean you are looking for reasons not to do it. Whoever cannot simply decide on the spur of the moment to be his own man must live as others' slave for ever.—As you please!—May you live well, according to your own lights.—Our paths diverge" (717–22). And Nathan, in spite of himself, is horrified by the idea that Al-Hafi is disregarding his financial responsibilities. "Al-Hafi!" he says admonishingly, "surely you will first square your accounts?" (723–24). Nathan belongs in the real world and thinks in a basically worldly way, a condition he is powerless to change. It would be wrong, even for a ruined Nathan, to accept Al-Hafi's proposal.

But still, even this prosperous merchant is seriously attracted by the idea of total retreat. Since he is shown as a wise man, his temptation prompts us to question objectively the desirability of the world (at least as it is depicted in the play), and when we question, we discover that the world in which Nathan chooses to remain, despite flashes of enlightenment, is quite thoroughly barbaric. This applies, moreover, not only to the Christians, whose general tendency toward narrow-mindedness is stressed repeatedly. Even in some very perceptive discussions of *Nathan* we hear of "the enlightened Sultan Saladin,"[11] and I suppose the word "enlightened" refers to Saladin's apparent religious tolerance, to statements like, "I have never insisted that all trees grow the same bark" (IV.iv.309–10). But actually this tolerance springs from a general good-hearted indifference, not from any positive rational conviction. Saladin is a simple man: "One cloak, one sword, one horse—and one God! What more do I need?"

(II.ii.203–4); he has his God, and as far as he is concerned others are welcome to theirs. His simplicity is expressed most clearly in a speech which seems to deny it: "Unfortunately I too am a thing of many 'sides, which often refuse to jibe with each other" (IV.iv.333–35). He does not care if his actions are inconsistent; he does what occurs to him at any given time and lets logic worry about itself. In the midst of an enlightened conversation with Sittah, for example, about the blind prejudice that restricts Christians to marriage with Christians, he is capable of reverting suddenly to his own irrational obsession with the malevolence of the Knights Templar (II.i.102–13), an obsession to which he gives vent by simply removing the head of every Templar he gets his hands on. Every Templar, that is, save one; and this one Templar, by being a brave, likeable, and relatively enlightened human being, is living testimony to the barbarity of the general practice.

Saladin's famous generosity, moreover, is attacked vigorously and justifiedly by Al-Hafi: "You would not call it hypocrisy, to oppress, impoverish, plunder, martyr, and throttle men by the hundreds of thousands, and then to pose as a humanitarian with individuals?" (I.iii.480–83). His generosity is nothing but recklessness at best, and in this it is specifically contrasted with Nathan's. When Saladin finally feels the pinch and sees himself becoming "hard" (IV.iii.230), the result is only that he becomes confused and offensive, as with the messenger Ibrahim (V.i). His generosity is sustained neither by practical seriousness (in order to stay generous one must devote some effort to staying rich) nor by that true rational humanity which avoids the damage that can come from generosity misplaced—as Nathan avoids this with Al-Hafi (I.iii.437–41).

The world in which Nathan lives—and the world in which, though he is seriously tempted by Al-Hafi, he specifically decides to continue—is a basically barbaric world, and Lessing adds a number of more or less gratuitous touches to emphasize this. When Sittah invites Saladin into her harem to discuss how they shall deal with Nathan, she could easily mention that she wishes to show him, say, a new set of chessmen; what she actually mentions, however, is a slave (II.iii. 355–56), and slavery is at least in principle irreconcilable with enlightened humanity. Slavery is in fact used twice within the play itself as the image of an unworthy human condition (II.ix.720; V.iii.93). Nor is historical accuracy an excuse here; Lessing is not obliged to display this motif at this point. Or we may return to Saladin's religious toleration and note that he apparently practices it with the same unenlightened and potentially disastrous recklessness that characterizes his generosity; for he has made a "Capitulation" (IV.ii.193) with the Christians whereby he himself admits that it will not be easy for him to avoid becoming a second Pilate by allowing Nathan to burn at the stake (IV.iv.422–23). Indeed, Saladin's view of Nathan's paternal rights—"What claim does he have to her, if he is not her father?" (IV.v.462–64)—is more narrow-minded than that of at least two Christians, the Templar himself when he has calmed down (V.iii.98–100) and the lay brother (IV.vii.624–41).

In a Jerusalem ruled by Saladin, Nathan is perhaps walking on even slipperier ground than he knows. Al-Hafi has pointed out that Saladin's good nature is all too ingratiating (I.iii.459–60), and even Nathan is apparently to some extent fooled by it; for at the very end he entrusts an important decision to Saladin and expects the latter to give it careful rational consideration. The danger of incest is past, and Nathan now gives Saladin the breviary that proves Assad's identity, saying, "The Templar and Recha as yet know nothing. What they shall learn is up to you alone!" (V.viii.682–83). Clearly he hopes Saladin will consider whether it is truly in the interest of the young people to know all the facts about their family. Assad himself had concealed these facts; the Templar has said that he does not want to hear about his father (V.viii.639–40); and as for Recha-Blanda, who is going to find it difficult enough adjusting to a new family, a new name, and a new religion, is it really necessary to tell her that she is also a Moslem princess by birth? But Saladin mistakes Nathan's motive completely and answers: "Shall I not acknowledge my brother's children, my niece and nephew, my children? Not acknowledge them? Leave them, perhaps, to you?" (V.viii.684–86). Here, where a rationally humane consideration of others' interest is required, Saladin only accuses Nathan unjustly of selfishness. Again, Saladin is by no means genuinely enlightened, and his rule is therefore no real protection against the world's barbarity.

This exchange between Nathan and the Sultan shows also that Nathan not only accepts, but deliberately promotes, the irrationalness of the world. He has given Recha as rational an upbringing as possible, but he also understands that reason by itself is not a sufficient basis upon which to build and order one's life. He understands that without the sense of belonging firmly to a single family, a single culture, a single religion, without the irrational but compelling restrictions of "nature and blood" (IV.vii.707), our existence tends to become disordered and aimless. We are given an example of just this sort of disorder in the person of the Templar, whose sense of belonging to his culture is disturbed by his vague knowledge concerning his father.[12] On the one hand this makes it easier for him to discard his prejudices (III.viii.618), but on the other hand it also leads him into violent extremes of opinion and behavior; he can exhibit Christian bigotry at its grossest, for which Saladin severely chides him (IV.iv.405, 408), and a few scenes later he can dismiss Christianity contemptuously as "rank weeds" (V.v.325). A contrast to this is shown in the figure of the lay brother, who, although he never questions for a moment his own Christianity, is still every bit as open-minded as the Templar but without the latter's instability.

The firm bonds of blood and tradition, arbitrary and erroneous as they may be from a strictly rational point of view, are necessary in human existence. Nathan loves Recha, but his love is tempered by rational altruism, and this is why he has always intended to give her back to her blood relatives, and back to the institutionalized error of Christianity, as soon as possible. This is why he has always asked of Daja not permanent resignation but merely "patience" (IV.vi.422–24); this is why he asks Saladin to think a bit before revealing the whole truth at the end; and this same balanced altruism, this concern for people's security as well as for their enlightenment, explains why he has not worried Recha with hints about her future and her past. Even in his enlightened parable of the three rings, Nathan does not advocate full rational enlightenment for all men but rather envisions a situation in which various orthodoxies compete for preeminence—"Let each of you strive to demonstrate the power of the stone in his own ring!" (III.vii.527–29)—a situation in which men will strive toward moral improvement for the greater glory of their own religions. Nathan not only accepts the barbarous world as it is, but he also advocates and promotes that separateness among particular cultures from which at least a good part of human barbarity stems,

in spite of his own apparent belief that the world would be a better
place if men could learn to regard themselves and each other as
human beings rather than members of their "Volk" (II.v.520–22).

3

However we seek to explain this paradox, at least it remains
clear that for the author of *Nathan*, an enlightened knowledge of
the need for human brotherhood is not sufficient to bring such
brotherhood about. Saladin, especially, is a case in point. As far as
his principles are concerned, he is enlightened; he could trade
maxim for maxim all day with the best of the Wolffians. But his
reasonableness does not go deep enough, it has not taken root and
flourished as wisdom. Therefore he constantly either forgets himself or blunders in the execution of his principles; and therefore,
as Nathan's questioner on religion, he shares with the Patriarch
the dubious distinction of representing Hauptpastor Goeze. Evidently Saladin lacks something that Nathan possesses, and this
something is not definable in terms of knowledge or maxims
alone.

Or yet again, the end of the play is by no means merely a uto-
pian vision. The point has been made often enough that Nathan
himself is not part of the happy family he has brought together;
Saladin in fact brushes him off rather rudely before plunging into
the ecstasy of embraces. Something is wrong with this universal
family of mankind if the wisest of all, the man whose wisdom
makes it possible in the first place, is excluded, and this sense of
wrongness is compounded by the question of what is going to
become of Leu and Blanda von Filnek, formerly known as the
Templar and Recha. Will they remain in Jerusalem and become
Mohammedans? Or remain in Jerusalem as Christians, despite the
Patriarch and despite the renewal of hostilities (V.ii) which will
make this a ticklish position? If Saladin had kept quiet about the
breviary, Recha and her brother could have gone back to Europe
and led a relatively uncomplicated existence. But Saladin lacks
Nathan's capacity for self-sacrifice; he is going to do everything he
can to keep his new-found "children" with him. And even if they
do go back to Europe, can they ever be fully content there, knowing that the "Promised Land" (III.viii.616) under its "paternal
sky" (III.viii.626) is as much their true home as Germany, under

that "bleak sky" (V.viii.623) which had proven unbearable to Assad? Will they not be homeless?

It may be objected that the question of what happens after the play is over does not concern us. But in this case that question is asked within the play, when Nathan suggests to Saladin that it is not self-evidently in everyone's best interest to reveal the whole truth. Moreover, the purpose of scene ii, Act V, is to remind us that the war is still in progress, which aggravates the anomalous situation of Assad's Christian children; and the story of the wanderings of Assad and his wife reminds us that homelessness is a real possibility for people in such a situation. Indeed the whole atmosphere of the play, the emphasis on money, for example, compels us to be aware of the immediate practical questions that arise from the plot. And Lessing himself, finally, says that drama ought to interest the spectator in its characters' future beyond the end of the play (*HD* 35, p. 333).

In this case, therefore, we are meant to be disturbed about the fictional future, and this disturbedness in turn reminds us that the embraces at the end do not represent a real solution to the problem of humanity. Here, as also from the example of Saladin, we learn that it is not sufficient merely to advocate, however rationally or passionately—or in the case of the audience, merely to see, however clearly—the idea of universal humanity. Somehow our mental attitude must be characterized by something deeper than the mere knowledge or feeling or vision that all men are truly brothers.

What is it, then, that Nathan has but Saladin lacks? The idea of wisdom is pertinent to this question, and I have suggested that the idea of self-sacrifice is as well. But the word that names Nathan's advantage most exactly is *irony*. Saladin—like the resolutely naive spectator who weeps at the end and supposes this is all that is required of him—is capable of affirming the notion of universal human brotherhood, but he is not also capable of examining this notion critically. Full affirmation combined with clear critical detachment—in other words, a kind of irony—is what distinguishes Nathan, and is what causes the discrepancy between his words and his actions. In what he says, especially in his pedagogical conversations with the young people (I.ii. and II.v), he advocates a rational appreciation of sheer humanness as the single truest bond among men; but what he does, after his first meeting with the Templar, is directed mainly toward establishing people's "true" identities, that is the irrational but realistically necessary blood-bonds on which their existence must be based. In fact Nathan's very existence is ironic in structure. He recognizes and deplores the world's actual barbarity—hence his temptation to join Al-Hafi—but at the same time he also belongs to the world and accepts it as it is.

Or let us consider the parable of the three rings. Saladin forces Nathan into a corner, where he can no longer simply preach rationality as he does to Recha and the Templar. Now he must find a way of expressing his whole thought on religion, and he accomplishes this by advocating, at the same time, both a rational transcendence of religion—the recognition that one cannot be sure about the truth of one's belief, that "the real ring was not discoverable" (III.vii.446–47)—and a commitment to the religion of one's fathers—that one should be firm in one's belief anyway: "Let each of you firmly believe his ring genuine" (518–19). But can one truly believe when one knows that one's belief is a rational necessity derived from the premise that no belief is reliable? In logic these opposites are irreconcilable, but in actuality they must be combined. Scholars have raised the question of whether Nathan is still truly a Jew, or whether he has not rather excluded himself from his religion by being too thoroughly rational,[13] and the answer to this question is that somehow, by an irony that defies logic, both alternatives are true, Nathan is both a Jew and a more-than-Jew: "Is being a Christian or a Jew prior to one's humanity?" (II.v.523–24), he asks; but he also says, "Sultan, I am a Jew" (III.v.325–26). Or we think, again, of the last scene, where Nathan, who is the cause and the very soul of the family reunion that is taking place, is also excluded from it. All these are symbols of his ironic situation: his acceptance of an unacceptable world, his Jewish non-Jewishness, his simultaneous membership and non-membership in the great family of mankind. One must be what one is, Jew or Christian or whatever, and yet at the same time retain sufficient rational independence to be able to encounter other men on the level of their humanness as such; one must appreciate and advocate the ideal of universal human brotherhood, while also retaining sufficient critical detachment to recognize that this idea does not exempt one from the necessity of belonging to the particular cultural tradition into which one is born.

4

But why should Nathan's irony be an advantage, and why should it be equated, or at least associated, with wisdom? Why must the wise man, despite his knowledge of the truth and desirability of universal human brotherhood, still accept the world as it is, with all its barbarity? Why does he avoid interfering with people's commitment to the cultural tradition of their birth, even though such traditions are mainly fabrics of prejudice? Part of the answer is given, interestingly, in Saladin's excuse for losing the chess game: "I wasn't really paying attention, I was distracted. And then: who always brings us these smooth, functional chessmen which do not actually represent anything? Was I playing with the imam?" (II.i.50–55). Saladin claims that he cannot concentrate on a game where the pieces are not recognizable, where each does not have its own shaped character. As a reason for losing the game this is false, but as a metaphor it is profoundly expressive. If the ideal of brotherhood ever actually triumphed in the world, if all men discarded their prejudices and embraced each other in the universal religion of man, the result would be a world of "smooth chessmen," an inhuman world lacking all true religious feeling and all incentive to moral action. Nathan practically says as much in his parable, where he points out the advantageousness of the division of monotheistic religion into three separate branches which compete and so spur each other on.

In the life of an individual—even for persons who have not attained the stage of wisdom—commitment to a particular culture need not be a hindrance to rational enlightenment. The comparison between the Templar and the more deeply committed lay brother shows the Templar's insecurity as the main hindrance to his rational development. And Al-Hafi, who combines a fanatical religiousness with uncompromising reason, is an extreme, not an ideal; but his case does show that reason and religion are not necessarily opposed. For the sake of each individual's progress toward enlightenment, therefore, as well as for the sake of the world as a whole, the wise man must to an extent violate his own highest ideal and promote the sense of narrow cultural identity which, as long as it exists, is always capable of producing not only

fruitful competition, and not only a secure basis upon which the
individual's reason may build, but also gross barbarity.[14]

Yet if this is the case, then why does Nathan constantly preach
rational humanity, especially to the young people upon whom
such preaching can be expected to make an impression? Clearly
our commitment to the culture we are born into is necessary not
for its own sake but for the sake of the maximum realization of
universal human brotherhood, paradoxical as this may appear on
first glance. We must first be what we are, but then we must also
use what we are toward a higher human goal. We must not only
honor and keep our own native religion, but we must also develop
and expand it (as the sons in the parable are explicitly enjoined to
do) in the direction of a universal humane belief. This idea is
exemplified by the two most thoroughly religious characters in
the play, Al-Hafi and the lay brother. Both respect Nathan as a
human being, and for this reason they both pay him what seems to
them the highest compliment; they regard him as a co-religionist:
Al-Hafi when he invites Nathan to accompany him on his pil-
grimage, and the lay brother even more explicitly, "Nathan!
Nathan! You are a Christian!" (IV.vii.688–89). For the lay brother,
being a Christian is man's highest state, as is for Al-Hafi being a
contemplative ascetic on the banks of the Ganges. But in both
men, particular religiosity has developed to such a depth that
man's highest state has become equivalent with rational human
virtue as such, so that Nathan qualifies. In the right sort of personality, then, even a strict and narrow religious commitment can
further man's rational progress.

Thus, to return to Nathan himself, the wise man must preach
universal brotherhood, yet in practice promote the integrity of
individual religions. A problem arises, however, when we consider the wise man's personal life. On the one hand, his irony, his
necessary constant readiness to preach humanity (and to maneu-
ver his way around the unanswerable questions his preaching
raises), prevents him from ever integrating himself securely into
his own native situation, into the particular life of family and
culture; and on the other hand, his recognition of people's real
needs and best interests also prevents him from committing himself unreservedly to the ideal he preaches.[15] Hence, again, the
family-tableau at the very end, with respect to which Nathan is in
a sense successful but also in a sense excluded. The wise man

must be both a Jew and a non-Jew, both a father and a nonfather, which in practice means neither-nor; his life is one of unceasing self-restraint and unfulfilment. Hence the association of wisdom with self-sacrifice as well as irony. The wise man's daily existence, to pick up a concept applied to the Jews in *Die Erziehung des Menschengeschlechts* (par. 32), is "heroic," and in almost the same way that self-conscious existence as such becomes heroic in the theater of Kleist.

5

This brings us to the question of *Nathan der Weise* as drama. We have seen the depth and unresolvedness, for Lessing, of the problem of drama in general; we have seen that *Emilia* already tends in the direction of radical dramatic experimentation; we have seen, in this regard, some parallels between *Emilia* and *Nathan*; we have seen that the function of *Nathan* in the Goeze controversy is no reason to deny that it is conceived with an eye to dramatic problems; and we have noticed the uncomfortable experimentality of its verse, which appears to be aimed at transforming naturalness itself into one element of an emphatically artificial configuration. If it can be shown from the text, therefore, that there is at least a possible parallel between Nathan's ironic wisdom and the situation of an audience in the theater, then we can conclude that this parallel is not likely to be unintended, especially if it involves the categories of illusion and detachment, the main poles between which drama had presented itself to Lessing as a problem.

Such a parallel does exist. The problem of drama arises from the nonperfectibility of dramatic illusion, which implies a discrepancy between drama's immediate and ultimate aims. A certain intellectual detachment on the part of the spectator is unavoidable, even when it is not specifically encouraged—and it is specifically encouraged in *Nathan* by the verse and the exotic-allegorical setting, by the food for philosophical thought that is constantly offered, by our perception of Nathan's own self-detachment or irony. Yet, on the other hand, drama by its nature aims at total illusion; otherwise, "Why the drudgery of dramatic form?" If we wish to think about philosophical problems or the implications of a fictional story, we do not have to go to the theater to do it. We would not go to the theater in the first place if the theater did not offer us something more than books do, and given the actual physicalness of poetic images in the theater, must this "something more" not at least include an especially compelling sensory vividness?

This is not only a problem for the dramatist, however; it is also a problem for the spectator, who is experiencing here and now the attempt of a dramatic performance to affect him. We are intellectually detached as we sit in the theater, we are aware of our intellectual detachment, but we recognize that there is something wrong with this detachment, something contrary to the clear immediate aim of the form of drama. Poetry in general "seeks not only to be understandable," but to sweep away our consciousness with "illusion" (L xvii, p. 101); and yet our consciousness has not been swept away. Drama in particular "makes no claim to a single definite teaching which must be derived from its fiction; it aims either at the passions or at pleasure" (HD 35, p. 331); and yet, especially in Nathan, we are constantly invited to reflect upon the play's doctrine. We find ourselves in a state of intellectual detachment mixed with a kind of regret, with the feeling that our detachment excludes us from an immediacy of participation which is implied by dramatic form as such, and these conflicting pulls on our mental attitude, toward both detachment and participation, create within us a condition comparable to the ironic situation experienced by Nathan. Like Nathan we can never either completely involve ourselves or completely detach ourselves from the world that unfolds on the stage.

Or if this is not clear enough in the abstract, let us consider the Patriarch's disapproval of theater. The Patriarch wishes to know whether the Templar's story of a Christian child raised by a Jew is fact or mere "hypothesis" (IV.ii.133): "For if the case in question is only a mental game, then it is not worthwhile to consider it seriously. Go instead to the theater, where such speculative pros and cons are applauded loudly" (IV. ii. 141–47). This speech tends very strongly to break the dramatic illusion; it not only mentions the theater but also reminds us that the events on stage are mere hypotheses, not facts, and that these hypotheses are set up in order to explore an abstract intellectual problem. At the same time, however, we associate the Patriarch's disapproval of the theater with his character as a whole, which is thoroughly disagreeable; thus we are led to question whether the hypotheticalness of the theater is a valid argument against it. Again, we are pulled in two directions at once. We are reminded that our intellectual detachment may be regarded as an imperfection in our relation to the work we are watching; but it is also suggested (via our presumed antipathy toward the speaker) that we should perhaps seek to affirm and justify our detachment anyway. That the Patriarch's speech, moreover, is located at a crucial point in the plot, where Nathan is in actual danger, a point at which the illusion ought by rights to become especially compelling, only increases its ironic effect.

Let us recall, however, that the problem of detachment and involvement is not unique in *Nathan*, but rather, at least to Lessing's mind, is inherent in the very form of drama. The reader of a work of narrative is also detached, but in narrative this detachment can be made to take the form of a "free play" of the imagination which serves ultimately to strengthen the illusion. The "living painting" of drama, on the other hand, allows our imagination only minimum freedom, which means that if our detachment is not eliminated altogether—the illusion in drama must be "weit stärker" (*HD* 35, p. 333)—it will necessarily take the form of an intellectual detachment that conflicts with the illusion. Given, therefore, that a total theatrical illusion is impossible, it follows that the problem of detachment and involvement is a special generic problem in drama, and in *Nathan*, by means of various devices, this problem is intensified for the audience, not relieved; the audience's awareness of the problem is deliberately sharpened. Why does Lessing do this?

The answer to this question is contained in the parallel between the spectator's situation and Nathan's. Merely to relieve the problem of detachment and involvement, to dull the spectator's awareness of it, is never more than a compromise; what Lessing attempts to do in *Nathan*, however, is to solve the problem of drama by building his play around the figure of an ironic wise man. If the problem of drama is a conflict between detachment and involvement, then the obvious solution is to create a synthesis of these two forces, to make them identical, and Lessing attempts this by means of an extraordinary but simple paradox. Our intellectual detachment from the play, namely, itself constitutes the deepest possible sympathy on our part with Nathan, the painfully *self*-detached wise man; and our involvement, our human sympathy with Nathan, provided we sympathize with his irony and

the necessity of it, itself in turn constitutes a kind of ironic detachment. The more we sympathize with Nathan, the more we
find ourselves sharing his uncomfortable but necessary irony; and
the more we are intellectually detached, the more we find ourselves involved sympathetically in Nathan's self-detached state of
mind. Our detachment thus is our involvement, and our involvement is our detachment.

The way in which the audience is approached here, moreover,
is clearly anticipated in Lessing's theory, if not worked out in
detail. Lessing thinks of the audience's situation in the theater as a
kind of practice for real life; tragedy is practice in "Mitleid" (pity)
and comedy is practice in laughing at the laughable. Now, however, one step further is taken and the theatrical situation is ex-
ploited as practice in wisdom. What appears to be an insoluble
problem, the tension between detachment and involvement, now
turns out to be a valuable didactic tool; by being subjected to this
tension in the theater (in as intense, as unrelieved a form as possible, like our subjection to self-consciousness in *Prinz Friedrich*)
and by recognizing the analogy with Nathan's ironic attitude, we
are led in the direction of a truly wise and self-sacrificing attitude
toward our own existence, an attitude which combines faithful-
ness to our own cultural situation with the intellectual detachment that enables us to wield and develop our situation humanly.

This procedure, moreover, can be related directly to the
religious-polemical occasion of the play's composition. Why
write a play about a Jew in order to make a point about the present
state of Christianity? We can answer this question by understanding the implied historical progression among the three
monotheistic religions represented in *Nathan*. Judaism is the old-
est religion and its representative is thoroughly ironic, whereas
Mohammedanism is the most recent religion and its representatives could hardly be more thoroughly unironic. Al-Hafi has ethi-
cal problems that are related to his religion, but his religion itself,
his unreserved commitment, is no problem for him, any more than
for Saladin. Religions are shown, therefore, as tending to develop
from simple belief toward profound irony, and the details of this
process are suggested in *Die Erziehung des Menschengeschlechts*,
in the argument on the Jews' "heroic obedience" (par. 32). Religion becomes a problem for the Jews, a "knot" (par. 28), when
they find it impossible to reconcile the unjust distribution of

goods in the world with their God's apparent promise to reward
virtue and punish evil. That they continue to be Jews, despite this
problem, that they continue to practice the obedience enjoined by
their scriptures, is therefore heroic, or as I have suggested, ironic.
The Jew is detached from his religion intellectually, by his awareness of its imperfection, its lack of absolute validity, but at the
same time he still resolutely belongs to it. Not every Jew will
automatically be a wise man, but an ironic wisdom like Nathan's
is more likely to occur among Jews than among adherents of a
religion not yet grown problematic.

Mohammedanism in *Nathan* is not yet problematic; but when
Nathan says, "Sultan, I am a Jew," Saladin answers, "And I a
Moslem. The Christian stands midway between us" (III.v.325–27).
Christianity is between Judaism and Mohammedanism, both in its
age and in its stage of intellectual development; it has not yet
reached the point of profound heroic irony, but as represented by
the vacillating Templar it has begun to become problematic. And
this is the stage at which Lessing felt Christianity had arrived, not
during the Crusades but rather in his own time. In the commen-
tary on Reimarus, in the architectural parable and *Eine Duplik*
and the *Erziehung,* Lessing indicates that Christianity has arrived
at a crisis, since the Christian may no longer believe implicitly in
his religion's historical foundations. It is time for Christianity to
stop taking its historical factualness too seriously; it is time for
Christianity to transform itself into a more generally rational and
humane belief. This is the reason for the way in which the three
religions are represented in *Nathan.* Mohammedanism represents
Christianity's uncomplicated past; the Templar represents Christianity's problematic present; and Nathan represents, or at least
suggests, what Christianity can and should become in the future,
as an older and ironically wiser religion. But Christianity will not
automatically become wise, and the dramatic structure of *Nathan*
is calculated to foster and encourage the sort of wisdom that
eighteenth-century Christians must learn, by subjecting its audience to the aesthetic tension between detachment and involvement, as preparation for the more general mental tension which is
wisdom, the tension between believing and yet also transcending
one's belief intellectually. This is Lessing's ultimate progressive
strategy against Goeze's reactionary dogmatism.

A question is still left, however. Why is the plot of *Nathan* so complicated and mysterious? Does the plot not distract from what should be the main focus, the hero's character? The two relatively clear answers to this question reveal yet further the depth to which *Nathan* is conceived as a theatrical work. First, the complexity and prominence and obvious allegorical quality of the plot give to the whole work the air of an instructive parable, so that the scene between Nathan and Saladin becomes a play-within-the-play, which invites us to reflect upon our situation as spectators and raises the question of whether a reaction like Saladin's in Act III, scene vii, is adequate. Nathan's parable does not express a doctrine so much as it poses a problem, the problem of how to reconcile a knowledge of the relativity of all belief with a commitment to the belief of one's fathers; and not only the ending of the larger parable in the plot but also our situation as reflective spectators is significantly analogous to this problem. The structure of parable-within-parable thus encourages precisely that reflectiveness which in turn makes both parables immediately meaningful for an audience.

Second, if the plot were handled less mystifyingly, if our interest were focussed entirely upon Nathan's character and upon the constant potential anguish inherent in his way of looking at things, the result would be an invitation to experience emotional empathy. We have seen, however, that what the play actually aims at is a more perfect form of identification with Nathan, which does not circumvent but rather includes our reflective detachment, and from this point of view the tendency of the plot to engage our intellectual curiosity is an advantage. The atmosphere in *Nathan*—created by the repartee in dialogue and by the image of chess, for instance, as well as by the plot—is that of an intricate game, but a game tinged with sentiment and having a certain melancholy depth; this is in turn the atmosphere of existence itself for the wise man, who is constantly obliged to juggle the irreconcilable opposites embraced by his mental attitude, and for whom this endless intellectual test of skill must also involve a constant sense of exclusion or less. Once again, our identification with Nathan is encouraged as an aspect of the total theatrical situation, not by an appeal exclusively to our feelings. And again the parallel with *Prinz Friedrich* appears, now in its deepest form, in that the actual situation of the spectator (the fact that he is sitting in a theater watching a particular kind of play) is itself utilized as a central and indispensable expressive device.

6

To recapitulate, the intellectual component in an audience's relation to drama is as important in *Nathan* as in *Prinz Friedrich,* and important in essentially the same way, as the source of an irony which is meant ultimately to become part of the spectator's cultural situation; the irony we learn and practice in the theater is meant to spill over into real life and become part of the way we deal with existence in general. For Kleist as for Lessing, moreover, the intellectual component in drama begins by constituting a serious problem, but in the end a way is found to exploit it for the sake of a more profound and immediate expressiveness than could possibly be achieved by an attempt to by-pass the intellect.

The idea of intellectual detachment brings us in turn to the idea of our culture as something which, while belonging to it, we must nevertheless also be able to wield consciously for the sake of a higher goal. In *Prinz Friedrich,* which was written later than *Nathan* and responds to a different situation, the humiliation of a bookishly inactive Germany in Napoleonic Europe, the revitalization of human society, rather than its cultural or spiritual elevation, becomes the main problem; but the tendency is basically the same as in Lessing. *Prinz Friedrich* is meant to teach us—or more precisely, to enable us to learn by our own experience—that true freedom is entirely compatible with the apparently external demands made upon us by the community, that our freedom is in fact to an extent inseparable from such demands; and in *Nathan,* correspondingly, it is the wise man (or the potentially wise man in a problematic culture) who recognizes that his life in the community is governed by arbitrary external rules which are still somehow inwardly binding. The irony of the Elector throughout, and of the Prince's heroically sophistical speech at the end, is in a sense the reverse of Nathan's irony; Nathan preaches universal reason but in practice promotes the necessity of particular cultural limitations, whereas the Elector and the Prince preach obedience to a particular law but in practice work toward a universalizing of law by its transformation into the organ of fundamental human freedom. The categories are thus shifted somewhat, in *Nathan* there is less emphasis on freedom, in *Prinz Friedrich* there is less on reason; but the human condition is still understood in essentially the same way, as a tension between opposites which are irreconcilable in logic but inseparable in actual experience, and expressible with unique intensity via the form of drama. In fact a direct transition between the type of drama represented by *Nathan* and that represented by *Prinz Friedrich* is observable in Goethe's career. I shall argue that *Iphigenie*, while closer in spirit to *Nathan*, is also a step on the way toward *Egmont*, which in turn (despite Kleist's low opinion of it) defines the type of drama to which *Prinz Friedrich* belongs.

A related tendency in late eighteenth-century Germany has to do with the inherent but not obvious suitability of drama as a vehicle for dealing with man's inner life. I refer here neither to the sentimentality of the bourgeois drama nor to Kleistian psychological depth, nor to the often-noted shift, say, in Lessing and Lenz, away from the Aristotelian emphasis upon action and toward an emphasis upon character as the soul of drama. These tendencies reflect the general development of aesthetics in the few decades around 1800, but the crucial event in the history of drama is the discovery—initiated in *Nathan*, then triumphantly vindicated in *Prinz Friedrich*—that the theater is by nature a model of human self-consciousness. In the theater we are both powerfully involved and clearly detached with respect to the unfolding fiction, in the same way that a self-conscious being is necessarily both involved and detached with respect to his own self. When we sit in the theater, therefore, the basic self-conscious structure of our existence, which we normally take for granted, is revealed to us in an intensified form; we do not learn about our self-consciousness abstractly or parabolically or by seeing it turn morbid in a fictional character (like Werther, or Hölderlin's Hyperion), but rather we experience it directly in the psychological complexity of our situation as spectators. Thus drama is not by nature any less "inward" a form than the novel, despite the narrator's ability to give details of his characters' inner life which can never be shown on the stage.

Narrative still offers greater possibilities for the depiction of inner life, but drama has the special capability of producing a sense of inner heroism. Drama in the German manner, since Lessing, places us in a situation where our self-conscious existence is intensified to the extent that its inherent difficulties affect us noticeably—the complex ironies that we quickly slide over in our dealings outside the theater, the inward self-sacrifice and self-restraint that are needed merely to live in our self-conscious, thus self-divided condition. In the theater-prologue to *Faust*, Goethe's Director compares the surging of the crowd past the box office to a woman's labor spasms; when we enter the theater, that is, we undergo a kind of birth; we live not the fictional characters' lives but rather our own life with an intensity that makes it seem completely new. We learn to appreciate our own mere existence as the constant overcoming of difficulties which in logic are insuperable, and this heroic overcoming is then reflected symbolically on the stage, in Nathan's self-sacrificing maintenance of an inner ironic equilibrium or in Prince Friedrich considered as a projection of the audience's mental state. It is all very well to say that the heroic no longer has a place in modern theater, but the heroic and the dramatic are not that easily separated. Otherwise, "Why the drudgery of dramatic form?" The effort and energy that go into producing a play, the perennial festive atmosphere of the theater, the singling out of one action or fate for stylized presentation upon a raised platform before an assembly of diverse individuals, all these effects suggest the presence of some monumentally significant cause that brings them forth, even in the case of comedy, where the fictional world does not as a rule include an image of that cause. If, therefore, for whatever reasons, the great deeds of our cultural ancestors, the rulers and heroes of our past, no longer appear usable as myths or symbols of the force that brings us together in the theater, then some other sort of greatness or monumentality must take their place.

Finally, because Lessing's own perfunctory answer to his basic question about drama had involved unverifiable psychological assumptions concerning the theater audience, it is important to understand that the deeper answer to Lessing's question, the answer implicit in *Nathan*, does not involve such assumptions, although it does give the audience an indispensable role in the genesis of dramatic meaning. No specific emotion, and no specific degree of emotion is required of the spectator. All that is required of him is his status as a self-conscious being, plus a good portion of mental alertness and intelligence. What is required—in *Nathan* as in *Prinz Friedrich*—is that he understand the work's subtlety.

Once this is accomplished, the parallel between the situation in the theater and that on the stage must become clear, and the spectator's consciousness of this parallel is alone sufficient to establish the intended relationship between him and the work. These plays, to be sure, are demanding, but they do not demand anything that a critically intelligent spectator cannot supply. In particular, they do not demand that our unconscious or instinctive reactions follow some specific, predictable pattern; and this is the crucial point, for any work of art that does make such a demand—any drama, for example, that is merely theater of shock or theater of sympathy—must be defeated by the simple fact that people always turn out not to be predictable after all.

4 *Iphigenie auf Tauris* and Goethe's Idea of Drama

That the first version, in prose, of Goethe's *Iphigenie auf Tauris* was being composed at the same time as *Nathan der Weise*, is a very interesting coincidence, for the two plays are almost identical in theme and approach: the fictional situation in both is highly contrived, with a view to expressing the idea of universal humanity; in both there is a preponderance of dialogue over action; and the exotic setting in both contributes to a sense of artifice and distance from the audience. But if this is mere coincidence to begin with, it does not remain so; for although *Nathan* and *Iphigenie* were begun around the same time, the final version of *Iphigenie* was not completed until seven years later, long after *Nathan* had been read and admired by Goethe.[1] The relationship between the two works, then, is a combination of *Zeitgeist* with direct influence, and certain less obvious aspects of this relationship are important in the history of drama. In particular, Goethe's attitude toward German culture is essentially the same as Lessing's toward Christian religion, and *Iphigenie* represents essentially the same kind of experimenting with dramatic form as *Nathan*.

It is not difficult to show that *Iphigenie* is important in the development of Goethe's thinking on drama and theater. The play represents a clear departure from his earlier style, even in the first version; it was undoubtedly his major creative effort in the service of the temporary amateur theater at Weimar (1776–83); and letters

97

of mid-March 1779 to Carl Ludwig von Knebel show that questions of performability and theatricalness significantly affected its
composition. Despite certain obvious points concerning stylistic
classicalness, however, it is not easy to define the theoretical and
practical advances embodied in *Iphigenie*. Let us approach this
question by looking first at the play's larger genesis, culminating
in the final version of 1786.

1

  Iphigenie was a painful birth, a "Schmerzenskind,"[2] but it was
by no means the only work that Goethe carried around a long time
before finishing. Of the dramas interrupted for the sake of the
verse *Iphigenie*, for example, *Egmont* was finished fairly soon
afterward, in 1787, but *Torquato Tasso* took two years longer, and
Faust dragged on all but endlessly. The long genesis of *Iphigenie*,
however, appears to bear a specially close relation to the genesis
of the first version of the theatrical novel *Wilhelm Meisters theatralische Sendung*. According to Goethe's diary the first book of
the *Sendung* was completed in January 1778; but despite indications later the same year that work was going forward, it seems
fairly clear that the letter to Charlotte von Stein of 5 June 1780,
and perhaps even the letter of 21 June 1782, allude to portions of
this first book which were still not in satisfactory form.[3] In any
case it is not until mid-1782 that we begin to hear about the completion of the second book, and it seems probable, therefore, that
in 1778, after finishing a draft of the first book, Goethe found
himself at a creative impasse; he continued thinking and working
occasionally, but toward the end of 1778 diary and epistolary
references to the *Sendung* peter out altogether for over a year, and
it is at just about this time, early 1779, that the first *Iphigenie* was
begun and quite rapidly completed.
  We can make a conjecture about the significance of these facts if
we recall that the early chapters of the second book of the *Sendung*, the chapters which had apparently stymied Goethe when he
turned to *Iphigenie*, are the point in the novel where he first
attempts to delve into the theory of drama and theater. May we
regard his turn from the novel to the play as a conscious turn from
the abstract to the concrete, as an attempt to develop theory by
applying it in practice? There are several quite specific relationships between Book Two of the *Sendung* and Goethe's remarks

about *Iphigenie*. In Chapter 4, for example, Wilhelm discusses with Werner the problems that arise from the heterogeneity of audiences: "Artistic excellence must first of course be recognized and proclaimed by connoisseurs; but if it is truly human, it must also have a positive effect in general, especially on those who cannot form a judgment about it" (*WA*, LI, p. 136). And just these problems crop up in the early genesis of *Iphigenie*, with specific reference to the concept of the "human," for Goethe is by turns defiant and worried about his feeling that this play will be accepted only by the select few who either possess exceptional poetic judgment or else experience their humanity in an exceptionally "pure" manner.[4]

Or we think of Wilhelm's insistence (in Chapters 4 and 5) upon the primacy of action in drama, for one of the main experimental features of *Iphigenie*, and one of the main reasons Goethe was worried about the reaction of a large public, is this play's lack of action. I do not mean that theory and practice, the *Sendung* and *Iphigenie*, are opposed on this point. On the contrary, Wilhelm's insistence that thoughts and feelings must be completely subordinated to action is clearly meant to be regarded by the novel's reader with a certain amount of irony, for we hear immediately that Wilhelm's sister and friend, in the very process of conceding his point, also manage to come up with examples that disprove it (*WA*, LI, p. 146); and of course one of the climaxes toward which both the *Sendung* (Book Six, Chapters 7–11) and *Wilhelm Meisters Lehrjahre* are directed, is Wilhelm's learning to defend the relative actionlessness of *Hamlet*. But on the other hand, Wilhelm's point that "descriptions and metaphors," if given too much room, are "the death of drama" (*WA*, LI, p. 134), must not be taken too lightly—especially in connection with a play like *Iphigenie*, where fully a sixth of the dialogue, 363 lines (307–432, 803–917, 949–1070) of a total of 2174 in the final version, is devoted to describing the true and false family histories of various characters, not to mention the prayers to the gods, which in a modern play we can probably reckon as metaphor. Apparently, in both the *Sendung* and *Iphigenie*, Goethe is attempting to redefine what constitutes dramatic action.

In any event the genesis of *Iphigenie* continues to be intertwined interestingly with that of the *Sendung*. In 1781, after two unsuccessful attempts at revision,[5] Goethe apparently leaves the play alone for the time being, and in 1782 he resumes work on the novel, which he continues sporadically until, on 30 December 1785, he writes Knebel that the sixth book, the last book of the manuscript that has come down to us, is finished. In 1786, however, work again slows down, and when Goethe heads for Italy, though he continues collecting background material for *Meister*, what he actually works on represents another decided turn toward practice; first he completes the verse *Iphigenie*, and then, in his letter to Charlotte von Stein of 20 January 1787, he speaks resolutely of "finishing" *Egmont, Tasso*, and *Faust*. To be sure, there is a practical reason for this resoluteness, in his wish to round out the forthcoming collected edition of his writings; but still a pattern of alternation between dramatic theory and practice, as represented by *Meister* and *Iphigenie*, emerges clearly enough.

This brings me to my main point, that the inner relationship between *Iphigenie* and the *Sendung* is not merely a matter of details but has to do with the novel's principal theme, the quest for a true German national theater. Given the situation in which *Iphigenie* was conceived, this concern should not be surprising, for the Weimar amateur theater had been started as a competitive German effort alongside the aristocratic French-speaking theater group that had entertained Weimar in 1775–76.[6] But Goethe does not merely intend his play as a model for what the German theater might accomplish; in fact the plot of *Iphigenie* is meant to *symbolize* the birth of such a theater. The Germans, as Lessing reminds them in *Laokoon*, are barbarians or not far from it, and in the *Hamburgische Dramaturgie* their lack of national civilization or civilized nationhood is blamed in part for the lack of a true German theater.[7] Goethe's response to these ideas is to show on stage the encounter between a sophisticated Greek lady and a barbarian, Thoas, who has a number of clearly marked German characteristics, especially his aversion to subtle verbal maneuvering and the value he sets on an individual's sincerity and directness. This encounter represents, among other things, the relation between a relatively uncivilized Germany and the tradition of drama as it comes down to us from the Greeks.

2

Iphigenie is not merely an allegory; the theatrical situation involves far too much irony for this. But it does contain an allegory. If Burckhardt is correct when he sees in *Iphigenie* "the world of a

language school," in which Iphigenie herself, through contact
with barbarians whom she has come to respect, must learn to
speak in a new and deeper way, "to speak as an individual,"[8] then
there is quite a close parallel with a later work of Goethe's in
which another Greek lady, Helen of Troy, is also taught to speak
by a barbarian; and at the end of Part Two, Act III, of *Faust*, Helen,
like Iphigenie, leaves her barbarian with nothing tangible to show
for their encounter. Iphigenie's emergence from the rigid, protective forms of hieratic language into the openness of direct personal expression, and her subsequent insistence upon trusting
Thoas absolutely, are parallel (though on a level of much greater
psychological verisimilitude) to Helen's emergence from trimeter
into the "strange and friendly" language of rhyme (*Faust*, l. 9368),
along with her subsequent quasi marriage to Faust; the obviousness of the cultural allegory in the Helen episode represents only a
shifting of emphases, the drawing forth and working out of what
had already been a significant but submerged element of the earlier play.

If the Germans succeed in creating a true drama, the allegory in
Iphigenie implies that some sort of fruitful interchange will be
required with the culture of ancient Greece, where drama, for
European purposes, is born. This will be an interchange, not
merely an imitation of the Greeks; the Greek notion of drama will
as it were learn something; like Iphigenie, it will change and
develop at the hands of the relatively uncivilized Germans. In fact
the Germans' lack of a highly developed civilization with a firm
tradition in drama may even prove to be an advantage; Lessing
argues that the vaunted sophistication of the French theater only
falsifies the ancient tradition,[9] and in *Iphigenie* Arkas says: "Benevolence, when it descends from heaven in human form, establishes its empire nowhere more quickly than where a new people,
confused and unpolished but vigorous, courageous and strong,
bears on its own shoulders, with trepidation, the burdens of
human existence" (1477–82). If we can show a connection between this idea of "benevolence" [*Milde*] and the idea of drama, if
we can show that Goethe imagines drama actually capable of
building an "empire," making a real contribution toward the establishment of civilized society, then part of what this passage
expresses is the hope that drama as a civilizing force will enjoy an
especially rapid growth among the unspoiled Germans.

At any rate, we can now make at least a tentative judgment

concerning the phase represented by *Iphigenie* in the development of Goethe's dramatic thinking. As in Lessing and in the
Sturm und Drang, so in earlier Goethe, Shakespeare is the guiding
star, for two basic reasons: first, the nearness of his genius to
nature—"Nature! Nothing is so wholly nature as the men Shakespeare creates" (*WA*, XXXVII, p. 133)—which means that we can
understand and presumably even emulate Shakespeare merely by
virtue of our natural humanness; and second, a certain affinity
between Shakespeare and the specific character of the German
people, as opposed to the decadent "Frenchies," the "Fran-
zösgen" (*WA*, XXXVII, p. 132).[10] A more soberly critical attitude
toward Shakespeare emerges in the *Sendung*, however, and if we
consider *Iphigenie* as well, then it is clear that neither of these two
reasons for studying Shakespeare remains valid. Obviously the
author of *Iphigenie* does not believe that drama is produced by
unsullied nature. Drama must be learned, by an imaginative but
conscientious study of existing tradition back to its roots in
Greece; Goethe is already moving toward his later idea that all
European drama is the specifically scholarly revival of an ancient
form, "from the dust of old academe" (*WA*, XIII, 1, p. 82). And
even if Shakespeare is somehow more a German than a French-
man, this fact is irrelevant, since the German dramatist's job is
not to discover a latent autochthonous style, but rather to accept
his situation as the member of "a new people," without any style
of its own but willing to experiment and learn. This is not to say
that Goethe no longer believes in the possibility of a true German
drama; what he no longer believes in (if he ever had, really) is the
possibility of translating the German national character directly
into a dramatic idiom.

Let us keep these ideas in mind while discussing the text of
Iphigenie. We shall not deal with any version but the final one in
verse, for our aim is not to trace in detail the growth of Goethe's
thinking on drama, but rather to grasp one or two neglected points
about what the thinking of Goethe's classical phase, in its broad
and relatively stable outlines, really is.

3

What, first of all, is the theater, and what is supposed to happen
there? In Book One of the *Sendung*, Wilhelm asks: "Where is
there such another sanctuary against boredom as the theater,

where is society cemented more pleasantly, where are men more inclined to admit they are brothers, than when they all hang on the lips of *one* man and are all swept up in *one* feeling? What are paintings and statues against the living flesh of my flesh, against that other ego on the stage, who suffers, is happy, and touches directly every similarly tuned nerve in myself? (*WA*, LI, pp. 50–51). There is a certain amount of irony here, primarily with respect to Wilhelm's subsequent inference concerning the supposed virtuousness of actors as a class, but the basic idea is still important and is by no means Goethe's exclusive property; Schiller, for example, who at this time was not in contact with Goethe, says something very similar in his early essay "Die Schaubühne als eine moralische Anstalt betrachtet." The significance of this idea is that it represents an attempt to understand drama by way of its one undeniably unique characteristic among literary types, its realization as performance. Drama is capable of evoking an especially strong sense of human brotherhood because it is an actual physical event (made literally of "flesh") in human society.

But how is this quality of drama to be developed artistically? Is it (as Wilhelm seems to think) only a matter of portraying natural emotions in such a way that the audience is moved to sympathize? In any case, *Iphigenie* is obviously not meant to function by this mechanism of direct emotional resonance. The idea of universal human brotherhood is central in the play's thematic structure, and it is reasonable to infer, therefore, given the thinking of the *Sendung*, that human brotherhood is meant to be created in the theater during a performance, via the play's "effect on pure human beings" (Goethe's diary, 6 April 1779). But the question of how remains unanswered. If one puts German burghers on the stage, then one can at least hope that some "similarly tuned nerves" in the German audience will reverberate with the characters' emotions.[11] But is one really aiming for this effect when one presents a miraculously rescued Greek lady and involves her in a plot that depends on questions concerning human sacrifice, inherited evil, and the proper method of interpreting divine oracles? Throughout *Iphigenie* there is an emphasis upon the artificiality of the fictional world, upon the cultural distance that separates it from the world in which the audience actually lives—a much greater distance, for example, than in *Tasso*, which is set at a small European court that can be imagined as analogous to Weimar. And I have already remarked upon the extraordinary amount of dialogue devoted to a detailed history of the house of Atreus, for which there is no obvious analogue in the life of the audience.

This cultural distance between the audience and the fiction, however, can itself be useful in expressing the idea of pure humanity, as an analogue to the cultural distance between Iphigenie's and Thoas's peoples.[12] In *Iphigenie*, as in *Nathan*, the cultural differences among the characters are the very source of the idea of humanity—humanity, by definition, is that which bridges cultural differences—and the same principle applies to the difference between fiction and audience. If we do, in the end, experience any real sympathy with the characters in *Iphigenie*, then we must attribute this sympathy not to our Germanness but to our humanity as such. The interaction among the characters on stage is thus an exact image of the intended interaction between fiction and audience in the theater. Like the characters, the spectators must leap a cultural gap in order to experience their pure humanity.

The trouble, however, is that there is an intellectual component in this process, that it is not merely a matter of the emotional reverberation postulated by Wilhelm Meister. Our immediate impression as we watch is of artificiality and differentness; the play is not by any means emotionally gripping, at least not early on. Before we can make the necessary cultural leap, therefore, we must recognize, from the characters' example, that such a leap is required of us; having grasped intellectually the theme of universal humanity, we must first interpret the stage as a symbol of the theater and *then*, presumably, adjust our own attitude in such a way as to correspond with this interpretation. But is it possible for human sympathy to arise from an intellectual grasp of the need for it? Is our understanding of the intended relation between stage and theater ("Man spürt die Absicht") not itself a source of alienation? The problem in *Iphigenie* is thus essentially the same as in *Nathan*: to effect a synthesis between intellectual detachment and emotional involvement in the audience.

The creation for the audience of an especially deep experience of pure humanity is unquestionably part of the play's intention; we convince ourselves of this only more firmly as we penetrate further into the text. Why, for example, in the last act, are there two separate resolutions of the conflict, and why are they permit-

ted to jar with one another as they do? First Iphigenie brings the
truth out into the open (1892–1992), and on this indispensable
basis O:estes and Thoas, with Iphigenie's help, learn to know and
respect each other (2027–94); then there is an ominous turn as
Thoas recalls the existence of a problem which mere human
understanding cannot solve, the problem of who will get the
statue of Artemis (2095–106); and then, finally, Orestes remem-
bers to reveal what he should have said at the beginning, that this
problem no longer exists, since the oracle has been re-interpreted
(2107–17). Goethe carries this off very smoothly in the dialogue,
and there is a perfectly good psychological explanation for Orestes'
forgetting at first to mention that he no longer intends to steal the
statue. But still, in the scene as it is actually arranged, the solution to the god's riddle gives the impression of being a mechanical
device tacked on in order to allow the play to finish up, rather
than plunge into renewed conflict.

Without the solution to the riddle, all Iphigenie's heroic truthfulness, all her pleading against "might and cunning" (2105,
2142), would be futile. Iphigenie herself is driven by this knowledge to the brink of despair, for in her last speech before Orestes
clears up the oracle, she violates her own extreme aversion to
"lies" (1405) by at least stretching the truth considerably. She
claims, namely, that she had "immediately" suspected Orestes of
being an impostor and had questioned him closely (2076–81),
whereas she had actually done nothing of the kind; nor had she
had any need to, since Orestes had been the first to reveal himself.
Apparently she herself recognizes, as Thoas does, that the problem of the sacred image prevents all hope of peace, and she is now
desperately attempting to overleap this fact by sheer rhetorical
energy and invention. Again, therefore, the word-game of the oracle, which is necessary to save the otherwise hopeless situation,
appears to interfere with the play's main theme.

But let us consider what the aim of the last scene really is.
Obviously it is not to show the final triumph of Iphigenie's
humane persuasion; otherwise Goethe would have proceeded differently. The aim of that scene, rather, is to show that Iphigenie's
truthfulness is powerless in itself, that it does not actually change
the world, that it requires a firm independent commitment by
others in order to become effective. Orestes claims to have been
healed by Iphigenie's mere "touch" (2119–20), but when he ap-

pears with sword in hand it is clear that he has not really been healed in the true sense of Iphigenie's humanity; the oracle has *already* been deciphered—otherwise he would say "Now I know," not "Now we know" (2108)—but it has not even occured to him that this might be the basis for a peaceful accommodation. He is not really healed until, in the sudden illumination of his last speech (2107–45), he drops all thought of fighting and pleads for nothing but human reconciliation.

The case of Thoas, however, is more crucial, as can be seen from his relation to Orestes' final rousing summary of the play's message: "Might and cunning, men's highest renown, are put to shame by the truthfulness of this lofty soul [Iphigenie], and her pure child-like faith in a noble man [i.e. Thoas] receives its reward" (2142–45). The important point here is that this statement is conditioned by the plea to Thoas which immediately precedes it. *If* Thoas allows the Greeks to leave unharmed, then Iphigenie's "lofty soul" will have "put might and cunning to shame"; but on the other hand, presumably, if Thoas insists on fighting, then Iphigenie's heroic trustfulness will prove futile. Orestes, having himself decided for peace, conjures up a vision of Iphigenie's soul-purity as the basis for a newly reconciled humanity, and he now asks Thoas to cooperate in realizing this vision, or at least not to hinder it (2136); the whole message of the play, therefore, is contingent upon Thoas' willingness to let the play's action express it, his willingness to let the truth be true, even though he (unlike Orestes) will gain nothing by it.

This is crucial, for there is an analogy between Thoas's situation and that of the relatively barbaric audience. The disturbing dependence of the final plot-resolution upon the reinterpreted oracle is meant to remind us that the play does not, and cannot, demonstrate the triumph of "truth" over "might and cunning." The most it can do is hold out to us, as Orestes holds out to Thoas, a speculative vision of humanity reconciled by heroic truthfulness, and ask us to do our part in realizing it. We are asked, like Thoas, to affirm the play's vision, but without having been offered any compelling evidence of its validity or any guarantee that it will be of use to us; and as in the case of Thoas, the very meaning of the play is contingent on our compliance. The ending, with the riddle, is quite literally glib and thus confronts us all over again with exactly the problem it ostensibly solves, the problem of realizing trustful human openness in the actual conditions of human society. Our own humanity, by being confronted with this problem, is challenged, whereas it would merely be flattered by a more convincing denouement; the eloquent speech in affirmation of Iphigeneian humanness which Thoas conspicuously does *not* make at the end of the play is a speech that is meant to arise, in its own way, in the mind and feelings of the audience. Thus Goethe is here operating with more than merely a presumed sympathy between spectator and characters; he envisages an actual experience in the auditorium which transcends anything depicted, or depictable, on the stage.

Another way of interpreting the theme of the oracle is fairly obvious, but it leads to the same kind of conclusion. All deities, says Blake, reside in the human breast, or as is suggested in a speech of Iphigenie's, the gods are an "image" in our "soul" (1717). Therefore, if we receive an oracle that appears wrong or destructive, it means that our own thinking is confused and has somehow turned against us. When our thinking is cleared up, when we regain our mental soundness and equilibrium, then the oracles of the gods are automatically cleared up as well, and this is what happens to Orestes as part of his "healing." The reinterpretation of the oracle at the end thus expresses the idea that those potent beings to whom man attributes divinity are only objectified aspects of his own humanity, the idea that man must take upon himself the responsibility for managing his own world, rather than entrust his fate to outside agencies; and this idea is also suggested by Iphigenie's refusal to accept the externally imposed necessity of deception.

The trouble with this idea is that the fictional plot is based on an undeniable miracle which an actual god has carried out. Therefore, if we perceive the play's "human" meaning in the fullest possible sense, if we understand that all deities reside in the human breast ("Läg' nicht in uns des Gottes eigne Kraft ... "), then we must also understand that this meaning is strictly applicable only in the auditorium, as distinct from the fictional world depicted on stage; Iphigenie herself, after all, cannot possibly doubt the external existence of the gods. Our attention is thus drawn yet again to our own situation, to the fact that the play presents us neither with a convincing picture of the world nor with a reliable guide to action or feeling, but rather with a speculative vision for which we alone are in a position to provide the full realization.

Both the interpretations I have suggested for the oracle bring us back to the necessity that a specially intense experience of humanness arise in the auditorium, beyond any mere reverberation in us of the characters' emotions, if the play is to achieve its full meaning. Something like what Wilhelm Meister imagines must happen in the theater, the spectators must find themselves participating in a ritually intensified experience of human brotherhood. Yet once again, this experience includes an intellectual component which Wilhelm does not take into account, especially to the extent that it arises from an ironic appreciation of the theme of the oracle; the experience must include an intellectual awareness of our obligation to experience it. Thus we are brought back to the problem defined above, the problem of how such an experience can possibly arise.

4

In order to deal with this problem we must first understand more about what we mean by "human," and we can begin by attempting to explain the apparently excessive amount of dialogue devoted, in *Iphigenie,* to past history. There appears to be only one reason for this prolonged dwelling upon the bloody outrages of the Tantalides: namely, to make the point that by objective standards the civilized Greeks are a good deal more barbaric than the barbarians, who have practiced a bit of human sacrifice, but apparently stop short of serving up their nephews in a stew. Again the parallel with the Helen episode in *Faust* emerges strongly, for one main purpose of the "Classical Walpurgis Night," out of which the Helen episode grows, is to bridge the gap between classical civilization and northern or "Romantic" barbarism by reminding us that the supposedly serene and symmetrical Greek imagination was every bit as capable as the German imagination of producing the grotesque or the ugly.

The Greeks are every bit as capable as the Tauridians of unreason, inhumanity, and absolute bestiality; yet the basic superiority of Hellenic culture is never questioned. Iphigenie herself, although she has received a perfectly good proposal of marriage, never swerves from her resolve to return home as soon as possible, even after she hears of the internecine outrages that have marred the victory at Troy; Arkas repeatedly stresses the gratitude of the simple Tauridians for the taste of higher civilization their new priestess has given them; and the very form of the play emphasizes the continued pre-eminence of Greek artistic models in modern Europe. But the Greeks are a bloodthirsty crew. Even Orestes forgets to mention in the last scene that there may very well be no further reason for fighting; it does not occur to him that negotiation might now be possible, for his imagination has been captured by the heroically self-flattering idea that he shall bring true civilization to Tauris, and indeed "love" (2056), by hacking up only one native rather than a whole bunch. Orestes may not really be bloodthirsty, but when faced with a difficult situation he is instinctively attracted more to the idea of killing someone than to the idea of talking things out. What is the definition of culture or civilization that is operating here?

The answer to this question is symbolized by Orestes' fate and development. The Greeks are not civilized because they are purer than other peoples but because they somehow manage simply to put the gross impurity of their existence behind them, as Orestes eventually puts behind him his own horrible crime. Orestes' dream (1258–1309), though set in the underworld, is an exact image of Hellenic culture. Like every other people, the Greeks are adulterers, murderers, usurpers, and traitors; what distinguishes them is that in the very process of bearing these heaviest "burdens of human life," they are also capable of acting civilized, of carrying on social existence so that it presents an ordered and harmonious appearance. Civilization is pretense, but it is a valuable pretense, a "schöner Schein" (beautiful illusion) without which life would not be livable. This pretense does not diminish man's titanic desire for unwholesome power, which is symbolized by Tantalus' continued suffering (1306–9), beneath the surface of the dream image of universal reconciliation. What civilization does, rather, is overcome man's tragic tendency temporarily, and never more than temporarily, by simply disregarding it, as the shades do in the dream, by refusing to take it as an occasion for hypochondriac despair—which is the lesson both Orestes and Wilhelm Meister must learn, and the lesson Werther fails to learn. At the very end of the play Orestes' and Iphigenie's exalted rhetoric gives the impression of perfect resolution (2117–73), but apparently only bewilders Thoas, who gets in edgewise a total of four syllables, since his own problems have not diminished in the least. Civilization, as exemplified by those two eloquent Greeks at the end, is a method by which men make the best of a bad situation. It lightens "the burdens of human life" by the expedient of pretending that they do not exist; the essential selfishness of Iphigenie's and Orestes' complete preoccupation at the end with their own happiness is rendered harmless not by being overcome but by being dressed up rhetorically as a vision of realized human brotherhood.

By "human," therefore, in the context of *Iphigenie*, we do not mean "natural"; the play presents a vision not of natural human goodness but rather of natural human incorrigibility which must be dressed up or sublimated by civilization, since it cannot be eliminated. In this connection we might recall that the *Sendung* (Book Two, Chapter 5) contains an interesting allusion to the *Hamburgische Dramaturgie* (no. 76) on the subject of public executions; Lessing quotes and agrees with Moses Mendelssohn that the spectators all basically desire the criminal's pardon, regardless of his crime, whereas Goethe (or at least Wilhelm) insists that there is a certain basic barbarism in us by virtue of which, in spite of ourselves, a last-minute pardon of the victim disappoints us. Again, man is naturally incorrigible and must make his condition tolerable to himself by art; hence the preferability of "those executions which poetry presents for us" (*WA*, LI, p. 151), which do not deny but rather sublimate our natural but uncomfortable barbarism.

It follows that the human brotherhood which is advocated, envisioned, and, in Goethe's intention, actually created by *Iphigenie* is not a natural but rather an artificial phenomenon, a "schöner Schein," since on the level of mere nature it does not exist. What I have called the intellectual component in an audience's perception of the play, therefore, is not only acceptable but indispensable. Drama in general, *Iphigenie* in particular, is not meant to generate an instinctive emotional resonance in its spectators; its aim, rather, is to provide the spectators with a training in civilized artifice and conscious sublimation. By the very act of sitting in the theater, especially at a play like *Iphigenie*, we find ourselves participating in a markedly artificial social ritual; in theme, however, this particular play has to do with pure humanity, with universal understanding and brotherhood, and we, being spectators,

cannot hope to experience such brotherhood as a natural emotional surge, since we are already intellectually conscious of it as
an idea; this in turn obliges us to question whether natural human
brotherhood is really what is required of us in the first place. In
fact the question of consciousness as an impediment to natural
feeling and action is itself an important theme in the play. Pylades
warns Iphigenie against thinking too much (1660–64), and
Iphigenie herself later says to Thoas, "In order to do good, no
thinking about it is needed" (1989); but these words clearly conflict with her own experience, for it had been only her repeated
reconsideration (against Pylades' advice) of the choice facing her,
that had culminated in her momentous decision to speak the
whole truth. Thus we are led—both by the apparent anomaly of
our situation in the theater, the requirement that we experience
directly something we have already grasped intellectually, and by
certain ironies in the dialogue—toward the understanding that
true human brotherhood arises not from instinctively shared feelings but from the deliberate sharing of thought, that it is an artificial but nonetheless valuable phenomenon toward the creation of
which we must work consciously with other men. And, provided
we understand and accept the artificial, ritual quality of the activity we are engaged in, this is what we do in the theater, in that we
consciously participate[13] in the socio-poetic creation of a temporary
artifice which glorifies (however unjustifiably) our humanity.

We can now also understand why Iphigenie speaks the frequently misinterpreted words, "In order to do good, no thinking
about it is needed," and follows them with the statement, "Doubt
alone is what makes good into evil. Don't think! Act generously,
as you feel!" (1991–92). These words, considered at their face
value, do not in any sense express directly the play's meaning. In
the first place, Iphigenie's own experience does not correspond to
what she says. It is, to be sure, her feeling that prompts her to
trust Thoas, but it is not a sudden access of feeling which she
immediately obeys; if she had followed her initial feeling about
Pylades (1382–83), then she would presumably have acted in the
spirit of his advice, "cleverly" (1581), and would now be safe on
shipboard. In fact, the whole of Act IV, 398 lines, as well as a good
deal of Act V, scene iii (1804–1919), is focussed upon the slow
emotional-intellectual brewing of her decision, her uncertainty
about *which* of her natural feelings to follow. And in the second

place, what Iphigenie says is not at all inconsistent with the hypothesis that she herself possesses a thoroughly civilized understanding of the necessary artificial or intellectual component in all expressions of true human community. Civilization is artificial, but although every civilized man knows this, no truly civilized man ever *says* it, since to do so would violate the whole aim of civilization, which is to sublimate human nature, to resist consciously the hypochondriac despair that must follow when one insists on looking too far beneath the civilized surface of existence. Therefore Iphigenie suggests that the only way to do good is by following one's feelings, a doctrine which flies in the face of everything any reasonable man would infer from the history of the Tantalides. Iphigenie is not here explaining the truth objectively, but rather, as Burckhardt suggests, she has learned to talk in a new way, and she uses this new way of talking in a civilized manner.[14] In content, what she says has to do with natural human feeling, but her mode of speaking is no less artificial than Helen's rhyming in *Faust*. Civilization is pretense, and here, between Iphigenie and Thoas, it is the pretense that natural feeling can function as a reliable guide to action.

5

It is important, moreover, that Iphigenie's appeal to Thoas' feelings is not a normal Greek way of talking; Arkas and Thoas are the characters in whose speeches honesty, human understanding, and sincerity of self-expression are prime values, whereas one result of Orestes' cure in Act III, scene iii, is that he no longer resists Pylades' typically Greek, that is unashamedly devious and violent plan of action. Iphigenie has thus learned something through her contact with the barbarians; but this does not mean that she has simply surrendered her civilized Greek character to a Tauridian way of thinking. On the contrary, she has, in a characteristic Greek manner, transformed Tauridian values into a new civilizing device, a rhetorical device, a device for creating in a new way the conscious artifice by which true human community is made possible.

And if we bear in mind that Tauridian values, especially the value set upon the feelings of the individual, are obviously similar to German values, then we can say something about the implied relationship of a nascent German drama to its Greek models. On one hand, the Germans cannot simply reproduce Greek art but must modify it; Greek drama in Germany, like Iphigenie in Tauris, must learn new tricks, as is also clear from the obvious difference between Goethe's and Euripides' treatment of the same plot. But on the other hand, at least a temporary encounter with the civilized Greek example is still necessary. The German native character, as a natural phenomenon, cannot produce the true human community which is the aim of drama; in order to achieve this it must first undergo transformation into a conscious device. It is not enough that the Germans merely *be* themselves; what they must learn, in addition, is to *wield* their being consciously, in order to create by artifice what nature left to itself can never bring forth, a genuine, if never reliably permanent brotherhood of man.[15]

The Germans must learn from the Greeks, not how to be, but rather how to realize their being, through conscious artifice, on the level of appearance, how to realize "Sein" as "schöner Schein." The outrages of the house of Atreus show that on the level of being the Greeks are no better than the Tauridians, and by extension no better than the Germans. Where the Greeks excel is in the artistic sublimation of being, the creation of bright images by which humanity is glorified (with or without any real justification) and men are encouraged to respect themselves and each other. We recall, in this connection, a very important speech of Pylades to Orestes: "We would prefer that all our deeds be as great, in the doing, as they later become when the song of poets has rolled them around the world for years, like a growing snowball. What our fathers did sounds so beautiful to us, when in the evening stillness a young man sings it to the lyre; and what we do is—as their deeds were to them—nothing but piecemeal drudgery" (681–89). Our ancestors' deeds, while being performed, were every bit as laborious and unsatisfying as our own deeds, and this point holds not only for the apparent difference between generations but also for that between cultures, between Greek and German culture for example. Our own existence is intrinsically no less significant than the Greeks'; indeed, as Iphigenie herself points out, the mere telling of the truth can involve as much genuine heroism as the deeds celebrated by Homer (1892–1919). The difference, again, is only "the song of poets," the Greeks' talent for sublimating existence, for turning their back upon its everyday sordidness and raising it into the light as a symbol of glorified humanity. For the Germans there are two lessons to be learned: first (this is Pylades' point), that they must not despise their own existence because of its relative colorlessness, for this colorlessness, this "piecemeal drudgery," characterizes all human existence; and second (this is the point of the play as a play, as conscious artifice), that they must also not merely be content with their own existence, but must use it consciously as material for the engaging artifice by which true human community is made possible. Thus the idea of natural drama and the idea of a strictly native German drama are both transcended in *Iphigenie*.

6

But Lessing, at the end of the *Dramaturgie*, argues that the Germans cannot yet hope to have a national theater because they are not yet even a nation, and this point seems to make rather more sense than the theory implicit in *Iphigenie*. Can true human community begin in the theater? Does the awakening of communal feeling in the theater not presuppose a sense of community in the society at large? Otherwise how can the audience be expected to respond correctly? Goethe, in the *Sendung* (e.g. Book Two, Chapter 3), and Lessing are both worried about the conflict between commerce and dramatic poetry; the Germans are too business-minded for the theater, too occupied with what "fills the purse."[16] If they concern themselves with the theater at all, they always expect from it something more tangible than it is prepared to give, if not actual material profit then at least a clear moral profit in the form of definable maxims for living.[17] Thoas' wish to marry Iphigenie, to receive from her not only a civilizing impulse which must then be developed independently, but also the solution of his own personal and political problems, is a clear allegory of this state of affairs. In reality drama can provide neither Thoas nor the Germans with any real improvement in their condition, and the aggressively artificial quality of *Iphigenie* is meant to impress this point upon the audience. If the Tauridians or the Germans are to achieve a higher level of culture, they must do so for themselves, and drama can only point them in the right direction.

But can drama do even this much? A certain guarded optimism on this point is expressed in the mechanism of Orestes' healing. The trouble with Orestes when he first appears is that he cannot communicate; he has fallen into an obsessive hypochondriac despair which distorts everything others say to him, so that he and Pylades spend all of Act II, scene i, talking at cross purposes. Even the best possible news, that the priestess is his lost sister Iphigenie, is immediately transmuted by his mode of thinking into bad news (1174–1254); "between us," he says to Iphigenie, "let there be truth!" (1080–81), but even the truth is still "between" them as a wedge, not a bond, for their thinking about it moves in opposite directions, they have not yet reached each other. Orestes' trouble is that he is utterly alone, in a self-created mental universe where, by definition, no one can follow him.

Then, however, comes the crisis. Orestes falls into a sleep or trance in which he perfects his withdrawal from reality by joining the sad society of the underworld (1258–1309). And he is still living in this imaginary human community when he speaks, to Iphigenie and Pylades, the immensely important words: "Have you also come down here so quickly? Sister, for you it is best so! That leaves only Electra; may a gracious god, with gentle arrows, send her down speedily as well. You, my poor friend, I pity! But come, come with me, to Pluto's throne, as new guests, to greet our host" (1310–16). For an instant, and on the level of complete illusion, Orestes achieves contact with his sister and his friend; for an instant he is convinced that they are at last sharing the same experience with him, that he and they are no longer living in disjoint universes. And then, when Iphigenie and Pylades make clear that they, for their part, are still living in the real world (1317–40), that instant of totally illusory communication proves a strong enough thread to pull Orestes back into the real world as well. Now he is healed, and not an instant earlier. The mere illusion of direct human contact is what heals him, for if we even imagine ourselves in contact with others, this is already a step toward openness, toward a social rather than an obstinately individual mode of perceiving and acting.

The relevance of this to Goethe's theory of drama is clear enough. Like Orestes in his dream, we in the theater, faced as it were with a substantial dream, are afforded momentarily the experience of a more perfect human community—provided we are willing to accept and participate in the artificiality of the proceedings; and in the case of *Iphigenie* we can hardly avoid doing so unless we leave the theater. We are made aware that sublimation and stylization of existence are indispensable in order that the "human" arise as an affirmable ideal around which a true community of men may shape itself, and we are aware of this truth in the very process of putting it into practice as the social ritual of drama. Shall we not, like Orestes, continue to feel at least something of this new artistic bond with our fellow citizens, this totally illusory bond of which the play teaches us that its illusoriness, its artificiality, is precisely its true human value?

The Germans need to learn how to sublimate their own normal existence and transform it into a consciously wielded symbol glorifying humanity; but a truly native German drama, if there were such a thing, would fail to accomplish this, for it would speak directly to its audience on a deeper-than-conscious level, as it were Wagnerianly, and so only strengthen, without elevating, their Germanness. Perhaps it is therefore to the Germans' advantage that drama must appear to them heaven-sent rather than earth-grown, that it comes to Germany by way of a scholarly tradition, a tradition of conscious minds, and so cannot hide its artificiality. And to take up the other suggestion in that speech of Arkas with which we began (1477–82), perhaps it is also to the Germans' advantage that theirs is not a highly developed civilization; for a too well-developed order of manners in everyday life would smother those stirrings of stylized existence that follow upon our experience in the theater. True human community, or true civilization, is the conscious cooperation of individuals toward the creation of a sublimated image of humanity; but civilization itself, when it stagnates (as it does) into mere unconscious habit, eventually interferes with such community.

7

The deeper parallels between *Nathan* and *Iphigenie* are now clear. For Lessing, now that Christianity has grown problematic, the Christian must learn to stand both inside and outside his belief; he must be a Christian, yet also be able to wield his Christianity in the service of a purely human ideal, and this is exactly what is required of the Germans and their Germanness in *Iphigenie*. Moreover, in both *Nathan* and *Iphigenie* the ironic cultural stance suggested by the play's meaning is incorporated into the theatrical situation, in that the audience is subjected to a distinct tension between intellectual detachment and emotional involvement. In both plays, the advance beyond drama of shock or

sympathy is the same: the requirement that the spectator understand the play and be aware of exactly what it demands from him,
the exploitation, therefore, of the intellectual component in our
relation to the stage, which in turn points clearly in the direction
of Kleist. Just as we must be aware, in *Prinz Friedrich*, that the
creation of a symbolic vision on stage reflects a similar event in
the theater, so in *Iphigenie* we must recognize that the leaping of
the gap between Hellenic and Tauridian reflects a leaping of the
gap between stage and auditorium; and the ironic force of the
avoided tragedy in *Prinz Friedrich* is comparable to the irony we
must sense in *Iphigenie* at the solving of the riddle, or the incompleteness of the family at the end of *Nathan*. This intellectual component in the relation between stage and spectator, again, plays a
crucial part in the development of German drama in general.

Let us conclude by dealing with a later theoretical utterance of
Goethe's which appears to contradict this point. In the essay
"Über epische und dramatische Dichtung," which is meant to
summarize both his own and Schiller's thought on the topic,
Goethe says that the mime or dramatic actor "presents himself as a
definite individual; he seeks to involve us in himself and his
surroundings exclusively, to make us feel the sufferings of his
soul and body, share his embarrassments, lose ourselves in
him. . . . The spectator must by rights be kept in a state of constant
sensory exertion; he may not collect himself mentally, he must
follow passionately; his fantasy is utterly silenced, no demands
may be made upon it" (WA, XLI, 2, pp. 223–24). When reading
this passage we are reminded of the later essay "Shakespeare und
kein Ende," in which the appeal to the "fantasy" of his listeners is
cited as an untheatrical element in Shakespeare.

But at least Goethe does not mean here that drama should produce a perfect illusion of reality. Throughout his career, in the
early introduction to Mercier, in *Iphigenie* and *Faust* and his
various masques, in the 1788 essay on men in female roles, in his
practice as a theater director, and in the conversations with Eckermann (e.g. 28 March 1827), Goethe distinguishes very carefully between theatrical effectiveness and resemblance to nature.
Moreover, in the essay "Weimarisches Hoftheater," he praises the
Weimar audience for its ability to appreciate plays that present an
intellectual difficulty, plays in which, after the first performance,
"some things are still obscure, even disagreeable" (*WA*, XL, p.

79). And in fact, in the essay "Über epische und dramatische Dichtung" itself, he says earlier on, "The epic poem presents mainly its persons' activity, tragedy mainly its persons' suffering; epic shows man's actions *directed outward*, tragedy the *inward-directed* man" (*WA*, XLI, 2, p. 221). How shall we reconcile this logically with the passage from the same essay quoted above? How can an audience sympathize or identify (*teilnehmen, mit-fühlen*) with an inward-directed character if its apprehension of this character is purely sensory?

With regard to *Egmont* more will be said about the representation of inward-directed characters on the stage, but a certain amount of deliberate verbal subtlety is already clear in the first quotation above. "By rights" ("von Rechts wegen") the theater audience ought to react in a wholly sensory manner to what it is presented with; in other words, the techniques employed by the dramatist and the actor must be calculated to encourage maximum sensory involvement. But drama cannot actually succeed in shutting off completely the spectator's thought and imagination. Such an idea would run counter to the whole development of eighteenth-century thought on the subject of artistic illusion, which is understood for example by Mendelssohn, and later by Schiller as well (who supposedly shares the thinking of Goethe's essay), as an involvement of our senses which leaves the intellect free, as a compelling sensory experience of which our intellect recognizes the illusory nature.[18] The immediate aim of the devices employed by playwright and actor, therefore, is not necessarily identical with the ultimate effect of drama upon its audience. Schiller argues repeatedly that, while drama does everything possible to capture our senses and emotions immediately, still our intellect, of its own accord, rises above this enthrallment and brings forth an idea of its own moral freedom, which is the true ultimate goal of the genre. And Goethe himself, to Eckermann on 28 March 1827, argues that the moral effect of Sophocles' plays arises as it were in spite of their author's workmanlike concentration upon his "subject matter" and his "métier."

I therefore take Goethe's argument concerning the sensualness of drama as a discussion of drama's immediate, not ultimate goal, and I cannot see that the argument is logically consistent otherwise. The actor and the dramatist must bend all their efforts toward creating as perfect an artifice as possible, an artifice which, while not for a moment deluding us into believing it real, still keeps us occupied on the sensory level by its coherence and energy; for the ultimate aim of drama, the metaphysical-social *meaning* of artifice, the relation between conscious artifice and true human brotherhood, requires this engagement on our part. The more compelling the artifice, the more clearly must the general meaning of artifice emerge when we reflect (seemingly in spite of the poet) upon its artificiality. If, on the other hand, the poet attempts to do our thinking for us, if he neglects his "métier," if he does not himself rejoice in artifice, but rather leaves it to one side as a mere tool, and speaks instead directly to our intellect about conscious artifice as the necessary basis of true community, then in the very act of speaking the truth he is also contradicting it, since he is attempting to communicate with us precisely by avoiding artificiality. Therefore—to take a particular instance— Iphigenie's statements about natural feeling are fitted smoothly into the give and take of conversation and, within the text, are not questioned with regard to their general validity; no author's representative is there to guide us, we must find our own way through the logical difficulties those statements raise in the play's larger context. Once the relation between human community and conscious artifice is understood, along with the centralness of this relation in Goethe's idea of drama as a genre, there is no contradiction between our own argument concerning *Iphigenie* and the argument in "Über epische und dramatische Dichtung." The poet goes to work as though his aim were to shut off our thinking altogether, but this serves to direct our thoughts—when, as we must, we do reflect upon his work—toward a more perfect apprehension of his ultimate meaning and of the significance of the theater itself as an institution.

Even more can be said on this point if we recall Goethe's idea that drama, or at least tragedy, presents "inward-directed" characters with whom we are meant to sympathize. For how shall this sympathy be achieved unless we too, for our part, are somehow inward-directed while watching the play, somehow led into ourselves? This is another aspect of the dramatist's single-minded concentration on what Goethe calls the sensory, on the perceivable outward smoothness and wholeness of his construct. That the dramatist refuses to operate with the infinitely pliable material of our imagination (as the epic poet does), but rather places everything before us in the form of tight, directly perceived actualness, that he thus refuses to encourage our thinking or imagining, ought to make clear to us that our thoughts about his work, and about the significance of the communal ritual in which we are participating, are strictly our own, so that we are led, strictly speaking, "inward" with respect to ourselves. A similar point has been made above concerning Kleist, and we shall return to this general idea below.

5 *Egmont* and the
Maelstrom of the Self

It will be useful to begin our discussion of *Egmont*, the next phase in Goethe's dramatic thinking, by making a diagram, which I think will not only reveal the play's meticulous architecture but also refute the perennial criticism of the ending as too "operatic."[1] The play is constructed as a spiral that leads gradually inward toward the center of Egmont's being (we recall Goethe's assertion that tragedy shows "inward-directed" man), so that the Clärchen dream, the transformation of the stage itself into the interior of Egmont's mind, is an entirely natural and aesthetically necessary ending.

1

The spiral structure is defined by three axes or radii that represent three areas in which Egmont's existence unfolds: (A) the streets of Brussels and the life of the Netherlandic people; (B) the palace and the world of Spanish politics; and (C) Clärchen's house, where Egmont lives his private, as opposed to his public, life. For the sake of simplicity, I have given the scenes of the play consecutive numbers:

Act I: 1 = "Armbrustschiessen" (I, i)
        2 = "Palast der Regentin" (I, ii)
        3 = "Bürgerhaus" (I, iii)

Act II:	4	= "Platz in Brüssel" (II, i)
	4a	= "Egmonts Wohnung" (II, ii)
	4b	= "Oranien kommt" (II, ii)
Act III:	5	= "Palast der Regentin" (III, i)
	6	= "Clärchens Wohnung" (III, ii)
Act IV:	7	= "Strasse" (IV, i)
	8	= "Der Culenburgische Palast" (IV, ii)
Act V:	9	= "Strasse" (V, i)
	10	= "Gefängniss" (V, ii)
	11	= "Clärchens Haus" (V, iii)
	12	= "Gefängniss" (V, iv)
	13	= "Egmont (allein)" (V, iv)

Numbers 4a and 4b constitute an anomaly in the pattern, but an anomaly by which the meaning of the pattern is made especially clear. Act I introduces the play with a complete cycle, a street scene (axis A), a palace scene (axis B), and a scene in Clärchen's house (axis C). Then, in Act II, another cycle begins but is interrupted, between the street scene and the palace scene, by Egmont's conversations with his secretary and Orange, his only real business conversations in the whole play; and this suggests that it is somehow in Egmont's interest to arrest the play's forward motion by establishing an equilibrium between the life of the Netherlands and the politics of Spain (axes A and B). Indeed, the image of equilibrium, or of threading one's way between opposed forces, occurs twice in the conversation with the secretary, in Egmont's idea of himself as a sleepwalker balancing on a ridgepole[2] and in the metaphor of the sun-chariot guided precariously between a rock face and a precipice (220); moreover, the position of "Egmont's House" between axes A and B corresponds to Egmont's personal position between the two names he bears, "Graf Egmont" and "Prinz von Gaure" (190). In any case the repeating sequence of axes, A–B–C, then resumes and keeps pace strictly with scene changes in numbers 5, 6, 7, 8, 9, so that numbers 4a and 4b are felt as what Goethe and Schiller might later have called a "retarding" element in the work's progress.

The spiral structure of the play is charted in Diagram 1. The asterisks indicate scenes in which Egmont appears, and with the exception of number 13 these are all even-numbered scenes

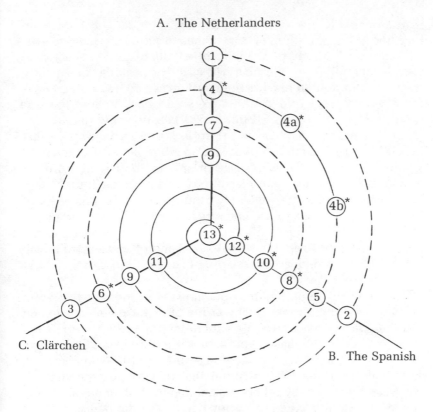

Diagram 1.   The spiral structure of Goethe's *Egmont*

(4, 6, 8, 10, 12), so that Egmont's appearances constitute a duple rhythm which is set off against the triple rhythm of progression from axis to axis. Moreover, the first three of the Egmont scenes (4, 6, 8) cross the axes in reverse order (A–C–B), again suggesting Egmont's interest in arresting the overall development.

Number 9 occurs twice, on axes C and A, because it is a Clärchen scene but takes place in the street and turns into a Netherlanders scene halfway through. A parallel situation is found in number 11, in which we first see Clärchen alone, whereupon Brackenburg arrives with news of what is happening in the streets, this being why the line from number 11 crosses axis A; the anomalousness of number 11 is underscored by the ambiguity

in Clärchen's earlier words, "Nach Hause!" (280), her decision
that her home is no longer *her* home. In all of the later scenes,
although the basic rhythm is still intact, the distinctions between
axes become blurred. Number 10, strictly speaking, is a palace
scene, but Egmont in his dungeon still refuses to believe that he is
cut off from the world of the streets and of Clärchen; the line
from number 12 crosses all three axes because now the "walls"
(282) by which Egmont is cut off do in a sense give way, in that
Ferdinand turns out to be not only a Spaniard but also an inspired
admirer of Egmont (like the Netherlanders), and is now finally
drawn to Egmont by a simple human affection not unlike Clärchen's; and number 13—where Egmont, inspired by his vision of
Clärchen, shouts imaginary encouragement to the Netherlanders
as he goes forth to meet his Spanish executioners—must be located on all three axes. Thus there is a sense of accelerated movement toward the end, an overleaping of axes, a sense of the spiral
as a devouring maelstrom.

It is especially important to appreciate the strong, steady rhythm
by which the spiral moves *inward*. This centripetal movement
has four phases, each of which includes three of the numbered
steps, and the only phase at all difficult to understand is the one
including numbers 4 (with 4a and 4b), 5, and 6. Numbers 1, 2,
and 3 obviously have in common that they show Egmont indirectly, as he is seen by others; and numbers 7, 8, and 9 show the
closing of the trap, the sealing of Egmont's fate: that is, the appearance of Alba's troops (no. 7), Egmont's capture (no. 8), and
the refusal of the burghers to start an uprising (no. 9). Numbers 4,
5, and 6, however, are the key to the whole progression, for they
show the nature and effect of Egmont's *conscious political thinking*. In number 4 Egmont is very stern with the burghers about
keeping the peace—"A respectable citizen, earning his living
honestly, always has all the freedom he needs" (211)—and in
number 4b, the conversation with Orange, he refuses to be a part
of anything that might smack of open rebellion. In number 4a,
however, by the image of the "sun's horses" (220), he compares
himself to Phaëthon, a standard classical example of excessive
ambition, and his next speech suggests this idea even more
strongly: "My station is high, but I can and must rise higher still; I
have hope, courage, and strength. The limit of my growth is not

yet attained; and when I have once attained it, I will stand firm up there, not trembling" (221). Precisely where is "up there"? Where does Egmont think he is going? In numbers 4 and 4b he appears mainly as a defender of the status quo. What sort of ambition does this indicate?

I think there is only one possible answer. Egmont believes, though he does not say so openly, that he will become the next Spanish regent of the Netherlands. I have argued this point in detail elsewhere,[3] but we do not need much argument to convince ourselves of the basic fact. Egmont knows that the Netherlandic people would like nothing better than to have him as regent; Jetter says so twice (178, 212). He also knows that the situation in the Netherlands has begun to worry the Spanish court, so that a change of regent may be contemplated; and obviously the most reasonable way to calm the Netherlanders would be to give them their own home-grown choice. Machiavell says exactly this (189), and exactly this is the point Egmont attempts to impress upon Alba, "that the citizen wants to be ruled by someone born and raised with him" (269). Egmont knows further that in the competition between himself and Orange for the regentship (Margarete mentions this [189]), his own carefree mode of living has given him the advantage, since it has aroused in the Spaniards less suspicion "that he always has something up his sleeve" (241). In a world of reasonable men, therefore, men unwilling to be "unjust and foolish" (225), Egmont knows that he would have the inside track for the regentship. In talking with Clärchen he compares himself explicitly to a soldier waiting quietly in ambush until his plans mature (239); all he needs to do, as far as he can see, is wait until the natural course of events secures his ambition for him. The one event that could thwart him is a violent disruption of the present situation; hence his policy (4 and 4b) of keeping the peace.

Numbers 4, 4a, and 4b allow us to see Egmont's conscious political aim, whereas number 5 shows that this aim is doomed—since Philip and his advisors are not following a reasonable policy—and number 6 shows the personal consequences for Egmont of his secret ambition, which is "an alien drop" (230) in his blood. By nature Egmont is a soldier who likes to "use his fist" and assert the soldier's "inborn right over the whole world" (282). That he is

now playing a patient political game therefore causes an inner
disharmony in him which amounts almost to schizophrenia, and
this is what appears in number 6. After the strain of numbers 4,
4a, and 4b, Egmont goes to Clärchen for a dose of "nature" to restore his inner balance, for "a gentle remedy to bathe the brooding
wrinkles" from his brow (230). Here, at last, we expect to see the
true natural man, "Graf Egmont" as opposed to the "Prinz von
Gaure"; but when Egmont (in 6) finally throws open his arms to
Clärchen, it is to reveal his Spanish uniform. The schizophrenic
complexity of his present situation is thus brought home to us
with something of a shock, and it is no accident that the ensuing
conversation is where he himself talks about the existence of two
Egmonts in conflict with each other (243). Even his private existence (axis C) is poisoned by the self-conscious tension arising
from his concealed ambition.

Thus numbers 1, 2, and 3 show Egmont as he is seen from the
outside; numbers 4, 5, and 6 show the futility and complications
of his conscious existence; and numbers 7, 8, and 9 show the
sealing of his fate. That this third phase represents a movement
further inward, toward the center of his nature, is an idea expressed by Egmont himself: "A man thinks he conducts his own
life; but his inmost self is irresistibly drawn toward his fate" (301).
Fate and the "inmost self," says Egmont, are identical, so that fate
(7, 8, 9) represents a deeper level of the self than consciousness (4,
5, 6). But if numbers 7, 8, and 9 show the external aspect of Egmont's fate, then numbers 10, 11, and 12 probe deeper still by
showing this fate in the process of being internalized and accepted. In essence these last three numbers constitute a single
inner dialogue. First (in 10) we see Egmont thinking to himself
and still deluded in his hopes of being set free. Then (in 11) Clärchen characterizes herself as a "part" of Egmont's "essence" (284)
and in this capacity resigns herself to the inevitability of death.
We do not see Egmont, but we witness a coming-to-terms with
Egmont's fate (including its public aspect, via Brackenburg's report) such as Egmont himself has not yet achieved (in 10) but will
achieve (in 12). Indeed, some of the things Clärchen says reveal
Egmont's situation more than they do hers: "Now I am free, and
my freedom contains the dread of powerlessness.—I am fully conscious, yet unable to make a single move that would help him"
(284). Egmont had been free, but his freedom had been utterly

futile from the start; Egmont had been conscious of himself, of his advantages and his aim, but this very consciousness, his internal tension and the rigidity of his concentration upon what he had believed to be his destiny, had rendered him incapable of lifting a finger against the present danger. Through Clärchen's words, as she specifically suggests, we hear Egmont's "essence" communing with itself.

And then, finally (in 12), comes Egmont's conversation with a second edition of himself, an aspiring young Egmont in the person of Ferdinand. This is the scene in which Egmont at last becomes fully reconciled to his being and his fate. By conquering Ferdinand's despair he conquers his own tendency in that direction; by discussing his downfall in detail, he faces and accepts it; and the sight of his own reflected image in Ferdinand's admiration and affection is what awakens in him the idea which then inspires him (in 13), that by having lived he also continues to live in the thoughts and feelings of others.

This brings us back to our main point. The conversation with Ferdinand is Egmont's deepest and most honest conversation with himself; it represents Egmont's arrival at a central point in his own nature, at the end of a steady progression from the beginning of the play, from the periphery inward. There is therefore no reason for it to come as a surprise when in the next scene (13) the stage itself is transformed into the interior of Egmont's mind. This progression does not explain why the last scene takes exactly the form it does; but once we understand the basic spiral structure of the play, we can conclude at least that the last scene is not merely tacked on to make room for a few heroic sentiments.

2

We can rephrase this point by saying that Egmont's nature pervades the whole play, including the scenes where he himself does not appear; the structure of the play is a kind of diagram of his personality, leading by a spiral path from the periphery toward the inmost depth, until the stage ceases altogether to imitate reality, and begins to imitate the interior of his mind. Even if we did not have the remarks in the last book of Dichtung und Wahrheit, therefore, we would still be able to recognize the applicability to Egmont of Goethe's idea of the "demonic."[4] Of the occasional individuals in whom this power manifests itself with special clarity, Goethe says: "An enormous force emanates from them and they exercise an incredible power over all creatures, even over the elements, and who can ascertain the limits of such a power? Moral forces are helpless against them; it is in vain that perceptive men accuse them of being dupes or deceivers, for the mass is still attracted to them" (*WA*, XXIX, p. 177). In a sense Egmont could be said to be a deceiver, in his concealment of his actual ambition, and in a sense he could be said to be a dupe, in that his ambition is hopeless from the outset. But such perceptions do not touch Egmont's demonic essence; they do not touch "the immeasurable vitality, the boundless self-confidence, the gift of drawing all men to himself, the ability, thus, to win the favor of the people, the silent affection of a princess, the outright love of a natural girl, the sympathy of a politician, the ability to win for himself even the son of his greatest adversary" (*WA*, XXIX, p. 175). Indeed, there is more to Egmont's demonic power than Goethe indicates here, for even when Egmont is not present on the stage, a force radiates from him which shapes everything that occurs. Egmont's "essence" is always there, and this suggests not only the idea of the demonic but also the related idea of "daimon." In his comments on the first strophe of the "Urworte" poem in *Über Kunst und Alterthum*, Goethe says: "Daimon refers here to that necessary, limited individuality which is asserted immediately at a person's birth; it refers to that by which the individual is distinguished from everyone else, even from those most similar to him. . . . Daimon has been reckoned the source of all of a man's future destiny, and it is easy to be convinced that a peculiar inborn force, more than anything else, determines our fate" (*WA*, XLI, 1, p. 216). This passage suggests immediately Egmont's association of his fate with his inmost self, the idea that fate does not merely happen but is determined from within, as the inborn law of one's being.

For the demonic individual like Egmont, then, daimon has both an active and a passive aspect. It is a power by which the individual's nature imposes itself upon the external world "demonically," but it is also a power by which the individual is helplessly determined. Therefore Goethe says, referring specifically to *Egmont*, that the demonic is "at work on both sides" (*WA*, XXIX, p. 175), both for the hero and against him. This is the central paradox in Egmont's destiny, that the source of his power is also the source of his helplessness. Egmont is destroyed not by arbitrary external events but "by the universe itself" (*WA*, XXIX, p. 177), by a mechanism of compensation built into the very order of things. He is the vessel of an overwhelming quasi-divine power which imposes his character irresistibly upon external reality; but this power, operating through his "inmost," also determines his own inevitable fate. "Nemo contra deum nisi deus ipse" (*WA*, XXIX, p. 177); the demonic in the end works against itself and destroys its own vessel.

It is not necessary to know *Dichtung und Wahrheit* in order to perceive this paradox, for Goethe brings it forth vividly on the stage by a variety of devices. The sense of futility that pervades most of the dialogue, the hopeless confusedness of the burghers, the political powerlessness which reduces Margarete's conversations with Machiavell to empty verbiage, the inconclusiveness of Egmont's conversations with his secretary and Orange, even the much criticized fact that the debate with Alba is known from the start to be pointless—the fact, in other words, that what the characters say or think never actually changes anything, gives very strongly the impression that events are moved by a force utterly beyond control or comprehension; and the play's spiral structure, the ubiquity of Egmont's nature, even when he is not present, identifies this force as his own personal fate. Goethe's handling of the figure of Alba, for instance, about whom not a single kind word is said before we see him, is brilliant: Orange calls him a "dragon" (229), Margarete finds him abominable (234), the burghers think of him as a spider (251). Here, we are led to believe, is a positive evil force, a counter force to the power that operates through Egmont. When Alba actually appears, however, he turns out not to be the devil after all, but merely a human being with an extremely difficult job to do—a man of great military and diplomatic skill, as Gomez tells us (253), a man who is firmly determined upon his course, but not so fanatical as to be free of doubt (260–62), a man with a genuine if hard-boiled love for his son, a man of rigid but considered principles, who is by no means unequivocally bested in the debate with Egmont. That Alba appears in this way is not merely an example of Goethe's supposed inability to depict evil; it is, rather, a deliberately calculated shock for the audience. The evil force we had been led to expect now turns out suddenly not to exist; Alba is as much at the mercy of events as anyone else, and it is thus suggested once again that these events are moved by only one force, Egmont's daimon or fate.

This is one side of the paradox; we sense that there is a power emanating from Egmont which determines the whole shape and action of the play. But on the other hand, Egmont himself, as we see and hear him, does not at all give the impression of being a powerful individual. As Schiller points out correctly, what we see of Egmont is not his strength but his weaknesses;[5] and we have discussed above the confused schizophrenic helplessness in his thinking. When Egmont says to his secretary, "If I were a somnambulist, walking on a dangerous roof peak, is it a friend's part to call me by name, to warn me, wake me, and kill me?" (219), the curious switch to the indicative in mid-sentence shows that Egmont wishes to think of himself as *actually* a kind of sleepwalker, guided solely by nature and instinct, as opposed to consciousness. He needs the sleepwalker's natural balance and agility because he in fact is walking a kind of tightrope: he must keep the peace and stay on good terms with the Spaniards in order to protect his chances for advancement, but at the same time he must deliberately allow a certain amount of unrest to develop—as both Alba (265) and even Margarete (192) suspect him of doing—in order that a change of regent may be contemplated. He must maintain an extremely delicate equilibrium between Spanish politics and Netherlandic freedom, but the fact that he *thinks* of himself as a naturally balanced sleepwalker contradicts the idea of unconscious instinctiveness implied by the image. Egmont is too conscious for his own good. He is walking in the dark, but not with the somnambulist's natural grace; he is groping, rather, and stumbling, confused, already doomed to fall.

Egmont is the vessel of a divine power which transforms the whole of the fictional world into a single huge spiral image of his being; but he himself is at the mercy of this power which is now also his doom. As the play unfolds, we receive the impression that what radiates from Egmont is not power so much as confusion. In the first three scenes we are shown Egmont's influence on others, not his actual person, and in each of these scenes we see a confused situation. The burghers have their preferences and catchwords, but they lack any sense of direction, either individually or collectively; they are, as Egmont himself later characterizes them, a "mob with which nothing can be accomplished" (243). Then, in the conversation between Margarete and Machiavell, we hear that Egmont is source of political and religious disorder in the realm. And Clärchen's home, finally, has been totally disrupted by Egmont; neither the mother nor Brackenburg nor Clärchen herself has any real prospects for the future, and they all know this. The world we are shown is an aimless and thoroughly unsettled world, and at its center, as the vessel of its governing power, stands the confused, self-divided figure of Egmont. The world is governed by Egmont's presence and shapes itself as a reflection of his being, but the form in which it reflects him reveals precisely his own stumbling helplessness. The demonic, as Goethe says, operates "only in contradictions" (WA, XXIX, p. 173); Egmont's power is identical with his helplessness; in one sense he resists the play's inexorable forward motion (in 4a and 4b), but at the same time he also embodies and radiates the power by which the spiral of fate fulfils itself.

3

And yet, how is it possible to say that the demonic operates both for and against Egmont? Is this power not in the final analysis simply identical with Egmont's being, including both his strength and his weakness, both success and failure, both his effectiveness and his doom? When we say that the demonic is "at work on both sides," we mean "on both sides" with respect to Egmont's *conscious* desires and perceptions; and self-consciousness is thus the necessary vehicle by which the demonic is realized as paradox. Our inmost self, says Egmont, is drawn irresistibly toward our fate, but this is not a movement "against" us except insofar as it opposes what we consciously imagine and desire as our destiny.

Again, it is not necessary to go beyond the text itself to see the importance of self-consciousness in *Egmont*. In Act I we are shown the force of Egmont's being by way of its effect on others, but at the same time we recognize that there is something wrong with this force, that it tends toward confusion rather than clarity. Then in Acts II and III (nos. 4, 5, and 6, the second phase of the spiral), we perceive that the source of this confused tendency is the self-conscious confusion produced in Egmont himself by his concealed ambition. Egmont not only possesses demonic power, but he also knows about this power, which he compares to the mysterious instinctive force that guides the sleepwalker, or to the irresistible forward drive of the Horses of the Sun; he knows that he has been swept aloft ("in die Höhe getragen" [243]) by a feeling which he inspires in others without even trying (240–41), by a power which appears to reside in his very nature. Indeed, he not only knows this, but he is actually banking on this innate power to produce a specific result in the world, to carry him higher still, to the regentship. He believes that he has understood his own destiny, and he is now operating consciously, constantly re-balancing himself upon his roof peak, in such a way as to help his destiny along. Even Alba's arrival does not shake his commitment to this supposed knowledge; even against Alba he trusts in his personal power, and in the power of his argument "that the citizen wants to be ruled by someone who was born and raised with him."

Egmont, in other words, attempts to *harness his daimon* and make it work for him in the real world. This is the deepest sense of his comparison of himself to Phaëthon, who attempts to harness and guide the overwhelming natural power of the Horses of the Sun. (It is no accident that the sun is also an image of daimon in the "Urworte," and an image of "god's own power" within us, in the poem "Wär' nicht das Auge sonnenhaft.") But Egmont's supposed knowledge of his destiny is what confuses him and ultimately exposes him to his doom; his conscious attempt to fulfill the supposed law of his nature is what brings him into conflict with his nature. He is not constitutionally a peaceable man, but rather, as he himself says—and in the privacy of his prison, where he has no reason to dissemble—he is happiest "where the swift-striding soldier asserts his innate right over the whole world, and in his terrible freedom, like a hailstorm, roams destroying through meadow, field, and forest, respecting no boundaries drawn by man" (282). Egmont is above all a soldier, who strikes first and asks questions later, but his consciousness of what he perceives as his destiny forces him into the unnatural role of peacemaker and defender of the status quo, so that he becomes unable to take the vigorous steps necessary to save himself.

Self-consciousness, then, is indispensable to the working of fate in *Egmont*. We are shown the radiant power of Egmont's being (in 1, 2, and 3), but we also recognize a disturbing tendency toward confusion in its effects. Then (in 4, 5, and 6), we detect that Egmont has his own vision of where his daimon is leading him; and we recognize that by operating consciously in accordance with his vision, he is actually only struggling against his nature, thus causing confusion not only in himself but also in his universe. This confusion, however, Egmont's over-conscious betrayal of his nature, is what makes him resist Orange's advice and so exposes him helplessly to the doom which breaks over him (in 7, 8, and 9); whereupon (in 10, 11, and 12) he gradually manages to come to terms with the idea that his doom represents a deeper level of himself than his conscious thinking had grasped. There is an obvious parallel here to the myth of Oedipus, who fulfills his fate by attempting consciously to avoid it.

Perhaps, on this basis, we can also say something more about the exact relation between "daimon" and the "demonic," and about the origin of demonic power. Daimon, by definition, is a property of every individual, and the demonic, according to *Dichtung und Wahrheit*, pervades all existence. How does it happen, then, that certain individuals appear to possess the demonic as a unique personal trait? The contradictoriness of the demonic, its operation "on both sides," depends logically on the individual's self-consciousness. Is it possible to argue that a certain specially intense type of self-consciousness is the *source* of a demonic power like Egmont's?

Goethe, in a conversation with Eckermann (11 March 1828) in which he discusses the demonic at length, identifies Napoleon's distinguishing characteristic as a state of unceasing "illumination," as opposed to "cloudedness," with respect to his self and mission; since daimon is associated with the image of the sun, the demonic individual (like Napoleon) is perhaps definable as one whose daimon fills him with light, with conscious certainty that it exists as a power that radiates into the world and shapes his fate, thus with something like "the boundless self-confidence" which characterizes Egmont. Everyone has his daimon, but the demonic individual is *one who is intensely aware of his daimon and strives mightily to realize it*. Even the perverse or paradoxical aspect of the demonic is implied by this definition. Daimon is by nature unknowable; the totality of one's self and fate cannot be grasped consciously, because consciousness is only one limited component of the self.[6] This state of affairs does not have too great an effect in the life of the average individual, who is more or less content to remain in the dark about his true self; but the Egmonts of this world are intensely aware of their daimon and intent upon knowing and using it, so that the necessary inadequacy of their supposed self-knowledge becomes a danger. Their self-consciousness, by virtue of its intensity, tends to become self-conflict, an internal self-division that disrupts the same self-unity it pretends to understand (we think of the paradox implied by Egmont's using the image of the somnambulist with reference to himself); the very power of such individuals, therefore, their own dauntless self-confidence, like Egmont's in facing Alba, their unswerving commitment to an increasingly faulty idea of themselves, is what eventually ruins them.

Goethe, it is true, denies the possibility of explaining demonic power by any single "concept" (WA, XXIX, p. 174). But the idea of the demonic as an especially intense and intent and determined form of self-consciousness does explain at least one important aspect of Goethe's thinking; and it is a particularly useful idea for the interpretation of Egmont, for it enables us to recognize that Egmont's is not merely a case of healthy nature thwarted by brooding consciousness, but rather of self-consciousness "on both sides" in Egmont's internal struggle. Moreover, there is a fairly obvious relationship with the motif of striving in Faust; and the definition of the demonic individual as one who commits himself consciously to the harnessing of his daimon also helps clarify the deep connection between Egmont and Iphigenie. The idea of harnessing one's daimon is a development from the idea, in Iphigenie, of consciously wielding one's native condition.

4

Rather than let his fate happen to him, Egmont is intent upon harnessing his daimon. Like Napoleon he is "erleuchtet," illuminated, filled with a burning awareness of his daimon's existence and power, and with the indefatigable will to experience and control that power in the same way that the rider controls a "noble horse" (268), by making use of its own natural bent. Or to put it differently, Egmont is a man in quest of his true self, and the spiral structure of the play marks the progress of this quest. In the end he does find and realize his true self, but what he finds is not what he had striven for; hence the suggestion in structure (4a and 4b) that his activity is a retarding factor in his own destiny. He finds in the end not power but ruin; he finds that precisely his conscious meddling with his daimon had set in motion the process by which his doom now catches up with him ("You have killed yourself" [300], says Ferdinand). This is the demonic, "which does with him utterly as it pleases, and to which he surrenders himself unknowingly, in the belief that his actions are his own" (Eckermann, 11 March 1828). The end of the quest, the center of the spiral, is death. When one actually finds oneself, one also destroys oneself thereby, and again there is a clear parallel with Oedipus, the relentless interrogator into his own true identity.

This idea, that the center of the spiral, the arrival at one's true self, is equivalent to death, implies logically that life by contrast is error, that by living we always necessarily pursue "life's misleading labyrinth" (*Faust*, 1.14), that as long as we continue to live we must continue to be deluded about ourselves, and this in turn brings us back to the idea of self-consciousness. Life, for a human being, necessarily involves consciousness, and as soon as we are clearly conscious of anything—as soon as we are able, for example, to formulate our consciousness verbally—we are already in error: "As soon as we speak, we begin to err" (*WA*, II, p. 279). The order of conscious thought has the effect of distorting the basic order of nature, twisting it out of shape—as Egmont's pretended knowledge of his destiny causes a disharmony within himself— and so necessarily leads us astray. Therefore Faust concludes, in the scene "Nacht," that the only way to achieve absolute self-realization or total communion with nature is death.

But once we see the central problem of *Egmont* in these terms, it becomes clear that this problem is not unique to the lives of demonic individuals. It is, rather, a general human problem, insofar as all men are self-conscious and necessarily in error with respect to their true selves. Nor is Egmont's quest for the self an experience from which we are excluded in our ordinary lives, for the very process of self-consciousness constitutes such a quest. We cannot think about ourselves without attempting to understand what we in truth are; we cannot say the word "I" without asserting by implication that there exists within us a basic unity of person which includes all the apparent accidents and inconsistencies in our experience. There is, to be sure, a difference between the average person's self-conscious meandering toward his true self and the demonic individual's unswerving drive. Goethe, in a letter to Friedrich Rochlitz of 23 November 1829, compares self-knowledge to the bull's-eye in a target and suggests that it is not in general advisable to insist upon being too good a marksman—which image of course recalls Egmont's skill with the crossbow (174). But the quest, the target, the ultimate goal, is the same for all of us.

The self-questing or self-assertion which Egmont carries out with unique intentness and energy is thus an integral part of our own experience. The demonic individual is an intensification or *Steigerung* of our ordinary self-conscious existence; we see in him not ourselves as we actually are, but ourselves as we potentially are, glorified, raised into the heroic, with the petty problems of our everyday experience revealed as tragic problems with a metaphysical dimension. Egmont, in other words, is a magnified projection of the spectator in much the same sense that I have argued Kleist's Homburg is; and the similarity between Goethe's play and Kleist's, in this respect, will emerge more clearly still as we go on.

The self, then, is a maelstrom which sucks us irresistibly toward a goal that turns out to be death. In every instant of life, by virtue of our self-consciousness, we find ourselves drawn toward the ineffable center of our being, whether or not we specifically desire this. Existence itself is constantly heroic, if in most cases inconspicuously so, a constant daring somnambulism at the brink of the abyss, a constant balancing between centripetal and centrifugal forces, between self-attainment and self-preservation; and the actual hero, the demonic individual, is the one who hurls himself into his dangerous situation with affirmative energy, like a soldier into battle, the figure through whom we are therefore able to see most clearly the true nature of our own existence. This, in its turn, explains the attractiveness of the demonic individual; it is a vision of *ourselves* that attracts us in a figure like Egmont, a vision in which the intrinsic heroism of self-conscious existence becomes wholly manifest. The force that draws us is the force of the maelstrom itself, our own self-consciousness, our irresistible tendency toward a true but deadly knowledge of ourselves, toward daimon or unity of person, toward the center of our own being.

This point is supported by a significant parallel between *Egmont* and *Nathan*. In Lessing's play, the spectator's sympathy with the hero is engendered not by a putative emotional resonance, but rather as an aspect of the situation in the theater, and the same type of argument applies to *Egmont*. The spectator, provided he understands the meaning of the play's developing structure, recognizes that the whole of the fictional world is a diagram of Egmont's being. But he must also recognize that Egmont's position is not essentially different from his own; Egmont's problem, and his doom, is that he is a conscious spectator in relation to himself, insisting on an interpretation of his own daimon. The spectator finds his way toward Egmont by the same path on which Egmont finds the way to himself, and that our perspective upon Egmont is thus essentially an interior perspective is revealed unambiguously in the dream scene, where the stage no longer even pretends to imitate external reality.

By watching the play, therefore, and by watching it with the conscious detachment which is unavoidable for a dramatic audience, we find ourselves participating in Egmont's uncomfortably detached conscious relation to himself. Or to look at it the other way round, our own self-consciousness (magnified by the tension between detachment and involvement which we normally experience in the theater) is transmuted into Egmont's self-consciousness via our understanding of the play's structure. At least as early as *Iphigenie*, Goethe reckons with an intellectual component, a conscious detachment, in the relation of an audience to his work; and yet he also insists that the immediate aim of drama must be to involve the spectator as directly and totally as possible, so that we may speak, as in Lessing, of a tension between detachment and involvement. In *Iphigenie*, moreover, this tension is emphasized by the suggestion that we must leap the cultural gulf between stage and auditorium in the same way that the characters finally bridge the gap between Hellenism and barbarism; and in *Egmont*, the hero's fictional attractiveness reminds us that we are meant to be swept up emotionally, while on the other hand the Netherlanders' unwillingness to risk their necks reminds us by analogy of the necessary incompleteness of our involvement. In Goethe as in Lessing, therefore, the natural tension in the spectator between detachment and involvement is specifically encouraged; and in *Egmont* this tension is the vehicle of our sympathy with the self-divided hero. As in *Nathan*, by being detached from the hero we find ourselves in sympathy with him, and our sympathy with him must include a correlative to his own painful self-detachment. His consciousness and ours are merged.

But for this relationship between Egmont and the audience to be realized, the audience must know of Egmont's concealed ambition to become regent. Why, then, does Goethe not let Egmont say anything about this, at least in the privacy of a monologue? The answer to this question is that Egmont does not say anything specific about his ambition, even to himself, because he is determined not to think about it. He recognizes the danger of his own divisive self-consciousness—as in the sleepwalking metaphor, or in the speech to Clärchen about his two selves—and therefore seeks to suppress his secret thoughts altogether; he recognizes that Orange had lost his chance at the regentship precisely by not doing this: "Orange has gotten himself the reputation of always having something up his sleeve" (241). He is counting on nature itself to make him regent; and he understands that by not thinking, by ironing flat "the brooding wrinkles" in his brow, he will arouse minimum suspicion among the Spaniards and maximize his chances. Of course this plan is doomed from the start; the deliberate suppression of consciousness is itself a conscious meddling with nature. But Egmont's attempt not to think, his attempt to avoid interfering with what he imagines as the natural sure-footedness of his daimon—comparable to the instinct of a spirited horse—is sufficient to explain his silence on the subject of his ambition.

There is more to be said, however, about the specifically dramatic significance of that silence. The thought of the regentship, which Egmont attempts to suppress, is a thought we, the audience, arrive at only indirectly—by inference from Egmont's mention of wishing to "rise higher" and his hint that he has "purposes" and a "secret reserve" (241) in his dealings with Margarete, or from the apparent inconsistency of his actions and his obvious self-conscious confusion, or from Margarete's mention of the competition between him and Orange. For us, therefore, as for Egmont, the thought of the regentship exists only subterraneanly, without being made explicit; thus another analogy between the structure of our consciousness and Egmont's is created. I suppose that the dramatic convention of the monologue might still permit Egmont to state his ambition without interfering with the credibility of his desire to suppress his consciousness of it; but if such a monologue existed, then the thought of the regentship, from our point of view, would be entirely unconcealed, and our relationship with this thought would no longer be similar to Egmont's.

Again, merely by watching and thinking about the play, by undergoing that tension between detachment and involvement which is mirrored in Egmont's difficult self-consciousness, by experiencing the thought of the regentship as a secret thought which gradually dawns on us—as it must at some point have dawned on Egmont that his daimon was leading him in that direction—merely by being spectators, therefore, we find ourselves participating, here and now, in Egmont's consciousness, and this is what justifies our interior perspective upon him.

5

The ideas and heuristic definitions we have been operating with serve well enough until the end of the play, the center of the spiral, where something unexpected happens. As the spiral moves inward by its four phases (Egmont reflected in others' consciousness, the problems of Egmont's own consciousness, the realization of his fate, and his inner reconciliation with his fate), as we move toward the center, we move toward truth and unity, until Egmont acknowledges that his doom and his inmost self are identical. But at the end, where the stage becomes Egmont's mind, what appears is not truth but *illusion*. Egmont says of his dream-vision of Clärchen: "With bloodstained feet she appeared before me, the hem of her garment stained with blood. It was my blood, and that of many noble men. No, it was not shed in vain. Forward to your goal, my worthy people!" (304). In history, however, Egmont's execution in 1568 was not the signal for a successful Netherlandic revolt against Spain. The union of the northern provinces under Orange was not effected until 1579, and Belgium, where the scene is set, was still under foreign rule when Goethe wrote his play. Indeed, even if we did not know this, it would be clear from the street scene between Clärchen and the burghers that this "worthy people" does not deserve freedom anyway. They are still only a "mob with which nothing is to be done"; and if Egmont later appears to contradict these words, in conversation with Alba, then he has a political reason for doing so. He is aiming to persuade Alba that the supposedly noble Netherlanders, these "men worthy to tread God's earth" (267), cannot be ruled by force and must therefore be granted their own aristocratic "brother"

(269)—Egmont himself—as regent. Throughout most of the play, therefore, Egmont appears to understand quite well the limits of what can actually be expected from the Netherlanders.

But at the end, where we expect one more step in the direction of truth, we find Egmont in the grip of a gross illusion; he imagines Clärchen at the head of an aroused populace, and exactly this vision has been cruelly parodied only four scenes earlier. It seems, moreover, that he is *knowingly* deluded, for immediately before his dream he addresses Sleep as follows: "You undo the knot of ordered thought, you mingle all images of joy and pain; the circle of inner harmonies flows unhindered and, swaddled in an agreeable insanity, we submerge and cease to be" (303). Is it "pleasing insanity" that we find at the center of Egmont's being, and thus, by analogy, at the center of our own being as well? Only one scene earlier, in the conversation with Ferdinand, Egmont appears to be headed in exactly the opposite direction, when he speaks of his "concern for this land": "If my blood is shed for others, bringing peace to my people, then let it be shed. Alas, this will not be the case. But it is not right to brood where one can no longer act" (301). Nothing could be more thoroughly sane than this. Egmont's earlier concern for peace, in the conversation with Orange, had not been entirely sincere—coming, as it had, from a man whose "fond memory of happiness" turns out to be a dream not of peaceful joy but of soldiers' raging "in terrible freedom, like a hailstorm, destroying, through meadow, field, and forest" (282). Earlier, Egmont's advocacy of peace had been self-serving, since a break with Spain would have ruined his chances for the regentship. But now he appears to desire peace genuinely, since Ferdinand has reminded him of the consequences of the huge miscalculation he has made—"You could have, and should have, preserved yourself for us" (300). He has succeeded only in reducing the Netherlanders' chances for freedom, by depriving them of their most capable and inspiring military leader, himself, and if mere chaos and purposeless bloodshed ensue, this will be largely his fault; therefore peace is now the most he can hope for. And yet, even his awareness of his own crushing responsibility is tempered by the sane reflection that brooding upon it is no use.

In the next to the last scene, then, Egmont sees the whole disastrous situation, his own and his country's, with calm clarity; but in the last scene he returns absurdly to the illusion he had appar-

ently left behind in his first monologue (no. 10), the illusion of an
aroused and purposeful Netherlandic people. As in the case of his
advocacy of peace, there has been a shift from the self-seeking
toward the altruistic (in no. 10 he hopes for his own freedom, in
no. 13 he does not), but this does not make him any less deluded,
where only a moment before (in 12) his sight had been perfectly
clear. If we are to understand the last scene as a final step in the
direction of truth, then our idea of "truth" needs to be refined; and
the possibility of such a refinement is suggested by a parallel with
the end of *Faust*, where Faust is literally blinded by "Care" (also
Egmont's archenemy [230, 282, 301]) and is grossly deluded about
the nature of what he hears (*Faust*, ll. 11539–43). Faust's encounter with "Care," like Egmont's, is not a defeat but a victory,
and leads to a triumphant inner vision—"Night seems to penetrate me more deeply, but within me is a bright light" (ll. 11499–
500)—which reminds us of the inward transformation of the stage
at the end of *Egmont*; indeed, it would not be at all inappropriate
for Egmont, in his pre-vision of a Netherlandic revolution, to speak
Faust's last words, "In the anticipation of such high happiness, I
now enjoy the supreme moment" (ll. 11585–86). But why, in both
Faust and *Egmont*, is triumphant inner vision associated so
strongly with the motif of delusion? What is truth? And where is
truth, if not at the gates of death?

We have seen the importance in *Egmont* of the idea that life
involves error or illusion, that the truth about ourselves, in the
sense of total knowledge of our own daimon, is inaccessible to us.
Existence for us takes the form of self-consciousness, which always entails self-division and error, so that perfect self-unity can
be achieved only when we no longer exist; the unhindered flow of
"the circle of inner harmonies" occurs only when "we cease to
be." But this means that even Egmont's sane awareness of his
situation (in 12), like Faust's awareness of his guilt in the matter
of Philemon and Baucis, does not constitute a knowledge of truth.
Egmont (in 12) perceives and acknowledges the facts of his situation, but the sane objectivity of his attitude springs from a delusion, the delusion that he has now fully understood and accepted
his fate. Again, there is no such thing as knowledge of one's fate. It
follows that Egmont's "agreeable insanity" (in 13) does after all in
a sense represent one further step in the direction of truth, for the
pretense of calm, final, objective knowledge has now been aban-

doned. Egmont is once again thoroughly, willfully, and energetically deluded about facts, but this energetic self-delusion is a
truer submission to man's fate (since man's fate *is* to be deluded)
than the quiet, apparently knowledgeful submission of the scene
preceding. Egmont (in 13) becomes once again his true self,
whereas (in 12) he had been uncharacteristically subdued. Once
again (in 13), he is "erleuchtet," filled with a burning vision of his
unconquerable daimon, of a mission that he will continue to carry out even after dying, and it does not matter that this vision
constitutes a delusion with respect to facts; what matters is that
Egmont is now truly affirming his fate, not merely accepting his
approaching death (as in 12) but also affirming deliberately—"insanity" is his word—that demonic intensity of consciousness
which had caused his ruin in the first place.

But where does this leave us, the audience? We understand that
what we are witnessing is the maelstrom of the self, a relentlessly
narrowing spiral. We understand, moreover, that the problem of
self-consciousness, with which we see Egmont struggling, is also
a problem in our own existence, so that our experience in the
theater ought ideally to be a journey toward the center of our own
being as well. And yet, at the very end, we are forcibly dissociated
from Egmont, in that we recognize the gross illusoriness of his
vision. We see that the path toward truth, for Egmont, has ended
in illusion, and this must raise doubts about where the spiral path
of the play has led us. Have we learned anything from the play
about our own being, or are we as deluded as Egmont?

What happens at the end of the play is that we are made aware
of an uncomfortable but logical development of the parallel between Egmont's situation and our own. "If my life was a mirror in
which you gladly viewed yourself, then let my death also be
such" (300); these words are spoken not only to Ferdinand but
also directly to us, the audience, as a signal. Egmont's life has in
fact been presented as a flattering "mirror" to our own life, as a
glorification of the problems of self-conscious existence; now, like
Ferdinand, we must draw the inescapable conclusion from this,
which means we must face even Egmont's deludedness, in spite of
our ability to see through it, as an image of our situation in the
theater. The vision of an inspired Netherlandic uprising stands in
the same relation to Egmont as the whole theatrical vision stands
to us; we are flattered by the play, a tragic depth in our own

existence is revealed, but the idea that we have thereby come to a true knowledge of ourselves is delusion. Egmont's death is the result of necessary deludedness, and by accepting Egmont's death as a mirror, we accept the necessity of our own deludedness.

"If my life was a mirror in which you *gladly* viewed yourself," says Egmont, however, "then let my death also be such." Not only must we recognize that the theater can never provide us with anything more than a pleasant illusion, an "agreeable insanity," but we must also rejoice in our delusion, like Egmont. And this idea brings us back to the main point in our discussion of *Iphigenie*: the true business of civilization, and the special function of drama within civilization, is to promote human brotherhood by suppressing the sordid facts of the human condition, by creating and consciously affirming an artificial image that glorifies mankind, whether or not such glorification is justified. The ultimate lesson of *Egmont*, as of *Iphigenie*, is that we go to the theater not to learn truth but rather to practice and reaffirm the conscious act of self-delusion upon which all civilized society is founded, without which human life would degenerate into hypochondriac despair. Again, the ultimate aim of drama, as opposed to its immediate aim, is not to obliterate or transcend our self-consciousness but rather to intensify it, to lead us ever deeper into ourselves and show us finally the way in which we may raise ourselves up by conscious artifice, the way in which we in fact are raising ourselves up, by participating in the artistic ritual of the theater. Man's job is to sublimate his condition by art, not to pick endlessly among the depressing facts of his condition.

Let us note, moreover, that the paradoxical relation between detachment and involvement not only continues to function at the end of *Egmont*, but is intensified. Our recognition that Egmont is deluded constitutes a certain detachment on our part; we apparently see more than Egmont does. But at the same time we understand that Egmont, by being deluded, has become that much truer an image of our own situation as willingly deluded spectators in the theater; thus our sense of identification with him is strengthened. And yet, this sense of identification, the idea that by watching Egmont we are learning something about ourselves, following a spiral path to the center of our being, is what we have now learned to recognize as a mere illusion on our part. There is no logical way out of this paradox; there is no single, final state-

ment that can be made concerning our relationship to the character Egmont. What counts, rather, is the process in which this relationship develops, the tension of detachment and involvement by
which our own self-consciousness is exercised and deepened, in
order that we may experience intensely the whole difficulty,
hence also the whole potential glory of the human condition, as it
were "Himmelhoch jauchzend/Zum Tode betrübt" (237).

6

   Egmont thus represents an advance beyond *Nathan*, as well as
beyond *Iphigenie*, in that its structure is simpler and more compelling, requiring less detailed intellectual work on the part of the
spectator. In *Nathan* we must piece together the whole of the
hero's intricate inner life before we can appreciate our own relation to the artistic vision, whereas in *Egmont* we are presented
with only one real intellectual puzzle, the question of Egmont's
hidden motivation; once we have solved this (which we ought to
have done by the end of Act II) the rest of the artistic pattern falls
into place without much trouble: Egmont as the harnesser of his
daimon, Egmont as the man in search of his true self, the self as a
maelstrom. The basic intention of *Egmont* still involves a difficult
artistic problem, for Egmont must be shown as both overwhelm-
ingly powerful and utterly helpless, but Goethe's solution is brilliant. The idea of Egmont's power is built into the structure of the
play, the idea that the whole world shapes itself as an image of his
being, and is reinforced by what we see of other people's feeling
for him. Thus the whole central paradox becomes clear to us as
soon as we begin to reflect upon the hesitancy and helpless confusion shown by Egmont when he actually appears.
   But it is still not entirely clear how the meaning of *Egmont* is
related to the nature of drama as a genre. We have seen that in
Lessing's opinion the tension between detachment and involvement is uniquely strong in drama (since in good narrative the
reader's detachment becomes a "fruitful" imaginative activity
which strengthens the illusion); the form of drama is justified for
any poetic construct, like *Nathan*, of which the meaning requires
an emphasis on that tension. But is Lessing's opinion on this
matter valid, or does it represent merely one way of coming to
grips with the still unsolved problem of drama? It is true that the
tension between detachment and involvement is important in

Egmont; but whereas in *Nathan* this tension functions as the goal of the play, as the mental state by which the spectator is enabled and encouraged to move toward the achievement of wisdom, the goal in *Egmont* appears to be quite different. Egmont at the end appears to have discovered a new source of overwhelming vital energy, a way out of the painful self-consciousness and unnatural self-restraint in which he had been trapped earlier. *Nathan* ends with ambiguity and irony; *Egmont* ends with "triumphal music" (305). What does this have to do with Goethe's idea of the form of drama?

To answer this question we must go back to the idea of the theater as a social or communal institution, the idea suggested in the *Sendung*, where theater is seen as fostering a sense of human brotherhood in the audience. Tragedy for Goethe is meant to lead the spectator, as well as the hero, "nach innen," toward the center of his own being; this basic idea is shared later by Schiller (tragedy acquaints us with our true moral freedom) and later still by Nietzsche (tragedy enables us to experience our identity with the one true ego, the divine creative force behind all phenomena). But for Goethe, the way inward appears to lead outward as well, toward social contact with others. Orestes, in the moment of his deepest withdrawal, experiences a vision of reconciled human community on the basis of which he imagines contact with Pylades and Iphigenie, and this illusion of human contact then develops naturally into the real contact and social reintegration that constitute his cure. Can a similar argument be made for Egmont? Both Egmont and Faust, in their final blindness, their withdrawal and aloneness at the end, experience a vision of human community, the vision of an aroused people that takes its life into its own hands and creates it anew in the presence of a chaotic danger symbolized by the sea. Does this vision have to do with the intended function of drama and the situation of the audience in the theater?

Egmont, in fact, is alone throughout most of the play. He encounters other people, but he is not really together with them; he is "surrounded by friends to whom he may not open himself" (243), and even with Clärchen he is not entirely open. His self-consciousness, his "reserve," his suppression of the deepest thoughts concerning himself, isolates him even in company with those toward whom he feels affection or respect. And yet, at the

very end, when his intellectual isolation is realized and compounded by physical isolation in prison, it turns out that he is
humanly isolated no longer. First Ferdinand appears, to whom he
propounds a doctrine of transcendent human togetherness: "Men
are not only together in each other's presence; the distant or de-
parted can also live for us" (300). Then Clärchen appears by a
miracle. And finally, by an act of self-delusive but characteristically heroic energy, Egmont imagines himself spiritually present
at the center of a great communal uprising. Again, the way inward, at its end, appears to reveal itself as a way outward, toward
human contact and fellow feeling.

A genuine appreciation and affirmation of human fate, I have
argued, is expressed not by calm resignation (no. 12 in *Egmont*),
but rather by the energetic commitment to illusion (no. 13). Resignation, or the stoic acceptance of one's fate, is a state of compounded delusion, inasmuch as it involves the pretense of knowledge, the pretense that by facing facts one has faced, once and
for all, the truth. A man who truly accepts and affirms his fate,
a man who, like Egmont, actually arrives at the center of his being, must not only accept the facts of his situation, but also affirm
energetically that inescapable self-delusive tendency in his self-
consciousness by which his situation has been produced. The
problem is how to be oneself as fully as possible—not merely how
to know oneself (which is out of the question anyway)—and one
accomplishes this by committing oneself to as fruitful and powerful a vision of oneself as one can, regardless of its illusoriness. But
what does this mean in practical terms? How shall we distinguish
the state of energetic self-consciousness (or demonic illumination) from mere insanity? The mad boy in *Werther*, after all, also
has an extremely clear vision of himself to which he is deeply
committed. What is the difference between him and Egmont?

The difference is that Egmont understands the necessary illusoriness of his vision. He understands this not only with respect
to the final vision, his "agreeable insanity," but also with respect
to his earlier vision of himself as Spanish regent of the Netherlands. Otherwise he would not be aware of any danger in his
enterprise, he would not compare himself to the teetering sleepwalker or the doomed Phaëthon; he would simply be submerged
in his totally false idea of the world, like the mad boy. The demonic individual, then, is aware of the ultimate unreliability of

self-consciousness, and yet remains fully committed to his own self-conscious vision. How is this possible? How is it possible to affirm, rather than resist, the maelstrom of the self? If one knows that self-consciousness leads to ruin, how can one remain committed to a particular self-conscious vision of one's own destiny? An idea cannot command our unreserved commitment unless it possesses validity for us, and how can we consider a conscious notion of ourselves to be valid if we know that self-consciousness as such is delusive?

There is only one possible source of objective validity for an idea or vision known to be illusory. The idea must be shared by others; it must have communal status. Therefore Egmont's final vision, like Faust's, is a vision of inspired community; and Egmont's earlier idea of himself as Spanish regent of the Netherlands must include the knowledge that the Netherlanders desire it and the belief that it would be best for them. Energetic or committed self-consciousness requires that one's vision of oneself be integrated with what one may assume to be the energetic belief of others. The idea of man presupposed by one's vision of oneself must be an idea, however deluded, which one is confident others share. Otherwise our self-consciousness (which we know to be unreliable) cannot attain an Egmontian intensity of commitment, but must remain mere daydreaming, by which we are "clouded" rather than "illuminated," a dreaming to which we could never commit our lives without going insane and becoming totally immune to self-doubt.

The path into the center of the self thus leads logically to the idea of energetic self-consciousness, to which we are fully committed while still recognizing its delusiveness, and this in turn implies the idea of participation in the communal; at the very center of our individual being we thus discover our nature as social creatures. The path inward reveals itself finally as a path toward contact with others. But there still remains the question of how we can be confident concerning the energetic belief of others. Egmont does not have a great deal of confidence in the Netherlanders, that "mob," and yet precisely the idea of an aroused Netherlandic people makes possible his final vision. If human community is the only possible basis for the fruitful existence of the self, then what is human community from the point of view of the individual? How does the individual experience it?

This question is not answered within the text of *Egmont*, but rather an answer to it resides in the nature of *Egmont* as drama, in the simple fact that we are participating in the ritual of the theater. Human community, as in *Iphigenie*, is the conscious cooperation among individuals in producing an artificial image, an illusion, by which humanity is glorified and life is made to appear worth living. Logically, of course, the result is a circle: energetic self-consciousness, a meaningful vision of ourselves and of man in general, presupposes a human community in which this vision is shared, and human community in its turn presupposes coopera- tion among energetically self-conscious individuals in producing a sublimated human image. But the logical insupportability of this structure does not alter the fact that we, in the theater, here and now, are engaged in the conscious communal production of a glorified image of man and of ourselves, an image, moreover, which, by analogy with Egmont's vision, we know to be illusory. If the performance of *Nathan*, therefore, is meant to be practice in wisdom for the audience, then the performance of *Egmont*, in the same way, is meant to be practice in energetic self-consciousness, in a self-affirmation which, like Egmont's, includes and over- comes the knowledge of its own deludedness. Thus the under- standing spectator does in a sense arrive at the center of his being; and the parallel with the self-transcending illusoriness of the message in Kleist's *Prinz Friedrich*, incidentally, is clear.

This idea of drama as practice in energetic self-consciousness is the aspect of meaning in *Egmont* that is not accessible to a reader—except in the abstract, by a logic that is not satisfactory as logic. If I read the text and understand its implications concerning the intrinsic heroism of all self-conscious existence, then I shall experience at most a moment of ambiguous inner self-exaltation, clouded by the understanding (also derivable from the text) that my identification of myself with Egmont is an illusion. If, on the other hand, I am a spectator at a performance, then my idea of the play's meaning, despite my knowledge of its illusoriness, assumes a certain objective validity, since I have reason to believe that it is shared by the others in whose company I am perceiving it. I am not merely daydreaming but actually participating, here and now, in the creation of an admittedly illusory but communally effec- tive, therefore affirmable and fruitful, vision of man and of myself, and the community of spectators and actors in which I find myself (or at least my own idea of this community) in a strong sense actually fulfills Egmont's vision of an aroused Netherlands; we in the theater are a community that insists upon freedom, in the sense of imaginative human self-determination as opposed to a slavish acceptance of the facts of life, and we are a community which for the sake of its freedom is willing to risk utter chaos (Egmont compares Netherlandic self-liberation to the bursting of dikes [304]) by asserting its sublimated idea of man in the face of its own knowledge that this idea is nothing but a contrived artistic illusion.

It is of course true that my idea, as a spectator, of the community in the theater, is as questionable as Egmont's final vision of the Netherlandic people; but both Egmont and I are aware of this, and neither of us is deterred by it. True human community can never be a solid object of belief or an entity to which it is possible to belong passively; it exists, rather, only by virtue of the conscious creative activity of the individuals who participate in it; each participant must be as it were "complete in himself, a little king" (267), in that he asserts on his own account the sublimated vision of man by which the community is defined. The community pre-supposed by my energetic self-consciousness, the communal understanding of the play in the theater, *may*, for all I know, not exist; but it *can* not exist, for me, if I wait for clear proof of its existence—if I do not take the first step myself and insist imagina-tively upon that heroic sense of self-conscious human existence which the play both expresses and calls into question. The lesson of Egmont's "agreeable insanity" therefore makes sense only by virtue of the spectator's situation at a communal event, and so would not make sense as the lesson of a work in any genre but drama. Thus also, as in *Iphigenie* and *Prinz Friedrich*, our under-standing that our thoughts about the play must be strictly our own, that the text's transmissible message is not complete in it-self, is an integral part of the poetic meaning.

Finally, we have discussed above not only philosophical and symbolic patterns in texts but also patterns of significant analogy between stage and auditorium; for if the relationship between stage and auditorium does not have a necessary function in ex-pressing the work's meaning, then it is hard to see how the form of drama is aesthetically justified. There are several obvious ways in which the situation in the theater can be integrated into a work's expressiveness: the technique of play-within-play, for example, as used in Goethe's time very subtly by Kleist, and not at all subtly by Tieck; or the various techniques of illusion-breaking, as in, say, Grabbe or Brecht. But the obvious ways are not the only ways. In *Egmont,* for instance, the spectator is faced at the end with the question of how it is possible for the hero, knowing what he does, to hurl himself into the gross self-delusion of the scene number 13, and the text as such offers no answer. The answer must be supplied by the spectator on the basis of his own situation in the theater; we understand what Egmont is doing only by understanding what we are doing.[7] Thus *Egmont,* as much as any play of Brecht or Pirandello, but without employing obvious alienating devices, depends for its complete meaning on the presence of a theater and a self-conscious audience.

It ought perhaps to be stressed, incidentally, that when we speak of "the situation in the theater," we are referring not to any real theater or audience but rather to the situation implied and (ideally) generated by the text. It seems quite clear that Goethe, for example, was never fully satisfied with his real audiences. In *Iphigenie,* considerable confidence in the audience is implied, but in *Egmont,* with the image of the unreliable Netherlanders, the effect is rather more admonitory; then, in *Tasso* and *Die natür-liche Tochter,* the mirror held up to the spectator is distinctly unflattering, if still challenging; and in *Faust,* finally, dramatic form itself is called into question. But even if Goethe's growing disillusion with audiences is justified, even if none of the plays we are treating has ever been appreciated properly in a real theater, this fact would not affect the validity of the argument. What really happens in the theater cannot be verified anyway; and my aim, again, is to show that the ideal notion of the theater in Germany exercises a crucial influence in the development of modern drama as a whole. *Nathan, Iphigenie, Egmont,* and *Prinz Fried-rich* provide evidence of how deep an effect the theoretical or ideal question of drama had on the development of the form in Germany around 1800, and how deeply this question was bound up with philosophical problems arising from ideas of human self-consciousness and community. This evidence is sufficient to enable us to speak of a flourishing poetic genre in the period, and our next task is to see how the tradition of German drama develops.

6 The Importance
of Being Egmont

Egmont is not the most popular of Goethe's plays, nor is it by any means universally admired of later German dramatists; in fact, several important German plays were conceived specifically in opposition to it, as attempts to supersede it. And yet, beneath the surface, behind the obvious differences and disagreements and oppositions, there is a solid core of continuous development in which the direct and indirect influence of *Egmont* plays an extremely important part.

1

The basic cohesion of the German dramatic movement, at least in its early phase, is fairly clear; and in order to go beyond this, toward the idea of a German-centered European tradition, it will be necessary, later, to make some points about German philosophy, especially Hegel and Nietzsche. But even if it can be shown that nineteenth-century German philosophy forms a link between the German movement and modern drama as a whole, this link would still not guarantee any continuity of poetic spirit. Therefore, in the present chapter, I shall treat not only influences, but also a pattern of significant affinities in spirit between German drama of the Classical period and modern European drama in general. If it is shown later that the German movement is an important historical factor in the growth of modern drama, then it will follow without much trouble that the historical process in

question preserves poetic spirit, or in other words, that it has the
character of a poetic tradition.

Let us begin with *Faust*. If the parallels discussed above are
granted, then it follows that the association of delusion with inner
truth at the end of *Faust* represents as it were Goethe's influence
on himself, from *Egmont*. This association of ideas may not
strictly originate in *Egmont*, but as far as I can see, it is not expressed earlier in Goethe's work with anything like the symbolic
clarity of the Clärchen dream and Egmont's subsequent exaltation.
Thus at least one crucial element of the *Faust* structure owes its
existence to *Egmont*; and this element is especially significant
with respect to drama as a genre, for it involves the imposition of a
strict limit upon the extent to which we may consider the dramatic vision a vehicle of truth. It is obvious that the structure and
style of *Faust* are intended to keep the spectator self-conscious
concerning his situation in the theater; but it is interesting for our
purposes that some of the techniques employed (including what
we may call the agreeably insane final scene, "Bergschluchten,"
in which Gretchen's reappearance is parallel to Clärchen's in the
dream) were first successfully applied by Goethe in *Egmont*.

Yet other major parallels can be drawn. We have seen that the
whole structure of *Egmont* is an image of the hero's being, progressing by a spiral path from the periphery to the center; Egmont's inner life is not only revealed by what he says and does,
but also diagrammed in the totality of what we see, in that the
spiral path by which we are conducted is also the mental path by
which he arrives at that knowingly deluded self-affirmation
which constitutes his truest self-knowledge. *Egmont* has been
called "anthropocentric" drama, in the sense of Goethe's and
Lenz's idea of a drama focused upon the personal power of one
central individual. But it is more than just this; it is an example of
what I should like to call *phrenographic* drama, in which the
physically perceived action and dialogue on the stage form an
actual *picture* of the central character's inner life.[1]

And if *Egmont* is subtly phrenographic, then *Faust* is obviously
so. Faust himself functions only sporadically as a character in a
connected dramatic action; his personality, insofar as we can
speak of it as a single entity, is bodied forth by the structure of the
work as a whole, not developed by action and dialogue. If *Egmont*
is constructed as a spiral, then *Faust* is a pulsing spiral, beginning

at the center, at the very gates of death, then widening to include the whole world—which is shown, however, not realistically but allegorically, as an emanation of Faustian desires and needs—and then, at the end of Part Two, returning to the center, where Faust conquers "Care," affirms his own necessary deludedness, in this sense achieves his true self, and dies. Thus the characteristic Goethean rhythm of expansion and contraction, diastole and systole, is used phrenographically, to represent the rhythm of man's inner life, the tension and interplay (as in Egmont) of centrifugal and centripetal forces with respect to the absolute center of our being at which we experience both truth and death.

Egmont is therefore an important forerunner of Faust with regard to at least two prominent aspects of structure and meaning, and Faust, in these two aspects, is an important forerunner of modern European drama from the late nineteenth century on. I say "forerunner" because it is not easy to pinpoint the actual influence of Faust; for most later European authors, Faust is simply an accepted poetic monument in the background of their work and thought. The idea of the "Faustian" is a commonplace, the idea of homo faber, man's striving to build his own world; and this idea, with varying overtones of seriousness or parody, appears in Ibsen's Master Builder, in certain resolutely modern figures in Hauptmann, in Wedekind's eternally insatiable Keith, in the "new man" vision of the expressionists, in Brecht's Marxist insistence on the alterability of the world, indeed in the very notion of attempting, by drama, to exercise a vitalizing or reforming influence on human society. Or we think of the mythopoeic aspect of modern drama—the revival of ancient myths, whether Mediterranean or Irish or Norse, and the attempted creation of new myths. Again, Faust is not always a demonstrable influence, but it is always there in the background.

The same applies to the two aspects of Faust we have singled out as coming from Egmont. It is true that the use of irony in modern drama, the technique of playing upon the spectator's self-consciousness and calling into question the validity of the vision, can be traced in part to comic traditions a good deal older than Faust, and in part also to the adaptation of ironic techniques from the narrative genres; but again, especially in German drama, the presence of Faust provides constant encouragement and sanction. And in the case of the phrenographic, Faust does exert a direct influence, in *Peer Gynt*, for example, and in Strindberg and the German expressionists, as well as an indirect influence in the "theater of the absurd"—provided we agree that absurdist stage techniques are meant to reflect (phrenographically) a state of mind rather than a definable state of external reality.

Or let us consider one other important feature of modern drama, the generalized world-theater image, by which I mean not merely the metaphorical suggestion that all the world is a stage, but rather the attempt to create, in the theater, a world that is somehow more authentic than the real world outside. Modern drama receives this function by way of the idea—whether existentialist or Marxist or the result of social or cultural disillusionment—that modern man's relationship to his world and his community has decayed, that the "real" world is no longer as real as it ought to be. Hence, in both the naturalistic and the Brechtian theaters, the attempt to use the relationship between spectator and stage as a means of confronting the spectator with social realities to which he routinely blinds himself; hence, in the theater of what may loosely be called the aesthetic movement, say in Yeats or early Hofmannsthal, the attempt to create in the auditorium an infinitely delicate interweaving of metaphorical and sensual impressions by which the spectator is meant to be reinitiated into the authentic but forgotten poetic character of his existence at large; hence also Hofmannsthal's attempt later on to transform the Salzburg festival into the nucleus of a new, unified European community;[2] hence the attempt to create a new world on the stage by subjecting huge masses of material to a relatively simple order, in Wagner for example, or Claudel's *Soulier de satin*; hence, in the expressionist and absurd theaters, the attempt at a violent metaphysical disorientation and reorientation of the audience as they sit there.

The idea of a radical renewal of human community, to be sure, is an important part of the general revolutionary cultural movement of Romanticism, and there is a relatively clear relationship between this idea and the idea of a specially receptive, art-oriented little community in the theater. Only in Germany, however, do the three or four decades around 1800 see a serious attempt, in practice as well as in theory, to develop the possibilities of this little community, to transform the ritualistic social gathering of the theater into at least the nucleus of a more authentically communal human world. We have discussed this aspect of four plays, by Kleist, Lessing, and Goethe, and we shall deal similarly with Schiller. But the most conspicuous vehicle by which the generalized world-theater idea is introduced into German and European dramatic tradition, the work most obviously intended to generate a world of its own in the theater, is *Faust*.

There is of course some question as to whether the proper auditorium and audience for a performance of the whole of *Faust* can exist, but this very question underscores the world-theatrical aspect of the work. *Faust* is written as drama but bursts open the walls of any conceivable theater and so, in its unfolding, becomes equivalent to the world at large. It demands a theater that does not and perhaps cannot exist; it calls for a radically new theater, a theater somehow thrown open to the total ebb and flow of human experience, in order not merely to represent that ebb and flow, but also to control it, to throw up dikes, as it were, and bring forth a new self-created artistic homeland for man. *Faust* does not necessarily exert a direct influence upon every work of modern drama in which a similar tendency can be detected; there are important modern intellectual movements by which the idea of such a world-theater is at least suggested, and the influence of other genres upon drama, the creation of "epic theater" for example, also has the effect of bursting the insulated interlude-character of theatrical works. But *Faust* is always there in the background, at the gateway to the modern age, as a constant classical precedent for experiments in this direction.

And in this respect, as in others, *Faust* is a development from *Egmont*, the first of Goethe's major plays in which the integrity of dramatic form is burst (by the elimination of the boundary between external and internal experience) in such a way as to suggest the possibility of new human community here and now, in the theater. In Goethe's career, the idea of such a community can be traced at least as far back as *Iphigenie*, and it is true that precedents for the disruption of form in *Faust* can be found in the *Sturm und Drang*, in German Romanticism and in the genre of opera. But the combination of the technique with the idea, the disruption of dramatic form for the sake of an immediate renewal of community in the theater, is achieved in *Egmont*, if not absolutely for the first time, then at least with such brilliance and force as to make this apparently actionless tragedy the most important predecessor of the later super-drama which was Goethe's life's work.

2

But the importance of *Egmont* is not exhausted by its position as a predecessor of *Faust*. In several other historically pivotal German plays, for example Kleist's *Prinz Friedrich*, the influence of *Egmont* is clearly felt. It is probably true, as Burckhardt argues, that Kleist wrote his play in opposition to *Egmont*, but the two plays are far more similar in spirit than Kleist would have admitted. Both are built around a central figure whose heroic stature and energy are impaired by self-consciousness; in both plays the hero reasserts and reachieves his heroic exemplariness precisely by way of self-consciousness; and in both plays the audience's consciousness of the situation in the theater is used to generate a sense of profound identification with the hero, an identification which does not depend on any instinctive emotional response. Both plays, moreover, end with a dream vision in which the hero receives a laurel wreath from his beloved, and it is clear that Natalie is in general conceived as a supersession of Clärchen; whereas Clärchen is willing but helpless, Natalie actually devises and executes a stratagem to save the Prince.

Or we think of yet another of the most influential nineteenth-century German dramas, Büchner's *Dantons Tod*.[3] As far as I know, there is no extrinsic evidence for a direct connection between *Danton* and *Egmont*, but Büchner's exceptional admiration for Goethe in general can be demonstrated (e.g. from his letter to his family of 28 July 1835), and it seems to me that the internal evidence in the two texts is conclusive. The basic atmosphere of *Egmont*, especially the sense of aimlessness and futility in dialogue, is reproduced and magnified in Büchner's play. The inconclusiveness of Danton's conversations with friends and associates, the pointlessness of his talking directly to Robespierre, the intellectual confusion of the citizens in the street and the deputies at the National Convention, all have precedents in *Egmont*, although these are not developed so far toward the grotesque. The source of this atmosphere in Büchner, moreover, as in Goethe, is an excessive or strained self-consciousness. The citizens and the deputies have been made aware of themselves as a historical force, which is what causes their blundering—how shall one follow a reasonable course of personal conduct if one starts by thinking of oneself as the instrument of something as impersonal as the natural laws St. Just speaks of?[4]—and the intellectual and moral positions of both Danton and Robespierre are undermined by morbid self-doubt. "Danton, deine Lippen haben Augen" (DT, p. 22), "your lips have eyes," says Marion, and the same words, with some justification, could be spoken to Egmont, who visits his mistress with the ulterior intention of adjusting his emotional equilibrium.

Egmont and Danton also have much in common as characters. Both are fatalists; neither believes that any fundamental change can occur, either in the world at large or in his own personal condition. Egmont insists that "things will go their course as always,"[5] despite the efforts of any Spanish official, and for Danton it is the self-determining history of the Revolution that mocks any individual's attempt at significant action: "We are puppets on strings held by unknown powers" (DT, p. 41). For both Egmont and Danton, however, this fatalism has a positive aspect; it is the basis of Egmont's belief in the eventual fulfillment of his destiny, or at least his belief in his own safety, which is paralleled by Danton's repeated insistence that he has become too integral a part of the scheme of things to be done away with (DT, pp. 25, 33, 39). Life is a "habit" (Eg., p. 299; DT, p. 61) which appears unbreakable, "a feeling of permanence" (DT, p. 39) on the basis of which both Egmont and Danton are willing to risk playing with deadly political realities as though they were a game: "Is there high treason in a mere carnival play?" (Eg., p. 219), asks Egmont, and Danton, when asked why he has created tension with Robespierre's party, answers, "They got my goat. I've never been able to see people playing Cato that way without giving them a kick. That's how I am" (DT, p. 12).

And yet, when they are faced with the immediate prospect of dying, both Egmont and Danton at least waver in their fatalism; both long for something like death in battle, where one has at least the illusion of being able to defend oneself, as opposed to the relentless process of imprisonment and execution which corresponds more exactly to the idea of unalterable fate. Not death itself is fearful, but rather "the dungeon, a picture of the grave, loathesome to the hero as well as the coward" (Eg., p. 281), or as Danton says, "To be killed so mechanically!" (DT, p. 60). Both heroes, moreover, despite their fatalism, also experience an uncomfortable sense of responsibility—Danton for the September Massacres and the present confusion in France (*DT*, p. 69), Egmont (in his conversation with Ferdinand) for the foreseeable futility of the coming bloodbath.

This brings us to a crucial question in the interpretation of both plays, a question by which the deep connection between them can be seen clearly. What does it mean that both cunctatious heroes, after their fate has been sealed, suddenly become self-assertively deluded in a way that on first glance does not seem characteristic? The parallel between the two plays in this respect is quite exact. The stirring but not entirely sincere speeches which Egmont throws in the face of his worst enemy Alba, not knowing that he has already been condemned, are echoed by Danton's speeches before the Revolutionary Tribunal, speeches equally stirring, equally suspect as to their sincerity, and equally futile. And then Danton, after receiving the comforting assurance that Julie will die with him, begins to make boasts concerning his place in history, boasts which even his friend Hérault mocks as "slogans for posterity" (*DT*, p. 70), just as Egmont, after the comforting vision of Clärchen, begins to imagine himself as the great martyr-hero of Netherlandic freedom. Danton's boasts, to be sure, are tinged with irony and accompanied by self-mockery ("Es ist nicht so übel seine Toga zu drapieren und sich umzusehen ob man einen langen Schatten wirft" [*DT*, p. 71]), but then Egmont's is a knowing self-delusion as well.

In order to test how deep this parallel goes, we should require a complete interpretation of *Danton*, which would lead us too far astray. Let it suffice to say that in *Danton*, as in *Egmont*, the hero's posturing at the end is related to the question of the nature and usefulness of theatrical performance; this relation is developed very subtly in *Egmont*, but in *Danton* the questionableness of theatrical representation is established as an explicit theme, in Danton's early speech about making a good exit ("wir stehen immer auf dem Theater" [*DT*, p. 32]) and in Camille's more extended diatribe (*DT*, p. 37). In both plays, therefore, it appears that the question of why the hero bothers to rouse and delude himself at the end is related to the question of why we bother to go to the theater, and this question is vital to the whole modern dramatic tradition from Lessing on.

In any case, there can be no doubt about the direct influence of

Egmont on *Danton*. Numerous other parallels in detail can be cited: Julie's and Clärchen's suicides, by poison, in order to accompany their executed lovers; Camille's desertion of Robespierre for Danton, as Ferdinand deserts Alba for Egmont. The motif of Egmont's clothing, which occurs visually in the scene with Clärchen, also occurs verbally, when his fine Spanish attire moves Jetter to blurt out, "His neck would be a real temptation for the headsman" (*Eg.*, p. 212); thus Egmont, like Danton (who is doomed finally by the words, "Danton has nice clothes" [*DT*, p. 64]), is too well-dressed for his own good. Or we think of Egmont's metaphor of the Horses of the Sun and Danton's dream of riding on a runaway world (*DT*, p. 41), or of the significant claustrophobic images that crop up in both plays (*Eg.*, pp. 245, 281; *DT*, pp. 61, 66). And when we hear Danton say to Lacroix, "they had warned me" (*DT*, p. 49), we recall Egmont's admission to Ferdinand, "I was warned" (*Eg.*, p. 301).

Thus the poetic and dramatic power of *Egmont* is propagated not only by way of *Faust* but also by way of at least two other important and forward-looking German works. The direct influence of *Egmont* on late nineteenth- and twentieth-century drama is harder to document—the only demonstrable instance I can think of is Hofmannsthal's *Der Turm* in the 1925 version with its visionary ending. But we shall see that indirect influence is enough to place *Egmont* at or near the center of at least a coherent German tradition.

3

Why *Egmont*? What is there about this play that makes it important to such dissimilar authors as Kleist, Büchner, and Goethe himself (as the author of *Faust*)? In the first place, it is a play about *the reconstitution of a hero*. As he first appears, Egmont is what we might call an ex-hero. We hear a great deal about his earlier heroic exploits and character, but when we actually see him, as Schiller points out, we see only his weaknesses, we discover that his heroism has been sullied by self-consciousness. He is now internally self-divided, confused, and inactive; he has forced himself into the unnatural role of peacemaker and bider of his time; he seems to have lost that simple, unhesitating unity of attitude which had once inspired absolute devotion in his followers. But at the end of the play his heroic stature is miraculously reconstituted; somehow he manages to become his true self again, transcending his consciousness.

From a strict interpretive point of view this re-achievement of the heroic is an extremely complex process which cannot be understood without taking into account the relation between stage and auditorium; but the immediate impression of Egmont as a reconstituted hero is created simply and powerfully. The play leads us to understand that Egmont's had been a heroic nature, but is now sullied by conscious self-restraint, self-concealment, and insincerity; and there is therefore a distinct sense of relief when in the first dungeon scene Egmont admits that what he really desires is not the peaceful welfare of the Netherlands, but rather the soldier's feeling of exultant power when he storms forth and "uses his fist." In themselves these sentiments are neither heroic nor especially attractive, but since we associate Egmont's debilitation with the evident insincerity in his speeches to Orange and Alba, the revived candidness of the first dungeon monologue at least prepares us for the idea of a reemergence of the heroic.

Then comes the scene with Ferdinand, which contains one of the finest moments in the history of drama. Ferdinand is at first all tears, but Egmont is all business and asks about the possibility of escape; Ferdinand replies that there is no hope whatever, and Egmont's reaction—a stroke of the purest genius on Goethe's part—is to stamp his foot (Eg., p. 299)! This is a gesture neither of despair nor of stoic resignation, but of *annoyance*, the gesture, for example, of a piqued Clärchen (Eg., p. 238). Egmont is informed, after having hope rekindled in him, that he has lost his life, and he reacts with the petty gesture of a man who has lost his collar button. This is Egmont the hero, and not all of Goethe's rhetorical skill, not a stage full of horses and swords, could express this heroism more perfectly. Egmont's sudden angry gesture shows that he is fully aware of his fate, not merely insensitive or resigned; but at the same time he is strong enough to regard death as a mere petty nuisance which allows him to remain petty himself—not only in his childish stamping, but also earlier in his vicious personal attack on Alba (Eg., p. 293–94), an attack which we, having seen and heard Alba, know is unjust. Death stings Egmont, but the specter does not have sufficient power to inspire high pathos in him, or deep introspection. This is the reconstituted hero, the man who feels the presence of death in its worst form, yet is not moved by this to become anything other than his old self; and we are reminded, interestingly, of the unrepentant last stanza in the Villon-parody with which Brecht's Macheath prepares himself to be executed. Just as he had impatiently and incorrectly dismissed Margarete's actions earlier by saying, "She is a woman" (Eg., p. 222), so Egmont now impatiently and incorrectly dismisses Alba's motives as personal jealousy; and at the very end he then hurls himself one more time into the same sort of energetic self-delusion that had characterized his whole existence. The question of how to create a truly credible modern hero is answered by the deep structure of Egmont; but the question of how to make the hero seem a hero is answered simply by letting him retain all his natural deludedness and prejudice even in the face of death.

On its surface as well as in its depth, therefore, Egmont is a drama of reconstituted heroism, and so is a kind of allegory for the dramatic movement of its time; Germany must find its way back from self-conscious fragmentation to the unifiedly communal art of drama in the same way that Egmont finds his way back from self-conscious confusion to the unified personal state of the hero. Drama as such, by virtue of its unalterable character as a public ceremony, generates the expectation that its meaning will include something of monumental communal significance, and this is part of what motivates the intense German quest for drama in the late eighteenth and early nineteenth centuries. Germany as a united culture with a solid poetic tradition does not yet exist; therefore dramas are required, communal poetic ceremonies in which the proper audience for a coherent and potentially "classical" national literature[6] will grasp the necessity of its existence and so come into being.

Heroic drama is not the only possibility open to aspiring German cultural pioneers; neither Iphigenie nor Nathan is heroic in exactly the Egmontian sense. But heroic drama is one of the most obvious possibilities, drama in which the audience's cultural identity and vitality are mirrored in a single character, a leader who is at once representative and extraordinary; for such drama will not only convey its meaning within the theater, by the subtle interplay between stage and auditorium, but will also create a visible and enduring image of its meaning, a new cultural myth, in the bright figure of its hero. The trouble is that heroic drama, for all its desirability, seems strictly impossible in a fragmentedly self-conscious age; how shall a heroic figure be credible if the sense of vital communal coherence he represents does not *already* exist in the culture at large? If modern heroic drama is possible, then the heroic must arise directly from its antithesis, from that enervating and self-isolating modern consciousness which is *our* common experience; and this recognition is the main reason for the Germans' tireless preoccupation with what they regarded as the prime example of a heroic tragedy of self-consciousness, *Hamlet.*

Here, then, is the problem confronted by the author of *Egmont;* and Goethe's solution was sufficiently striking and brilliant to inspire at least two other major authors, Kleist and Büchner. In *Prinz Friedrich* and in *Danton,* as in *Egmont,* we are informed indirectly of the central figure's qualities as a leader and hero; but these qualities, in the hero as we see him, appear smothered by excessive self-consciousness. Then, by way of the encounter with death in an unexpected and particularly unpleasant form, the hero regains his heroic stature, not by changing but by refusing to change, by remaining resolutely, indeed outrageously himself. Egmont at the end becomes more Egmont than ever, despite his recognition of where being Egmont has led him; and the same is true of both Homburg, who turns even Brandenburgian submission into an act of willful defiance, and Danton, who reasserts the decadent "Epicureanism" which had ruined him, in that he experiments now with the ironic enjoyability of creating a monumental historical figure for himself.

This pattern, again, is an allegory of the general cultural situation in which the three plays were written. As is suggested in *Iphigenie,* the Germans do not need to change their way of being in order to achieve a higher level of civilization; what they must learn, rather, is to wield their nature self-consciously in the production of a symbolic glorification of man. Self-consciousness must be affirmed, not resisted; it must be realized as a heightening rather than a distortion or violation of our true being, and Egmont, Homburg, and Danton, the self-conscious heroes who refuse to change, represent this general cultural process mythically. They are, so to speak, speculatively conceived heroes. They are meant to inspire in the theater, thus to initiate in the society as a whole, precisely that cultural self-discovery of which they are the quasi-mythical representatives; or at least they will be mythical representatives if such a cultural self-discovery takes place. It is not possible—by the nature of the question—to decide whether Egmont and his progeny actually achieve the status of mythical heroes within a coherent German culture; but it is clearly possible to speak at least of an Egmontian school of heroic drama, in which the problem of credible heroism on the modern stage is explored with special depth and subtlety.

4

In the eighteenth and nineteenth centuries, there is a tendency among dramatists to concede, at least by implication, that the heroic—as we imagine this manifestation of the human to have been understood in antiquity or in the Renaissance—is no longer readily available as a basis for communication between artist and audience. The community to which a modern audience belongs, it is felt, no longer possesses the sort of cohesiveness that is necessary for an individual heroic image to be translated directly, by the spectators' normal mental processes, into a fruitful communal feeling. Grillparzer's Rudolf von Habsburg says to his defeated enemy Ottokar, who had aspired to bestride the world: "The world is there for all of us to live in, and true greatness belongs to God alone. Earth's youthful dream is finished, and the age of heroes and mighty men is past, like that of the giants and dragons."[7] Community nowadays requires self-sacrifice rather than self-assertiveness of the individual. Our cities no longer have a Grove of the Furies, where their welfare is linked with the sacred memory of an individual's enormous crime against nature. None of us, not even the Goethes among us, are really "great heathens"; like Lessing in his intellectual struggle with Richard III, we are hemmed in by the idea of purely moral limits beyond which the individual ceases to be tragic.

The age of heroes, says Grillparzer, is past; drama will now have to get along without those eminently useful individuals who represent the community not by such abstract qualities as public spirit or moral soundness, but rather by an extraordinary quasi-divine power they possess, a power mysterious in its origins but obvious in its effects, like the demonic in Egmont. And yet the basic task of drama remains the same—to reflect and (by using as a model or nucleus the little gathering in the theater) to intensify the life of the community as a whole. Thus the heroic, for all its unattainableness, remains a desideratum, especially in an age where drama takes on the task of creating that deeper communal sense of life on which its own function depends; for the hero, if he can be made credible, will serve as a memorable focus of the dramatic meaning, a symbolic rallying point for the society.

Hence not only the theme of the reconstituted hero in Goethe, Kleist, and Büchner, but also the enormous variety of heroes or hero-substitutes or heroes via irony—or indeed figures so monumentally unheroic that this itself becomes a heroic quality—on the modern stage: from such obvious examples as Hofmannsthal's tragic Sigismund and comic Hans Karl Bühl, or Eliot's Thomas, or Anouilh's, from Wedekind's Keith, a hero by remaining himself, to Ibsen's deeply questionable but unquestionably monumental Brand, Peer Gynt, Solness, from Shaw's variously modernized and ironized but thus affirmable versions of Caesar, St. Joan, Don Juan, all the way to Caligula or King Ubu, two possibilities of creating a kind of hero from sheer negation. None of these figures is heroic in the sense of being unqualifiedly admirable, and none of them is a reconstituted hero in the way Egmont is; but they are all endowed with a special vital energy within their works, and all represent the attempt—by irony or intellectual paradox or the significant play on assumable conventions—to anthropomorphize, in something like a modern myth, some actual or potential essence in our communal life.

Brecht is especially useful as a test case, for while on the one hand he attacks at its very root what we ordinarily think of as the heroic, by arguing specifically against the value of individual feelings or drives in the modern world, still, on the other hand, such figures as Baal, Macheath, Mutter Courage, Azdak clearly possess something comparable to heroic stature. These figures are not meant to arouse an immediate emotional response; "alienation" is involved in the presentation of all of them, even those created before Brecht developed the idea theoretically. But Brecht himself is careful to point out that alienation does not exclude a kind of empathy: "The artist's self-observation, an artificial and artful act of self-distancing, prevents any complete empathy or submergence on the part of the spectator, and creates an impressive remoteness from the fictional events. And yet, empathy of a sort is still employed. The spectator identifies with the actor, as one observer with another; thus an attentive, observing attitude is cultivated."[8] If the play is acted properly—and in Brecht's plays, the proper method of acting emerges from the texts alone, without any specific authorial directions—then the spectator will experience empathy not with the character but with the actor. This means in turn that the spectator is invited to participate, or to feel as if he were participating, in the *creation* of the character; seeing and hearing, says Brecht, are "activities"[9] and must be encouraged as such, not used as avenues by which to captivate the spectator. The world as a whole, and especially the world of human society, in this "age of science" (KO 14), is known to be an arbitrary, therefore changeable, human construct; therefore, if the theater audience are made aware of themselves as critical participants in the arbitrary creation of the vision that unfolds before them, this awareness will be practice for a more socially "productive" attitude in the world at large, since the "productive" in Brecht's sense, as the knowledge and use of man's ability to change the world, is the same as the "critical" (KO 21, 22, 25).

But the Brechtian hero is not merely an intellectual postulate. He is endowed with an immense, burgeoning vitality and energy, far more than is required merely to state his case (which is usually about as far as the characters get in the plays of Brecht's imitators); and it is not immediately apparent what the function of these humanly engaging qualities is, if the spectator is meant primarily to preserve his distance. Is their sole function to provide that "entertainment" which Brecht insists is the very nature of drama (KO 1–3)? If so, then the entertaining aspect of the play and its socially productive aspect are distinct, which is not at all what Brecht implies (KO 77).

The answer to this question is simple and far-reaching. If we are aware of ourselves as participants in the creation of the Brechtian hero, then we must refer the hero's outrageous vitality to a corresponding vital energy *in ourselves*. In a sense, therefore, we do empathize with the hero, but without sharing his opinions or feelings, which are kept from us by theatrical alienation; we ourselves live in the hero's vitality (this being part of what is suggested by the verb *sich produzieren* in KO 77) and so become aware of a vital energy within us which, properly employed, is the force that must change the world. "Society can derive enjoyment even from the asocial, as long as the latter shows vitality and greatness, for it then often reveals rational powers and abilities of special value, albeit destructively applied. Society can even enjoy a catastrophic flood, if it knows itself ultimately capable of controlling the river, for then the river belongs to society" (KO 25). If, by means of theatrical alienation, we are provided with a point of view from which the conquerability of the hero's asocialness is clear, then his power becomes our power, an overflowing vital power which is not only enjoyable but also instructive, in that it supplements the play's teaching of *what* we must do to change the world, by teaching in addition, through an imaginative flexing of our own muscles, *that* we can do it (cf. KO 46).

It follows that we understand a Brechtian hero fully, and experience him as a hero—in other words, experience his individual energy as our own communal energy—only by understanding what we are doing in the theater, our active role as participants in the creation of an enjoyable and edifying vision for ourselves; and clearly there is a similarity here with the process of understanding *Egmont.* I do not mean that *Egmont* directly inspired either Brecht or any of the other attempts at a modernized version of the heroic. But *Egmont* and the Egmontian school represent the first important attempt to revise radically the very idea of the heroic so as to make it usable on the modern stage, and to accomplish this by using the spectator's detached consciousness as an indispensable constituent element in his experience of the heroic, not merely as a point of view. We think again of the paradoxical engendering of empathy by way of detachment, in both Goethe and Brecht.

Even if the neo-heroic aspect of modern drama is based in part on dramatic traditions that by-pass eighteenth-century Germany, or on nondramatic intellectual traditions like that of vitalistic philosophy, still the importance of *Egmont* as a forerunner is indisputable, and we shall therefore not be surprised if in recent drama we occasionally find quite clear parallels to *Egmont,* whether deliberate or accidental. For example, if we did not know from extrinsic evidence that this is quite unlikely, we could easily take *Die Dreigroschenoper* as a parody of *Egmont.* Macheath, like Egmont, is a hero who is clearly warned of his impending doom but refuses to change his habitual mode of living, his Thursdays at the whorehouse; like Egmont, he still has hope, even after being imprisoned, but his fate, like Egmont's, is sealed by what happens in the streets, except that in Brecht the streets are too full of people, whereas in Goethe they are too empty; and like Egmont, who plans to leave his soldiering behind him and become a ruler, Macheath plans to go into banking. Macheath's switch from business to emotion at the end of his wedding with Polly, moreover ("And now it's time for emotion. Otherwise a man becomes the creature of his profession"),[10] corresponds grotesquely to Egmont's distinction, for Clärchen, between his two selves, the "creature of his profession" and the lover; and the relationship with Tiger Brown, who is attached to Macheath emotionally but belongs officially to the opposition and is forced to play a part in Macheath's capture, corresponds to the relation between Egmont and Ferdinand. Alba and Peachum of course represent completely different social forces; but at the end, when Peachum announces, "we have thought up a different ending,"[11] we are reminded of the apparently illogical, "operatic" ending of *Egmont*. Thus the spirit of *Egmont* not only lives subtly in modern dramatic techniques and tendencies, but also from time to time appears quite close to the surface, and we shall question later whether such phenomena are entirely accidental.

5

There is another set of tendencies in modern drama which is related not to Goethe's achievement in *Egmont* so much as to the problem underlying that achievement, the problem of a historical age in which the heroic is no longer meaningful, an age of excessive self-consciousness, individual isolation and indirection, of the loss of all vital communal sense. In particular, this historical vision produces a melancholy tragic mode, now that the necessary communal basis for the cathartic joyfulness of earlier tragedy is assumed to be missing. If heroic tragedy is no longer appropriate in the modern theater—or if the author has not sufficient theatrical imagination to produce the heroic via irony, as in *Egmont*— then at least a melancholy shadow of tragedy can be created by holding up the mirror to that decadent state of human community which prevents the shadow's original from appearing.

A prime example of this tragic mode is Schiller's *Wallenstein*. Like Egmont, Wallenstein is an ex-hero, a man whose impressive deeds lie in the past, and who is now in the position of having thought so much about his destiny that he has become inactive. As Egmont refuses to make a clear choice between Spanish and Netherlandic interests, and excuses himself on the grounds that he is merely playing ("Ist ein Fastnachtsspiel gleich Hochver-rath?"), so Wallenstein, with similar excuses (esp. *Die Piccolo-mini* II.v.861–70), refuses to make a clear choice between the Empire and the Swedes; as Egmont insists upon trusting his daimon, so Wallenstein insists upon trusting the stars. But Wallenstein is never reconstituted as a hero; as his doom closes over him he achieves a certain basic human stature, but a sense of vigorous heroic energy, comparable to that generated in *Egmont*, is lacking. Wallenstein is a realist (in the sense of "Über naive und sentimen-talische Dichtung") whose situation and state of mind now require idealism, the assertion of intellectually free moral categories; but he can liberate himself intellectually only to the extent of becoming a kind of dreamer (which is how we see him) and thus a melan-choly mirror to the Germans, who are excellent at speculation but ignorant of the secret inner path to vigorous action.

This melancholy tragedy of hero-turned-dreamer embodies a particular interpretation of *Hamlet*, and there is already a ten-dency toward it in *Dantons Tod*, although Büchner's wit and imagination manage in the end to achieve something more. But in Grillparzer, especially the two Habsburg tragedies, the melan-choly mode appears in full bloom. Even in the first act of *König Ottokars Glück und Ende*, in the midst of Ottokar's triumph, we are shown that he has no real power; his vainglory is an empty dream, the destructive blundering of an inflated idea of his own personal destiny; and the action of the play is essentially only his confron-tation with reality, his temporary submission to it, and his final, futile rebellion against it. There is some consolation for the audi-ence in the figure of Rudolf von Habsburg, the earnest advocate of the Habsburg Imperial ideal; but Grillparzer, later in life, took steps to insure that this consolation would not be regarded as his last word, for in *Ein Bruderzwist in Habsburg*, the Imperial ideal, now represented by a second Rudolf, is also revealed as an empty dream. The day, in the end, is carried by reality in a very depress-ing form, and heroism, or brilliant individual achievement as a focus of communal life, is simply not possible.

The importance of this melancholy tragic mode for naturalist and symbolist drama around the turn of the century is clear enough, in Ibsen, Chekhov, Hauptmann, for example, who present a vision of the individual's helpless subjection to his own past, his heredity, his milieu. This vision results from a number of factors, including modern political and scientific developments and traditions in narrative, but it is important to recognize that a solid dramatic tradition is also in operation here, a response to the disappearance of the hero as a valid symbol in drama—a response, in other words, to the Egmontian problem, as distinct from the Egmontian achievement. There is no room for doubt, as far as I can see, that Ibsen reckoned Goethe, Schiller, Grillparzer, and Hebbel among his immediate artistic predecessors, say what one will about the extent to which he either echoed or superseded them;[12] and while the case of Russian drama down to Chekhov, Gorky, and the Moscow Art Theater is not quite so clear, still there is sufficient awareness of the Germans to enable us to speak of a Russian development at least parallel or sympathetic with the German-centered growth of a melancholy tragic mode.[13]

The idea of the heroic is crucial in "realistic" dramatic style around 1900 precisely by virtue of its absence or questionableness, and is what differentiates this style, for example, from the essentially sentimental "bourgeois" drama of the eighteenth century, in which the heroic, or the surpassing of existing human norms, is generally speaking not a problem.[14] In modern drama the concern with the heroic has to do with the question of drama as a genre, the legacy of German Classicism. When Synge says, "On the stage one must have reality, and one must have joy,"[15] he is deriving a principle of dramatic language from the basic communal character of the theater. Drama must have "reality," in the sense of immediate meaningfulness for the community represented in the auditorium, but it may not just mirror the community's inadequacy or incohesiveness; a dramatic performance, unlike the reading of a novel, is a festive social event, and the reflection of the community in a dramatic work must therefore always have something like a mythical or heroic dimension, something basically festive or joyful.

Even if there is such a thing as realistic or factual drama, still realism will not develop so easily or naturally in drama as in the narrative genres, which are more closely related to the expository essay and thus intrinsically better able to absorb and transmit material conventionally assumed to be factual. Drama contains as it were an innate resistance to the idea of reality as a force that overpowers human will and aspiration; the overpowering force in drama is traditionally not reality but *fate*, which is mysteriously identical with the human self it conquers. And this resistance in drama to the category of reality is necessary, I think, to account for the frequency with which visionaries or artists or dreamers occupy an important place in modern dramatic works more or less realistic in style. Such characters, in their yearning beyond reality (whether or not they are particularly attractive as human beings), represent a tendency of the genre itself; if they are defeated by reality in the end, their defeat, like Ottokar's, is drama's attempt to exploit the tragically pleasurable potential of its own threatening obsolescence, perhaps an attempt to awaken in the audience a sense of communal cultural daring, at the brink of the theaterless abyss. Occasionally the artist-figure in realistic drama surpasses his function as an indicator of the absence of the heroic, and actually achieves heroic stature—this can be argued of Ibsen's Solness—but the more typical case, in its most perfect artistic realization, is *The Cherry Orchard*, where the audience finds itself in exactly the situation of that absurdly festive company on the stage, enjoying its sovereign communal humanness (i.e. its situation as a theater audience) as a kind of delusive aristocratic pleasure in a house that will soon be torn down.[16]

The sense of reality in such authors as Ibsen, Hauptmann, Chekhov—again, reality as an implacable *external* force, not fate, which is anchored in our own being—is not merely the result of a particular view of the world, but also a phase in drama's dealing with the problem of the heroic, a development of the melancholy tragic mode that can be traced back to *Wallenstein* and *Egmont*. Some interesting test cases support this point. One is Hauptmann's *Die Weber*, often cited as the definitive work of German dramatic naturalism because it supposedly leaves behind the idea of the individual altogether, hence also the idea of the heroic, in order to show the intolerable but inexorable mechanics of modern social reality. If there had ever been a connection between modern naturalism and the German-Classical problem of a revival of the heroic or mythical in drama, this connection now appears to be severed; even the suggestion in Heine's famous poem that the downtrodden weavers are weaving the fate of "Altdeutschland" is not taken up by Hauptmann.

One passage in *Die Weber* appears in fact to be an attack on the idea of the heroic or mythical at its root in theoretical aesthetics, at the end of Act II, where old Baumert learns the militant

"Dreissiger-song." Part of the function of the heroic or mythical in art, if there is such a function, must be to transfigure our merely factual existence, to liberate us from the immediate oppressiveness of reality, and this function implies Kant's idea of aesthetic perception as divorced from selfish personal interest, since our interest, in this sense, is a force that binds us to reality. But when old Baumert hears the song from Jäger, a song that could not be more inadequate as poetry than it is, he experiences a caricature of aesthetic rapture in which he savors each phrase as a man with a more advanced critical vocabulary might savor Rilke—and this, it seems to me, is meant to raise the question of whether our Kantianly acceptable enjoyment of more sophisticated texts is different in character. When we experience aesthetic disinterest, when we "shake the day's dusty burdens from our shoulders" (*Die Weber*, Act IV), are we perhaps merely following our own personal interest less honestly than Baumert? Are we, as aesthetic enjoyers, merely insisting on a privileged social position, like Dreissiger in his game of whist? If so, then the heroic or mythical in art is nothing but a sham.

But in spite of this, the problem of the heroic is central in the structure of *Die Weber*. In each of the five acts there is one figure who starts out in the direction of becoming a hero and is then swallowed up by events, Bäcker in Act I, then Jäger, Wittig, Kittelhaus, and old Hilse in Acts II to V. This series of characters forms a complete circle: the rebellious weaver (Bäcker), the ex-weaver with broadened horizons who returns to lead his people out of bondage (Jäger), the nonweaver goaded by his experience of social injustice into becoming a rebel leader (Wittig), another nonweaver (Kittelhaus) who risks life and limb in a morally sincere effort to quell the uprising, and old Hilse, who returns to the beginning by taking a stand for the value of simply submitting to the weaver's lot. Thus every possibility of something like heroic leadership is covered, and all prove futile. The play, as it were, tries to have a hero but by the nature of things cannot, and this struggle places it firmly in that branch of the German dramatic tradition in which the unavailability of the heroic as a valid artistic symbol becomes the source of tragic feeling. Ultimately there is a strength in Büchner's Danton which contradicts his own words, "We have not made the Revolution, but rather it has made us" (*DT*, p. 32); but this strength is no longer available in *Die Weber*, where potential heroism is a futile struggle in the toils of a blind historical convulsion. This is not inflammatory drama; it is essentially melancholy drama, carried one step further in the line from *Wallenstein* through *Ottokar,* but still belonging to this line, in that it expresses in structure an unrealizable desire for the heroic. What is tragic is not the plight of the weavers or of society in general, but the impossibility of any humanly fruitful relation to the reality depicted, the absence, in other words, of anything for the theater to celebrate or mythologize. Precisely by being "realistic" drama, *Die Weber* is also tragedy in the melancholy mode, and the scene with old Baumert and the song can perhaps be read, alternatively, as a grotesque epitaph on the possibility of a communally uplifting art which is still truly art.

Or to take an even more significant example, let us consider the dramatic-historical ancestry of Ibsen's Nora, who is often regarded as purely a creature of the modern world. The scene in *Egmont* where Clärchen goes forth into the streets and attempts to start a popular uprising represents an important response (which in subsequent German drama becomes a typical response) to the problem of dramatizing an unheroic world. Egmont himself has the makings of a hero, but his countrymen lack the ability to use him as a hero. The age of heroes is dead, or at least threatening to die, not because of any lack of powerful individuals but because communal existence lacks that vigorous, cohesive spirit by virtue of which the hero can become representative of us. Thus a mere girl, with the special emotional tenacity which is habitually attributed to women, finds herself in the awkward position of trying to rouse by force a spirit in her compatriots which, in a less decadent age, would arise of its own accord. Immediately we are reminded of Schiller, of the obvious parallel in *Die Jungfrau von Orleans* and also Leicester's words to Mortimer in *Maria Stuart:* "Have you seen how things stand at this court, how the rule of woman has constricted our spirits? Where is the old heroic energy of this country? Everything is subjected, in thrall to a woman, and all our courage is hamstrung" (II.viii.1933–38). It is clear from what we see of Leicester's own character that he is reversing cause and effect here; female rule has not destroyed the nation's heroic spirit, but rather the self-conscious degeneration of heroic spirit has made possible, indeed necessary, an oppressive female rule. The nobles of England are no better than the burghers of Brussels;

the strong feelings of Leicester and Mortimer are no more use to Mary than the burghers' feeling for Egmont is to Clärchen. The whole England of *Maria Stuart*, in one aspect at least, is a huge, harshened echo of Clärchen's night in the streets.

One basic theme operates here, whether the female figure happens to be an oppressive ruler or an active (Clärchen) or passive (Mary) advocate of heroic resistance, the theme of the historical degeneration of both the world and the theater, the emergence of a situation in which the conventional male roles of governor and hero can no longer be filled by men truly equal to them, even where such men still exist, as in *Egmont*. And this theme can be followed without difficulty down to the twentieth century. It appears with a morbid intensity in Kleist's Penthesilea, then variously modified in Grillparzer's Medea and Libussa, and in Antigone and Joan of Arc as frequent subjects for modern revival (Shaw, Brecht, Anouilh); it appears especially in the image of a clash between powerful women, as Mary and Elizabeth, Brunhild and Kriemhild, or the prime classical example, Electra and Clytemnestra, seen variously by Hofmannsthal, Giraudoux, O'Neill, Hauptmann. There is a hint of this theme, at one end of the spectrum, in the Countess Cathleen, a gentle female Faust, and there is a grotesque exaggeration of it at the other end, in say Strindberg, Wedekind, Dürrenmatt.

But the especially important case in literary history, which provides the connection with Ibsen, is that of Friedrich Hebbel. Hebbel's first major work, *Judith*, which we know was written as a kind of rejoinder to *Die Jungfrau von Orleans*, involves an obvious instance of a woman's having to do the job her menfolk are no longer equal to; but it also redoubles this theme in that the man Judith must destroy, Holofernes, is himself the last representative of a dying heroic age, a man of overflowing energy and outrageous personal style, whose heroic potential, thwarted by the lack of a worthy opponent to test him, has begun to turn back on itself self-consciously and degenerate into a pose. Thus the emergence of dread power in a woman is associated doubly with the idea of a historical development by which the heroic becomes obsolete.

But Judith is more than merely the vessel of a historical process; she is also a modern woman, in the sense that she is deeply conscious of the difference between her personal identity and the role assigned her sex by convention. The conventional development of her life had been disrupted by her husband's impotence, and she now has an uncomfortably sharp outsider's perspective upon what it means to be a woman; she submits to her destiny as a manipulable object—if not in the hands of a husband, then in the hands of God Himself—but at the same time she cannot deny her awareness of herself as a person, and in this respect she anticipates (naturally enough) Hebbel's later Mariamne and Rhodope and especially Klara in *Maria Magdalene*, whose socially untenable situation is the result of her submission to Leonhard, her convulsive attempt to deny her personhood and retain her conventionally given status as a mere object.

Thus in Hebbel's Judith the type of the woman as a vessel of power or heroic resolve gives birth, as it were, to the type of the modern woman torn between self and role, and this is significant because it can be demonstrated that Hebbel's developing vision of the latter type exerted a considerable influence on Ibsen.[17] The relationship between *Maria Magdalene* and *A Doll's House* or *Ghosts* is not as striking as that between Hebbel's *Gyges und sein Ring* and *When We Dead Awaken* (in the figure of the woman who is defiled by being exposed to view), but given what we know about Ibsen's admiration of *Maria Magdalene*, it is hard to imagine that Nora and Mrs. Alving have nothing in them of Hebbel's Klara, who is also the victim of unthinkingly conventional responses from the men in her life, her lovers and her father. Obviously other factors are at work here as well; but from Ibsen's idea of women's problems, which is in turn highly influential in later drama, it is still possible to trace back a chain of influences via Hebbel and Schiller at least into the intellectual vicinity of *Egmont*; and the continuity of this chain—from *Egmont* to *Wallenstein*, *Maria Stuart*, and *Die Jungfrau von Orleans*, to *Judith* and *Maria Magdalene*, to *A Doll's House* and *Ghosts*—will be even clearer after we have dealt with Schiller in more detail.

Again, therefore, the negative aspect of *Egmont*, the bare problem of generating true dramatic meaning in what Erich Heller might call a disinherited theater, has repercussions at a greater distance than one might suppose. Clärchen and Nora are dissimilar figures, but the chain of influences connecting them is not superficial; for the relation between the problem of woman and the problem of a degenerating society, a society in which interpersonal attitudes have become poses by which individuals (the burghers of Brussels or Norway) protect their own interests and illusions, remains constant throughout, and this problem implies in turn the problem of a communally valid art, or in particular the problem of drama as a genre. The focus is different in Ibsen, but the underlying poetic and cultural problems are a direct development from those in Goethe. As in the case of *Die Weber*, a clear relation exists between modern "realistic" drama and the legacy of *Egmont*.

Again, I do not wish to deny the importance of extra-dramatic and non-German factors in the genesis of such phenomena as the neo-heroic, the melancholy tragic mode, the powerful woman, and the modern woman. But I do mean to show that there is a cohesive modern dramatic tradition, a woven pattern of influences, inner relationships, echoes, common concerns, and significant oppositions, all of which have to do with the nature of the genre, and many of which reflect clearly the importance of German theory and practice from the late eighteenth century on, especially as these are summarized in *Egmont*. That there are other forces which affect modern drama is not an argument against the existence of such a tradition.

6

If we review the various dramatic problems and tendencies that radiate through *Egmont*, we discover that the array includes, *in potentia*, a complete catalogue of the works of Schiller's later dramatic phase. *Wallenstein* is suggested by the idea of the ex-hero whose energy and resolve are undermined by self-consciousness. The assumption of leadership by woman in an unheroic world points toward *Maria Stuart* and *Die Jungfrau von Orleans. Die Braut von Messina*, as Schiller makes clear in his preface on the use of the chorus, is an attempt to reassert and exploit the necessary artificiality of the theater, an attempt, thereby, to rescue modern man from his excessive inwardness and reconstitute the public or communally valid character of poetry: "The palace of kings is now closed, the courts have retreated from the city gates into the inside of buildings, writing has supplanted the living word, even the people, the sensually vital mass, where it is not merely a brute power, has become the state, thus an abstract concept, and the gods have gone back into the human breast. The poet must open up the palaces again, he must bring the courts out under the sky, he must re-establish the gods."[18] And Schiller's Wilhelm Tell, as some fine recent interpretations have indicated,[19] represents yet another response to the Egmont problem, the problem of reconstituting the heroic in a self-conscious age, in that he is a hero who is subject to inner weakness and disharmony but is willing to accept this condition in order to survive and be of use in the world, rather than merely go down in a blaze of glory. In this sense, he is a forerunner of Rudolf in Ottokar, who resolutely renounces all claim to personal heroic stature, and in another sense he is perhaps a forerunner of Kaiser's Socrates, or of the humanized hero in Shaw or Giraudoux.

This branch of the tradition is not so clearly traceable as the development of the modern woman, but still Schiller's Tell comes quite close to satisfying Brecht's demand, in Die Massnahme, that the individual be willing to sully his inner self for the sake of his social goal. Egmont, for example, is an expert with the crossbow, does not have a particularly high regard for human life, and is notorious for his willingness to play outlandish games (Eg., pp. 190–91, 219). But even Egmont would never allow himself to be maneuvered into the situation of having to shoot an apple from anyone's head, let alone his own son's, to satisfy a tyrant's whim; still less would he ever stoop to shooting his enemy from ambush; and least of all, as is clear from the scene with Alba, could he ever bring himself to beg forgiveness as Tell does of Gessler (Tell III.iii.1873). Tell is in some ways very similar to Egmont. His conversation with Stauffacher (I.iii.414–45), in which he declines to take part in anything like a rebellious conspiracy, contains clear echoes of Egmont's conversation with Orange; and his insistence on going to Altdorf despite Gessler and the hat—and on allowing his son to go with him!—is comparable to Egmont's disastrous insistence on continuing to live his life as if there could be no serious change in the existing order of things. But Tell is prepared to violate his inmost feelings in a way that Egmont is not, and the result is that whereas Egmont, with a grand heroic gesture, in the end accomplishes nothing, Tell the bushwhacker makes a significant contribution to human freedom in the real world.

Tell could easily be a direct answer to Egmont, almost a Brechtian answer—although Brecht apparently did not recognize this. Tell's motivation is rather more complex than what is advocated in Die Massnahme, but Schiller's play is still a clear step in

Brecht's direction—Grusche's questionable risking of her child's life on the bridge is perhaps even a direct echo of Tell's questionable apple shot—and a step that starts out from the basic *Egmont* problem of creating a valid heroic image on the modern stage, in an era of divisive and debilitating self-consciousness.

It can be argued that Tell's character degenerates in the course of the play. At the beginning he insists on complete independence, self-unity, and moral clarity. Like Egmont, he recognizes that talking and thinking interfere with action, which is why he will not attend the rebellious deliberations; if his friends are ever truly in need, if they can ever confront him with the clear moral necessity of helping a fellow-creature, then he will act (I.iii.440–41), but he will not let his actions be sullied by excessive advance consciousness. In Act III, however, Gessler teaches him an important lesson (one which Egmont never learns): that inner harmony is not necessary for action, that one can shoot the crossbow, for example, even when every fiber of one's being resists doing so. And Tell then simply applies this lesson when he murders Gessler. He has become not an idealist but a desperate and dangerously self-divided individual; his character, as he had striven to maintain it at the beginning of the play, is in ruins, and his heroism his exemplariness, consists in bearing this burden, not breaking under it even when faced, in Parricida, with the terrifying image of what is now at least potentially himself. This in turn indicates by analogy the lesson the spectator must learn as a spectator: to participate affirmatively in the theatrical celebration of man and of human freedom despite his knowledge (which the play is calculated to awaken) of the self-disruption and inner difficulty by which freedom must be purchased. Again, as in Lessing, Goethe, Kleist, and Büchner, the idea of the heroic is ultimately referable to our own daily steadfastness in bearing the anguish of self-conscious existence; *Tell*, like *Prinz Friedrich*, is a reaction against *Egmont*, but a reaction that still propagates the inner spirit of Goethe's play.

And yet, is it a direct reaction? Obviously the relation between *Egmont* and any of Schiller's later plays will be less accidental than the parallel in *Die Dreigroschenoper* probably is, but is there any special reason for singling out *Egmont* as a shaping force in late Schiller? In fact there is. For *Wallenstein*, by all accounts the key work in Schiller's late period, is a specific response to *Egmont*. This point is of considerable consequence, for it is hard to overestimate the importance of Schiller's late plays in subsequent German drama. Nineteenth-century drama echoes them repeatedly in theme, language, and structure; and if, toward the twentieth century, there is an increasing tendency to rebel against their influence, artistic rebellions of this sort tend to preserve as much as they destroy. That Schiller is parodied in *Die heilige Johanna der Schlachthöfe*, for example, and perhaps also in *Mutter Courage*, by no means implies that his work had no positive effect on Brecht.[20] If we can show, therefore, that in *Wallenstein* Schiller's dramatic creativity was rekindled mainly by an intellectual confrontation with *Egmont*, that *Egmont* thus provided an important impetus in Schiller's late phase, then we shall have said a good deal about the indirect influence of *Egmont* in and through practically all German drama down to the present.

There is some extrinsic evidence. That Schiller devoted serious thought to the question of how *Egmont* might be improved is obvious, since he rewrote Goethe's play for the stage; and he says afterwards to Körner, "Egmont has been not without usefulness as preparation for my Wallenstein" (10 April 1796). Curiously enough, however, this "preparation" seems to have slowed Schiller down rather than speeded him up, for there is no evidence that he even thought about *Wallenstein* for the next six months; and this is significant because almost exactly the same thing had already happened once previously. In September 1794, shortly before his visit with Goethe in Weimar, Schiller writes to Körner that he is now grappling in earnest with *Wallenstein* (4, 12 September), but when he gets to Weimar, what he discusses with Goethe is apparently not *Wallenstein* but the plan for *Die Malteser* (letter to Charlotte Schiller, 20 September); in fact, as later in 1796, he now abandons *Wallenstein* altogether for an extended period. And it is during that visit in 1794 that Goethe first offers him the job of revising *Egmont* for the stage. Does the contact with Goethe, and specifically with Goethe as the author of *Egmont*, discourage Schiller in his *Wallenstein* project? Does the prospect of actually revising *Egmont* appear to Schiller as a substitute for working on *Wallenstein*? In either case, the conclusion that Schiller regarded *Wallenstein* as a response to *Egmont* is implied.

Schiller's attitude toward Goethe, with regard to his work on *Wallenstein*, is clearly ambivalent. On the one hand he relies on Goethe for moral and technical support (e.g. letters to Goethe, 24

January 1797, to Körner, 7 April 1797), but on the other hand he is nervous about venturing too far into what he regards as Goethe's poetic domain. He writes to Wilhelm von Humboldt on 21 March 1796, concerning *Wallenstein*, "It is true that on my present path I shall get into Goethe's territory and shall have to measure myself against him; and it is certain that I shall lose by the comparison." The context of this statement is a discussion not of *Egmont* but of the distinction between "realism" and "idealism" as worked out in the essay "Über naive und sentimentalische Dichtung"; Wallenstein as a character is "genuinely realistic," therefore difficult to manage for an author of Schiller's temperament. But if we turn to the essay itself, we read of the realist:

> The circle of his knowledge and action extends to everything that exists conditionally; but he never gets further than conditional knowledge, and the rules he derives from individual experiences are valid, in the strictest sense, only for one case each; if he develops the rule of one moment into a general law, he will inevitably plunge himself into error. . . . His acuity depends on the recurrence of similar cases, and when things follow one another in orderly fashion, he can judge correctly; but when something unprecedented happens, all his wisdom is nullified. [*SA*, XII, pp. 252–53]

And these ideas are strikingly applicable to Egmont, a good deal more so than to Wallenstein. It is true that Wallenstein tries to infer general rules from his past successes and from his past relations with Octavio Piccolomini; but Egmont's, at least on the surface, is much more exclusively a tragedy of miscalculation or error, rather than fate. Indeed, Egmont, who explicitly bases his action or inaction on the premise that "things will continue in their course," and is brought low by an *unprecedented* act of tyranny, could hardly be a more perfect illustration of what Schiller says in general about the realist; and it is hard to imagine that Schiller, once the reviewer and now the prospective reviser of *Egmont*, is unaware of this.

Wallenstein, then, is in Schiller's own view the first true realist he has attempted to use as a dramatic hero, but the description of the realist in the essay on naive and sentimental poetry fits Egmont better. From this we can learn something about the direction in which Schiller wishes to improve upon *Egmont*. One of the main problems posed for Schiller by *Wallenstein* is the development of the historical material into a tragic action from which the idea of fate will emerge clearly; we read in a letter to Goethe of 28 November 1796, "Fate in the strict sense still contributes too little, and the hero's own faults contribute too much, to his misfortune." Again we think of Egmont, and we recall the emphasis in Schiller's review upon Egmont's lack of stature, the obviousness of his weaknesses; the trouble with Egmont is that he is merely a realist, that his downfall is merely the result of the realist's characteristic intellectual limitedness, rather than the working of fate in some larger sense. In *Wallenstein*, by contrast, Schiller wishes to create what he considers a true tragedy, which will reveal a tragic aspect of the human condition in general, not merely a particular human flaw. Wallenstein is meant to surpass Egmont in the direction of human universality, which is why his particular personal weaknesses must be suppressed, along with those weaknesses that are characteristic only of a realist's mode of thinking (see e.g. letters to Körner, 28 November 1796, to Böttiger,[21] 1 March 1799); and this in turn is why Wallenstein the finished product is not so exclusively a realist as Egmont, who had been an important influence in his creation.

Wallenstein and Egmont, both ex-heroes whose self-assured heroic energy has been undermined by self-conscious brooding on a misguided idea of personal destiny, are both faced with a choice between conflicting loyalties; and both, in that they refuse to make a clear decision, think of themselves as playing a game in which their personal freedom is preserved. The major difference between them lies not in their characters but in their situations, in that the decision toward which Orange pushes Egmont is morally defensible whereas that toward which Illo and the Terzkys push Wallenstein is not; and this is how Schiller tries to develop an Egmontian character in the direction of human universality. Egmont's inaction, his allowing himself to slide into the position of a supposed traitor against Spain, is amoral, whereas Wallenstein's inaction, his allowing the decision for a momentous act of treason to be made in spite of himself, is clearly immoral. *Egmont*, therefore, in Schiller's view, shows a *discontinuity* between morality and the realist's mode of thinking, whereas *Wallenstein* shows a *conflict*; or in other words, whereas *Egmont* (again, in Schiller's view) demonstrates only the limitedness of a particular way of looking at things—the realist's inability to make a genuine moral

judgment—*Wallenstein* reveals a fundamental and always potentially tragic contradiction in the human condition as a whole—the
way in which the process of thinking about oneself empirically, as
if one's destiny were a knowable object, leads eventually to a
perversion and violation of true human freedom, even without
one's deliberately committing a crime, the way in which man's
unavoidable quality as a percipient being tends to take on the
character of an act that violates his rational or moral being. This
aspect of Schiller's intention explains the importance of Max Piccolomini in the play. It is Wallenstein who actually undergoes the
process by which percipient self-questing (as opposed to rational
self-determination) becomes of its own accord a violation of moral
human nature; but Max—who also thinks of Wallenstein's being
as a kind of natural law (*Picc.* V.i.2548–54; *W. Tod* II.ii.733–35),
and whose moral sense tears him loose from Wallenstein in the
end—is necessary as a measuring instrument, to reveal, in his
utter despair, the depth of inner human contradictoriness involved in Wallenstein's fate. Wallenstein is capable of undergoing his fate, but not capable of experiencing it fully, which
is why Max is necessary to bring out its inner or humanly universal significance.

In *Wallenstein*, then, Schiller attempts to surpass *Egmont*, but
he still uses *Egmont* repeatedly as a source of techniques, images,
and human configurations. The basic method of characterization
employed in *Wallensteins Lager* and in the first act of *Die Piccolomini*, the initial depiction of Wallenstein by way of others'
perceptions of him, is indebted to Goethe's procedure in the first
act of *Egmont*. The relationships among Wallenstein, Max, and
Octavio are parallel to those among Egmont, Ferdinand, and Alba,
in that Max is a passionate admirer of the man his father must
destroy. Both plays give prominence to the idea that true fate, as
opposed to the conscious idea of one's destiny, is identical with
one's true self or heart (*Picc.* III.viii.1840; *W. Tod* I.vii.655–56;
II.iii. 953–56). Many of the arguments for and against Imperial
rule in *Wallenstein* are arguments used in Egmont's debate with
Alba, Illo's image of the army as a horse that needs the right
rider (*Picc.* I.ii.202–7) being an especially clear echo. Illo's exhor-
tation of Wallenstein—"Will you, by hesitating, simply await the
worst?" to which Wallenstein replies, "Better that than to *choose*
the worst deliberately!" (*Picc.* II.vi.925–27)—recalls Orange and

Egmont; and his warning about how the army's communal enthusiasm will fade with time and pressure (*Picc.* 945–57) describes exactly what happens to the burghers of Brussels. Max's
argument with Octavio (*Picc.* V.i and iii; *W. Tod* II.vii) about
whether Wallenstein is actually guilty or whether his basic innocence is being transformed into guilt by others' suspicion (e.g.
Picc. 2632–35) recalls Margarete's first conversation with
Machiavell as well as Vansen's and Ferdinand's descriptions of
how an innocent man may be convicted. And Wallenstein, like
Egmont, when he feels himself seriously threatened, compares
himself to a mutilated tree (*W. Tod* III.xiii.1791–94).

But if Schiller's aim is to surpass *Egmont*, why does he still
remain so close to it? Why does he enter into this difficult ambivalent relation with Goethe? Or to put this question into a form in
which it has been asked by many critics, why, if it does not suit
his temperament, does Schiller insist on writing a tragedy with a
realist as the hero?[22] Once we understand the connection between
Wallenstein and *Egmont*, the answer is clear. Schiller wishes in
Wallenstein to write *a tragedy of self-consciousness*. The rational
or at least cerebral quality of the modern age, this enlightened
eighteenth century, poses a serious threat to the communal function of art and hence to the very existence of drama; our relationship with the world is mediated by abstract concepts which close
us off from nature, not by sensually compelling myths, and as
Schiller argues repeatedly in his aesthetic writings, this is not
healthy even from a moral point of view. Somehow—we think
both of the early "Schaubühne" essay and the late essay on the
chorus in drama—the immediate public nature of drama must be
recaptured; and one way to do this is to develop our cultural
disease itself into a tragic vision, for the communal, quasi-
mythical resonantness of such a vision will be practically assured;
it will show, after all, what we *are*. We must make a myth, in other
words, out of our self-conscious exclusion from a mythical mode
of experiencing. And this, in turn, given Schiller's basic distinction of human types, means that the new tragic hero must be a
realist, since for an idealist self-consciousness is not tragic. The
idealist's self-consciousness is by definition an act of moral self-
determination, which under certain circumstances can lead to his
downfall, but is never identical with it. The realist, on the other
hand, as Schiller says, "plunges himself *unavoidably* into error"

(my emphasis) when he becomes intensely conscious and tries to draw general conclusions about himself and the world; self-consciousness as such disrupts the fabric of his being and is in effect his downfall, even if, like Tell, he manages to survive.

Schiller is aiming at a tragedy of self-consciousness, the poetic intensification of an unheeded anguish inherent in all our normal experience, and it is evident that he sees Egmont (the quintessential "realist") as a step in this direction. In his revision of Goethe's play there is a good deal more bustling about than in the original; Egmont's secretary now becomes rather a nuisance, interrupting not only the interview with Orange but even that with Clärchen. This bustle, however, throws into sharp relief Egmont's own inactivity, his character as a hesitant brooder on the one hand, and on the other hand a man whose natural courage has become self-conscious affectation, now flaring up as blind obstinacy—in both of which traits Wallenstein follows him. Egmont, in Schiller's version, turns quite unpleasant to his secretary for worrying Clärchen, and then deliberately gives a drunken party to flaunt his unconcern at Alba's arrival.[23] He even speaks the line, "And to bathe the brooding wrinkles from my brow, there is, I know, a gentle remedy" (NA, XIII, p. 25)—despite Schiller's earlier objections (SA, XVI, pp. 183, 185), and despite the ease with which it could have been deleted—I believe because this line reflects with exceptional clarity the hopeless paradox involved in a conscious attempt to suppress or transcend consciousness. For Schiller, Egmont must be an extreme example of character degenerating self-consciously, and it is significant that the one speech in which Egmont reveals his true self most clearly, his monologue in prison on freedom as the soldier's exultant exercise of brute power, is deleted in the revision (NA, XIII, p. 63); for this speech compels us to recognize, unless, like Schiller, we have reason to resist the recognition, that Egmont has been consciously dissembling, that Alba's thrusts do not entirely miss the mark, that Egmont is not merely the victim of an unaccustomed inward self-division.

Again, Schiller in *Wallenstein* wishes to transform the communally disruptive, debilitating, anti-dramatic self-consciousness of the age into a tragic vision by which, at least within the theater, our sense of community will be restored paradoxically, and "a living monument" will be erected "in the feelings of the noblest and best men" (*W. Lager*, "Prolog," 45–46). This is why *Wallen-*

stein, even if not originally conceived as a response to *Egmont,* inevitably becomes such a response in the course of its genesis; Schiller, in his continuing occupation with *Egmont* as its reviser, soon recognizes that the weaknesses he had once criticized in the hero's character are weaknesses of self-consciousness, therefore capable of being developed into symbols of a general tragic contradictoriness in the human condition.

Once we understand this, we are able to see quite a clear unity in Schiller's overall development, for if *Wallenstein* is a response to *Egmont,* then *Don Carlos,* in a similar way, had been a response to *Hamlet.* Again there is some extrinsic evidence: "Carlos, if the comparison be permitted, has the soul of Shakespeare's Hamlet" (to Reinwald, 14 April 1783). And again the extrinsic evidence is dispensable, given the evidence in the text. The situation of Carlos' parents—his natural father has remarried—is the reverse of Hamlet's, but the state of acute discomfort occasioned by this situation is similar. Carlos, who has recently returned from school, like Hamlet, despises the basic attitudes of his father, against whom he attempts to form an alliance with his mother, as Hamlet does; and Philip, like Claudius, entertains the notion that the young man's behavior indicates sickness, which in Carlos' case actually is love, in Hamlet's only supposedly. Posa, although his role eventually develops out of all proportion, corresponds to Horatio, Princess Eboli to Ophelia, and at the end even the idea of a ghost walking the ramparts is introduced.

The details of the relationship between *Don Carlos* and *Hamlet,* however, need not concern us here. What is important is that it is *Hamlet* Schiller had chosen to rearrange, as he later rearranges *Egmont* in *Wallenstein;* for *Hamlet* represents to Germans of Schiller's period the prime example of a tragedy of "Seele," of inner life and brooding self-consciousness.[24] *Wallenstein,* therefore, is not nearly so radical a departure from the series of early dramas, ending with *Don Carlos,* as has often been supposed. In both *Don Carlos* and *Wallenstein,* Schiller starts from an existing tragedy in which the problem of self-consciousness is central, and rearranges the characters and situations with an eye to greater universality of tragic meaning. If Egmont, in Schiller's view, is not as tragic as Wallenstein, then Hamlet is also not as tragic as Carlos, for in the end he does get his revenge, and the world sets itself right despite his self-consciousness; Carlos, however, achieves nothing whatever toward the task he has been set, the furtherance of human freedom, especially in the Netherlands, and his world remains "out of joint" because of his tragic inability to stop talking and get a move on for Brussels. In both cases, the unavoidable tragic contradictoriness of self-consciousness is reflected in a second character—Posa, corresponding to Max—whom the hero's self-violation forces into a position where he must in effect commit suicide.

In *Wallenstein*, Schiller thus does not simply leave behind the failure of *Don Carlos*, but rather he tries to repair it by taking up the same problem from another angle. Nor is *Don Carlos* the first of Schiller's works in which this problem is central. We have only to think of the "tintenklecksendes Säkulum" against which Karl Moor conducts a rebellion he knows to be futile, this age in which knowledge and cerebration have usurped the place of active human greatness. The hopelessness of our Hamlet-like situation amid the rottenness of the present age—our intense knowledge of our historical obligation to become heroes or geniuses, and yet our awareness that this weight of obligation impedes and enfeebles us—already receives full expression in Goethe's *Werther*; but Schiller, even in *Die Räuber*, with its curiously moralistic ending, attempts to go beyond Goethe in a positive direction. Gradually the idea of a tragedy of self-consciousness takes shape for him, the idea of a homeopathic remedy, an overcoming of our self-conscious despair by transforming this despair into an inspiring communal celebration in the theater; and *Don Carlos* is the attempt to create such a tragedy, taking *Hamlet* as the starting point.

Don Carlos, however, is a failure, and the "Briefe über Don Carlos," though ostensibly a defense of the play, is really the beginning of Schiller's struggle with the question of why it fails. Gradually, in his thinking about *Egmont* and then more systematically in his own aesthetic essays, Schiller works out the idea of the realistic hero, the only possible heroic type in a true tragedy of self-consciousness, and the result is *Wallenstein*, which in turn is the basis on which a further development, constantly referable to the idea of consciousness, leads eventually to the both grim and joyful quasi tragedy of Wilhelm Tell.

7

In earlier chapters, we established certain relationships among Lessing, Goethe, and Kleist with respect to the problem of drama as a genre, and we have seen now that *Egmont* serves as a stimulus by which the dramatic thinking of Kleist, Büchner, Schiller, and Goethe himself is developed and clarified. We have shown a relationship between technical problems of drama, especially those arising from the inevitability of a detached intellectual component in the audience's attitude, and certain philosophical problems associated with the ideas of self-consciousness, human community, and the heroic; and we have seen that these ideas can be followed from *Egmont* through Schiller to the major mid-century dramatists, and beyond. We have not yet treated Schiller's idea of drama as a genre in full detail, and we will not have space to treat Grillparzer's and Hebbel's. But even if these last authors do not possess as subtle a formal mastery of the genre as Lessing, Goethe, Schiller, or Kleist, even if their sense of the genre itself as a problem is not as clear, still I think they are unquestionably heirs to the general complex of ideas that grew up in German Classicism. Even if in Grillparzer the melancholy mode tends to become exaggerated at the expense of drama's basic festiveness, and even if Hebbel, in his dogmatic historical theorizing, is attempting the re-establishment of tragic drama by way of a theatrically unfounded shortcut, still both the melancholy mode and the seeking of a basis for authentic tragedy in the modern age are elements of the Classical tradition. The tradition may diversify, but it still exists, specifically as a dramatic movement, an array of ideas and tendencies that has its principal source in the problem of drama as developed mainly by Lessing and Goethe.

My main purpose, however, is to show the importance of the German movement in modern European drama as a whole. Therefore I have not said much about the *Sturm und Drang*, I have barely touched on the highly modern drama of extreme irony in Tieck and Grabbe, and I have not mentioned either the immensely popular but trivial plays of Kotzebue and Iffland or the important Austrian playwrights Raimund, Nestroy, Anzengruber. The drama of extreme irony, in which self-conscious mental processes are allowed to play havoc with the conventional integrity of the stage, belongs at least on the periphery of the German movement, and the Austrians (including Grillparzer) all incorporate something of the tradition from Classicism, by either parody or influence, into their own separate theatrical tradition; but these points are not of special significance with regard to the growth of modern drama. The question of the *Sturm und Drang*, especially Lenz and early Goethe and Schiller, is less easily settled, for this movement does exercise a demonstrable independent influence on a number of important modern playwrights. When we come to naturalism and expressionism, and then to Brecht, it will take some arguing to show that the deepest-running current remains the tradition from Classicism.

Egmont, to recapitulate, is an important link in several chains of direct influence leading into the twentieth century, and exerts a strong but less tangible influence by way of *Faust*, which serves as a kind of amplifier for Egmontian techniques and tendencies that then become important in modern drama. It is also a significant forerunner in spirit of modern drama, especially with regard to the idea and dramatic function of the hero; *being* Egmont is not merely a matter of being depicted as a certain type of person but rather involves a web of analogies between stage and audience by which the fictional person is endowed with something like mythical stature, and similar endeavors are important in the development of drama from naturalism onward.

In any case the unity of the German movement arises not from a specific theory of drama, but rather from an especially intense concern with the problem of drama, and I shall attempt later, in discussing German philosophy, to say something more definite about the actual avenues by which this movement exerts its influence. First, however, we must have a clearer idea of Schiller's place in the picture.

7 Schiller's Theoretical Impasse and *Maria Stuart*

For Schiller, drama meant tragedy, at least in practice. There is a curious passage in "Über naive und sentimentalische Dichtung" where some quite extravagant claims are made concerning what comedy *would* accomplish if it ever actually arrived at its goal,[1] but Schiller speaks only in the subjunctive here, as if suggesting that comedy in its true form is an unrealized ideal. Later on, to be sure, in a letter to Körner of 13 May 1801, he also speaks somewhat deprecatingly of comedy, excusing his own incapacity on the grounds that this genre has not sufficient "depth" to engage him as an artist; but as described in "Über naive und sentimentalische Dichtung" the goal of comedy—"the highest thing man has to strive for," a state of perfect equilibrium and accord with the world—is still at least very similar to that "Totalität" which is posited in the aesthetic *Briefe* as the ultimate goal of art in general: "It cannot be true that the cultivation of particular abilities in us necessitates the sacrifice of their totality; or even if this is a strong natural tendency, still it must lie within our power to restore the totality in our nature, which art disrupts, by means of a higher art" (*SA*, XII, p. 24). And this—regardless of whether one considers the *Briefe* primarily a philosophical or a technical work—is unquestionably a profession of faith. If Schiller had been able to write a comedy (or alternatively, a "sentimental idyll"),[2] a work by which the wholeness of the human condition could be restored, he certainly would have done so. But he was not able; he was committed to a tragic view of man.

1

Ilse Graham is doubtless justified when she cautions against confusing Schiller's philosophical opinions with his opinions on artistic technique, and she may even be correct in asserting that "integration of the individual"[3] is achieved by some of Schiller's tragic figures. But I cannot agree with her reading of *Tell* as basically nontragic. If Tell practices "a quite deliberate constriction and narrowing of the field of vision," it does not follow that "his eye and his heart, his sensual nature and his mind work here in flawless unity";[4] on the contrary, the deliberateness of his self-limiting constitutes an inner hiatus, an attempt to suppress consciousness by consciousness, the *Egmont* problem. Some of Schiller's heroes, especially the heroines Mary Stuart and Joan of Arc, may achieve full self-integration in the end; but in accordance with the tragic law of *Egmont*, they also achieve death thereby—unlike Tell, who survives to bear with exemplary steadfastness the burden of an ineradicable self-division—and their self-integration therefore does not represent directly that viable totality which is the aim of art.

Wrong as it may be in general to confuse philosophical and technical issues, it remains true that Schiller limits himself in practice to the tragic and that he feels this necessary because of his own philosophical appraisal of the limitations of his age: "Our tragedies would be obliged to struggle against the powerlessness, the flabbiness, the characterlessness of the time, against our base way of thinking; our tragedy must show force and character, it must shake our mind and elevate it, not relax it. Beauty is for a happy generation, but an unhappy one must be moved by the sublime" (to Süvern, 26 July 1800). These unhappy features of the age are associated in Schiller's mind with an unbalanced and debilitating self-consciousness. His own artistic mission is to write a definitive, perhaps therapeutic, tragedy of self-consciousness, and we have discussed his sense of this mission as it develops through *Wallenstein*.

Graham herself, it seems to me, confuses philosophical and technical categories somewhat. She deals accurately with many of Schiller's characters and arrives at the important perception "that the hubris of the Schillerian hero, which constitutes his tragic guilt, lies in the predominance of his *Person*";[5] she relates this idea to subtle patterns of imagery in the plays, and she pulls together character and imagery into a clear sense of Schiller's poetic vision. But then she equates this vision, which is basically philosophical in nature, with what is meant actually to happen in the theater. This is a mistake. Again *Tell* is the obvious example. The vision of a perfect harmony of man and nature is unquestionably present in the play; but the effect of the play (the intended effect, as I have argued) is derived precisely from the contrast between this vision and Tell's inner state, as a parallel to the contrast between poetic vision as such and our own situation as a knowing modern audience; this contrast or inner tension we must bear, indeed bear joyfully, as Tell presumably does his in the end.

2

Since drama therefore means tragedy for Schiller, the problem of drama becomes the problem of why man should use art to inflict tragic visions upon himself, the problem of the early essay "Über den Grund des Vergnügens an tragischen Gegenständen." Schiller's thinking in this essay is quite primitive, but foreshadows the basic line he takes later on. The main category with which he operates is "Zweckmässigkeit" (expediency, suitability toward an end), and he defines the realm of tragedy as including "all possible cases where a natural is sacrificed to a moral expediency, or one moral expediency to another which is higher" (*SA*, XI, p. 146). This idea has to do only with the content of a work being considered, not with its form, but Schiller nevertheless approaches the notion of genre by his insistence upon a particular relationship between such content and the responses of an audience or reader. Our reaction, for instance, when we are presented artistically with the spectacle of martyrs dying for their cause, is described as follows: "the apparent senselessness of nature, which rewards virtue with misery, the unnatural denial of self-love, etc.: all this, since it awakens so many ideas of thwarted purpose, ought to cause us the acutest pain; but why should nature trouble us, with all her goals and laws, when by thwarting us she becomes the occasion of revealing our own moral purposefulness in sharpest contrast?" (*SA*, XI, p. 147). The pleasure we take in tragedy thus depends on the existence of a free moral purposefulness *in ourselves*, which is excited through being challenged by a tragic vision of nature's moral intractability. Tragedy shows nature as thwarting our moral purposes, and this arouses a feeling of moral independence in us, a feeling so intrinsically good that we are even tempted to love its evil cause, "to be reconciled with evil" (*SA*, XI, p. 147). Our pleasure in tragedy is our sense of victory in a struggle *against* the substance of the artistic vision, for "only resistance makes a power visible" (*SA*, XI, p. 146).

This general idea, that the spectator at a tragedy is engaged in an inner struggle against the vision of man's fate that is being presented to him, remains more or less constant in the writings of Schiller's theoretical decade (preceding the completion of *Wallenstein*), for example in the idea of the sublime. In Stahl's concise and accurate formulation: "A sublime object defeats our sensuous nature while enabling our rational self to triumph over it. Such an object evokes an awareness of our rational superiority over our senses which have proved inferior to another and more powerful material force."[6] The thinking of "Über den Grund des Vergnügens . . ." is refined, to be sure, in the later essays. Already in "Über die tragische Kunst" Schiller moves closer to a generic idea of drama by concentrating on the idea of "Mitleid" (pity) as a state of actual suffering which still includes an element of detached mental freedom, so that it serves as training in how to deal with the immediate sufferings of real life; only a short step is necessary (and is then taken in the *Briefe*) to get from here to the idea that the artificiality or play-character of art has an essential function with regard to art's moral effect. In "Über die tragische Kunst," moreover, it is the necessary vividness of the sense of suffering evoked by a tragic work that gives drama the advantage over narrative (*SA*, XI, pp. 167–68). As nearly as possible, we must undergo directly the hero's sufferings—we must be able "to exchange persons with him" (*SA*, XI, p. 169)—for only thus can our rising above these sufferings be a true moral victory.

These are refinements, but the basic thought remains unchanged, so that Berghahn is quite correct in summarizing Schiller's view of the dramatist's mission as follows: "He is master of the whole scale of emotions, from delicate sympathy to terrible inner upheaval, and he knows how to vary and gradate these emotions until our sympathy has reached the point where we must react with an opposing force which lifts us above all moral duress and reveals something entirely permanent in ourselves. . . . Schiller's idea of pity or sympathy thus implies the experience of the supersensual, with which tragedy is meant to familiarize us."[7] Drama in the first instance offers us an experience by way of the senses, and our job as spectators is to react *against* this experience in order to recognize, affirm, enjoy, and so develop our own active and supersensual moral freedom.

This, on the level of theory, is Schiller's way of coming to grips with what I have called the intellectual component in an audience's attitude toward the stage. But Schiller's thought on this subject is rather more extreme than that implied in Lessing or Goethe or even Kleist. The audience, in order to derive pleasure from tragedy, must actively *resist* a major aspect of the tragic vision presented them, and this idea is not easily reconcilable with the idea of the work of art as constituting an organically integrated whole. Schiller argues, to be sure, that in the case of a martyr tragedy we take pleasure even in the martyr's sufferings, not only in his (and our) triumphant strength; but these are two quite different sorts of pleasure, the former a good deal less direct than the latter. Can it be that, in order to appreciate a work of art, we must take it apart in our imagination and elevate ourselves so as to leave an important portion of it beneath us? That Schiller was aware of this difficulty in his theory is suggested by his emphasis in later essays, especially "Über das Erhabene," on the idea of not merely overcoming, but rather actively *affirming* our suffering nature, transforming even death into an act of will. "The morally cultivated man, and only he, is entirely free. Either he is able to subdue nature, or else he is in agreement with her. Nothing that she does to him is coercion, since it has already become *his own action* before it reaches him; the operation of nature does not touch him, because he freely relinquishes everything within its domain" (*SA*, XII, p. 266). The emphasis in this passage is especially significant with regard to the genre of drama; for if a theater audience can be made to think of tragic suffering as an expression of its own will, then the discrepancy between two different modes of experiencing will vanish, since active volition is also what raises us above our suffering. Or we think also of the "play-drive" in the *Briefe*, another idea by means of which it is possible to argue that the whole of a tragic structure satisfies us in a single way.

These ideas, however, the play-drive and the transformation of fate into will, are entirely speculative; they say nothing about how drama approaches its audience. Schiller's answer to the question of why there should be such a thing as tragedy in the first place is still inadequate, for it still implies that our purpose in the art of tragedy is to inflict on ourselves a kind of flagellation against which our free moral being must in the end rebel; and his own basic dissatisfaction with this idea can be seen by comparing what he says some years later in the essay "Über den Gebrauch des Chors in der Tragödie":

> True art, however, is not merely a transitory game. It is seriously concerned not merely to provide man with a momentary dream of freedom, but rather to *make* him free, really, here and now; and it does this by awakening and developing in him the power to interpose an objective distance between himself and the sensible world, which otherwise merely oppresses us as gross matter or blind force, the power to transform the sensible world into a free work of the spirit, and so to dominate the material by the ideal. [*SA*, XVI, p. 120]

This, it seems to me, involves more than merely a difference in emphasis from the essays preceding *Wallenstein*. The aim of tragedy as flagellation had been not to relieve the burden of the sensible world, but rather to exploit it and call forth our reaction against it; now, however, Schiller argues that art actually makes us free, by exercising our *Geist* or intellect rather than challenging our will. Now it is implied that the very process of watching tragedy somehow liberates us as we sit there, not that we achieve our freedom only outside the theater, by reacting against the vision.

The *Briefe* on aesthetic education to an extent foreshadows these later ideas; especially the idea that art makes us free is anticipated by the notion of the aesthetic state as a necessary transitional phase between the sensual and the moral. But from a practical point of view the idea of art in the *Briefe*, and especially the implied idea of drama as a genre, is still unsatisfactory. In practice, neither the state of nature nor the state of perfected moral culture actually exists: "Man, one might say, was never in a purely animal state, but he has also never entirely escaped that state" (*SA*, XII, p. 94). And the same is apparently true of the aesthetic state, that "condition of pure determinability" or "fulfilled unlimitedness" (*SA*, XII, pp. 77, 80) which must presumably be the state of the audience in a theater; otherwise the practical division of beauty into a relaxing and an energizing type (16th letter) would not be necessary. Moreover, even if the aesthetic state of the Briefe did exist in the theater, it would still be merely a step on the way, a transition; it would be what Schiller in the essay on the chorus calls contemptuously a "dream of freedom," not freedom itself. The dramatic vision and our mood in experiencing it would still exist for the sole purpose of being superseded by a more solidly moral attitude. Indeed, the figure of Wallenstein shows clearly how the attempt to prolong a quasi-aesthetic state of determinability, rather than relinquish it in favor of a firm moral choice, must lead to disaster.[8]

In the essays preceding the completion of Wallenstein, at least with regard to the question of drama, Schiller reaches a theoretical impasse. The road from theory to practice is blocked because theory, even in its refined form, leads repeatedly back to the idea that the tragic vision which unfolds on the stage must somehow be mentally superseded by the audience, and this idea cannot possibly serve as a basis for creative activity. The poet, in order to create, must be convinced of his vision's immediate positive value and enjoyableness (even in the case of satire, which is fun); if he starts out by understanding that his audience's true enjoyment and edification will be achieved only in spite of his craftsmanlike efforts, whence shall he derive the energy to continue those efforts? Schiller's struggle with aesthetic theory in the 1790's thus does not help him as a working dramatist, but rather tends to hinder him—as ought to be clear anyway from the long, tortured genesis of the Wallenstein plays. Wallenstein is by no means simply a case of theory put into practice.

Only one of Schiller's ideas from the 1790's holds out hope for a solution to the problem of drama, the idea of not merely overcoming the intractability of nature, but rather somehow affirming it. In "Über das Pathetische" we read of Vergil's Laocoon that "his death becomes an act of will" (SA, XI, p. 262), and in "Über das Erhabene" it is clear from the basic focus of the discussion ("man is the creature that wills" [SA, XII, p. 264]) that will is the faculty by which a man must transform his natural helplessness into his own action. But in the Briefe, in connection with the play-drive, there is a passage in which this idea begins to deepen. Schiller defines beauty, or the object of the play-drive, as "living form," and says of the beautiful object (taking the example of a work in marble): "Only in that its form lives in our feeling, while its life takes shape in our understanding, is it living form, and this is always so if we judge it beautiful" (*SA*, XII, p. 55). The context here is limited but the formulation is highly suggestive; if we extrapolate from it in the direction of drama, it implies that the natural or sensual or fated aspect of a work (its "life") is affirmed by an act of *intellectual re-creation*, by "taking shape" in our understanding. This is a movement, though still only a tentative one, in the direction of the later essay on the chorus, where the job of art is to transform nature into "the free product of our formative spirit" (*SA*, XVI, p. 121). Art must place us in a position where we affirm the world of fate not merely by willing it but by shaping it, by relating ourselves to it *as if it were our own artistic creation*; if this can be accomplished, then the details of a tragic vision will no longer have only negative significance and the basic difficulty in Schiller's thinking will have been eliminated.

This idea, however, is not yet available to Schiller in the 1790's, and in fact it is not developed fully into a theory of drama even in the essay on the chorus. Once he reaches the impasse I have described, Schiller turns firmly from theory to practice (in *Wallenstein* and *Maria Stuart*) in order to resume his struggle with the same problem from another angle. When drama reaches a dead end in *Don Carlos*, Schiller turns to theory, and when theory bogs down, he turns again to drama.

Schiller's dramatic thought, moreover, at its crucial point in the idea of affirmation of fate, appears to have been deeply affected by Lessing's. The discussion of Laocoon in "Über das Pathetische" is developed explicitly from Lessing, the essay "Über das Erhabene" opens with a quotation from *Nathan* on the subject of will, and the passage from the *Briefe* on "living form" recalls Lessing's idea of drama as "living painting." In fact the whole opposition between "life" and "form" recalls Lessing's distinction between actions and objects as artistic content; and Schiller, like Lessing, develops his opposition by arguing that the total experience of beauty occurs only with the aid of what is supplied by the mind of the spectator. When we come to *Maria Stuart* we shall see the full eventual depth of this affinity with Lessing.[9]

3

Schiller often suggests in letters that he regards *Wallenstein* primarily as a technical problem, since he feels no emotional attraction to his hero, and critics have been quick to take up this suggestion.[10] But it is incorrect to conclude that *Wallenstein* embodies directly the results of the theoretical essays. Schiller's theorizing does not get him substantially beyond the idea of tragedy as flagellation, or at best as "an inoculation of unavoidable fate" (*SA*, XII, p. 279), an idea with which he himself is not satisfied; and the clearest sign of his dissatisfaction is *Wallenstein* itself. By choosing a hero with whom he is not in sympathy, and one he does not expect to arouse deep sympathy in an audience, Schiller deliberately reduces the "pathetic" intensity of his work and thus attempts to *avoid* his own concept of flagellant tragedy.

There is, then, a curious negative relationship, with regard to technical dramatic questions, between *Wallenstein* and Schiller's aesthetic essays; but the corresponding positive relationship with regard to philosophical questions is not affected. Schiller's goal in *Wallenstein* is the creation of a more-than-Egmontian tragedy of self-consciousness, and self-consciousness, accordingly, is understood in the *Briefe* as one of the two irreducibly fundamental elements of human experience, the other being feeling, "Empfindung":

> Self-consciousness cannot depend on the will, which presupposes it. It is a primal expression of the personality, to possess which is no merit and to lack which is no fault. Reason, or absolute consistency and universality of consciousness, can only be demanded of him who is already self-conscious; prior to this he is not human, and no human act can be expected of him. . . . Neither abstraction nor experience can lead us back to the source of our concepts of generality and necessity; it is enough that self-consciousness exists, and with its unchanging unity is given also the law of unity in everything that exists *for* man and everything that arises *through* him, for our knowledge and our actions. . . . Thus feeling and self-consciousness arise entirely without the help of the subject, and the origin of both lies as much beyond our will as beyond our cognition. [*SA*, XII, pp. 74–75]

Now tragedy as flagellation, which uses "the pathetic-sublime" (*SA*, XII, pp. 316–20), approaches its spectator first by way of "Empfindung" (the faculty through which we experience "pathos"), whereas self-consciousness, "the experience of his absolute existence" (*SA*, XII, p. 75), is the basis on which the spectator eventually knows himself elevated above the world of feeling and suffering. But in *Wallenstein*, in order to create a tragedy *of* self-consciousness, Schiller attempts to reverse this procedure. *Don Carlos* is what we might call a pathetic tragedy of self-consciousness; inside the fictional world self-conscious confusion is a principal source of the tragic, but the appeal to the spectator is primarily emotional. In *Wallenstein*, on the other hand, the work's pathetic or emotional intensity is deliberately reduced and the spectator is approached primarily by way of his self-consciousness. Wallenstein struggles not with his condition (the object, in general, of "Empfindung") so much as with "the law of unity," with the mystery of an ultimate wholeness in us (such as that postulated by astrology) which includes both self and world, and we are meant to recognize that this striving for form or destiny, for knowledge of a true unity in existence, is an element of our own mental life, equivalent to our existence as "Person." Wallenstein's way of searching for unity or totality, especially his "realist's" idea of freedom, is misguided; but the fact *that* he searches is something we have in common with him, insofar as we are self-conscious beings equipped with the concepts of "generality and necessity."

Self-consciousness, for Schiller, is a mixed blessing. On one hand it is the experience of our "absolute existence" and so enables us to create an order of morality and culture surpassing the accident of nature. But on the other hand, nature and culture then exist in disharmony for us, so totality of being or complete humanness assumes the character of a distant dream; and this aspect of self-consciousness becomes tragic in the person of the realist, who unavoidably plunges himself into error when he tries to apply the idea of generality or totality within his own mode of experiencing.

We can go a bit further in this reasoning if we follow Käte Hamburger's lead in understanding that there is no such creature as a pure realist.[11] The realist claims to act strictly in accordance with "natural necessity," but Schiller then puts a question to him: "Where do you get that idea of natural necessity? Surely not from experience, which presents us only with particular natural phenomena, not with nature (as a totality), only with realities, not with necessity. You therefore always go beyond nature and determine yourself idealistically, whenever you wish to *act morally* or even *avoid suffering blindly*" (*SA*, XII, p. 260). A realist who generalizes on his experience, plunges himself into error and thereby undergoes the tragedy of self-consciousness, in other words, is a realist who is being only honest with himself. The tragedy of self-consciousness is not an aberration of realism, but rather is inherent essentially in the realist's mode of being and can be avoided only by a complex hypocrisy; every realist, by being human, is also an idealist, and his basic realism tends naturally to make him a blundering and potentially tragic idealist like Wallenstein. If we understand, moreover, that realism in its turn is an ineluctable aspect of the human condition, to which even the idealist submits whenever he performs a particular action—"for all particular existence is subject to temporal conditions and operates according to empirical laws" (SA, XII, p. 259)—then it follows that Wallenstein's fate must reveal a tragic tendency not merely in every realist's, but in every man's self-conscious existence, even the most confirmed idealist's. The tragedy of self-consciousness can be realized fully only by a particular type of individual; but no self-conscious individual, in Schiller's view, can fail to find the preconditions for such tragedy in himself.

Wallenstein, then, approaches us primarily by way of our self-consciousness rather than our feeling. But if the suggestion above is valid—that Schiller here deliberately reverses the procedure of pathetic tragedy—then it holds by analogy that, whereas the vehicle of the tragic in Wallenstein is self-consciousness, the vehicle by which we are eventually liberated from tragic despair must be feeling ("Empfindung"). And this is in fact the situation Schiller attempts to create. In "Über naive und sentimentalische Dichtung" he discusses the incompleteness of both the idealist's and the realist's "systems" as follows: "The idealist pays for his system's faults with the loss of his individual temporal existence, but he despises this loss; the realist pays for the faults of his system with the loss of his personal dignity, but he is not aware of this loss. His system works for everything of which he has any knowledge or need; what does he care for treasures he neither knows nor values?" (SA, XII, p. 257). What is really tragic about the realist is not his temporal ruin so much as his failure to recognize that he has lost something higher, his failure to experience his own tragedy as a tragedy. This is the reason for Max Piccolomini's prominence; Wallenstein undergoes his tragedy, but Max is necessary as the mirror in which the tragic shows itself as tragic.

If we bear this in mind, the whole structure of Wallenstein falls into place. Wallenstein's mystical groping and inaction, his vision of freedom and his inevitable ruin, are an intellectual pattern by which the spectator is made aware of the constant tragic potential inherent in his own self-consciousness. But the spectator's *feeling* of this pattern as tragic, in which he is aided by Max, raises him one step above Wallenstein; our feeling for Wallenstein's tragic sacrifice of human dignity, to which he himself is insensitive, places a distance between him and us. The play reveals a tragic potential in all self-consciousness, but it shapes this into an objective image to which we react via feeling, and this feeling in turn is testimony to a basic idealism in us by which the tragic potential of self-consciousness is at least balanced. Thus the procedure of flagellant or "pathetic-sublime" tragedy is exactly reversed; our self-consciousness involves us while our feeling liberates us.

But in spite of this, *Wallenstein* is still basically a kind of flagellant tragedy. Two distinct modes of experiencing are required of the audience, and the intention is to cause us suffering in order that we may rise above it and learn a deeper truth about ourselves; tragedy is still meant to function as an "inoculation," now an inoculation of the inner contradictoriness of self-consciousness, in order that this contradictoriness no longer hinder us in the realization of self-consciousness as a positive force. The problem of tragedy as a fully unified art-form is thus unresolved, for one crucial idea has not yet been brought to bear on the actual dramatic structure of *Wallenstein*, the idea of the artificiality of the artistic vision, which opens the possibility of our affirming the tragic as our own intellectual creation. This idea, the idea of the necessary and salutary and joyful artificiality of art, becomes quite prominent in Schiller's later theoretical works of the 1790's, especially the *Briefe* and "Über das Erhabene," and is stressed even in the verse prologue to *Wallenstein* itself: "Life is serious, art is cheerful" ("Prolog," l. 138); but not until *Maria Stuart* is it actually incorporated into dramatic structure. In style *Wallenstein* is not at all realistic, but the central tragic problem in it is still meant to be a real threat to the spectator, against which he must defend himself, not an intellectual edifice in the creation of which he participates and rejoices.

The problem of the intellectual component in a theater audience's attitude is therefore central in Schiller's development. The early dramas, from *Die Räuber* to *Don Carlos*, all involve difficulties of self-consciousness within the fiction, but they are also what

Schiller would later term pathetic tragedies, which attempt primarily to arouse the spectator's feelings by resonance with the characters' feelings. After *Don Carlos*, however, Schiller is prepared to admit that complete emotional resonance between audience and hero can never be achieved, and indeed is never really aimed at in drama; now he tries to justify his own earlier practice by understanding tragedy as flagellation, in which the spectator's intellectual detachment, his ultimate freedom from the tragic suffering of the fiction, plays an indispensable part. But this idea leads to an impasse because it conflicts with the idea of artistic unity and provides no direct positive justification for the details of the tragic vision; tragedy becomes an art that assumes its full meaning only when we turn our backs on it. Therefore, in *Wallenstein*, Schiller attempts to use the intellectual component in our attitude as the primary vehicle of the tragic, so that our self-consciousness will no longer constitute a turning away from the vision. And although the result, for the time being, is still essentially tragedy as flagellation, the basic idea is sound, needing only to be combined fruitfully with the idea of theatrical artificiality in order to produce Schiller's greatest drama, *Maria Stuart*.

4

That *Maria Stuart* is to some extent a repudiation of *Wallenstein* can best be seen in two characters, Mortimer, who is a kind of travesty of Max Piccolomini, and Leicester, who bears the same relation to Wallenstein. Leicester represents what has become of the self-conscious hero, the Hamlet type. Like Wallenstein, he hovers inactive between conflicting loyalties, and his inaction, like Wallenstein's, proves disastrous. The locked room in which he is compelled to experience Mary's execution (V.x) is an example of what I have called phrenographic theater; it represents his entrapment within himself, his inability to undertake any outward-directed action and so escape from the self-conscious circle of his own thoughts. And that it is this scene by which the execution is represented on stage indicates that we are meant to think of Mary's death, at least in one aspect, as an event *within Leicester's mind*, as the disaster of self-consciousness, as the final collapse into utter despair of a fruitlessly self-preoccupied mental attitude. Graham's treatment of the play is perfectly accurate to the extent of implying that Mary symbolizes *man's hope for per-*

sonal integration and wholeness, for "totality":[12] she represents this for Elizabeth, to whom she in effect offers the opportunity to become reconciled with a repressed sensuality; for Mortimer she is the symbol of reconciliation with the sensible world; for Leicester she is the hope of escape from a humanly unworthy situation; she herself has hoped to heal the rift between England and Scotland (I.vii.829–31), which symbolizes inner human self-division; and she also represents a hope of human totality for the audience. But Leicester, like Wallenstein, does nothing but play for time; he hopes for personal integration by prolonging indefinitely a state of hovering determinability, and the futility of this mental procedure is symbolized by the spectacle of hope's death (i.e. Mary's death) in the locked room of his mind.

Leicester, however, is not really a Wallenstein but the travesty of a Wallenstein, for he lacks Wallenstein's (and Egmont's) grand sense of personal destiny. In Wallenstein and Egmont, the insistence on remaining determinable (*bestimmbar*) reflects a courageous if misguided commitment to the idea that they embody as individuals an irresistible natural force, a law of destiny; but there is no such demonic element in Leicester. His conversation with Mortimer (II.viii) is a grotesque parody of Egmont's with Orange; he has no sense of direction whatever, no personal substance, but rather maintains his determinability for its own sake, as an image of freedom which he himself knows is delusive. *Wallenstein* remains an achievement in its own way, but Schiller, by parodying its hero in Leicester, indicates that *Maria Stuart* is meant to be a different kind of tragedy, still having to do with self-consciousness, but no longer admitting a Wallenstein as its focus.

And Mortimer in turn obviously represents a perversion of Max's idealism. He perhaps does not quite fit Schiller's description of the "fantast" (SA, XII, p. 263), but we must be careful not to regard even his dying attitude in too positive a light.[13] He does not in the least redeem himself by his death; in one of his last speeches, to the guard who is about to overpower him—"What is it, you hired slave of tyranny? I laugh at you, for I am free!" (IV.iv.2805–6)—he echoes the very last words of *Egmont*; but the opinion he expresses here is *false*, whereas Egmont is really defying the overdisciplined servants of a tyrant. Mortimer simply does not know what he is talking about, for Schiller repeatedly makes the point that Elizabeth has conducted her reign with scrupulous justice, and in consequence is genuinely beloved of her people. It is true, as Elizabeth admits (IV.x.3208–11), that she has practiced justice only because she has had to, so that in the depths of her heart she is perhaps a tyrant after all. But the fact remains that her officers (like Paulet and the officer of the guard) and her court (which includes men like Shrewsbury, and even Burleigh, who may not be moral but is still selflessly loyal) follow her because they believe in what they are doing. There is nothing mercenary or servile about them, and Mortimer's words to the guardsman, "hired slave," thus ring strongly false.

What Mortimer means by "freedom" is expressed all too clearly a few lines later when he shouts, "And in my last moments, my heart must open itself freely, my tongue proclaim it! Curses and ruin upon you...; (IV.iv.2809–11). Freedom for Mortimer is freedom to shout the worst insults he can think of as loudly as possible. This is the "freedom" Mary had availed herself of in Act III but later specifically renounces, for the sake of a truer freedom, when her time comes to die. Nor should we overlook the inconsistency in the image of a Catholic who talks about going to heaven in the very act of committing the mortal sin of self-destruction. Neither in Catholic doctrine nor in poetic feeling is there any sense of redemption accompanying Mortimer's death, and this lack is underscored by the words he addresses to Mary: "Beloved! since I could not save you, I shall set you a manly example in dying" (2818–19). We are meant to remember these words, because they are echoed later when Melvil says to Kennedy, "Let us lead her [Mary] with noble, manly composure," and Kennedy answers, "It is she who will set us the example of noble composure" (V.i.3372–78). It is Mary who provides the true "example" of how to die, and she does this precisely by refusing to follow Mortimer's example, by not committing suicide and not even stooping to remind Elizabeth that she is a bastard. Again, by contrast, Mortimer is shown as essentially a confused fanatic, even *in extremis*.

Thus Schiller dispenses with the character types represented by both Wallenstein and Max. *Maria Stuart* is a new kind of self-conscious tragedy, and in order to understand exactly how it works we can best begin with the question of Mary's Catholicism. Mary spends the whole play learning that true freedom must be achieved by submission. In Act I she submits nobly to the removal

of her personal possessions and even to the loss of her life, provided only that Elizabeth admit that "force," not "justice"
(I.vii.962, 965), is being employed; in Act III she does her best to
submit to Elizabeth directly; and in Act V we hear that she has
succeeded in submitting instantly to the inevitability of her
execution, with no complaint at all (V.i.3409). But why, then, will
she not submit to the necessity of dying without a priest? Church
doctrine, as Schiller certainly knew, does not make salvation contingent on the physical presence of an ordained priest, and in
cases of need, confession received by a layman is perfectly valid.
Furthermore, even if it is plausible that Mary should long for
the comfort of a priest, why does Schiller not take the opportunity to let her learn yet another lesson in submission and self-
sufficiency? Why does he grant her wish for a priest, at some
significant cost in plot probability? In fact Mary does learn the
ultimate lesson in self-sufficiency, when she says to Melvil, before she knows he is ordained: "What makes the priest a spokes-
man of the Lord? His pure heart and unsullied life. Thus you, ordained or not, are a priest to me, God's messenger, bringing peace"
(V.vii.3637–40). But then why not let Melvil simply be Melvil?
Why does Schiller insist on showing an official Catholic ritual, a
ritual which is now not only unnecessary from the point of view
of Mary's character—since she has in effect poetically ordained
Melvil anyway—but also likely to offend some of the audience?[14]
     If the play as a whole were at all Catholic in spirit, we could
understand this "miracle" at the end (3645). But the play is not
even sympathetic with the Roman church, which is shown in a
distinctly unflattering light, especially by way of its effect on
young Mortimer. Nothing is fundamentally wrong with Mortimer's personality. He exhibits much personal courage, and if
he tends toward passionate excess, then so do most young men.
Unfortunately his Puritanical upbringing has forced him to re-
press the passionate side of his nature, so that when his sensual
life is awakened in Italy he takes the extreme step of changing
his religion. But this step in itself is not disastrous, nor even necessarily unhealthy. What is both unhealthy and disastrous for
Mortimer is that his Catholic teachers take advantage of his now
burgeoning passionateness to convince him that the word of the
Church outweighs even the most basic moral truths; he and his
cohorts, as he boasts to Mary (III.vi.2502–26), have received ab-

solution in advance for the most outrageous crimes, which he now fully intends to commit. Catholicism is not necessarily incompatible with morality, but something is fundamentally wrong with an institution in which such a thing as Mortimer's absolution in advance is even conceivable; and the audience is clearly not meant to have any special respect or sympathy for this institution. Protestantism, in its tendency toward repressiveness, is perhaps no better, but this does not justify Catholicism.

Mary herself, however, the heroine, whose personality unquestionably grows toward glory in the course of the play, not only insists on her Catholic religion at the end, but insists on precisely what makes that religion dangerous, its ceremoniousness, its outward trappings; and not only does she insist, but her wish is miraculously fulfilled even after she has succeeded in renouncing it. Why should this be?

A partial answer to this question is provided by the crucial idea of affirming fate, transforming it into one's personal creation. The highest freedom is achieved not in the assertion of "person" against "condition," but rather in the unification of the two by a voluntary or creative act, and the scene between Mary and Melvil is a symbolic enactment of this process. The Catholic Church, for the purposes of this scene, is an established order in the physical world, which bears to an individual primarily the relation of external authority (rather than inner conviction) and so belongs essentially to the realm of "condition." Mary, in her speech "ordaining" Melvil, is prepared to accept inner conviction and purity of heart as a substitute for actual priesthood, but this is a compromise apparently dictated by circumstances. What her heart truly desires (V.vii.3643) is a ceremony fulfilling in detail the strict physical requirements of the Church; and this, as I say, is a symbol of the unification of person and condition, will and fate. Mary's most earnest desire has become one with a submission to even the grossly arbitrary manifestations of external authority; and her desire, although the circumstances are contrived so as to make it practically absurd, is then immediately satisfied. This indicates allegorically that true freedom, the only possible successful assertion of personal will, lies in the insistence on external limitations, not in their removal. Hence also Schiller's stress on the negative aspect of Catholicism. If it were even remotely possible to equate Catholic belief with true morality, then by the same token it would be possible to regard Mary's insistence on Catholic ritual as the insistence on a universal law (hence an aspect of that universal reason which operates through "Person") rather than on a particular, arbitrary and definitely questionable condition. The purpose of the scene, however, or one purpose of it, is to suggest symbolically not the victory of person over condition but rather the unification of the two; the Church, not the prison, must function symbolically here as Mary's condition, to which universal validity is by definition not attributable.

I say that this scene "suggests symbolically" the union of person and condition, not that it depicts this union. In order to do the latter, Schiller would merely have had to let Mary submit willingly to her circumstances, i.e. to the absence of a priest. But the scene in this form would not have expressed the idea of free will. The free willing of external necessity is a strictly internal process which by nature cannot be depicted. If a situation is necessary, then it will occur whether or not the subject wills it, and there is no way for an observer (or a theater audience) to judge adequately concerning the subject's freedom; that a dramatic character, for example, says he wills his fate, does not of itself convince us that he is not simply making the best of his situation. But Mary's insistence upon Catholic ritual is an expression of free will, indeed outrageously so, since what she wills is apparently impossible; and yet the object of her will is not liberty, but rather full submission to what we know is an arbitrary and morally questionable external authority. Thus a symbol (not a realistically verifiable occurrence) of the union of free will with externally imposed order is created. And the miraculous fulfillment of Mary's desire expresses symbolically the idea that true salvation, or human self-realization, can be achieved only by way of such a union.

Thus *Maria Stuart* is meant to surpass *Wallenstein* in the direction of the idea of a union of person and condition, or will and fate. But how is this idea related to the question of drama and the situation of an audience in a theater? Why does Schiller, after finishing *Maria Stuart* and helping direct the first performance, write to Körner, "I am at last getting a handhold on drama and beginning to understand my craft" (16 June 1800)?

5

It has been remarked that there is a relationship in *Maria Stuart* between the outward ceremoniousness of Catholicism and the inescapable need of poetry for palpable symbols, but sufficient attention has not been paid to the more specific relation between Catholic ritual and the ritual art of drama.[15] Mortimer, in advocating the "power of art," inveighs against Protestantism's reverence for "the disembodied word" (I.vi.430–33), and the connection with verbal art—with the disembodied word of books, of degenerate "Schrift" (cf. *SA*, XVI, p. 124), as opposed to the embodied language of drama—is therefore easy enough to make. Moreover, it is quite clear that something of intellectual Germany's need for the physical, actionful art of drama reverberates in Mary's answer to Mortimer's description of his experience in Rome: "Spare me! No further. No longer unfold before me the vivid tapestry of life.—I am miserable and imprisoned" (451–53). The Germans, in their unfriendly clime, are also imprisoned—by their own inwardness and intellectuality—and unable to make contact with the full vital physicalness of art. One of Schiller's principal aims in all his aesthetic writings had been to justify art on moral and intellectual grounds, thus to reconcile its sensual playfulness with the characteristic over-seriousness of German thinking.

The Germans, in the general field of poetry, require the physical and communal art of drama in order to balance their habitual tendencies and complete their humanness; and the symbol of Catholic Mary stranded in Protestant England therefore has a deep affinity with the symbol of Iphigenie among the barbarians. Like Goethe's lady, Schiller's seeks her homeland "with her soul" (*Iph.*, l. 12), especially in Act III, scene i; as in Goethe, her wish to escape is apparently answered by the appearance of an enterprising young man, Mortimer corresponding to Pylades, who however suggests an immoral plan of action she must reject; like Iphigenie, moreover, Mary is a kind of priestess of reconciliation, who offers Elizabeth an opportunity for human growth similar to the opportunity offered Thoas. *Maria Stuart* is a tragic version of *Iphigenie*, a version in which the childless barbarian monarch proves intractable. But a deeper affinity between Goethe's play and Schiller's is the relation of the two heroines to the art of drama, which is even clearer in Mary's case than in Iphigenie's; for the character of Catholicism as a religion in which the physical performance of prescribed quasi-dramatic rituals assumes prime importance is not only mentioned but demonstrated, in the scene with Melvil. In both *Iphigenie* and *Maria Stuart*, therefore, the appearance of a helpless lady on a barbarian shore is associated with the problem of how true drama is to be introduced and developed among the intellectual Germans, for the sake of their human growth and wholeness. Nor, incidentally, is it unjustified that we associate the "barbaric" with excessive intellectuality or self-consciousness; Schiller himself, perhaps following Lessing,[16] says that man becomes a "barbarian, when his principles destroy his feelings" (*SA*, XII, p. 13).

The parallel between *Iphigenie* and *Maria Stuart* can be carried a bit further, for Goethe's emphasis on the moral questionableness of Greek history and attitudes corresponds to Schiller's on the morally negative aspect of Catholicism; and a function of this emphasis in both cases is to make clear to the German audience that they cannot simply become Greeks or Catholics in order to have a theater, that it would be wrong to try to alter significantly their own native situation, despite its apparent disadvantages; the example of Mortimer shows what such self-abandonment leads to. But if the German cultural situation is in a strong sense antidramatic—Schiller stresses this, and stretches history, by associating Protestantism in general (via Paulet) with the special discipline of Puritanism—how shall Germany have a true drama without altering its situation radically? The answer to this question suggested by *Maria Stuart* is essentially the same as that suggested by *Iphigenie*. We must realize our own native cultural situation as an artistic symbol glorifying mankind; we must learn to wield our own particular character self-consciously.

The expression of this idea is another aspect of the scene between Mary and Melvil. By the time Melvil reveals his priesthood, Mary has already succeeded in reconciling herself to the lack of a priest; she no longer needs an official Catholic ritual to provide her with comfort and mental equilibrium in her final moments. Therefore, as we observe the ritual of Confession and Communion taking place on the stage, we know all the while that Mary is inwardly one step beyond it, that she is submitting to it not blindly but consciously and freely, that she has transformed the ritual into a work of art, her own creative act. She had been prepared to "ordain" Melvil as her personal priest, and the fact that he has also been ordained officially only completes the paradox, the idea that one and the same situation can be both externally imposed and a free creative act, "at once our condition and our deed" (*SA*, XII, p. 102).

This is basically the idea of unifying will and fate, but now in a more advanced form, as the idea of transforming fate into a conscious artistic creation, and our task henceforward is to understand how this idea is incorporated into the theatrical experience. The problem can at least be defined by recognizing that there is meant to be a parallel between Mary's confession and the ritual of tragedy to which the audience is submitting. Confession is ordinarily a form of flagellation in which the individual confronts himself with the faultiness of his nature and condition in order to rise above it; but Schiller is not satisfied with the idea of flagellant tragedy, and his dissatisfaction is expressed in Mary's transcending the ordinary process of confession, her freely creative relation to the ritual with Melvil. We must express and confront ourselves honestly in the tragic theater, but our doing so must have the character of a free self-affirming activity, not the mere suffering which Schiller had earlier posited as the tragic spectator's primary response. We must, like Mary, freely glorify our humanity in the ritual itself, not merely by the purified state in which we emerge and ultimately dissociate ourselves from the ritual.

For Germans around 1800 tragic drama is an especially serious matter, because of their sense of need for a vitally communal art form as cultural cement (i.e. a national theater); and *Maria Stuart* is even more serious than most tragedies from the point of view of a German audience, because it presents symbolically the death of precisely that hope for vital self-completion which drama as a form offers. Leicester's scene in the locked room shows Mary's death as a mental event, the destruction of human wholeness by excessive, indecisive self-consciousness. For us, therefore, if we recognize in ourselves that over-intellectual, confusedly self-conscious tendency which lies at the root of the tragedy—and of course we do not need to be Germans in order to feel this—the play is a ritual of anguished confession. Yet if Mary's "example" is valid, we are also supposed to regard the play as a free and joyful creative act on our part. How is this to be accomplished? How, for us as we sit in the theater, is the play meant to be our affirmation of our own limited cultural attitudes and the realization of these attitudes as a conscious artistic image glorifying mankind?

This question cannot be answered except by understanding how the spectator at *Maria Stuart* is induced to regard the stage images and action as his own artistic endeavor, and we shall come

to this point further on. First, however, it is important to understand a bit more clearly the way in which this play supersedes
Wallenstein. Like *Wallenstein*, *Maria Stuart* approaches us
through our self-consciousness; it is meant to function as a kind of
confession for the audience, provided the audience recognizes in
Mary the symbol of man's hope for self-reconciliation in the most
general sense, that hope for perfect human integration which our
self-consciousness both engenders and thwarts. But in *Wallenstein* we are offered a way out—our experience of the tragedy as
tragedy (with Max) elevates and in a sense exempts us—whereas
in *Maria Stuart* there is no such relief; Schiller places us, by virtue
of our self-consciousness alone, in the position of Mary's killers,
and not merely Leicester's scene in the locked room, but in fact
the whole plot makes this clear. Elizabeth is a victim, not a villain;
her role is basically passive. The two characters whose actions
directly precipitate the crisis that destroys Mary are Leicester and
Mortimer, and these characters represent the two inevitable per-
versions of self-consciousness: the degeneration of character into
indecisive brooding (Leicester, "flabbiness, lack of character," in
the letter to Süvern), and the equally hopeless reaction against
this degeneration, which takes the form of violent enthusiasm
(Mortimer, *Schwärmerei*). Thus we are offered no way out; self-
consciousness, as Schiller assumes his audience is experiencing
it, necessarily degenerates, either in Leicester's direction or in
Mortimer's, and this degeneration destroys the hope represented
by Mary.

But Leicester and Mortimer are also Mary's two lovers, which
complicates the situation. It is not merely self-consciousness that
destroys the hope of personal integration, but self-consciousness
in the form of a desire to possess that hope, self-consciousness
striving to overcome its own anguished dividedness, either by
way of a hovering, quasi-aesthetic "determinability" (Leicester) or
by way of violent self-abandonment (Mortimer). Our hope of reconciliation with ourselves, therefore, is thwarted precisely by our
conscious desire to hold it fast, and this paradox has obvious
consequences with respect to our situation in the theater; it is
implied that our understanding and affirmation, as an audience,
of what Mary represents, necessitates the tragic development on
stage, the vision of hope's death, not its triumph. Perhaps, by yet
another paradox, the death of hope is even valuable to us; perhaps

human self-integration first becomes possible when we no longer
hope for it, no longer impede ourselves consciously. We shall
return to this point.

Maria Stuart, again, surpasses *Wallenstein* in what we have
seen to be the direction of *Egmont* or *Prinz Friedrich*. *Wallenstein*
leaves open a way out of the divisive aspect of self-consciousness; but *Maria Stuart*, like Goethe's play or Kleist's, represents for its audience an uncompromised intensification of self-
consciousness, an exacerbation of the inner tension and paradox
of existence to the point where it verges both on despair (since
hope dies with Mary) and on a new strength (since the destruction
of an impossible hope is presumably preferable to its perpetuation
in the mental equivalent of an English prison). Does this mean
that *Maria Stuart* is merely another type of flagellant tragedy?
Obviously not. Flagellant tragedy presents us either with an intolerable vision of fate (our condition), thus forcing us to take refuge
in the moral freedom of our "Person," or else (as in *Wallenstein*)
with an intolerable sense of self-consciousness in its negative aspect, thus forcing us to take refuge in our corresponding sense of
its ideal or positive aspect. But *Maria Stuart* leaves us no refuge; it
confronts us with a hopeless paradox inherent in our mode of
being, and yet it does not objectify this paradox in a figure like
Wallenstein, but rather requires us to experience it as the very
process of understanding the play. There is no refuge; the only
possible way to deal with the intolerable experience offered us by
Maria Stuart is to affirm it somehow as our own conscious artistic
creation. This defines our main interpretive problem: how is this
dramatic ritual of confession meant to be transformed into our free
act? How can the audience be placed in a creative relation to the
stage action and images?

Maria Stuart aims at a ritual intensification of its audience's
self-consciousness in two different but connected forms; the audience is meant to recognize, confess, and so transform into a free
creative act, both self-consciousness in general and also a particular set of "barbarically" intellectualized cultural attitudes which
to Schiller's mind compose the German character. If these two
objectives can be united and simultaneously compassed, then true
humanness and true Germanness will have been fused, or at least
Germanness will have revealed its basic human dimension.
Germanness, in the theater, will have achieved the status of a true

culture—not merely a condition, a set of external limitations and unthinking habits by which individuals are chained to a meaningless social order, but rather a unification of condition and person, the constantly reinitiated process through which individuals both accept and actively create their community, and through which the community, as represented by the group in the theater, thus shapes itself and rises above nature to bring forth its own authentically human world.

And yet, must we not ask whether such an accomplishment is even conceivable, in the light of what Mary's alien presence among the English suggests about the relation between drama and German society? Can the Germans conceivably achieve true culture in the theater, when the communicativeness of theater appears to presuppose not only a certain un-German openness to the physical, but also exactly that communal cohesion which is yet to be created? Among the Germans, with their intellectual veneration of "the disembodied word" (as opposed to the Word made flesh, which is suggested both by the transsubstantiated elements of the Catholic Eucharist and by the physical realization of poetry in the theater), how can drama even begin to have meaning?

Schiller meets this problem by recognizing that it does not really exist. Again Mary's example is the key, in particular her alienated situation as a Catholic imprisoned in a Protestant land. An extreme situation, in which it becomes practically impossible to cleave to one's native cultural allegiance, is the situation most favorable to a *proper* relationship with one's culture (by which the culture becomes both condition and person, thus the union of the two); for such a situation gives one the opportunity to affirm one's ingrained attitudes as a free act, rather than accept them as routine. Under these conditions, moreover, the culture itself flourishes most perfectly; Catholicism in France and Italy, where it is taken for granted, produces beauty but has a tendency toward corruption, which we see via Mortimer, whereas Catholic ritual as practiced by Mary in prison is a sublime assertion of human freedom, which is what culture (man's victory over nature) ought to be.

Thus it follows, by the parallel between Mary and the audience, that an important part of the play's meaning is formed by the fact that it is a play. If German spectators appreciate this fact properly, then the conscious distance it interposes between them and their own cultural situation becomes the opportunity for a more authentic exercise of their culture. In the culturally inhospitable environment of the theater, and perhaps only in such an environment, German Protestant intellectuality can achieve that self-conscious activeness and human intensity with which Mary endows Catholic ritual.

This point, that the Germans *can* conceivably have a theater in which their Germanness is affirmed, must of course remain speculative until we have seen how Schiller does place his audience in a creative relation to the stage; but it is interesting that Schiller himself builds this speculation into the structure of his work. The historical event used in the plot took place less than a decade before the first known performance of a play by Shakespeare, thus on the eve of what many educated Germans of Schiller's day considered the greatest age of drama since ancient Greece; and this fact is important because at least since Herder, who makes the point with specific reference to Shakespeare, it had been commonplace to think of poetic works and movements as sprouting organically from their native cultural soil.[17] By depicting the age of Elizabeth, especially in a theatrical work, Schiller is describing at least one possible historical matrix of great drama; and what he describes is not an age of energetic, burgeoningly whole men, not an age populated by Shakespearean heroes, but rather a degenerate age, corrupted by self-consciousness, an age in which, as Leicester unworthily admits, heroic strength has fallen prey to brooding and intrigue, quite literally (given the importance of documents in the plot) an "inkslinging age," an age, therefore, which exhibits significant similarities to what the Germans of Schiller's day are dissatisfied with in their own age. And yet the age of Elizabeth then surpassed and immortalized itself in the field of drama, perhaps not so much in spite of its apparent disadvantages as because of them. Again, it is suggested that precisely the superficial nontheatricality of a particular community can make theater a valid and valuable instrument of cultural expression. Schiller had earlier proclaimed, "If we ever had a national theater, we would become a nation thereby," and had stipulated "patriotic content in drama" (*SA*, XI, p. 98) as the prerequisite for such a national stage; now, however, it dawns on him that at least in the case of Germany, a properly conceived drama can effect cultural consolidation and vitalization merely by being drama, by virtue precisely of the incongruity between its form and the temperament of its audience.

But what does this cultural consolidation entail for the spectator? Will he now be a fundamentally improved human being? Given the system of parallels discussed so far, we can approach this question by way of the effect on Mary of her apparent purification in the ritual with Melvil. Let us look, in particular, at her last words. The last words of any tragic character are important, but the last words of Mary Stuart, who is depicted as undergoing a rigorous education for death, will be subject to specially close scrutiny by an audience. And yet these words do not express peaceful reconciliation; they are a thinly veiled and highly effective verbal *attack* on Leicester: "Farewell, and, if you can, live happily! You were the suitor of two queens; you have scorned and betrayed a tenderly loving heart in order to win a proud one. Go kneel at Elizabeth's feet! May your reward not turn out to be a punishment! Farewell! I have finished with this earth" (V.ix.3832–38). The words "if you can," and the idea of kneeling before a proud lady whose favor is really a punishment, are deliberate barbs—which, incidentally, had been missing earlier in Mary's last message to Elizabeth (V.viii.3781–86). The speech, moreover, is spoken before witnesses, including Leicester's worst enemy, Burleigh—a circumstance Schiller could easily have avoided if he had wished—and Mary knows perfectly well (see V.i.3411–13) that if she succeeds in scoring a hit on Leicester, if her words produce any sign of emotional vulnerability on his part, this will tend to discredit him and place him in real personal danger. Her last speech, again, is an attack, and she thus dies not as an angel but as a human being; if she is now reconciled to herself, it is to her human self as she is and has been that she is reconciled, not to some idealized abstract. To the very last she is the passionate Mary Stuart, who can forgive practically anything— her own death, for example, at the hands of Elizabeth—but cannot forgive a false lover, not even for the sake of an oath (V.vii.3691) sworn to a priest who has been sent directly by the Pope himself.

This ending is important especially because it says something about the effectiveness of the ritual performed by Melvil, hence also about the humanizing effect of drama on its audience. For us, as we sit in the theater, the drama is a kind of confession; it is our ritual confrontation with a serious fault in our way of being.

But the experience of the play does not eliminate our fault, any more than the experience of confession eliminates Mary's; what it does is provide us with a certain conscious relation to ourselves by which we are enabled to wield our unaltered character artistically. Mary's speech to Leicester, again,is an expression of her passionateness, and yet not a helpless, convulsive expression like the attack on Elizabeth in Act III by which she demeans herself; it is, rather, a controlled expression by which she humanizes and ennobles herself. This is what drama is meant to do for us, not to change us but to place our character into our own hands, as a tool for self-expression and self-development, not merely a condition to which we are subject.

Or in general cultural terms, Mary's example shows that the aim of her drama is not to free us *from* our particular cultural situation but rather to free us *for* it, for a more authentic, essentially artistic commitment to it. The spectator is meant not to become "human" in an ideally purified sense but rather to remain as German as ever, if not more so; he is meant to enjoy the freedom of experiencing his own limited condition as a deliberate creative act. Only mediately, by way of his affirmed Germanness, is the spectator's humanness purified, in that he now experiences the union of person and condition; only by being truly a German (his condition) does he become more fully human.

These ideas, at this stage in the argument, are still speculative, but their history in Schiller's intellectual development can be traced quite clearly. In his earliest major essay on the subject, Schiller had imagined the effect of drama as a triumph of pure nature, "when men from all circles and regions and classes, throwing off the fetters of affectation and fashion, torn free from the oppression of fate, joined anew in *one* all-encompassing sympathy, dissolved anew into *one* race, forget themselves and the world, and draw near to their heavenly origin" (*SA*, XI, p. 100). And this idea of universal human brotherhood—which recalls Wilhelm Meister's naive enthusiasm in the *Sendung*—remains essentially unchanged in the *Briefe*, where the promise of the sixth letter, that human "totality" can be restored by "a higher art," is answered in the twentieth letter by the idea of the aesthetic state, a "state of real and active determinability" (*SA*, XII, p. 78). It is true that in the *Briefe* Schiller is talking not about freedom from particular cultural prejudices but about a state of indeterminacy balanced between two universal forces, the sensual and the rational. But the latter idea includes the former; the "step backwards" (*SA*, XII, p. 77) which art makes us take, out of an imperfectly rational state into a sort of limbo (the aesthetic state) from which we can begin the business of self-determination all over again, is evidently also an escape from our everyday cultural limitedness. The spectator in a theater is meant to feel himself man as such, with no allegiance to anything else.

Even in *Wallenstein*, where Schiller calls into question the dramatic implications of his own aesthetics, the situation is not substantially different. Wallenstein's attempt to maintain a state of uncommitted determinability, as an enjoyable but delusive image of human freedom, is not set up as a model. But it is meant nonetheless to reflect our inner situation as we sit in the theater, our aesthetic mood; only thus can it make us aware of a tragic potential in our own nature, in that necessary self-consciousness by which we first experience our being in a human way. The presupposition, in other words, is still that at least for the short time we sit in the theater, we are nothing but man, undergoing directly that fruitful but dangerous state of limitless determinability which is deducible from the facts of our existence but is present in our normal experience only as a dimly sensed undertone.

In *Maria Stuart*, however, a crucial development has taken place. Wallenstein is replaced by Leicester and in this form is relegated to a subordinate, inglorious role. The mirror that is held up to the audience now contains the image not of a *state* (like Wallenstein's or Leicester's determinability) but of an *action*, Mary's creative insistence upon the limited external authority to which she submits; this action is in progress even in Act I, where Mary has already begun, in the conversation with Kennedy, to translate the judgment upon her into her own terms, to re-create it in a form she can affirm, as payment for her real guilt (I.iv.321–22). And the inference, evidently, is that the audience, as they sit in the theater and are reflected in that mirror, are assumed to be carrying out an action of their own, a decisive self-limiting action like Mary's. This is what Schiller suggests later in the essay on the chorus when he says that art makes us free. True human freedom is not contained in a general state of determinability (*Wallenstein* already teaches this lesson, without incorporating it in form) but rather exists only in the particular self-determining action itself, and this action must somehow actually be taking place in the auditorium. We are not free in that we are *able* to determine ourselves, but only in that we actually *do* this.

Before attempting to follow this idea further into the structure of *Maria Stuart*, let us note that it implies a deep affinity with Lessing's *Nathan*. For Lessing man's proper excellence is a universal reason by which he is elevated above the limits of his particular culture or religion; but at the same time, true wisdom recognizes and promotes by irony the necessity that a man nevertheless belong to a particular culture, and a limited cultural allegiance (provided it is employed actively rather than followed slavishly) is in turn the indispensable instrument by which human reason is realized in the world. Both this thinking and the basic structure of symbols by which it is expressed, a clash of opposed religions, are picked up in *Maria Stuart*; and in fact, not long after finishing this play, Schiller did his own stage version of *Nathan*.

6

Although we have seen what is meant to happen in the auditorium at a performance of *Maria Stuart*, we have not yet seen how it is meant to happen. Mary is set up as a model, and if we are serious-minded, I suppose we may cast about for ways to follow her example. But is there anything in the work's poetic structure by which we are given the sense that our presence in the theater *already* constitutes a following of her example, a transforming of our externally imposed situation into a free creative act?

Maria Stuart both refers and appeals to certain culturally determined attitudes which the German of Schiller's day would be likely to recognize as belonging to his own make-up. But the poetic meaning of the play does not depend on the Germanness of its audience. If the spectator happens to be a German, and if he happens to understand that the plot, the strangling of human hope by self-consciousness, represents a characteristically German mental process, then his sense of participating in the creation of the tragedy will be automatically transmuted into a sense of creating artistically his own Germanness; he will be as deeply aware of the faults of Germanness as he is of the faults of Catholicism, and he will overcome these faults by a deliberate act of affirmative self-determination. This process, however, is secondary and not essential to the play's meaning. Of primary importance is that the spectator, any spectator, be maneuvered into the position of an active creator with respect to the artistic construct; if this is not accomplished, the play cannot have cultural significance anyway, in the sense in which we have defined it.

Schiller approaches his task largely by way of thematic structure, and it is thus necessary to form a precise idea of what the play's main theme is. The opposition between appearance and reality is of course important, as is that between verbal and sensual knowledge and that between true and apparent freedom; but the governing theme, from which these others radiate, is the opposition between feeling and opinion in relation to truth.

In Act I this theme is developed mainly in connection with the question of Mary's guilt. We recognize at the beginning that Paulet is a man of thoroughly sound moral character, and that he has no use whatever for Mary, whom he sees with "a crucifix in her hand, vainglory and worldly lust in her heart" (I.i.142–43). But in the conversation with Mary that follows, his unkind remark about her willingness to trust men (I.ii.177–79) has no effect on her at all; obviously she does not feel guilty in the sense in which he considers her guilty. He himself, though his tone remains self-righteous, does not venture to attack her again until she expresses directly her personal respect for him (I.iii.252–53)—in contrast to her initial distaste for Mortimer—and his retort at this point smacks of self-defense (256–61); he seems to be taking special care not to let himself drift into anything like a cordial or sympathetic relationship with her. Mary does not bother to defend herself against Paulet, but Paulet feels called upon to defend himself against Mary; thus her position, her inner certainty, appears clearly the stronger, and Paulet's opinion of her, despite his own uprightness, is revealed as questionable.

In the very next scene, however, alone with Kennedy, Mary positively insists on her guilt; and again it is essentially human opinion against which she asserts her inner feeling. Kennedy lists every possible consideration on the basis of which men in general might reasonably regard her guilt as a thing of the past, but Mary, as with Paulet, refuses to be moved. In the first four scenes, then, we are presented with Mary as a defender of the truth of feeling against the distortions of opinion. She stands fast against both a typical opinion of her guilt and a typical opinion of her innocence. She is guilty, but not as Paulet imagines; and if she is also innocent, her innocence is not exactly what Kennedy has in mind.

Then comes the scene with Mortimer, which is important because it reveals the flimsiness of human opinion by showing the mechanism of its genesis. Mortimer claims to have abandoned "error" (I.vi.487) and arrived at truth, but his own account of his conversion makes painfully clear that this is nothing but a primitive psychological convulsion in him, a typical youthful reaction against his upbringing. Opinion is here revealed not only in its ill-foundedness but also in its dangerousness, for precisely Mortimer's radical change of opinion, his direct experience of the changeableness of opinion, is evidently part of what now makes him so desperately insistent upon the truth of his new opinions; opinion is delusive, but our awareness of this only drives us further into delusion. The absurdity of Mortimer's intellectual position becomes especially clear when he tells how he has checked up on the authenticity of Mary's claim to the English throne (525–33), as if French jurists and historians could give him unbiased information. Mary herself, happy as she is to receive news from the Continent, becomes impatient at this point (534–35).

And now, after Mortimer has reported the judgment of the special court and so removed any possible suspense in this regard, comes Mary's dispute with Burleigh, which is concerned not with truth itself so much as with the validity of the opinions of particular people in particular situations. The basic question that arises is the question of how men can possibly make decisions in the real world. We have been shown clearly that opinion is by nature unreliable, and Mary produces a specific argument against the reliability of her forty-two judges (I.vii.762–86). But on the other hand, what *should* the English do in this situation? I think it is meant to be obvious that Mary has in fact been conspiring with representatives of Spain (929–30; cf. I.vi.608); her denial of this charge (935) is cleverly equivocal, in that it refers only to Burleigh's doubtless exaggerated assertion that she has incited "all the kings of Europe" (933) against England, and in the rest of her speech (935–58) she practically admits that she has developed her political power wherever possible. Should Elizabeth set free a clever and powerful claimant to her throne? Burleigh's speech about the excellence of the forty-two (737–61) is not without weight; these judges may not be exercising "justice" (798) in exactly the sense Mary requires, but on the other hand their judgment is by no means irresponsible.

The point is that decisions in the real world *must* rest on the shaky basis of opinion. Schiller himself points out that even the most dedicated idealist becomes a realist as soon as he wishes to carry out a particular action, for any action in the real world must be based on empirical judgment, on opinions concerning presupposable facts and expectable results. Mary can remain as steadfast as she likes against the influence of opinion on her inner sense of truth; the judgment of the forty-two may be highly questionable and in some respects manifestly unjust. But the fact remains that the judgment against Mary is not uncommonly arbitrary, not essentially different from any judgment on which real decisions are based. The question of whether Parliament has jurisdiction over Mary symbolizes the larger question of whether there is any such thing as "jurisdiction" in the first place, whether it is possible in general to base any real decision upon an unchallengeably valid judgment; and the answer to this question is no. Action presupposes empirical opinion, and opinion is by nature untrustworthy.

Then, finally, in the last scene of Act I, the idea of public opinion is introduced, the totally unreliable, truly irresponsible, but immensely powerful "Meinung" (I.viii.1015) of people in general, of "die Welt" (1019). This idea is important because it reminds us that opinion is not only the necessary basis of judgment in reality but also a factor which judgment must take into account. Opinion, as it operates in the political world, is doubly unreliable because it must include opinions about opinions, and in fact the clash and confusion of opinions about opinions (i.e., what public reaction can be expected in various contingencies) then constitutes a large part of the debate in Act II, scene iii, involving Burleigh, Shrewsbury, and Leicester. Thus we are presented with the image of a fundamentally unsound order of reality, a world fabric which not only engenders opinion but also includes this mercurial entity as a constitutive element. As soon as we leave nature behind and begin to act and build as rational men, as soon as we create civilization and polity, we discover that we have brought forth for ourselves a swiftly changing, frighteningly unpredictable world in which precisely the highest and most inflexible products of our reason, our ideas of the good and the true, are of no more immediate use to us than a suit of armor to a swimmer.

This is the world which then unfolds in all its dubious glory in Act II, and later reveals itself even more profoundly in Act IV, the world dominated by Elizabeth. If Mary resists opinion, Elizabeth is exactly the opposite in character; she opens herself so completely to the world of conflicting and confusing opinions that she becomes incapable of doing anything at all. Her weakness is that she thinks even of herself only as she exists in the opinion of others. At the beginning of Act II we find her engaged in a grotesquely complicated attempt to manipulate her image in the mind of the French envoys, and in the debate about Mary, as well as in the proposal to Mortimer, she is concerned mainly with how she will appear. This weakness, this wish to exist as a favorable image in all other minds, without committing herself to any specific course of action, is what makes her susceptible to Leicester's argument that she should meet Mary, and then to his thoroughly transparent stratagem in Act IV. Elizabeth, in her own eyes, *is* what others think of her; she signs Mary's death warrant with the words: "Am I a bastard, you say? Wretch! I am a bastard only as long as *you* live and breathe. All doubt about my royal birth is obliterated as soon as I obliterate *you*. As soon as there is no alternative for the Britisher, I shall have been born of a legitimate bed!" (IV.x.1343–48). Perhaps there is some common sense in the idea that Mary alive can always come to represent a choice for the British people. But basically Elizabeth proposes to eliminate the fact that in a sense she is a bastard by eliminating the mind that considers her a bastard. Fact itself, for Elizabeth, is merely a function of opinion.

If the whole civilized world is a treacherous place, as it were riddled with false opinion, then that particular place where Elizabeth sets the tone is even more treacherous than necessary; and it is in Elizabeth's England that Mary attempts to retain her dignity and self-respect by clinging to her own feeling of herself. But is feeling sufficient defense against the world's confusion? A major purpose of Act III is to show that it is not. Within the thematic structure of the play, Mary's joy at the beginning of Act III is derived from an apparently sound logical proposition. If the world becomes treacherous because of the way people think about it, why should the individual not rescue himself from its treachery

by insisting on the validity of his own feeling, by simply creating
his own private world? "I want to dream myself free and happy.
Why wake me from this sweet delusion?" (III.i.2089–90). But
clearly this is an excess, a weakness as great as Elizabeth's. If
Elizabeth, encouraged by her people's adoration, has gone to the
extreme of seeking to create a flattering image of herself in
everyone's mind, then Mary, encouraged by her successful resistance against Paulet, Burleigh, and even Kennedy, has gone to the
extreme of insisting that her own feeling assume the status of
reality. And she quickly pays for this error, for it puts her off her
guard. What Paulet and Burleigh think of her had not troubled her
in the least, but Elizabeth's gloating now proves too much, especially in the presence of Leicester; she reacts to the opinion of
herself now hurled at her by bursting out violently and in effect
killing herself. The firm reliance on feeling thus eventually leads
to an excess by which we are exposed all the more helplessly to
the treacherous world.

The remainder of Act III shows that an insistence upon the
validity of feeling is as much a cause of confusion as the unreliability of opinion. First Mortimer arrives, wrapped up in his feeling
of himself as Mary's lover, and succeeds in creating for Mary a
situation even more chaotically hopeless than the one she herself
has brought about by her weakness. Then Mortimer's plans in turn
are ruined by his ally Sauvage, who acts upon the inner drive to
become a martyr. Our feeling, our sense of the truth about ourselves, can counteract the emotional effect upon us of the world's
opinions; but when it is translated into action, this feeling produces chaos, precisely because it disdains opinion, cares for nothing but itself, does not bother to take externals into account.

Thus we are shown a very bleak picture of things in general, but
a picture which by rights ought to have a positive aspect. We are
shown that the civilized world is a treacherous place in which to
exist, but we are also shown that its treacherousness is man-made,
resulting from the functioning of human opinion. We are shown
that feeling is dangerous and disorderly in the sphere of action,
but we are also reminded that our feeling of ourselves, our self-
consciousness, which gives rise to the possibility of will, is reliable evidence of our ultimate freedom: "As soon as you wish, in
any instant, you can prove that your will is free" (II.iii.1332–33). If
the world, at least as it affects us, is man-made, if we are the

creators of our world, and if, in addition, we are truly free, it follows that we are capable theoretically of creating a better world, a genuine human order in things.

The question is: How? Empirical judgment falls short, and the individual's uncompromising assertion of his feeling overshoots the mark. How are we to realize the potential that seems by logic to inhere in our relation, even our present relation, with the world? An answer to this question is suggested at the play's true climax—the scene with Melvil[18]—in Mary's idea of the Church: "It is the high, holy Church which raises us a ladder to heaven; it is called universal, or catholic, because only the faith of all other men strengthens our own faith; where thousands worship and pay honor, the glow bursts into flame and the spirit takes wing for highest heaven" (V.vii.3607–13). As in *Egmont*, the only immediate source of validity for an idea or belief is its *communal* status. To the need for energetic self-consciousness in *Egmont* corresponds the idea, clearly derivable from the treatment of the themes of opinion and freedom in *Maria Stuart*, that no belief is justified except by being transformed into a free act. But according to Mary, the difference between a shared and an unshared belief is crucial; a "catholic" belief changes its very nature, as it were bursts into flame, takes on the quality of truth which supersedes opinion and feeling and heals the world.

Is this anything more than a dream? Catholicism as an institution is not advocated in the play. Does that truly free unanimity of belief which Mary envisions ever actually happen, in such a way as to order and heal our world? The answer is that, to a limited extent, it is happening here and now, in the theater; as in *Egmont*, we understand the full meaning of the play only by understanding what we are doing as an audience. The fictional world that unfolds on the stage derives its reality, its order, its very being, solely from the unanimous belief of those assembled to view it, and the belief of each spectator, as is suggested in Mary's speech, is strengthened by the belief of the whole company. It is true that we are not fooled by what happens on the stage; we do not react to it in the same way we react to what we see happening in the street. But this is precisely the point, that the stage-reality is created knowingly, hence freely, unlike our everyday reality (the opinion-corrupted world of civilization) which is also created by the way we think of it, but is created blindly and chaotically. What happens in the theater is a foretaste of what ought to happen in the world: the free artistic creation, by communal belief, of a fully human order—not merely an abstract ordering force like custom or law or morals, but an artificial order which yet appears before our eyes as something closely resembling the fullness of reality itself.

Hence the central artistic paradox in the play. The fictional world is presented as fundamentally unsound and disordered, a treacherous reality composed of unreliable opinions and ungoverned feelings. But the artistic form of the play, by contrast, is exceptionally polished, compact, and symmetrical. The verse shows few irregularities and often breaks into rhyme; indeed, in Act III, scene i, Mary speaks in rhymed near-stanzas. The acts form a perfect Chinese-box structure, with Acts I and V belonging to Mary, Acts II and IV to Elizabeth, and Act III showing their meeting. The arrangement and entrances of characters often assume dancelike patterns; in Act III Mary shocks Elizabeth with an unexpected outburst, whereupon Mortimer shocks Mary with an unexpected emotional assault, whereupon Okelly shocks Mortimer with unexpected news; and the debate in Act II, scene iii, is built on a perfect symmetry of opinions, Burleigh versus Shrewsbury with Leicester in the middle. The form of the play could hardly be more orderly; the world depicted could hardly be less so. Shall we speak, then, of a discrepancy between form and content?

In fact we do not have to. Form and content in *Maria Stuart* are perfectly coordinated in that they represent the two principal aspects of a single basic truth, the truth that conscious, rational man is ultimately the creator of the world he lives in. The play's fiction shows the negative aspect of this truth, a world undermined by the vicissitudes of opinion and the unaccountability of feeling, whereas the play's form reveals the corresponding positive aspect, the orderly perfection brought forth by a company of men (the audience) who agree freely to have their opinions and feelings in common, an order, moreover, which projects itself as a world to which the audience's unanimity lends immediate realness. By making the spectator aware, via the fiction, of his share of responsibility for the world's disorder, Schiller seeks also to make him aware of his corresponding indispensableness in the creation of the orderly human ritual of the theater. This is how drama is meant to "*make* men free." The audience in a theater is carrying out, on a limited scale, the free act of human self-determination, the creation of a valid, limited order in the face of the ever-potential chaos that characterizes the human world, and *Maria Stuart* is constructed in such a way as to to maximize the spectator's awareness of this.

This interpretation eliminates the contradiction between the play's form and its content, but it does not eliminate the paradox, the feeling of strain between form and content, which serves the important aesthetic purpose of drawing the audience's attention to the artificiality of the proceeding. Without the feeling of thorough artificiality, via that high stylization which is set off by the content, the spectator could not possibly be induced to regard himself as a participant in the creation of the artistic construct. Thus Schiller not only displays the artificiality of the theater, but he now weaves it into the fabric of his work, in that the tension between form and content, by which the work's artificiality is made to reveal itself as such, also expresses the two-sidedness of the idea that generates the work's main theme, including the notion that even our normal reality is man-made, blunderingly artificial, itself an unperfected work of art.

One important question remains, which brings us back to the beginning of our discussion of Schiller: Why is *Maria Stuart* a tragedy? If the audience are meant to understand that here and now, in the theater, they have in a sense solved the problem of human existence, that they are engaged in a free act of creative self-determination as a community, then why does the fictional world not reflect and depict this achievement, why does it show the death instead of the triumph of hope? The answer to this question emerges from a clear idea of the freedom the audience experiences. True freedom, once again, is neither the self-indulgence of inaction (Leicester) nor the violent action of uncompromising self-assertion (Mortimer) but rather the deliberate act of self-*limitation*—again, we experience our perfected humanity only mediately, by way of an affirmation of our own limited cultural condition—and the tragicness of *Maria Stuart* is meant to be felt as constituting an act of self-limitation on the part of the audience. Once we in the audience understand our role as participants in the creation of the artistic edifice, it follows that if hope's triumph were depicted on stage, it would represent a self-magnification or self-universalization on our part, not a self-limitation; we would be attempting to experience our perfected humanity directly, not mediately. Hence the tragedy. Mary, when she submits to the ritual of confession, has already in spirit transcended her Catholicism, but now affirms it unreservedly nonetheless; so also the audience, as an artistically self-creating community, have transcended the self-conscious death of hope, and so also they submit to this form of the tragic nonetheless, as the seal of their achievement. We might compare Kleist's *Prinz Friedrich*, where the triumph of hope in a sense is depicted, but where—for essentially the same reason that moves Schiller to remain within the bounds of the tragic—this triumphant vision must be tempered by deep irony.

Thus it is possible for the spectator to see in Mary a model for himself, yet also wholeheartedly affirm her tragic fate. The hope for fulfilled human totality, if we cling to it, necessarily involves a concept of such totality, which concept, by our hoping, is exposed to the divisive process of self-consciousness and degenerates in either Leicester's direction or Mortimer's. Only by hope's death, only by an act of free but strict self-limitation—the German's affirmation of his Germanness, the spectator's freely embracing the tragic plot as his own creation—can our full humanness be achieved. Mary, like Christ on the cross, dies for us, and the whole play in the end turns out to be a secularized ritual of communion as well as of confession (so that its reflection in the scene with Melvil becomes still more complete), a Last Supper at which the total humanity symbolized by Mary is lost to our sight, but by the same token incorporated in our being. Schiller has therefore solved the problem of his theoretical writings; there is no longer any need for the audience to resist or transcend the tragic aspect of the tragedy, and the dramatic work of art has at last been made a coherent and undividedly communicative unity. Schiller has learned his "craft."

But is true human order found only in art? How is the transition to be made between the play's poetic meaning and its intended cultural significance, between the spectator's free creative participation in the ritual and his development of a creative relation to his culture at large? The content of *Maria Stuart* suggests at least the possibility of such a transition. In the foreground, in the words and actions of the main characters, we discern mainly the tendency of the human world toward disorder; but in the background we constantly feel the presence of two huge, cohesive, communal human entities, the polity of England and the Church of Rome, and Schiller emphasizes repeatedly that both these entities are founded on the genuine belief (though not necessarily the free belief) of large numbers of people. In the real world civilization's tendency toward disorder is balanced by at least a tendency toward order; if creative unanimity of thought and feeling, in a form at least distantly related to what we experience in the theater, were not also a phenomenon in the real world, it would be impossible for anything like England or the Catholic Church to come into being. In the theater, then, the orderly aspect of human rationality is not merely deduced from first principles but also extracted from the confusion of real experience, as it were by filtration, in order to be sublimated and re-actualized as a communal artistic process. As a theater audience we experience in a purer form something which is already an integral part of our experience in general, and the idea of adopting an artistically creative attitude toward our everyday condition does not involve quite so much of a leap as it at first seems to.

The cultural, the philosophical, the dramaturgical implications all fit together in the end, and this fitting together reflects a brilliant and exceptionally comprehensive unity in the conception of *Maria Stuart*. Again, as in the case of the neo-mythical and neo-heroic, we cannot assert that the play succeeds in its intention, for to do so would involve unverifiable psychological assumptions about real audiences. But the intention, the design, is unquestionably grand, and grand, evidently, in essentially the same way as that of *Egmont* or *Nathan* or *Prinz Friedrich*, grand in what I think we may now confidently call the characteristic manner of the German dramatic movement.

7

After finishing *Maria Stuart*, Schiller says that he is now beginning to master the "craft" of drama. He has succeeded now in integrating the complex situation of an audience—which includes both detachment and involvement, both distance and sympathy, both a sense of reality and an awareness of the artificial—into the inner poetic and symbolic structure of his work. Now the experience of an audience (at least the envisioned experience) is no longer merely a preparation for freedom but has become freedom itself, and as such is identical with the work's deepest intention, which is now fulfilled directly by the community in the auditorium, not merely by a presumed reaction inside the mind of the individual spectator.

Now Schiller feels free to flex his muscles artistically as he never had before. He finishes *Maria Stuart* with a strikingly artificial formal polish, and the scene with Melvil, the crux of the play's meaning, comes close to being an obvious authorial intrusion. It is a highly improbable scene—Mary expresses eloquently her need for an authentic Catholic ritual, whereupon her interlocutor turns out to have been secretly ordained a priest—and if the play is considered merely a portrayal of human interaction, it is an unnecessary scene. But at this point in the play a sense of authorial intrusion is perhaps appropriate, for the aim is to provide the spectator with a sense of his own creative freedom relative to the vision; the author's intrusion reminds us of the play's createdness, hence of our own part in its creation. Now, in other words, the theater is being used as a theater, with something like full poetic exploitation of its complex nature.

Schiller never attempts what one could call radical irony in the theater, but it is significant that with *Maria Stuart* (not with *Wallenstein*) he begins moving in the direction of theatrical experimentation; realistic probability becomes less important and ironic devices of various sorts, calling attention to the theater's artificiality, become more prominent. In *Die Jungfrau von Orleans* the supernatural is introduced; *Die Braut von Messina*, with its choruses, is almost aggressively artificial; the performance of *Wilhelm Tell* is meant to become a kind of festival for the audience, a festival in which our participation is rendered only more significant by our understanding of the questionableness of Tell's inner state and of our own; and *Demetrius* was to have been a drama about an impersonator, thus calling attention even by its subject matter to the artificiality of what the actors are doing on the stage. Schiller—in a sense by way of his aesthetic writings, and in a sense in spite of them—has learned his craft and is now aware of his obligation to make advances in it.

The last plays, from *Jungfrau* on, embody the difficult quest for a new dramatic idiom. Schiller's sense of the corruptness of the present age necessitates tragedy as his basic dramatic mode; even satire is inadequate, for the corruptness of the age is not primarily political or social but metaphysical, a corruptness in the category of consciousness by which man is related to his own self. Therefore all the early tragedies have to do with consciousness as a theme or idea, whereupon *Wallenstein* attempts to use self-consciousness as the primary vehicle of the tragic; and finally in *Maria Stuart,* Schiller's crowning achievement takes the form of something very close to *Egmont,* an exploitation of theatrical artificiality in order both to indict and to justify the audience's self-consciousness. But where shall Schiller go now? The achievement of *Maria Stuart* involves something like a supersession of his own tragic vision. Now new forms and even a new sort of vision are required; and these are the objects of Schiller's quest in the uneven groping of the last plays.

8 Breakthrough in Theory: The Philosophical Background of Modern Drama

The influence of nineteenth-century German philosophy on modern literature in general, and on modern drama in particular, will probably not be disputed. The idea of the Dionysian, for example, often in forms Nietzsche would hardly have recognized, has had considerable impact. Individual dramatic figures in conspicuous variety—Liolà, Sigismund, the Hairy Ape, Sorge's Beggar, Baal, Caligula, Wedekind's Keith, Christy Mahon—embody aspects or interpretations of this idea, and the absurdist strain in modern drama includes a tendency toward "Dionysian" questioning of the distinction between subject and object. The dramatic theory of *The Birth of Tragedy* has exercised only a limited direct influence, mainly because it has not been understood; but the idea of the Dionysian, even superficially considered, obviously suggests drama as a form for its expression, for it includes the idea of the communal as opposed to the individual, the idea of art as a revitalized public ritual, the idea of transcending the realistic tendency of nineteenth-century narrative.

1

It seems to me that the inherent dramatic tendency of the Dionysian as an idea is typical for much of the intellectual material bequeathed to modern literature by the German philosophical tradition, and that the existence of this tendency is related to the existence of a flourishing German drama in the Classical period. I will argue, for example, that the theory of drama implied in *The Birth of Tragedy* is a direct development from Schiller, and that its spirit also informs Nietzsche's later critical and dithyrambic works, of which the impact on modern literature—in such diverse authors as Andreyev, Shaw, Brecht,[1] as well as in Strindberg and the German expressionists—is more clearly marked. Nineteenth-century German philosophy is an important *shaping force* in modern drama—not merely a source of content or ideas—and it assumes this function because of its fundamental relationship with the German dramatic movement.

The intellectual climate of Europe toward the end of the nineteenth century is composed largely of philosophical uncertainty and philosophical iconoclasm, tendencies most clearly represented by the two great anti-Hegelian Hegelians, Kierkegaard and Nietzsche: Kierkegaard, the self-questioning philosopher, at home in the inward depths beneath simple sayings and doings, the philosopher of irony: Nietzsche, the philosopher of the heights, who despises the depths, the philosopher of outrageous aphorisms which defy questioning and condense into hammer-blows upon the idols and ideas of the age.[2] Uncertainty and iconoclasm constitute, as it were, a co-ordinate system on which the intellectual life of nineteenth- and twentieth-century Europe can be plotted. The secularized world of the Enlightenment is still with us, but we no longer have an Enlightenment confidence in reason and progress; therefore we grasp at straws, faith in art or science or the class-struggle, faith in the sanctified Philistinism of D. F. Strauss or the sanctified atavism of Wagner, faith in any number of "gods that fail." And yet, our uncertainty also makes us philosophically hypersensitive, so every intellectual advance assumes exaggerated proportions. Darwin, Marx, and Freud, soberly considered, are excellent critics of their respective scientific traditions and responsible generalizers from their basic data; but especially in post-Enlightenment Europe—which had supposedly learned from critical idealism to appreciate the philosophical limitedness of any generalizations upon data—there is nothing inherently culture-shaking in evolution or psychoanalysis or socialist theory. A special intellectual climate of uncertainty is required for such scientific movements to assume the character of philosophical revolutions; uncertainty invites the iconoclastic, or indeed creates it, and the hammer-blows of iconoclasm in turn justify our uncertainty.

This is the intellectual climate of the post-Kantian era, now that German metaphysics, in its critical aspect, has challenged our basic assumptions about existence, and in its systematic aspect has whetted our appetite for a new kind of certainty, but not actually satisfied us.[3] Needless to say, this is a simplification; we cannot make the tradition from German idealism responsible for all recent intellectual history. But we can identify at least one very important area of our intellectual experience which is quite clearly continuous with the German tradition; we can speak, perhaps, of a *dialectical sense of life*, a sense of existence as unrelieved flux and vertigo in which everything immediately implies its negation, nothing stands fast, and iconoclastic upheaval is the norm, a sense of dialectical tension between self and world, resolved by its exacerbation and exacerbated by its resolution, the "journey" described by M. H. Abrams,[4] which is endlessly frustrating because we know it to be "circuitous" but cannot experience it thus. Not only in Hegel, but in Schiller, Fichte, and Schelling as well, Kantian thought is developed in this direction; then, after Hegel, Kierkegaard's concepts of irony and despair, as well as Schopenhauer's notion of a Will which realizes itself by thwarting itself and then thwarts its realizations, are clearly dialectical; and I will argue that a type of Hegelian dialectic informs Nietzsche's basic thinking in *The Birth of Tragedy*.

In the area of literary form, from Romanticism on, it is easy to recognize the importance of a dialectical habit of mind, in the production of forms from the negation of form, which leads eventually to anti-novels, anti-heroes, anti-memoirs and so forth. And in the area of drama we can be still more specific, for in recent years some very suggestive points have been made about the immediate importance of Hegel for two major and seminal modern dramatists, Ibsen and Pirandello. Brian Johnston has argued, if anything overconclusively, that Ibsen's plays from *The Pillars of Society* to *When We Dead Awaken*, constitute a dramatization of the essential structure of the sections on "Spirit" and "Religion" in Hegel's *Phenomenology of the Spirit*; and Anne Paolucci, although she is cautious about whether Pirandello "actually read Hegel," argues cogently that "Pirandello's dramatization of the experience [of self-consciousness, progressing from 'I-Thou' to 'We'] follows the course of the Hegelian analysis."[5] It seems to me that, given the existence of an important basic relation to Hegel in the works of Ibsen and Pirandello, there is in fact a fairly obvious way of going beyond both Johnston's and Paolucci's arguments. If the plots, characters, and action in Ibsen's realistic "cycle" are meant to suggest the Hegelian phases of spirit leading up to religious consciousness, and if we recall what Hegel says repeatedly about the necessity that spirit, in its later phases, repossess itself consciously of its own past, then it appears that this process of conscious self-repossession is what is supposed to be happening in the theater. The whole theater, including both auditorium and stage, is a model of the self-conscious mind; the audience is to the stage-vision as the developed spirit, moving toward absolute knowledge, is to its own earlier phases; theatrical performance is Hegel's hyphenated "Er-Innerung."[6] And the possibility of a similar argument is even clearer in the case of Pirandello, especially in such plays as the Six Characters and Tonight We Improvise, where the theater, like Hegel's self-conscious spirit, projects a vision, an object, an "other" which turns out to be itself.[7]

Thus we arrive by way of Hegel at something similar to the poetics of German Classical drama, the use of the theater as a model and intensification of self-conscious existence, rather than a form of escape from self-consciousness or an attempt to transcend it. This, as it had been in German Classicism, is essentially a dialectical theater, of which the very structure, the relation between audience and stage, is a projection of the dialectic of self-consciousness, and Ibsen and Pirandello are by no means the only modern examples. Shaw, Brecht, and Giraudoux, for instance, different as they may be in other respects, have in common one prominent tendency which is clearly attributable to the presence of dialectical historicism in their intellectual background: I mean the use of spirited repartee among obviously representative characters to dramatize the clash, interchange, and mutation of historical forces. And again it is not difficult to draw inferences concerning the intended character of the theater as an institution. The association of individual characters with historical states of consciousness reminds the spectator of his own relationship, as an individual, to history, and the dialectical interplay thus expands to include the auditorium as well as the stage; the relation of spectator to stage is historically self-conscious and self-developing. The same kind of point, moreover, can also be made for a very different type of drama, which includes the grotesquely exaggerated expressionist drama around World War I and the grotesquely unexaggerated "documentary drama" since World War II. Here the relation of physical distance between stage and audience is used as a wedge of intense consciousness between ourselves and the essence of our age and is meant thus to contribute to a dialectically self-overcoming tension in the age.

The importance of a dialectical sense of life in the shaping of modern drama—again, not merely in the content—has been demonstrated by critics who do not even mention Hegel. Guthke, for example, shows very clearly that an important segment of modern drama derives its form from the attempt not merely to combine the comic and the tragic but to synthesize these opposed forces in such a way that each implies the other.[8] It is possible to argue, as Guthke does, that the modernity and modern flower of tragicomedy have to do with "the disastrous chaos of the modern world" and specifically with a "particular uncertainty of the modern writer" with regard to his mission. But the concept of uncertainty or chaos is not sufficient to account for the phenomenon of tragicomedy which, as Guthke correctly insists, involves the recognition that the tragic and the comic, while remaining strict opposites, nevertheless imply one another; the manifestation of this sort of thinking in artistic form testifies, again, to a dialectical sense of life. Perhaps, indeed, this sense has become so much a habit that it costs us some effort to recall the importance of German philosophy in establishing it. David I. Grossvogel, in his interesting book *20th Century French Drama*, which addresses itself specifically to the question of "the self-conscious stage," does not touch on the nineteenth-century background of his own and his authors' dialectical thinking, even though French drama—not only in philosopher-dramatists like Sartre and Camus—tends to operate on a rather high level of awareness of its intellectual tradition.[9]

Two other questions, however, must also be kept in focus: the question of how dialectic philosophy is related to the German dramatic movement, and the question of whether its modern influence is such as to preserve and transmit the formal achievements of Classical German drama, whether, in other words,

German idealist philosophy may be regarded (without pretending that it is only this) as part of a modern dramatic tradition which includes German Classicism as one of its crucial phases.

2

By dialectic philosophy, the reader will have recognized, I do not mean merely the philosophy of progress proposed by Hegel, but rather I refer in general to those philosophical doctrines in which the self-opposing activity of self-consciousness is taken as the generating center, or at least as an adequate model, of the way things happen in nature and history.[10] Dialectic, thus understood, although it is frequently associated with the notion of either linear or circular progress, does not necessarily imply such notions, and the clearest proof is the work of Nietzsche. Even in *The Birth of Tragedy*, Nietzsche already attempts to turn Hegel on his head, not by rejecting dialectic but by pessimizing it. For Hegel, the dialectic of the spirit tends toward the goal of "absolute knowledge," a state in which the spirit knows itself as itself and so is finally at one with itself; but Nietzsche argues that the culmination of knowledge as such, unrelieved by salutary illusion, is suicidal despair. The mechanism of history is still basically dialectical—involving swings from illusion to deeper knowledge to more powerful illusion and so on—but the climax of this dialectic, the synthesis of brilliant illusion and appalling knowledge in the art of tragedy, is by nature a short-lived phenomenon which as it were commits suicide, whereupon the whole endless process begins yet again in a different way.[11] When Nietzsche speaks of "the terrible destructive dynamics of so-called world history" (52, vii), he is expressing a basic perception with which Hegel would have had no trouble agreeing;[12] for Hegel, however, there is ultimately a purpose behind the destructiveness which necessarily arises in a history governed by dialectical negation, whereas for Nietzsche there is no such purpose. What Nietzsche hopes for is a fully self-conscious Socratic culture, a Socratism that recognizes its true nature as art and thus becomes art, a "Socrates making music" (98, xv), an achievement, in other words, not unlike the integrated self-comprehension of Hegel's absolute knowledge; but Nietzsche never suggests that transfigured Socratism, once achieved, will be anything more than a transitory cultural phase which, having produced its great art, will be swallowed up like all the ages before it.

The most obvious dialectical element in the thought of *The Birth of Tragedy* is the tension between the Apollonian and the Dionysian. This is a true dialectical relation. The Apollonian and the Dionysian are not merely different forces which originate separately and then happen to meet and clash in ancient Greece; on the contrary, they imply each other logically while still remaining strict opposites, they are connected by "mutual necessity" (35, iv). The Apollonian perfection of Homeric myth can only arise on the basis of the Dionysian wisdom of Silenus (31–33, iii); and conversely, the stirring of "Dionysian powers" in our own time is proof that the Apollonian, even if still "wrapped in a cloud" (151, xxv), is present among us. The clash of the two drives tends not to weaken but to intensify and purify them until, at their highest level of purity, they merge in the dialectical synthesis of tragedy.

For our purposes, an especially interesting aspect of the Apollonian and the Dionysian is the way they reveal Schiller's influence on Nietzsche. In the *Briefe* Schiller bases his whole argument on the idea of two constitutive "drives" in human nature, the "material drive" and the "form-drive," which, despite their opposed tendencies, imply each other logically, since matter cannot achieve manifestness except in form, and form requires the existence of what it is applied to. These are constitutive drives; they do not belong to human nature; rather they *are* the basic structure of human nature, as "person" and "condition" are the basic structure of experience. But this state of affairs causes Schiller some perplexity. Can human nature be based on a contradiction, on drives that tend in opposite directions? Schiller's answer is that, if man exists as a unified entity, then there must, logically, be a third drive that mediates between those of matter and form, and this third drive, which the *Briefe* also attempts to demonstrate empirically, is the play-drive. Thus the play-drive, the source of all artistic creation and experience, is logically equivalent to the generic existence of man, and it follows that art is an indispensable humanizing force, without which man would not be truly himself.[13]

Nietzsche, like Schiller, is concerned to show that art is the very soul of human existence, not merely one human activity among others. Even religion and science, says Nietzsche, are only "names" for what are essentially forms of art (98, xv), and in fact existence itself can be truly justified "only as an *aesthetic phenomenon*" (43, v); that is, only by thinking artistically do we experience existence in such a way that life appears worthwhile, which means that art is the force that keeps us alive. Nietzsche, then, is arguing in the same general direction as Schiller, and like Schiller he derives the idea of art from the idea of opposed "drives" (21, i, *et passim*). The Apollonian and the Dionysian, moreover, like form and matter, are constitutive drives in human nature. Nietzsche specifically says that dreams and intoxication, those "physiological phenomena" (22, i) which some commentators to this day regard as the essence of the drives, are merely an *analogy* (24, i; 34, iv) by which the components of art's dialectic can be visualized. All existence, again, is essentially artistic in character; the world is "an idea imagined anew in every moment by the Primal One" (35, iv), and we ourselves are "artistic projections" (43, v) of the eternal creative process. Man, therefore, fulfills his true function and is most perfectly in harmony with existence when he himself is an artist—"the eternally achieved aim of the Primal One" is man's "creation of the redeeming vision" (35,iv)—which means that the dialectic of Apollonian and Dionysian, by which art develops, constitutes man's basic nature.

These parallels, along with frequent specific references in *The Birth of Tragedy*, make it clear that Nietzsche is attempting to develop the argument of Schiller's *Briefe*. But at one crucial point he does not follow Schiller. Can human nature be based on a contradiction? Schiller answers no, and therefore postulates the play-drive, whereas Nietzsche implies that human nature *is* based on a contradiction, a reflection or emanation of the "primal contradiction and anguish" (40, v; 47, vi). Nietzsche refuses to believe in the existence of a single concept which resolves the tension between the drives; man is not a given, conceptualizable entity but rather a dialectical entity whose very being is the tension between antitheses, and who thus always has yet to *become what he is*—in a characteristic phrase of Hegel's which then becomes a refrain ("Werde, der du bist") in later Nietzsche. Schiller, faced with a contradiction in human nature, infers the existence of a synthesis coeval with the antitheses; Nietzsche argues that the synthesis of the drives—the absolute completion of human nature in the ritual of dramatic tragedy—always lies in the future, as something to be achieved. Even when tragedy is successfully created, it soon dies of its own inner contradictoriness and the process must begin yet again.

Thus Nietzsche takes Schiller's basic thought and applies to it the more sophisticated dialectical technique of Hegel, but without the idea of a goal that can be achieved once and for all. And it seems to me that in doing this, Nietzsche overcomes the impasse in Schiller's aesthetics, that he solves in theory the problem Schiller could only solve in practice, with *Maria Stuart*. Schiller's problem, again, stems from the apparent necessity that the content of tragedy receive a negative valuation from its audience, that the audience somehow overcome the tragic vision. Comedy is easily justified, given the assumption that the comic vision is essentially a vision of self-reconciled human totality; but tragedy presents a vision of suffering and human fragmentation, and must this not be overcome by the reconciling process of art? Nietzsche solves this problem on the level of theory. If the single ground or source of total humanity actually exists, as something like the play-drive, then the aim of art must be to realize it or conform to it, which makes it difficult to justify tragedy. But if human nature is based on an utterly unresolvable internal antithesis, then tragedy, the ritual in which men affirm joyfully a vision of precisely the hopeless fragmentation of existence (the tearing apart of the god), will itself be the only possible synthesis or realization of total humanity, the only possibility of authentic (though paradoxical and temporary) self-affirmation, thus self-wholeness, for human beings. Tragedy can be this, moreover, only by virtue of our positive valuation of its tragic content—otherwise we are not affirming what is truly ourselves—so that Schiller's difficulty is at least circumvented.

What is especially interesting, however, is that Nietzsche's theoretical solution to this problem is not essentially different from Schiller's own practical solution. The audience of *Maria Stuart* must affirm its condition as a quasi-artistic act; there is no escape from the inner self-opposition of human nature, play-drive or no play-drive. Mary perhaps achieves self-wholeness, but like Egmont she does so at the cost of her very existence; as long as we continue to live we are constituted by an unrelieved inner tension;

the self-opposing process of self-consciousness in us, as we are reminded by the scene with Leicester in the locked room, necessarily strangles our hope of self-reconciliation. Yet it is possible to realize this hopeless situation as a symbol which glorifies mankind and authenticates culture. Mary's last words represent an expression of her faulty nature, an expression which, in its controlled dignity and force, elevates her nature without denying it; and we in the theater—to the extent that we follow the play's thematic drift and understand our own creative relation to the vision—are doing the same thing, expressing our own fundamentally faulty nature with a controlled ritual symmetry and formality which, for the moment at least, gives this expression the character of precisely that self-reconciliation we had ceased to hope for.

Thus Nietzsche's solution to the problem of tragedy in theory—the idea that the business of tragedy is not to *represent* a given, pre-existent state of human wholeness, but rather to *be* the achievement of a human wholeness which had not yet existed prior to the performance—is essentially the same as the solution Schiller arrives at in practice; and in this way Nietzsche's argument is clearly also the theoretical equivalent of the achievement in *Egmont*, and even in *Nathan* and *Prinz Friedrich*, although these last two plays are quite different from what we normally think of as tragedy. As far as I know, there is no indication that Nietzsche ever recognized the relation between his own thinking and the implicit poetics of German Classical drama; but that relation exists nonetheless, and is by no means accidental, since Nietzsche starts out directly from Schiller's grappling with the problem of self-consciousness in aesthetics.

Again, Nietzsche achieves his theoretical breakthrough by applying Hegelian dialectics to Schiller's system; thus his achievement is symptomatic of the ability of dialectical thinking to give drama a new shape and function. Schiller was hampered theoretically by what he felt was the necessity of understanding existing phenomena (e.g. humanity) as the realization of pre-existent concepts, and only by way of a considerable struggle did he manage to circumvent this obstacle in practice. Now, however, after Hegel and Nietzsche, the obstacle no longer exists; what Nietzsche does in theory is to *free drama from the idea of representation*—by which I mean not only the sensual representation of reality, but also the representation, in meaning, of existing concepts. Drama, to the extent that it is affected by a dialectical sense of life, no longer needs to restrict itself to the representation of past or present conscious states, but may now set out boldly to *create new states of self-consciousness* by the mechanism of the theater. (We recall the idea of the generalized world-theater image, the idea of the theater as itself a world more authentic than the world outside.) The way is thus open for a general European flowering of what had been anticipated in practice by German Classical drama. Dialectic philosophy includes the notion that every basic act of self-consciousness—especially communal self-consciousness, for the creation of which the theater is uniquely well-suited— generates a never-before-realizable state of human development; and precisely such conscious human self-renewal, *in* or at least *through* the theater, is a central endeavor in several widely different types of modern drama.

3

In order to understand Nietzsche's influence, however, we must first understand his theory of drama in more detail. *The Birth of Tragedy* does contain a theory of *drama*, not merely a theory of the tragic, and this theory is worked out in the discussion not of Wagner but of the Greeks. It is, moreover, as much a theory of modern drama as of ancient drama, and in particular—again, not by accident, considering its debt to Schiller's aesthetics—it can be applied with little modification to the dramas of German Classicism, although Nietzsche himself does not seem to have recognized this.

Let us begin with the idea of the audience of Greek tragedy. Nietzsche asserts "that the satyr, the simulated natural being, is to cultural man as Dionysian music is to civilization. Of the latter, Richard Wagner says that it is cancelled by music as lamplight is by daylight. In the same way, I think, the cultured Greek felt himself cancelled at the sight of the satyr-chorus. This is the immediate effect of Dionysian tragedy: that the state and the social order, all divisions between man and man, fade before an overpowering feeling of unity which leads back to the heart of nature" (51–52, vii). Does this mean that the audience at a tragedy are swept up in an intoxication which suspends their self-consciousness? It is clear that this is not what Nietzsche means. The word "simulated" (*fingirt*) ought already to tell us this. If chorus and audience were actually plunged into an absolute union with preconscious nature—nature in the Rousseauistic sense of utter undivided satisfaction—then there would be no reason to speak of the satyr as a "simulated natural being"; satyr and spectator, for the moment at least, would simply be one with nature.

And what does Nietzsche mean by "nature"? Rousseau's notion of a fundamentally good and satisfying nature is precisely what he is arguing against (e.g. 33, iii). What do we find when we get to the "heart" of nature? This question is not difficult to answer, given Nietzsche's repeated references to the "primal contradiction and anguish in the heart of the Primal One" (47, vi) or "the malignity in the nature of things, the contradiction at the world's heart" (65–66, ix). As a matter of fact, Nietzsche argues specifically that the Apollonian visions of tragedy, "those heliochrome-like images of the Sophoclean hero," are necessary as an "antidote" to counteract the audience's looking "into the subsurface horror of nature" (61, ix); and this viewing of "horror" at the heart of nature, which immediately precedes the appearance of the tragic hero, must refer to the audience's sense of unity with nature via the chorus. It is true that unity with the chorus is spoken of as a joyful experience, but this is the basic paradox of tragedy (not only in Nietzsche's theory): the experience itself is horrible but our inward relation to it is somehow joyful. In any case, union with "the heart of nature" clearly involves the experience of a "contradiction" even deeper and more horrible than the ordinary internal division of self-consciousness; the satyr himself is "sympathetic" (59, viii), which means that he actually undergoes the contradictoriness and suffering of the god (54, viii). When Nietzsche says "the Dionysian Greek," he does not mean the intoxicated Greek but rather the wise Greek, who desires truth, knows the horror of existence, and has a special "talent for suffering" (34, iii); "the Dionysian Greek wants truth and nature in their highest potency—he sees himself transformed into a satyr" (55, viii).

The Dionysian state of the audience in a Greek theater, then, does not imply an exemption from inner contradictoriness or a transcendence of it. Nor does it imply that the spectator is less than fully conscious of the artificiality of the drama. Nietzsche calls his reader's attention specifically to the essay "Über den Gebrauch des Chors in der Tragödie" (50–51, vii), in which Schiller emphasizes that the spectator of drama must never be allowed to forget the artificiality of the ritual, the fact that the envisioned world is a product of creative human *Geist*. Moreover, Nietzsche's whole argument depends on the idea "that all the famous figures of the Greek stage, Prometheus, Oedipus, etc., are only masks of the original hero Dionysus" (67, x); indeed the audience are actually supposed to *see* "not a crudely masked man, but rather an apparition born as it were of their own transport" (59, viii). But on the other hand, the mask, the particular form in which Dionysus appears, is by no means nonessential; the "epic" quality of the dialogue (60, viii), or "the Apollonian of the mask" (61, ix), is the necessary "antidote," by which our Dionysian knowledge of the abyss is balanced and the tragic effect completed. The audience, therefore, must see clearly and enjoy the surface action on stage, while also *seeing through* it to the cultic reality beneath, which is to say that the audience must appreciate the artistic illusion while remaining fully aware of its artificiality.

The audience are thus not "intoxicated" in the ordinary meaning of this word, not bereft of their senses. They experience, rather, a deep inner self-opposition and suffering, and they enjoy an artificial contrivance of which they recognize the artificiality. But on the other hand, they are not self-conscious in the ordinary sense either; the "cultural man" in each spectator is "cancelled," the normal self-consciousness of daily life no longer prevails. This can only mean that the daily self-consciousness of the Greek spectator is *replaced by a deeper or truer self-consciousness*, by the consciousness of a truer self, by an anguished self-consciousness belonging to man as such rather than to a particular person in a particular situation. Now we can begin to see the closeness of Nietzsche's theory to the inherent poetics of German Classical drama; Goethe, Schiller, Kleist, and to an extent Lessing, all aim at an intensification of the audience's self-consciousness, to the point where it assumes tragic proportions, where it becomes an absolute metaphysical anguish which no longer separates individuals but tends to bridge "the divisions between man and man"—and the same is true of Büchner as well. Daily self-consciousness, our awareness of our empirical self, is a confusing and irritating but still rather shallow affair, from which we find relief by imagining "that idyllic shepherd of our modern dreams" (55, viii); if, however, we seek not relief but truth, if we imagine not the shepherd but the satyr, then we discover that our ordinary self-consciousness is the expression of a metaphysical contradiction with which all existence groans.

The question remains of the exact relation between chorus and audience, of the "overpowering feeling of unity" that connects them. We can begin to answer this question by understanding the difference between dithyramb and tragedy. The original choral rites from which tragedy grew had the character of an epidemic natural phenomenon in which all the participants transformed themselves in the same way; but Nietzsche then continues: "The later constitution of the tragic chorus is the artistic imitation of that natural phenomenon, and so entails, it is true, a separation between Dionysian spectators and the enchanted Dionysian spirits they observe. But we must keep in mind that the audience at Attic tragedy recognized *itself* in the dancing chorus, that there was basically no opposition between audience and chorus; all are joined in one great sublime chorus of dancing and singing satyrs or of people who let themselves be represented thus" (55, viii). And yet, surely there is a difference between the natural phenomenon and its "artistic imitation," between actually dancing and "letting oneself be represented" by dancers. Does this mean that tragedy approaches but cannot quite reach the purity of the original rite? Obviously this is not what Nietzsche means. Art, we recall, is the highest and purest expression of humanity, and tragedy is the highest form of art. Therefore the separation in tragedy between spectator and dancer must be an advantage in some way.

I think we can make perfectly good sense out of Nietzsche's apparently conflicting statements if we pay closer attention to one rather curious locution. The Dionysian spectator does not become a satyr, but rather he "*sees himself* magically transformed into a satyr" (55, viii; cf. 57–58), which expresses the idea of unity (by transformation) while not excluding the idea of separation (in the process of seeing). This ought to remind us that the spectator's feeling of unity with the satyr and with nature does not imply a feeling of self-unity, but rather a feeling of self-separation, a participation in the "primal contradiction" of being. The feeling of distance between spectator and satyr (*sich sehen, sich repräsentiren lassen*) thus paradoxically increases the feeling of unity—insofar as the spectator experiences that distance from the satyr as a distance from himself, which self-separation is in turn the very nature of the satyr, whose half-bestial appearance expresses the dialectical truth that man, eternally unfulfilled, is always in the process of becoming what he is. In the theater our self-consciousness is intensified to the point where it becomes a feeling of unity with self-separated nature, with the self-separated satyr, and with all other men; but this feeling of unity implies self-separation for us as well, which is symbolized by our distance from the dancers.

Again, therefore, we have a striking parallel with German Classical drama, with the paradox of detachment and involvement in Lessing, Goethe, Schiller, and Kleist. The spectator's detachment from the chorus becomes the essence of his belonging to it, his participation in the eternal "contradiction"; precisely the division of that "great sublime chorus" into spectators and dancers makes it more unified as a communal phenomenon. Nietzsche does not use the word "self-consciousness," which in normal usage would have meant people's empirical awareness of themselves as particular individuals; but self-consciousness, in the broader sense in which we have understood it, is what he means, an anguished inner self-division which can be intensified to reveal metaphysical dimensions. This intensification, in Nietzsche's theory, is effected by the vision of the chorus as "a self-mirroring of Dionysian man" (56, viii)—a mirror which shows us ourselves by separating us from ourselves—and in German Classical practice it is effected by the transformation of the whole theater (phrenographically) into a huge symbol of self-consciousness, whereby our own self-consciousness is revealed as the tragic self-separation of existence itself, and in this form is realized, for the audience, as a communal phenomenon, the beginning of communal existence on a new level. There is an interesting double meaning in one passage where Nietzsche speaks of the community in the theater: "An audience of spectators, as we know it, was foreign to the Greeks. In their theaters, on the concentrically rising terraces of the auditorium, it was possible for everyone literally to *overlook* (*übersehen*) the whole cultural world about him and, in satiated contemplation, to imagine himself a member of the chorus" (55, viii). The verb *übersehen* means both "to survey" and "to neglect"; the Greek spectator, by being able to see his fellow citizens around him (which the modern spectator, in his darkened auditorium, presumably cannot do), is also enabled to "neglect" this surface cultural reality in favor of the essential community of satyrs or "true men" (54, viii) which it conceals. And in German Classical drama, as we have seen, the spectator's awareness of participating in a communal ritual is encouraged by various ironic devices, whereupon this awareness is meant to transform the theater-gathering into the nucleus of a more authentic community of men who are more fully human than they had been in daily life.

Once the audience's mood has been established, however, the tragic hero appears: "In this enchantment the Dionysian enthusiast sees himself as a satyr, *and as a satyr, in turn, he envisions the god*; i.e., in his transformation he sees a new vision outside himself, as the Apollonian completion of his state" (57–58, viii). Let us reconsider *Maria Stuart* in the light of this passage. The world of Schiller's play, we have seen, is a thoroughly confused world, corrupted by self-consciousness and by its unavoidable dependence on human opinion. In particular, it is a reflection of our own self-consciousness, our own confused cultural condition, and by being a reflection it potentiates our self-consciousness and begins to reveal the larger dimensions thereof. In Act I we are shown the discontinuity of conscious life; we are shown through Mortimer the suspect genesis of opinion and the suspect tendency of feeling; we are shown through Burleigh the inevitable confusion of justice and expediency in the world, as well as the confusing operation of public opinion. Then, in Act II, these recognitions blossom forth as the vision of a highly ceremonious, apparently orderly world which is in truth nothing but chaos; our own inner division is thus revealed as a general disorderly tendency in existence, not merely a private discomfort. And yet there is also a positive aspect to this revelation; the idea that worldly disorder has its source in individual consciousness suggests the corresponding possibility of communal consciousness as a source of deeper order, which possibility is in a sense already realized by the situation of the theater audience.

This much corresponds to Nietzsche's idea of the function of the chorus: first the revelation of self-consciousness as an undergoing of the eternal self-opposition of existence itself; then the realization of this anguished experience as the enjoyable participation in a community of "true men," a community based on human nature as a free power rather than a helpless state. Mary herself, however, the tragic heroine, is not a member of this higher community but rather a kind of projection of it. She represents, as we have seen, the hope of self-reconciliation, for Elizabeth, for Mortimer, for Leicester, for the divided realm of England and Scotland, and (once we understand the implications of our self-consciousness) for ourselves as well; her nature is thus derived logically from the anguish of self-division by which we in the audience are made something like a Nietzschean chorus. But at the same time, in her calm, uncompromising assertion of inner feeling in Act I, and then in her recaptured equilibrium at the end, she is also a vision of triumphant individual integrity. It therefore requires only a slight stretching of Nietzsche's terminology to recognize in her the "Apollonian completion" of the state into which the audience has been maneuvered. The suggestion of joyful reconciliation in her last scene before dying, moreover, could be explained in Nietzschean terms as corresponding to the audience's affirmation of the eternal contradiction that constitutes it, the transformation of disorder into order, of helpless anguish into vital power; the hope of reconciliation, in its Apollonian guise, is destroyed, but the agency that destroys it is precisely that "contradiction" which we have learned to experience as a new bond with our own nature and with nature in general.

It is not difficult to see that similar relationships with Nietzsche follow for Egmont and Homburg regarded as "projections" of the audience in the theater. Nietzsche, mainly under the influence of Schiller's aesthetics, starts out from essentially the same problems that occupied the poets of German Classicism, the problem of tragedy as a joyful vision of suffering and the problem of drama in general as a communal art form; but he brings to these problems more advanced theoretical techniques and so manages to traverse in theory the same ground covered by Classicism in practice. The parallels are both deep and striking, and the only real flaw in Nietzsche's thinking is his failure to appreciate the ability of verbal and mimic irony to generate the effects he ascribes to a Dionysian world-view in the audience; this is why he can apply his ideas only as a theory of ancient drama, which he then attempts unsuccessfully to force upon Wagner. Where Nietzsche insists on the necessity of a particular Dionysian "mood" (59, viii) produced by the chorus, the German Classical dramatists—and Brecht, we have seen—make use of the intellectual component in their audience's attitude to create a paradoxical unity of detachment and involvement which serves essentially the same purpose.

4

To give a really thorough treatment of the influence of German philosophy in modern literature, we should have to deal, at the very least, with Schopenhauer in France, with Hegel in Italy (in part via Croce), with the particular refraction of German ideas established in England by the Romantics and by such writers as Carlyle, with German literary criticism, especially the Schlegels, and with a host of minor figures who from time to time serve as intermediaries.[14] For our purposes, however, all this is not necessary. That numerous paths of influence exist, we may take as given; what we must ask is whether the influence of German philosophy is such as to preserve and transmit the spirit of German Classical drama.

In the case of Nietzsche, the dramatic theory of *The Birth of Tragedy* is closely related to the poetics of German Classicism, but apart from the widely misunderstood idea of the Dionysian, *The Birth of Tragedy* is not one of Nietzsche's most influential works. In what way, then, and to what extent, is Nietzsche's early theory of drama still present and effective in his later work?

Let us begin by looking at *Der Fall Wagner*. Does it follow from his repudiation of Wagner that Nietzsche has also repudiated his own thinking in *The Birth of Tragedy?* Wagner, in the later work, is described as the incarnation of decadence, not merely a sick man but the sickness itself,[15] and the specially pernicious thing about this sickness is that it is opposed to knowledge and logical thought. *Lohengrin*, says Nietzsche, teaches the morbid doctrine that "to be scientific is a crime against the highest and most holy" (p. 11); Wagner's "style," says Nietzsche, is based on the principle, "Above all, no thought! Nothing is more compromising than a thought!" (p. 18); and as for drama, "Drama requires *hard* logic: but what did Wagner care about logic anyway!" (p. 27). All this is typical of the late Nietzsche, from *Human, All Too Human* on— *sapere aude*, "philosophical pathos" (p. 8), the glorification of knowledge over feeling, of living in the cold air of the heights and daring to follow logic where it leads.

But again, does this constitute a repudiation of *The Birth of*

Tragedy, or had the admiration for Wagner in that early work been merely a logical inconsistency? I think it is clear that the latter is the case. The essential theory of drama in *The Birth of Tragedy*—which the Wagnerized terminology tends rather to obscure—is a theory of drama as knowledge, as authentic, anguished self-confrontation, not self-transcendence or self-deception; the aim of drama is not to soothe or flatter the audience but rather to make them experience human nature at the level at which it becomes a metaphysical contradiction, an unrelievable anguish which, by being experienced in this form, is transmuted into a kind of joy, essentially the same joy as that of *The Cheerful Science* or of Zarathustra, who discovers the possibility of affirming absolutely that which is absolutely unaffirmable. It is true that in his later work Nietzsche no longer regards the theater as a suitable vehicle for this higher philosophical joy[16]— he throws out the baby with the bath water, as if the Wagnerian theater were the whole of the modern theater. But he had originally derived his notion of philosophical joy from the idea of a particular non-Wagnerian type of theatrical experience, and his late works thus contain a latent theatricality, which is then retranslated into dramatic practice, by Strindberg, for example, and by Brecht and the German expressionists.

The principle of modern drama, in all of these cases, is neither the imitation of reality nor the alleviation of human anguish, but rather the intensification of our condition, precisely in its most difficult and disturbing aspects, in order that we face and recognize and, at last, enjoy it. Does modern man find himself in the state Hegel called "unhappy consciousness"? Then the business of the theater is to plunge him into it still further, until it becomes an act of exhilarating affirmation, like Zarathustra's biting off the serpent's head; and this idea in turn is a Nietzschean development of German Classical poetics. Is the modern world perverse? is it absurd? Then man, in the theatrical world he creates for himself, can and must be more so. We recall Paul Ackermann's words in Brecht's *Aufstieg und Fall der Stadt Mahagonny:* "See, that's how the world is: peace and concord don't exist, but hurricanes exist, and typhoons where necessary. And just so is man. He has to destroy what's there. Who needs a hurricane? What is the typhoon's terror compared to man when he is in a playful mood?" To which Begbick answers, in a parody of the famous *Antigone* chorus, "Bad is the hurricane, worse is the typhoon, but worst of all is man."[17] Drama mocks existence as Zarathustra mocks the adder; if existence is an adder, then man himself can be a dragon. Or we think of the third of Dürrenmatt's "21 Punkte zu den Physikern": "A story has been thought through to the end when it takes its worst possible turning."[18] Man, in the theater, surpasses and in a sense conquers reality by giving his own existence its "worst possible turning" and then actually enjoying it. Nor does it follow from this Zarathustrian poetics of drama that our enjoyment of the theater is destructive in character. On the contrary, both Brecht and Dürrenmatt envision at least the possibility of a positive social effect through drama, and in the case of Brecht this positive effect has to do with a sense of our sheer creative power relative to the world. We are reminded of both *Egmont* and *Maria Stuart*, where the audience is compelled to experience the human condition as an intolerable paradox; man's own conscious and emotional presence creates a world of culture which cannot possibly correspond to that sense of the ideal which makes him human. But this maximization of our anguish, this recognition of the world as not only our burden but also our fault, is transmuted by the nature of the theater into at least an enjoyable intimation of our power to create true order in existence.

The most important example of Nietzsche's influence in modern drama is Strindberg, whose influence upon later drama, and especially upon the development of dramatic form, is difficult to overestimate. What Strindberg actually owes to Nietzsche, whom he read relatively late, is debatable, but he at least had no trouble assimilating into his own style a Nietzschean or Zarathustrian poetics of drama. His whole early development—his Schopenhauerian pessimism, the sense of existence as inner anguish appropriated from Kierkegaard, his striving to out-Ibsen Ibsen in both the symbolic and the naturalistic manner, the early influence of such plays as *Die Räuber* and *Götz von Berlichingen* (all of which, incidentally, places him in the German dramatic tradition)—had predisposed him toward the idea of drama as a painful confrontation with the human condition at its worst; and in fact he suggests that the spectator's experience ought in a sense to be one of torment.[19] What is missing in the early Strindberg, however, is that Nietzschean component of joy or affirmation which does not really blossom forth until the great works of the

last period, *Crime and Crime, To Damascus, The Dance of Death,
A Dream Play, The Ghost Sonata* and *The Great Highway.*

All these plays were written after the crisis of 1896 in which
Strindberg turned to Swedenborg, but it is still correct to speak of
a Nietzschean rather than of a Swedenborgian affirmativeness in
them. As far as dramatic form is concerned, the essence of what
Strindberg learned from Swedenborg was how to apply Nietzsche.
The other-worldly aspect of those later dramas, the sense of mystical consolation in them, does not determine their form but rather
grows from it—to use one of Strindberg's favorite images—like
flowers from the fecund filth of the earth; Strindberg as an individual may have been deeply affected by Swedenborg (as he was
also, for example, by at least his own idea of Buddhism), but the
very idea of art demands that the ideas of any particular philosophy be rejustified in form, and it is in the essentially musical form
of Strindberg's later works that their affirmativeness is rooted.
Swedenborg showed Strindberg the general direction in which he
had to move, but Nietzsche showed him how he had to proceed as
a dramatist.

Perhaps we can see this by comparing *The Dance of Death* with
The Father. The vision of human life in the later play is certainly
not any more comforting or optimistic; on the contrary, the hor-
rors of human life, and especially of married life, are if anything
probed more deeply and developed more broadly in *The Dance of
Death.* In *The Father* the battle lines are clearly drawn. Both the
contestants know exactly what is involved in the struggle, and
both in fact know quite well what the outcome will be. The other
characters, the doctor, the pastor, and even the nurse, wish
merely to keep themselves out of the morass; they base their
action or inaction on the most obvious but shallowest possible
justification—the doctor on the technical existence of a crime of
violence, the pastor on his blood-relationship to Laura, the nurse
on a romanticized notion of her relation to the captain—and the
result is that they are in effect passive, mere tools or weapons in a
struggle they themselves avoid.

In *The Dance of Death,* on the other hand, there is no such
clarity. The basic struggle is the same, but the weapons, the al-
liances, the field of combat, and the stakes change almost from
minute to minute. The minor characters, Kurt and Judith, do not
simply allow themselves to be used, but rather strike ignorant

blows of their own—Judith actually administers the *coup de grâce* to her father—which confuse the situation between the main antagonists. The world of the play is entirely unbalanced by the morbidity at its center, and at the vague edges of this unbalanced world there are a significant number of unanswered questions: Is the captain an embezzler, and how does he avoid being charged? What is Kurt's real history, especially in America? Did the captain really engineer Kurt's loss of his children (a supposed fact for which we have only Alice's word)? The answer to the question of paternity in *The Father*, as Adolf himself points out, is ultimately irrelevant; but the unanswered questions in *The Dance of Death* bring home to us a basic epistemological flaw in existence. In *The Father* there is a solid underpinning to the action; Adolf is a serious and competent scientist, and Laura has a single concrete goal in her plans for her child. But in *The Dance of Death* there is no such underpinning; Edgar is in everything merely a sham, and Alice has no idea of what she hopes to gain; there is nothing to be known and no one to know it.

By objective standards, then, the world of *The Dance of Death* is worse than that of *The Father*; life is emptier, the morass of human misery is both deeper and wider. But at the same time *The Dance of Death* is clearly the more affirmative or even joyful work of the two; and this, I think, has to do with a basic musicality in its structure, perhaps not as obvious a musicality as that of *A Dream Play*, but serving essentially the same purpose. The structure of *The Father* is psychologically rational, the vision of human misery is limited by what two relatively well-founded characters can inflict on one another, whereas in *The Dance of Death* the very geometry of the fictional world is distorted by the misery of the central characters, so that these characters in turn appear mere manifestations of a larger force, as it were variations on a theme. Strindberg attempts to introduce this dimension in *The Father* by way of philosophical discussion of the general problem of the sexes; but these are abstract ideas, whereas in *The Dance of Death* misery as such is sounded forth in the whole shape of the vision and combined with itself contrapuntally in the interaction of the characters. *The Father* is built upon two relatively substantial characters to whom misery is added as an attribute, whereas the substance of the characters in *The Dance of Death* is misery itself. The whole world is but variously concretized misery, and the young love of Allan and Judith in Part II is no exception; it is perfectly clear from their first scene together—which ends with Judith's "I'll-pay-you-out!"[20]—that if they ever manage to get married, their marriage will be a carbon copy of Edgar's and Alice's, that the playful inflicting of pain in courtship is only a prelude for something more essential and horrible still to be revealed.

And yet this vision—not of man beset by misery but of perfect misery revealing itself in the form of man—has a distinctly affirmative component, which we can begin to understand by understanding Edgar's and Alice's moment of relative peace at the end of Part I. The source of this respite is not relief that a disaster has been averted, for Edgar does not share Alice's relief. What the two share, and for a moment experience as sharing, is the *power* of their unhappiness; "everyone who comes near us grows evil and goes his way" (p. 187), says Edgar at the beginning of the speech that moves Alice to laughter. And then he speaks his refrain, "Cancel out and pass on!"—which means pass on to ever new forms of torment, pass on willingly and in a sense happily, rather than merely accept one's misery grudgingly as something "destined" (p. 186). What he and Alice share is the momentary sense of freedom as *authors of their own misery*, a sense of having gone their fate one better, of having made themselves and others even more miserable than nature could make them, a pride in their willingness to commit atrocities as it were beyond the call of duty, like the travesty of a silver wedding they will now celebrate. We are reminded not only of Nietzsche's *amor fati* but also of Schiller (the idea of conquering fate by willing it).[21]

Of course this sense of sharing between Edgar and Alice cannot last; if it did, their misery would be alleviated and they would have nothing to share. But the feeling that unites them momentarily at the end of Part I is important as a reflection of what is intended by the play's *form*; the liberation of human misery from the confines of rational psychology, so that it may modulate, develop, and reflect itself as a single quasi-musical cosmic theme of which men are but the passing manifestations (as it were "dissonance in human form—and what else is man?"),[22] constitutes for us an artistic surpassing of our natural condition, similar to that carried out by Edgar and Alice. The company in the theater are meant to experience, at least for a moment, a sense of creative power as authors of their own condition; we are meant to experience misery itself as a communal work of art, not merely part of the work's content. And this, as I say, reflects a Nietzschean poetics of drama, a confronting the human condition in its extremest form in order to transmute it into a new philosophical joy, a poetics which Nietzsche had first developed in *The Birth of Tragedy*, and which can be traced from there, by way of Schiller's theory, back to German Classical drama. Nietzsche is not the only influence here; Strindberg's musically structured plays, the dream and quest plays, also represent one of the clearest modern attempts to revive and develop the dramatic style of *Faust*, the technique of using characters like musical subjects, allowing their situations to arise as a crystallizing of laws or forces inherent in the scenic-intellectual background. But this too can be traced back to *Egmont* and the center of the tradition from German Classicism, which tradition—despite all the obvious dissimilarity between say Artaud's "theater of cruelty" and Goethe's court-theater at Weimar—is thus essentially what is propagated by Strindberg's influence, especially in France and Germany.[23]

One of the key ideas in this historical development, finally—even if it is not always so explicit as in Schiller's *Briefe* or Strindberg's note to *A Dream Play*—is the idea of self-consciousness. While on one hand it is the indispensable condition of freedom or creative action, self-consciousness is also a source of confusion, self-division, unhappiness, Dionysian pessimism, Kierkegaardian despair; by its nature it strives toward a self-wholeness which, as *Egmont* teaches, is both salvation and death. Self-consciousness is thus both divinity and mortality, both power and helplessness, both freedom and bondage, and this paradoxical combination of ideas is characteristic not only of the Egmontian school of drama but also of the German idealist movement in philosophy from Kant at least to Nietzsche, from the idea of human self-determination, our free Kantian bondage, to Zarathustra's extreme vision of eternal recurrence, the great wheel on which our freedom is utterly broken yet immediately restored via the truth that every instant of existence is an infinitely affirmative act which initiates all history.

And in modern drama, especially in the Strindbergian contribution to dramatic form, this paradox of freedom and bondage, something like the Hegelian interchange of Master and Servant, becomes central. The musical structure of such plays as *The Dance of Death, A Dream Play, The Ghost Sonata,* has the effect of rendering human misery independent of any particular situation, thus subjecting us to it maximally, while at the same time and by the same device providing us with a sense of free artistic power relative to our subjection. Nietzsche, although he devotes little systematic thought to drama in his later period, makes a remark apropos Wagner which tends toward a similar idea: "The technical problem over which the dramatist often sweats blood, we know, is the problem of endowing his plot and its resolution with *necessity,* so that both are possible in only one way, and both give the impression of freedom (principle of minimum effort)" (p. 27). If we could read "independence" or "self-completeness" (*Abrundung, Abgeschlossenheit*) instead of "freedom" ("*Freiheit*"), the meaning would be clear: the achievement of strict necessity cuts a dramatic plot loose from the mind that created it; the plot stands on its own, as a self-determining whole. What is actually suggested, however, is that this logical rounding off of the dramatic plot produces an "impression of freedom" for the *audience.* The plot requires no specific imaginative or ideological contribution on our part; it stands over against us, independent, in such a way that our thinking about it, our perception of its meaning, is "free" in the sense of being strictly our own—which idea recalls *Prinz Friedrich,* and also Goethe's emphasis on the immediate "sensory" completeness of drama. Wagner, says Nietzsche, browbeats and subjugates his audience by being vague, whereas the true dramatist liberates us by his strictness. And if we substitute for the idea of necessity in plot structure the idea of a human misery so absolute as to be expressible only by relentless musical logic, we arrive at the late Strindbergian conception of drama. Thus, again, there is a parallel between Strindberg's poetics and that of German Classicism, and again Nietzsche appears to figure in the historical relation between the two.

It is especially interesting, however, that the paradox of freedom and bondage appears not only thematically and structurally in modern drama but also historically, as the tendency toward a division of styles. Naturalism and expressionism, for example, are commonly taken as stylistic poles; Bentley distinguishes between realist and anti-realist "traditions"; Eric Sellin, apropos Artaud, speaks of lunar and solar drama, drama that broods and drama that acts,[24] a formulation approaching maximum generality but difficult to apply. Perhaps we can subsume all these oppositions by distinguishing between *sensitive* and *energetic* dramatic style: drama that reverberates or responds to forces from outside itself, and drama that attempts to generate its own outward-directed force. This would enable us, for example, to include impressionist drama (a kind of poetic naturalism of the soul) in the former category, and social-didactic drama in the latter. But the distinction remains problematic. The opposites tend in practice to merge or change places; action and reaction, freedom and bondage, tend ultimately to become identical, as in Strindberg.

I suggest that this persistent sense of stylistic dichotomy, despite its failure to produce a strict separation of styles, has to do with the importance in modern drama of the German idealist tenet that man's subjection to his condition and his power over it are the horns of philosophy's most basic dilemma. This accounts not only for the ultimate untenability of the distinction between sensitive and energetic drama, but also for its superficial obviousness. A concern with the paradoxical unity of freedom and bondage— with a modern version of the paradox of the demonic in *Egmont*— obliges the dramatist to begin by separating the elements of this unity, so that the style of a given work will appear at first glance either sensitive or energetic. Modern dramatic style separates into two streams for the same reason that artistic beauty in Schiller, which is in essence one paradoxical phenomenon, must be divided for practical purposes into "melting" and "tensing" beauty.

5

In Strindberg the influence of Nietzsche's version of German idealism and the influence of German drama, especially *Faust*, tend in the same direction. In Ibsen and Pirandello, the influence of Hegelian thought produces effects which recall certain aspects of German Classicism. And in general a dialectical sense of life, as part of the modern period's debt to nineteenth-century German philosophy, tends to bring about affinities between modern drama and the German Classical drama of intensified self-consciousness. The question that needs to be dealt with, therefore, is that of the historical relation between German philosophy and German drama. Does the thought of Hegel and his successors, insofar as it influences modern drama, actually reflect and transmit the achievements in dramatic form of such authors as Goethe, Lessing, Schiller, Kleist?

There is, to begin with, a basic affinity between German drama and German idealist philosophy as a whole. Both movements arise in response to a feeling of helpless fragmentedness, of self-conscious alienation between man and nature, subject and object, individual and community, a feeling which in late eighteenth-century Germany becomes especially strong because of the Germans' sense of cultural immaturity and inferiority, their lack of a self-confident literary or artistic tradition, their dependence on foreign models. One of the principal goals of German drama in this period is to generate a cohesive and productive communal life for its audience, and essentially the same can be said of idealist philosophy; Kant is concerned mainly with establishing a durable basic for ethics, aesthetics, and religion in general, but the application to the Germans' cultural predicament quickly appears in Fichte and Hegel. The basic problem is substantially the same for both dramatist and philosopher: to exploit that quality of human consciousness which produces alienation or mere fruitless scepticism as the foundation for a solid reordering of man's generic and communal being.

In the case of Hegel, however, we can be a bit more specific, for Schiller's *Briefe* was an important influence in shaping the thought of the *Phenomenology*. Walter Kaufmann shows in fact that it was from the dialectical tendency of the *Briefe*, Schiller's point that human wholeness or Hellenic harmony had to negate itself for the sake of development toward a higher wholeness, that Hegel derived much of his attempt to surpass the Kantian system.[25] To judge from the *Aesthetics*, Hegel never appreciated the achievement of German Classical drama, and even Schiller's aesthetic writings do not give an adequate sense of this achievement. But the dialectical aspect of Schiller's writings—the recognition (later made explicit in the essay on the chorus) of self-conscious *Geist* as a creative power, not a hindrance—is what tends in the direction of *Maria Stuart*; and it is by means of Hegelian dialectic that Nietzsche later develops Schiller's thinking into an adequate theory of drama. In the *Phenomenology* Hegel as it were writes a theory of drama without knowing it, or at least lays the groundwork for such a theory, and this is in turn made possi-

ble by the influence of the tentative first step taken by Schiller
toward a descriptive poetics of German Classical drama.

German drama is therefore an important shaping force in
Hegel's thought and the source of a fundamental dramatic tendency in it. By this tendency I mean primarily the whole idea of
the world as dialectic of spirit; but it is also no accident that in the
Phenomenology, as later in the *Aesthetics,* Hegel recognizes
drama as the culmination of art's total development, as the most
thoroughly dialectical art form. His well-known argument that
tragedy is the clash between forces with equal moral justifiability,
for example, carries forward the discussion of a question that had
been acute not only in Schiller, but also in Lessing's worried
meditations on *Richard III,* the question of how our moral judgment of the tragic hero is related to our aesthetic judgment of the
tragedy. It seems to me that this question is finally put to rest by
Nietzsche's argument, in the spirit of German Classical practice,
that our relation to the hero (the hero as a visionary embodiment
of our own anguished communal knowledge) is such that no
moral judgment is required. But even in Nietzsche there is still at
least a distant echo of Hegel, in the idea of an "eternal vitality"
(52, vii; 104, xvi) which is revealed and glorified by the tragic
destruction of what turns out to be mere appearance; in Hegel,
we recall, the outcome of tragedy is a revelation of the ultimate singleness of spirit underlying its limited and destructible
manifestations.

Hegel's thought, as I say, has a fundamental dramatic tendency
which associates him with the theoretical wing of the German
dramatic movement from Lessing to Nietzsche, and a clear manifestation of this tendency is his intense concern with the question
of *the generic quality of drama* in its philosophical significance.
The particularization, "Besonderung,"[26] of moral powers or aspects of the spirit, so that they can appear as characters in an
insoluble tragic collision, is possible only in a dramatic performance; in narrative or in drama for the reader, the mere implied
presence of a general authorial consciousness, no matter how im-
partial or unobtrusive, must mediate between the antagonists,
who are in essence themselves modes of consciousness. Hegel
does not make the argument in exactly this form; he derives his
idea of the tragic *from* a general principle of drama which includes the necessity of performance. But the argument as I have

stated it is logically implied; the indispensable "lyrical principle" (*Ästh.*, 485) in dramatic poetry entails an exclusive relationship between the external fiction and the consciousness manifest in the form of characters, which relationship would be superseded by the presence of a narrating consciousness.

Or to look at it differently, drama is the only art form in which a fully adequate representation of the actual mechanism of dialectic is possible. Verbal works of art, since language both expresses and refers, by nature combine a basic inwardness with a basic outwardness, and so approach the totality of spirit in a way that nonverbal art cannot (see *Ästh.*, 222, etc.). But the nondramatic forms of verbal art, because of the presence of an authorial consciousness in the immediate artistic structure, reveal truth as a kind of stasis, mediated by that consciousness, whereas in drama truth appears in its true dialectical form, as that which is in the process of becoming what it is, as a resolution which is not fully accessible to any particular consciousness until it actually arrives through the operation of antitheses. We must not be misled by Hegel's statement that the dramatic poet ought to assert his own individuality more strongly than the epic poet. Hegel is here speaking of the poet's relation to his public, not to his work; and what he means is that we do not wish to experience the fictional world of drama merely as a kind of reality, "but rather, at the same time, we wish to recognize in the completed work the product of a self-conscious and original act of creation, the art and virtuosity of an individual poet" (*Ästh.*, 507). (Compare Schiller's essay on the chorus.) This does not imply, however, that drama can be in the least arbitrary, that it can express "the one-sided world-view of this or that subject"; on the contrary, drama demands "that in the progress and completion of the dramatic action, tragically or comically, the realization of that which is in and for itself rational and true be shown as achieved" (*Ästh.*, 508). Drama, then, must give the impression of self-conscious originality, of an individual poet's mind, while at the same time revealing not opinion but pure truth—which is to say, again, that drama must mirror the dialectical world-process itself, the ceaseless self-conscious production of historical realities which burst forth as if totally original, yet reveal themselves as strictly rational once they are realized. This is why the dramatist, of all poets, requires "the greatest openness and comprehensiveness of mind" (*Ästh.*, 486). If the

epic poet succeeds in effacing himself completely, then it is for
the purpose of giving the impression that his fiction is continuous
with our own established reality; if the authorial consciousness is
eliminated, then it is immediately replaced in epic by "popular
consciousness" (*Ästh.*, 507), an established, collective idea of the
way things really are. Drama's job, however, is to produce not
reality but truth, the catastrophic but rational process by which all
established realities are superseded dialectically.

Hegel therefore carries forward the German dramatic tradition
by inquiring intently into the unique generic quality of drama,
and his idea of this quality is intimately related to the essence of
his thought as a whole. Thus it is no accident, and has to do at
least indirectly with the German dramatic movement, that for
Ibsen and Pirandello dramatic form appears the proper vehicle for
expressing a Hegelian sense of things. Drama, again, is the most
thoroughly dialectical art form, and Hegel's awareness of this is
not limited to his theory of tragedy and comedy. Some passages in
the *Phenomenology*, for example, deal very subtly with the dialectical relation between the actor and his role,[27] a relation which
figures implicitly in the thought of Lessing and Schiller, somewhat more obviously in *Prinz Friedrich* (we recall the parallel
between the characters' staging of a vision for the Prince and the
actors' staging of a vision for the audience), and then centrally in
much modern drama, especially Brecht and the Brechtians. Or we
think of Hegel's basic definition of drama in the *Aesthetics* as a
synthesis of subjective and objective poetry, which recalls the
grappling of German Classicism with the problem of detachment
and involvement, or individual and community.

Perhaps more important for our immediate purposes, however,
is the special relationship between the genre of drama and a
dialectical conception of the human self. Hamlet says of his outward expressions of mourning:

> These indeed seem,
> For they are actions that a man might play:
> But I have that within which passeth show;
> These but the trappings and the suits of woe.

And then, in the monologue that follows ("O, that this too too
solid flesh . . . "), he reveals what he had been holding back. But it

soon becomes clear that neither this nor any of Hamlet's monologues succeeds in revealing the whole of what is "within" him. We see more and more of him as the play progresses, on the one hand through what he says and thinks, on the other hand through the gradual unfolding of his fate, but there is still always something of him, something like Egmont's "inmost self," which literally "passeth show," which does not exist in any form that could allow it to be revealed on the stage. And the presence of this unstageable something seems to me a uniquely dramatic feature of the work; precisely the inaccessibility, in drama, of the self on its deepest level, constitutes the truest possible representation of the self. In all forms of narrative, where the whole content, including the characters, is imagined, "vorgestellt" (*Phän.*, 558), thus mental or ideal in nature, the true self of each character exists on essentially the same ideal plane as its manifestations in body, thought, action, and fate; the fundamental *difference* between the true self and its effects is thus not part of the basic artistic structure. In drama, on the other hand, the true self, which "passeth show," does not exist on the main sensory level of expression; the existing realities, rather, are character and fate, in dialectical tension with one another—the light and dark sides of the hero's existence, as Hegel has it (*Phän.*, 561–62), or in Nietzsche's terms, the hero as himself and as Dionysus—and only by the gradual resolution of this tension does the true self first achieve its being, beome what it is.

This idea of the self in drama brings us into the vicinity not only of Hegel's thought but also of Maeterlinck's, Chekhov's, Andreyev's, Ibsen's and Strindberg's, Schnitzler's and Hofmannsthal's, even Allardyce Nicoll's, in short, into the intellectual vicinity of some widespread ideas in modern drama, the idea of the inward hero and the idea, by consequence, that action in what we usually take to be Aristotle's sense is dramatically dispensable. In our age, says Maeterlinck, "it is certain that the domain of the soul increases each day," and our age therefore produces dramatic figures like Ibsen's Hilda and Solness, "the first heroes who feel themselves living for a moment in the soul's atmosphere."[28] Drama now does its main work not by what it says but by what it does not say, or says secretly, not by what it shows but by its gestures in the direction of what cannot be shown (we recall the problem of demonstrating freedom in *Maria Stuart*), by a system of invisible relationships with the audience; drama's business, in Hegel's terms, is not to show reality but to reveal truth.

I will not claim that all ideas of this sort which appear in the context of modern drama are attributable to Hegel's influence. Hegel himself becomes rather unsystematic and unperceptive when dealing with modern drama, or drama of character; and in Maeterlinck, for example, the ideas I have mentioned have any number of sources, including medieval mysticism, Novalis, Carlyle, and Schopenhauer. But generally speaking, the ideas of the inward hero and the actionless drama may be regarded as the result of two very broad tendencies in nineteenth-century thought, in both of which Hegel plays a significant part—the tendency, first, to see history as progress toward ever greater interiorization of existence, which makes an ancient or Renaissance heroism of action obsolete; and, second, the tendency, culminating in such thinkers as Nietzsche, Mach, and Freud, to question the notion of the self or "ego" as a single operative entity, which tendency brings with it a questioning of the apparently simple procedure of creating dramatic characters and allowing them to act in accordance with what they are.

Both these intellectual tendencies have a deep effect on the modern novel, but they do not necessarily favor the novel as a genre. In the work of all the dramatists mentioned above, as well as in all existentialist drama and in Nietzsche's theory,[29] the radical difference between what appears on stage and what "passeth show" is recognized as a uniquely valuable artistic device for dealing with the inward dialectical complexity of modern existence. Thus Hegel, the philosopher of history as interiorization, the dialectical critic of what appears under various conscious circumstances as the individual's "ego," makes an important contribution to the shaping of modern drama even where his influence is not demonstrable; and this contribution preserves and develops the spirit of German Classicism, partly because of the influence of Schiller, and for that matter of Lessing and Goethe as well,[30] partly because of the basic community of origins and aims that connects German idealism as a whole with the "inward-directed" drama of the Classical period.

Perhaps we can best summarize Hegel's role in the development of the German dramatic tradition by saying that he is instrumental in keeping alive the *question* of drama as a genre. He himself attaches great significance to this question, even though the logical and empirical prerequisites for something like Lukács's basically Hegelian theory of the novel were available to him, and Szondi in fact argues that the dialectic triad epic-lyric-dramatic in the *Aesthetics* corresponds to the triadic historical progression from classical art through Romantic art to the ultimate synthesis of spirit, beyond art, in religion and absolute knowledge.[31] Thus Hegel's whole philosophical-historical system is as it were in danger of becoming a theory of drama; if Hegel had understood the achievement of German Classical drama, if he had not been able to see something like an absolute limit in Sophocles' *Antigone* (*Ästh.*, 556), then he might have had to agree, after all, with his old school chum Schelling, that art (which in his own system would have meant drama) is the culminating act of the spirit.

In any case, the immediate reason for Hegel's concern with the question of drama as a genre emerges from his association, in the German Classical spirit, of "humanity" with a "community of consciousness" (*Phän.*, 63). The single basic faith shared by Hegelians of all persuasions, and mocked by their opponents, is faith in the history and destiny of consciousness. The operation of consciousness in culture necessarily leads to a state of "unhappy self-consciousness" (*Phän.*, 571), skepticism, alienation, loneliness, confusion; but this state, which includes the Zarathustrian belief "that God is dead" (*Phän.*, 572), is not final, not self-perpetuating. It is, rather, the preparation for a new form of communicable knowledge, a new cohesion among men, which is brought about by yet another self-conscious movement. This faith in the ultimately "circuitous" or spiral form of man's self-conscious journey through culture is of course not exclusively Hegelian—it could be called Schillerian or Kleistian or German-Classical or Romantic—but Hegel and his followers still represent the most significant nineteenth-century intellectual force propagating it. And at least something of this faith, at least the belief that alienated consciousness can for a time overcome itself in the direction of the communal, is necessary in serious modern drama, in any serious attempt to reestablish communal art for our fragmented and groping age.

Hegel does not express any hope for new developments in the field of drama, but the general influence of his thought nonetheless tends to maintain or awaken a sense of the genre as a problem, a sense of drama as desirable and perhaps even possible in a new type of community, even though the old categories of action, passion, and heroism will no longer be applicable. The effects of this sense of drama as a problem can be traced in the development of what I have called the melancholy tragic mode, the attempt to derive tragic feeling from the knowledge that tragedy in the older sense is no longer possible. Or they can be traced in the tendency of the German movement, and then of modern drama, to use the artist or artist type as a dramatic hero, in Goethe's *Tasso*, Hölderlin's *Empedokles*, Grillparzer's *Sappho*, Johst's *Der Einsame* along with Brecht's answer to it in *Baal*, and the artists or quasi artists or visionaries in Chekhov, Ibsen, Strindberg, Hauptmann. This tendency is an aspect of the general attempt to install human inwardness as the new content of drama's communally accessible externality, to carry out the final dialectical step by which "unhappy self-consciousness" returns to the communal fold, and in modern drama it reflects Hegel's presence even where the influence of a Hegelian tradition is not so clearly marked as, for example, in German expressionism.[32]

Something needs to be said, finally, about the relation between historicism and modern drama. Pre-Hegelian historicism—or Herderian historicism—is anthropological in character and primarily biological in imagery; Shakespeare is seen as a plant growing in the soil of his time and nation. And this species of historicism does not encourage the development of modern drama. In an age characterized by individualism, self-consciousness, the decline of deep communal cohesion in favor of mechanical regulation by government, how can the "plant" of drama flourish? A number of characteristically Herderian and artistically unfruitful answers to this question are offered from the late eighteenth century on. Schiller, in the early "Schaubühne" essay, hopes to revive the German theater by using German subject matter, and Wagner later demonstrates what this leads to; both Ibsen and Strindberg waste some effort on Scandinavian myth and history; and the more unimaginative of the naturalists try to convince us that modern industrial and commercial society constitutes a new native soil for drama nowadays, an idea that conveniently excuses the dramatist from incorporating his naturalistic images into a genuine artistic structure.

This is where Hegel comes in. The idea that history moves forward by acts of free conceptual consciousness, not by some quasi-biological mechanism, is necessary if historicism in general is to be reconciled with radical innovation in artistic form. And especially in the case of drama, which by the late nineteenth century apparently required drastic measures to overcome a long dormancy, some such idea was necessary; the metaphor of slow vegetable growth was not applicable. I do not mean to say that free artistic experimentation can happen only in the context of Hegelian historicism; the artistic experimenter does not need to be a historicist in the first place. But only Hegelian historicism, only the idea that conscious originality is what produces the *logical* and *necessary* development of history, enables the artist to see his radical experiment as a classic in the making, as a fully communicative self-revelation of its culture. And again, this is crucial for the communal art form of drama. The nondramatic artist may reconcile himself to his work's remaining unknown, but there is something desperately futile about the dramatist who does this, like Grillparzer; for the dramatic work is not fully realized, it is not yet itself, except as a communal event, and if the dramatist cannot presuppose an adequately cohesive community for his work to exist in, then he must at least hope to create such a community.

Thus it is the Hegelian, or ultimately Schillerian, paradox of self-conscious freedom and strict historical-communal necessity that generates a proper atmosphere for the more drastic attempts to create a true modern drama by main force—say Jarry and Apollinaire, Marinetti's futurism, German expressionism. Or we think of the whole idea of the *Gesamtkunstwerk*, as it appears not only in Bayreuth but also in the efforts of Reinhardt or Copeau, the attempt—hopeless even when it is "delicate and in good taste" (Bentley on Copeau)[33]—to elevate drama from its status as merely one of the arts and establish it as a kind of super-art, the pantechnic celebration of a cultural unity which the celebration itself must first bring into being. But a certain debt to Hegel, and thence to Schiller and German Classicism, is also reflected in the dramatic experimentation of such authors as Ibsen, Strindberg, Brecht, Pirandello, Ionesco, in their experiments *as* conscious experiments, which are related via Hegel to the less conspicuous but no less radical dramatic experiments carried out in Germany around 1800.

6

In what sense, to come back to the main question, can one speak of a central modern dramatic "tradition" which at a crucial juncture includes German Classicism? German and Scandinavian dramatists in this century tend to be aware of certain parts of the German movement, but in other countries this awareness is much less developed. In order to understand the flourishing of modern drama we must have recourse to a number of general tendencies in nineteenth-century thought which have the effect of presenting drama as an especially difficult but important cultural problem: the ideas of metaphysical, psychological, and historical dialectic; the sense of a progressive interiorization of existence and a corresponding loss of communal cohesion, so that the shaping of communal life is in danger of being left to inhuman agencies; the need for a modern equivalent of myth and for a new sense of what makes the heroic individual. And I have attempted, accordingly, to show the importance of the German movement in the background of all these tendencies, especially as they affect drama.

What I am attempting to trace, therefore, is an intermittently realized tradition of spirit, or perhaps—I am borrowing this term—a "discontinuous tradition,"[34] and this sort of tradition is by nature harder to lay hold of than, say, the Scribean tradition of play-building, or the various traditions of farce that have a demonstrable effect on modern drama, or for that matter the "tradition" of the puppet theater, which influenced not only Jarry and Ghelderode but also Goethe. But while a number of stylistic features in modern drama can be traced without the aid of German Classicism, I think it is not possible to see modern drama as any sort of coherent whole without discovering German Classical drama in its background.

Perhaps one should not try to see modern drama as a coherent whole; perhaps one should simply be delighted by its variety. This would be a valid objection against the attempt to force a single rigid form onto modern drama, but I have not made any such attempt. My point is that there is a relatively unified German dramatic movement from Lessing on, which can be shown to include at least a few major modern authors—Ibsen, Strindberg,

Hauptmann, Brecht—and that the main unifying feature of this movement is its recognizable theatrical modernity: that is, its awareness and exploitation of dramatic performance as a social ritual; its integration of the audience's self-consciousness and the work's artificiality into poetic structure; its penetration, by consequence, of the hidden complexity and anguish and strength of everyday human existence. These, it will probably be agreed, are all aspects of modern drama, but their manifestations are so enormously varied that there would be very little chance of agreement about the extent to which they constitute an essence. Therefore I have approached the problem from the other direction. Rather than attempt to extract an essence from a large number of modern works, I have begun with the easier question of the unity of German drama and traced intellectual paths by which the spirit of that drama is transmitted to our century. This is not proof of the overall coherence of modern drama of course. But at least there is a strong cultural force tending toward such coherence.

Perhaps we can say something more specific about how this force works in practice by taking as examples two dissimilar authors, Shaw and Pirandello, who are both affected by nineteenth-century German thought, but neither of whom appears to be influenced directly by German Classical drama. If clear formal affinities with the German dramatic movement can be shown in Shaw and Pirandello, and if these affinities can be related to the general influence of late idealist and dialectic philosophy, then we shall at least have a measure of the scope of the phenomenon we are dealing with.

Let us begin with Shaw's prefaces. Are the plays really plays, or are they—as the prefaces might lead us to believe—really polemical treatises, which the author, for the fun of it, has written in dramatic form? It seems to me that the plays are in truth plays, and that even the prefaces have a dramatic function in that they serve to condition the spectator, whether he has read them or is merely aware of their existence. By means of his prefaces, essays, and articles, Shaw presents himself to the public at large as a man with a point to make, and the result, in the auditorium, is a kind of alienation. The spectator comes prepared to interpret what he sees, and then to agree or disagree with its point; he does not come prepared to suspend his disbelief and deliver himself emotionally to an illusory world.

I do not mean that Shaw's expository writings are not seriously intended, although it is not always easy to see exactly how serious they are. But they do also serve a dramatic purpose, in that they produce an alienation which enables Shaw to operate effectively with a minimum of artistic innovation, with characters (as he says himself) out of Dickens and with theatrical techniques out of a comic stock-in-trade since Molière. If we are intellectually detached, in the expectation that the author is making an assertion with which we must agree or disagree, then we shall accept relatively old-fashioned artistic conventions in the same way that we accept the old-fashioned conventions of grammar when listening to a lecture. The conventions occasion us no discomfort because the Shavian atmosphere disarms them; they do not require conventional responses on our part. "Effectiveness of assertion is the Alpha and Omega of style,"[35] says Shaw, and we are meant to apply this statement to his own works. The first audiences, presumably, distinguish between assertion and style, because the assertion is still controversial; later, when the assertion has been disproved—and "All the assertions get disproved sooner or later"—it functions as an element of style, in Shaw's case as the interposition of an intellectual distance which lends vitality to certain shopworn conventions.

But are Shaw's plays really characterized by effectiveness of assertion? Can an author make a serious assertion if he knows that all assertions are eventually disproved? Can the form of drama serve as a vehicle for assertions in the first place? Fergusson speaks, quite correctly, of "the true Shavian sense of human life as rationalizing in the void,"[36] and does this not apply to life in the auditorium as well as to the life on stage? Effectiveness of assertion, or at least directness of assertion, whether or not it is identical with style in general, is an indispensable element of Shaw's style, and Shaw's plays, accordingly, are written in such a way as to give the impression of such directness; the moral stripping of clan Shotover and Mangan and the Dunns in *Heartbreak House*, for example, contains a number of definite assertions about British society. But these assertions, on examination, prove very limited and all point beyond themselves in the direction of a question, a paradox, a chaotic "void" about which no useful assertion can be made: "Is this England, or is it a madhouse?" (V, 164). Shaw's own metaphor for this void, in *Heartbreak House*, is the open sea. The fact that Captain Shotover's quarter gallery or great cabin is part not of a ship, but of a house on dry land, produces an immediate sense of incongruity and potential chaos, a sense of being "at sea" after all. The Captain, upon hearing that the rector is now homeless, says: "The Church is on the rocks, breaking up. I told him it would unless it headed for God's open sea" (V, 177–78); and Shaw, not with the Church but with the theater, is apparently trying to avoid those "rocks."

The end of *Heartbreak House* is nothing if not ambiguous. Mangan, who corresponds to Chekhov's Lopahin and so is presumably on his way to inheriting the earth, is fortunately carried off by a German bomb plus thirty pounds of Captain Shotover's dynamite. The cherry orchard, as it were, is saved, but the result is merely to leave the world, or at least England, at the mercy of the Heartbreakers' cultivated omissiveness. And yet, the audience is not permitted the luxury of crying a plague on Heartbreak House, for the very last words of the play refer clearly to the institution of the theater. Hesione says of the bombing, "But what a glorious experience! I hope theyll come again tomorrow night," to which Ellie responds, "Oh, I *hope* so" (V, 181); and we are meant to reflect that the bombs *will* come again tomorrow night, and will again be greeted with an absurd joyous enthusiasm, as long as the theater continues to sell tickets. We, the audience, with at least our pretensions to culture, have by some absurd accident survived and even won the war, as the Heartbreakers have survived the bombing, and the fact that we are now deriving amusement from this in the theater proves that we have learned no more than they. Heartbreak House, like the Ranevskaya estate in Chekhov, encompasses the auditorium. Our relation to the war itself, as Shaw points out in his preface, had been that of theatrical spectators— appalled or excited or indifferent according to our prejudices, but always ineffective—and we are now carrying on as before.

Shaw's aim is to awaken a clear self-consciousness in his audience, but a consciousness which includes the recognition that consciousness does no good. Being stripped "morally naked" (V, 166), knowing ourselves to the bone, does not change our condition; Hector Hushabye, for example, understands clearly at least one aspect of the play's social lesson—"Think of the powers of destruction that Mangan and his mutual admiration gang wield!" (V, 175)—yet remains Hector Hushabye, with his own peculiar madness, to the end. What we are left with is rationalizing in the void, a knowledge of emptiness, which knowledge is the emptiness it knows; the "assertion" for the sake of which we had accepted the theatrical conventions now evaporates, and the conventions themselves become yet another symbol of emptiness, an image of our own hopeless thought processes. Something very close to a Nietzschean dramatic configuration has been created, a stage fiction which, in all its tight particularity and even topicalness, functions as the direct projection of a sheer nihilistic anguish experienced by the audience, a Dionysian knowledge of the emptiness behind all apparent reality. Like the characters themselves, we could now joyfully see Heartbreak House destroyed, in order to experience its essential emptiness as a *force*, a Nietzschean or Bergsonian *élan*, a defiant vitality, a "metaphysical consolation"; "I still have the will to live" (V, 177), says Hector and then, with perfect logic, lights up the house as a target. But as in Brecht, where the hurricane misses Mahagonny, or Kleist, where death misses Homburg, the irony takes us one step further. Precisely the absence of a catastrophic climax serves to establish an essentially tragic (not melancholy) experience of the human condition; as in Brecht and Kleist, the anticlimax reminds us that the situation on stage is a reflection of our situation in the theater, not a situation of bracing danger, but rather a self-reflected balancing on the brink of the abyss, heroic only in its everydayness.

Shaw's "Fantasia" is on one level "in the Russian Manner," but also in the German manner on a somewhat deeper level, and this is largely ascribable to the Nietzschean influence. Shaw is first of all a dialectical historicist; he understands that each age has its unique character, produced by a mechanism of conscious antithesis and assimilation relative to what had gone before, that artistic greatness, for instance, must be gauged in terms of a "philosophy" peculiar to its "epoch" (II, 41–48). But his historicism also incorporates Nietzsche's criticism of Hegel, the denial that history is rational progress, the recognition that the historical procession of philosophies or moralities or religions is a relatively superficial phenomenon which masks the recurrence of basic vital or psychological forces beneath; thus the god Ra can say "that men twenty centuries ago were already just such as you" (II, 166), and Cauchon, Lemaître, and Warwick can "make a twentieth-century audience conscious of an epoch fundamentally different from their own" simply by becoming themselves conscious of "what they were really doing"—which entails a "sacrifice of verisimilitude" (VI, 73–74) but not a sacrifice of plausibility, since self-consciousness changes nothing anyway. History is a dialectic of consciousness which leads nowhere. Darwin the simple naturalist and Joan the simple "visualizer" (VI, 33) initiate antithetical movements in history without having any idea that they are doing this; the antitheses are then sharpened by the gross ignorance of their opponents, whereupon, eventually, syntheses are arrived at; Joan and Darwin are both canonized by people who misunderstand them as much as their opponents had, and history blunders on.

History, in other words, is Captain Shotover's open sea, where everything changes but "Nothing happens, except something not worth mentioning" (V, 176), this something being the occasional spectacular disaster brought down by man upon himself. Nor is this idea of history at all modified by the views expressed in *Man and Superman* or *Back to Methuselah*. "Creative evolution" for Shaw, like Nietzsche's "Übermensch," is not an assertion about history, but rather a hypothesis designed to furnish modern man with a maximally self-alienated perspective within his own historical situation; the idea of creative evolution, which apparently says everything but actually accomplishes nothing, is a demonstration that self-consciousness, even at its highest tension (the state of being what Zarathustra calls a "higher man"), does not change either our basic or our immediate condition. Particular cultural situations are mere masks for the state of being at sea, but our knowledge of this does not liberate us from the particular vessel we happen to be riding.

Why, then, does Shaw not leave his audience in peace? What does he hope to accomplish with them? An answer to this question is apparently suggested by Captain Shotover's answer to Hector's question about the proper business of an Englishman: "Navigation. Learn it and live; or leave it and be damned" (V, 177). But can we take navigation here to mean something like political science, when Shaw points out in his preface that even if the Heartbreak people knew political science, they would have no opportunity to apply it (V, 16)? The open sea, as Captain Shotover imagines it, has storms to be weathered and reefs to be avoided, but no harbors, no ports to be made, and what is the use of navigation if one has nowhere to go? Evidently navigation as a metaphor must refer to the state of being at home on the open sea itself, and this idea is also suggested by the progression of stage settings in *Heartbreak House;* Acts I and II are set in a ship's cabin, but in Act III we pass out through the doors and find ourselves not only at home, on dry land, but on a piece of land which enjoys a kind of magical, if questionable (or indeed "damnably dull" [V, 181]) security. What does this mean in poetic or social or theatrical terms?

Let us think back for a moment to *Maria Stuart,* where Schiller attempts to reveal the social, political, and ultimately metaphysical dimensions of our individual self-consciousness by showing that the world of human culture, although it exists ostensibly for the sake of order, has an inescapable tendency in the direction of self-division and chaos, which tendency, however, also contains an intimation of our true freedom and destiny, our totally realized humanness. Our awareness of our freedom thus depends in Schiller on our experiencing the world as chaos; but on the other hand, the actuality of our freedom resides only in the act of firm self-limitation within an established but arbitrary order. This is Schiller's version of the idea of "navigation," as opposed to Leicester's drifting; somehow we must be, as it were, both at sea and at home. And the resolution of this paradox is for Schiller the idea of transforming the inevitable and inevitably arbitrary cultural givens of existence into a conscious work of art, an idea which is present in all German Classical drama from *Nathan* and *Iphigenie* on, in Schiller's theoretical notion of "play," and also in Nietzsche's early artistic or musical Socratism as well as in his later *amor fati.*

It seems to me that essentially this idea is what Shaw is aiming at as well. John Tanner writes of the need for the Superman, that "with Must there is no arguing" (II, 780); but it is clear from the rest of his argument that none of the specific measures required to pave the Superman's way can ever be carried out, except perhaps involuntarily. The "Must," for a moment—like Nietzsche's "threefold Must" in *Vom Nutzen und Nachteil der Historie,*[37] or Brecht's at the end of *Der gute Mensch von Sezuan*—wrenches us free from our old cultural order but offers us nothing tangible in exchange, and so leaves us no choice but to return to the fold as Jack himself turns to marriage, with the firm (but for all we know, hopeless) resolve to transform slavery itself into an energetic act of creation. The attempt to found a culture on solid ground, as a reliable system of institutions, is futile; the culture is then not on solid ground but "on the rocks," not founded but foundering. Institutions are inevitable, but they must be treated as a creative game; otherwise they soon become, dialectically, objects of negation, and eventually invitations to sudden social disaster (see II, 774–75). Freedom and bondage, therefore (the paradox of German idealism), must be not merely coexistent but identical, as must be also knowledge of the truth and knowledge of the futility of knowledge. The ability to balance on the horns of this paradox is what the Alpine German (Nietzsche) imagines as living in the cold air of the heights, and what the maritime Britisher calls "navigation." It is, moreover, an ability which the theater, as a creative communal game of the intellect that imposes on its audience the paradox of detachment and involvement, is specially well suited to foster.

The aim of Shaw's theater is essentially the same as that of German Classical theater, not education (except perhaps "homeopathically") but rather the revelation that here and now, in the theater, the audience is living life at its realest, not an idea or image but an intensified version of life itself.[38] Fergusson says much the same thing, though somewhat disapprovingly, when he says that Shaw involves us in his characters' rationalizing "for therapeutic reasons, . . . for the sake of a certain decent fitness in the moral void"; in the theater we experience intensely, thus therapeutically, what we experience only dimly outside it, namely a "moral void" which represents "outer darkness, the unmapped forces of the changing modern world"[39] in which we must live. Our business in life is navigation, an adroit balancing between the void of sheer truth and the world of gross institutional illusion, so that the void may become in a sense livable, the world in a sense truthful. And the theater, for Shaw, is where this process begins, for the theater is a real social institution (whereas the reading of a novel is purely private), but an institution which opens into the institutionless realm of the poetic imagination, into the void of Must without Can, into the cold Alpine air of truth, where reason rationalizes perilously at the brink of nonsense.

This sense of the theater, in earlier Shaw, is meant to generate a rapport between the audience and Caesar's "originality," his ability "to estimate the value of truth, money, or success in any particular instance quite independently of convention and moral

generalization" (II, 303). Caesar passes beyond convention, or beyond good and evil, but not in order to turn his back on convention and live wholly in the void; he lives, rather, in a world of
particular instances, in response to which he plays creatively with
conventions, infusing the qualities of "frankness, generosity and
magnanimity" with a new energetic spuriousness, in place of
their old institutionalized spuriousness. In other words, he practices that purposeless but necessary "navigation" for which the
theater trains us. And in later Shaw the same sense of the theater
places us, the audience, among Joan's admirers, but also among
her murderers. (The parallel with *Maria Stuart* is really quite
close.) Joan, in her uninhibited peremptoriness, is an embodiment
of our own experience of the ideal or poetic void beyond convention; this experience is revealed through her as an "evolutionary
appetite" (VI, 26–28), an unrealizable Must, which is thwarted by
the fact that as a theater audience, as willing participants in a
social ritual of the sort Joan by nature abhors, we also inevitably
join the ranks of her innocent murderers. But we are not quite so
"normally innocent" (VI, 72) as the people of her own time; for
her energy, the energy of her Must, remains an integral part of our
situation as poetic imaginers in the theater. Her energy has become our energy (we recall Brecht on the vital energy of the "asocial" character), now redirected into the paradox of "navigation,"
the paradoxical identity of world and void by which it becomes
conceivable, as Ladvenu's report in the Epilogue suggests, that
this "orgy of lying and foolishness" (VI, 192) which is normal
human society may yet somehow enter into a genuine relation
with truth.

Shaw's basic sense of drama and the theater perhaps grows
deeper after World War I, but it does not change essentially, and
the simplicity of the devices by which he puts it into practice
should not blind us to its significant affinity with German Classical dramaturgy. Shaw casts us as Joan's murderers for the same
ultimate poetic reason Schiller casts us as Mary's, to awaken us to
the possibility of infusing even this terribly imperfect world with
our own creative energy; that his techniques are in part diametri-
cally different from Schiller's—the Dauphin in a sense corresponds to Leicester—does not mean that his work is different in
spirit. And since the philosophical aspect of Shaw's dramaturgy is
Nietzschean, in the sense in which Nietzsche develops the

achievements of German Classicism, this affinity in spirit is also a historical link to the German movement.

Unlike Shaw's prefaces, Pirandello's well-known preface to *Six Characters in Search of an Author* gives the impression of being basically an interpretation. Unfortunately, however, although it does raise some deep interpretive questions about the play, it has also distracted critics from the even deeper questions which ought to be asked. Pirandello, in that preface, distinguishes carefully between the life of life and the life of art: "Everything that lives, by living, has form, and for the same reason must die: except the work of art, which lives forever precisely by *being* form."[40] And the same distinction clearly underlies the father's cross-examination of the director, in which he claims to be "more real" than the director.

> *The Father:* If your reality can change from one day to the next . . . .
> *The Director:* Of course it can change! It changes constantly, like everybody's.
> *The Father* (with a groan): But not ours! Do you see? That's the difference. Our reality does not change, cannot change, can never be otherwise, because it is fixed—thus—as "this"—forever—(sir, it is terrible) an immutable reality which ought to give you the chills when you encounter us. [p. 105]

A real person, by the natural logic of self-consciousness—"reflecting," as the father says, "that 'this,' as you now feel yourself (*come lei ora si sente*), all your existing reality of today, will inevitably strike you as illusory tomorrow"—is constantly in danger of feeling that he is not "someone" at all, but rather "no one," whereas "a fictional character has his own life in truth, marked by traits that belong to him, so that he is always 'someone'" (p. 104).

But does this distinction hold? The director, after all, is a character in a play. The difference is that the director (like most dramatic characters) does not know that he is a character, whereas the father does, and the effect of this self-knowledge is precisely to make the father *less* (or less consistently) a character than the director. The father insists that he is more real than the director because the latter's self-consciousness constantly reduces his existence to illusion, by lifting his immediate person (*come ora si sente*) out of it. But this argument can be reversed exactly and used against the father, whose consciousness of himself as a dramatic character constantly lifts *him* out of his "role." Not only the director makes this point (p. 105), but the father himself, earlier on, asserts that his own principal scene in the inner play is merely an illusory instant (p. 73) which does not really express what he feels himself to be, *come ora si sente;* he now applies to himself exactly the argument he later uses against the director, "that each of us believes himself 'one' but in truth is not" (p. 72).

The full significance of this interchangeability of positions between the father and the director ("for you are me" [p. 103], says the father) becomes clear when we consider the situation of the audience. We the audience are real human beings exposed to the confusion and uncertainty of self-consciousness, and our relation to all the characters in the play is therefore parallel with that of the director to the father; the characters are "somebody" in a quasi-eternal sense, they belong to an unchanging artistic structure which is their "reason for being" (p. 40), whereas we live constantly on the brink of being "nobody." And yet, if the relation between the director and the father is reversible, then so perhaps is that between us and the characters in general. In fact, this last relation is reversible in a fairly obvious way. Fictional characters, as the father boasts, are ideal or mental realities, by comparison with which our own changing reality has the quality of illusion. But in drama alone of all literary genres, the characters have a physical as well as an ideal existence, in that they are represented by actors, and this physical existence calls the unity of their ideal existence into question, as we recognize in the *Six Characters* when we see the same scene performed in two different ways. The dramatic character must be realized by performance; this, after all, is why the six characters have come to the theater. But every performance is *different,* which means that even within one moment of his existence the dramatic character is not unified, not constant; in this sense he is more changeable than we are, a mere "illusion of reality" (p. 102). We in the audience are less real, but also more real than he is.

When we enter the theater, we are presumably disposed to think, as the director does, that we simply are what we are and that the stage will be peopled with unreal figments; but the father's captious syllogisms, his "Demon of Experiment" (p. 64), quickly involves us in at least the possibility that our own supposed reality is mere illusion, and a flimsy one at that. Then, however, as we probe more deeply into the play's thought, as we understand the implications of the reversible relation between the father and the director, we receive a new sense of our reality which replaces the highly questionable everyday sense we have left behind. On one hand this new sense of our reality is only relative and ambiguous—we are at least *as* real as the characters in the play—but on the other hand, by virtue of the father's arguments, it also contains a striving toward poetic ideality, a potential absoluteness, which is lacking in the way we usually think of ourselves. We are also *as* ideal as the characters.

In fact, the crucial reversal of positions between director and father is meant to take place in our own state of mind as we sit in the theater; for as soon as it occurs to us that our situation is parallel to that of the director, this very recognition constitutes an act of self-consciousness with respect to our quality as spectators, so that our situation has automatically become similar to the father's, who is uncomfortably self-conscious with respect to his quality as "character." Thus we, the audience, are the intermediate term by which the father's words to the director, "lei è me" (you are me), make sense. As spectators we are identified with the director and his troupe, and in fact the father's plea, "Sir, we want to live! at least for a moment, in you" (p. 59), could as easily be addressed to us as to the director; it is after all in the minds of an audience ("da tutti immaginato" [p. 105]) that a dramatic character must ultimately "live." But as self-consciously disoriented spectators at a "comedy in the making," or in other words, as "spectators in search of a play" (possessing "being" without "a reason for being" [p. 40]), we are also identified with the characters in search of an author, especially the father. Moreover, the fact that it is possible for us to derive a sense of our own reality from our intellectual relationship with poetic creations allows us to participate in the father's earnest if questionable claim to immortality; there is, as I have said, a potential absoluteness, an eternal dimension in our reality as it is restored to us by this theater.

At least this particular play of Pirandello, therefore, exhibits affinities with the German movement which are both profound and specific. The play is not meant to show reality but to generate, here and now in the theater, a reality somehow realer than real, a direct intensification of human existence for its audience. And the method by which this task is approached is exactly the method employed by Lessing, Goethe, Schiller, and Kleist; the relation between stage and auditorium is made into a huge working model of individual human self-consciousness, so that the self-consciousness of the individual spectator is magnified, its inherent problems exacerbated, beyond all normal possibility, while at the same time it is also transformed into an orderly communal phenomenon and so in a sense transfigured, its problems in a sense resolved. This model of self-consciousness, moreover, as in the German plays, consists in a complex analogy between our consciousness as spectators and patterns of consciousness within the fictional world, the analogy between our relation to the stage and the reversible relation of characters and actors. And the message inherent in this structure, finally, is essentially the same as what could be called the general message of German Classicism, that self-consciousness, although it disrupts and undermines our existence constantly, must still be affirmed and developed as the only possible avenue to the true self, to an eternal or absolute humanity.

We might summarize these points by saying that *Sei personaggi in cerca d'autore* is a profoundly Hegelian work of art, perhaps the most perfect example available of how Hegelian thought transmits the spirit of German Classical drama and brings forth, or at least favors, a philosophical dramaturgy of self-consciousness in the specifically German manner. There are a number of relatively obvious Hegelian features in Pirandello's text: for example, the father's use of "questo" ("this," pp. 103, 104 in quotation marks) as something approaching a technical philosophical term, in a meaning similar to that of Hegel's "Dieses" (e.g. *Phän.*, 81–92, 579–80); or the presence of a character, the son, "who 'negates' the very drama that makes him a character" (p. 45), yet still plays an indispensable part, by withdrawing into his room where his mother then follows him, leaving the children alone in the garden. But on a deeper level, the whole dialectical movement between the director and the father ("lei è me") or between the audience and the stage action, the movement by which the self stands over against its opposite and in doing so reintegrates its opposite with itself, embodies a characteristic Hegelian criticism of such distinctions as "*the same* and *not the same, identity* and

non-identity" (*Phän.*, 594); and this in turn is a development of
the dialectic which is realized in German Classical drama (e.g., as
the demonic "on both sides," both for and against Egmont),
though still only latent in German Classical theory.

As far as I can see, no single passage in Hegel could be regarded
as a paradigm for the whole action of *Sei personaggi*, but there are
any number of significant possibilities. For example, the relation
between actor and character (or analogously, between audience
and stage fiction) recalls the development of consciousness in the
two aspects Hegel calls "Master" and "Servant." The characters
are quite an accurate metaphor for Hegel's Servant, that consciousness whose essence is "life or being for an 'Other'" (*Phän.*,
153); a character exists in the imagination of others, and the
characters without an author arrive on the stage searching for a
manifest drama, a structure to which they may bear the relation of
"dependence from a determined existence" (*Phän.*, 154). The actor, on the other hand, is a metaphor for the Master, in the sense of
"a consciousness existing for itself, which is mediated with itself
by *another* consciousness" (*Phän.*, 153); his essence is to exist
independently and self-relatedly, "for himself," but in such a way
that he needs to present himself to himself in the form of a second,
more limited consciousness, the fictional consciousness of his
role.

The second "act" of the play shows the Master's domination
over the Servant, the actors' imposition of their own ideas on the
characters' reality, culminating in the "cruel" use of the word
"illusion" (p. 102), which completes the characters' reduction.
But at this point the tables are turned; the father now advances on
the director and puts his weighty question, "Can you tell me who
you are?" (p. 103), and this peripety also has a clear parallel in
Hegel. By being dominated, the Servant ceases to function as a
true mediation of the Master's independent, undominated being,
whereupon the Master, who needs the Servant as testimony of his
own essence, loses his "certainty of himself" (*Phän.*, 155). And
correspondingly, if the actor has fully mastered the character, so
that the character (while remaining a necessary self-expression or
self-mediation for the actor) has become non-independent, then
the actor must begin to worry about the integrity of his own being,
"who he is." Meanwhile, according to Hegel, "servitude, as a
repressed consciousness, will withdraw into itself and so achieve

the turning to true independence" (*Phän.*, 155), which is exactly what happens to the *personaggi*, who are thrown back upon themselves and become at the end what they have been in truth from the beginning, uncomfortably but ineluctably independent self-consciousnesses.

The same process can be traced in the relation between the audience and the fiction as a whole. The spectator's is an independent self-consciousness (Master) which still requires from the fiction a mediation of itself with itself in the form of a meaning relevant to itself. But when the spectator masters the fiction by reducing it to its meaning, the fiction thereby loses for him that independent realness which makes its meaning believable, loses its spontaneity "and becomes a machine, an allegory" (p. 36). The spectator has thus received an idea of himself (the meaning) which by being understood is also undermined (like Egmont's or Homburg's self-understanding) and so calls his own ontic integrity into question. And yet, this self-questioning in the spectator, his despair, now, of fully understanding the play's meaning, endows the fiction with a new vital independence (the Servant frees himself) by which it is enabled once again to become genuinely meaningful, so that the circle is complete and, again, our existence is restored to us on a higher plane.

A great deal more can be said, even with reference to Hegel, about Pirandello in general and about the *Sei personaggi* in particular. I have not touched the religious aspect of the play, for example, the suggestion of searching for that "author" who is God, which perhaps makes the play a phrenographic image of Hegel's "unhappy consciousness." At the very end, almost in the words of the Psalm, the director asks for a "lamp unto his feet"— "Lasciami almeno accesa una lampadina, per vedere dove metto i piedi!" (p. 116)—and receives instead the image of the four remaining *personaggi*, before which he flees. Our search for the divine, in other words, is a Hegelian search for what we in truth are, but when this is offered us by self-consciousness in its "unhappy" phase ("lei è me," says the father), we cannot recognize it for what it is.

Still, however, *Sei personaggi in cerca d'autore* is unquestionably a crucial play in Pirandello's development, looking both backward, to the plays of complex psychology, and forward to the "myths," and it is also an example of how the effect of

Hegelian thought favors a dramaturgy in the German manner, involving complex parallels between consciousness *on* stage and consciousness *of* the stage. Pirandello's specific techniques may be derived from styles as old as the *commedia dell'arte* or as new as the *teatro del grottesco,* but his infusion of these techniques with a single philosophic spirit, an essentially Hegelian spirit, is what makes of them a true dramaturgy, a method of creating genuine and profound works of art for theatrical representation. Thus, in Pirandello as in Shaw, despite the lack of any significant direct contact with the German movement, the essence of German Classical drama receives new life, in that the theater is again used to bring home to its customers the heroism of daily life, the need for what Shotover calls "navigation," the complexity and difficulty and constant tragic potential of everyday existence in the form of self-consciousness, as this is being experienced here and now during the performance.

7

Both late eighteenth-century Germany (the cradle of idealist philosophy) and late nineteenth-century Europe as a whole (the heir to a fully developed and exported German idealism) are examples of culture pervaded by a dialectical sense of life: a brooding on the paradoxes of self-consciousness, the vision of a perverse "demonic" quality in our immediate experience and in the broad sweep of history. This state of affairs, which follows more or less naturally as a reaction to the rationalist overconfidence of the Enlightenment, takes a specially deep hold in eighteenth-century Germany because of the absence there of a solid tradition of acknowledged literary greatness; the situation of the "disinherited" thinker, exposed directly to the perverseness of reality and history, was experienced more intensely by the typical German author than it would have been if he had been able to regard himself as the heir to something comparable with Elizabethan or French classical poetry. And this experience, in all its potentially dramatogenic depth, helped along by a dialectically minded German philosophy, then catches up with all Europe about a century later.

But this quality of the general intellectual situation is not sufficient to account for the existence of a flourishing modern drama, any more than for that of eighteenth-century German drama.

Therefore we have discussed the direct and indirect influence of
German Classical poetics, especially its role in producing a fundamental and influential dramatic bias in the thought of Hegel
and Nietzsche—and also, we might add, at one further remove, in
much pre-existentialist and existentialist thought, say Kierkegaard and Heidegger, in the idea of the inadequacy of any
philosophical system as a static construct, the idea that philosophy must be an action in progress here and now.[41] We have seen,
moreover, how this bias in turn affects the idea of dramatic form
in at least four widely different modern authors, Ibsen, Strindberg,
Shaw and Pirandello. Precisely the differences here are important;
for my aim is not to reduce modern drama to a single type, but
rather to exhibit precisely its variety as evidence of the inherent
fruitfulness of the tradition by way of German Classicism. The list
can easily be extended; we might associate Sartre with Hegel,
Camus with Nietzsche,[42] Marxist drama with Hegel, expressionist
drama with Nietzsche, and so on.

There remains one rather simpler but extremely important question, which is hardly even asked, let alone answered, in dramatic
criticism, the question of where serious modern authors get the
idea of using drama in the first place—as distinct from the question of where their ideas on the nature and efficacy of dramatic
form come from. The novel, after all, is a much more characteristically modern form, having undergone (unlike drama) an enormous expansion of its possibilities in the nineteenth century.
Why, on the threshold of the modern age, is drama suddenly
revived by an extraordinary number of major authors? why is it
not left to languish on the boulevards and in the desk-drawers of
occasional geniuses like Grillparzer? The failure to ask this question is a flaw in the work of both Bentley and Brustein; and while
Fergusson's idea of modern theater's "partial perspectives," in
their striving for wholeness, does give a sense of the genre's larger
development, it does not come to grips with the question of tradition in sufficiently concrete terms.

The question has hardly been asked, yet the answer could
hardly be clearer. The idea of using drama as a specifically
modern form, the idea that drama is capable of doing much more
than it had been made to do during most of the nineteenth century, comes mainly from Scandinavia, especially Ibsen and then
Strindberg. Yeats, for example, may have been an anti-Ibsenite,

but it seems hardly likely that his willingness to devote endless effort to the project of an Irish literary theater (not to mention the willingness of his more Ibsenite associates) was not in large part inspired and challenged by the success of the Norwegian. Ibsen and Strindberg, however, as we have pointed out, owe their general perception of drama's possibilities principally to the direct and indirect influence of the German movement.

Or let us consider Wagner, whose work also functions as conspicuous encouragement for a serious modern renewal of drama. Wagner's own notion of an all-encompassing historic synthesis of the arts may be unrealizable, or even thoroughly perverse, and it may be true that his influence on aesthetic thought, say in late nineteenth-century France, was very slight;[43] but his theater owes a great deal to its background in dialectic philosophy, and the *existence* of Bayreuth in its turn played an important part in the genesis of, say, Villiers de l'Isle Adam's *Axël* and Paul Fort's Théâtre d'Art, both of which (to return to the example above) were influences on Yeats. Wagner's theater and the Abbey Theatre could hardly be more dissimilar, but with regard exclusively to the idea *that* drama is a major possibility for modern artistic renewal, as opposed to the question of *how*—and this idea by no means arises automatically in either Ireland or France—there is a chain of influences which connects them and which leads back ultimately to Schiller and the drama around 1800.

9 The Assault upon the Audience: Types of Modern Drama

"Merdre!" This word signals a very important but not very well understood movement in modern drama, which we may term "the assault upon the audience." The theater of Jarry and Apollinaire, of certain expressionists, of dada and surrealism and recent absurd drama, appears on first glance to be what I have called a theater of shock, a twentieth-century *Sturm und Drang;* but there are important distinctions to be made here. Artaud's Theater of Cruelty, for example, is a much more sophisticated endeavor than anything we encounter in the *Sturm und Drang,* an endeavor that would have been unthinkable without the growth of philosophical historicism and empirical anthropology and psychology in the nineteenth century. Like Wagner, Artaud attempts to create a theatrical situation in which man's "circuitous journey" will be completed by the return to a mythically ordered mode of existence; the only basic difference is that whereas Wagner flatters his audience (Nietzsche is correct on this point), Artaud sees the need for more drastic measures.

1

But let us begin with some earlier movements. *Ubu Roi* was first performed by live actors in Lugné-Poë's Théâtre de l'Oeuvre, which was the successor to Paul Fort's Théâtre d'Art, and Fort's theater in turn had been established in direct rivalry with Antoine's primarily naturalistic Théâtre Libre. Thus it appears convenient to infer the existence of a rivalry or contrast between naturalism and whatever movement it is that Jarry represents, a dichotomy between naturalistic and expressionistic style, between the sensitive and the energetic. It is even tempting to postulate a parallel here with the situation of drama in the mid-eighteenth century: the naturalistic would be to the expressionistic as theater of sympathy, or bourgeois drama, is to theater of shock, or *Sturm und Drang*.

Needless to say, this dichotomy does not characterize with any strictness the repertoires of the three French theaters mentioned; and we have seen, in general, that the sensitive and energetic tendencies of modern drama are essentially only aspects of a single basic paradox which is related to the idealist paradox of freedom and limitation. My point is that modern drama's assault upon its audience is an entirely different *type* of phenomenon from either theater of shock or energetic dramatic style, a phenomenon not at all incompatible with strict naturalism. The work of Gerhart Hauptmann is an obvious test case. In practically all naturalistic writing there is at least a covert aggressiveness, a "J'accuse" in the absence of which it would hardly occur to us to speak of naturalism in the first place. But in Hauptmann, of all naturalistic authors, the sense of social wrong seems most clearly to be overshadowed by a sense of human suffering, the mood of accusation by a mood of compassion.[1] In Hauptmann, therefore, if anywhere, we shall expect to find a modern theater of sympathy, certainly not an exact equivalent of eighteenth-century bourgeois drama, but at least something opposed to the modern theater of assault.

This is not the case. Not only do Hauptmann's dramas contain an assault upon their audience, but in fact this assault belongs to their very nature as art and is not different in essence from the assault upon the audience inherent in the form of expressionist or absurd drama. The text we shall concentrate on is *Die Weber*, for a number of reasons. This play, first of all, is in several ways the most thoroughly naturalistic of Hauptmann's works, the *ne plus ultra* of his early stark-naturalist phase, after which he turned to comedy in *Der Biberpelz*, visionary consolation in *Hanneles Himmelfahrt* and monumental history in *Florian Geyer*. Then also, *Die Weber* is the most innovative of Hauptmann's early naturalistic plays, hence the one in which his own personal idea

of naturalism as a mode is likely to emerge most strongly. And in
Die Weber, finally, Hauptmann appears to be aiming for an especially close relationship between human sympathy and social
consciousness; the focus on a group rather than on individuals
tends to transmute our human sympathy directly into an awareness of larger social issues. Thus, in the case of *Die Weber*, we can
speak of a theater of sympathy without even needing to question
the play's reforming tendency.

But is *Die Weber* really intended to produce either human sympathy or social reform? Hauptmann's own utterances suggest a
negative answer on both counts,[2] and I have argued above that the
play belongs to the German tradition of melancholy tragedy,
tragedy based on the impossibility of tragedy in the modern
world. The structure of the play expresses an unrealizable desire
for the heroic; the collective, as it were the Dionysian mass, is
supervaded in each act by an individual who could conceivably
become a hero, but is then immediately swallowed up in the tide,
and the real tragedy is that there is no longer any genuinely
human or satisfyingly cathartic way of relating ourselves to the
blind historical surge thus represented.

This point can be developed by way of the question of what we,
the audience, are doing in the theater. In particular, old Baumert's
learning of the rebellious song at the end of Act II calls into question not only the objective *validity* of a Kantian aesthetics of disinterest, but also the basic *morality* of such an aesthetics. Surely
we, in the theater, are being presented with a work of art at least
potentially as incendiary as the song. Conditions among the Silesian weavers in Hauptmann's time were not substantially different from what they had been a half century earlier; and while
the play does not attempt to fix the blame, it does depict the
conditions themselves with sufficient vividness to make clear that
something must be done. Surely an increase of consciousness is
all that is needed; once the weavers' plight, or any comparable
social situation, becomes widely enough known, the society as a
whole will be forced to take steps to correct it.

But Hauptmann reminds us with a certain rhythmic
insistence—once in each of the first four acts—that even in 1844,
the year of the rebellion, the plight of the weavers had been very
widely known, and that this had done the weavers not a bit of
good.[3] Knowledge is not enough, because knowledge, or con-

sciousness, necessarily includes a distance which separates us from the reality and urgency of the object. The parallel with our situation in the theater is clear. By adopting the attitude which the theater as an institution requires of us, by watching and sympathizing and understanding, we find ourselves merely re-enacting the ineffectiveness of all those shocked newspaper readers and "Weaver-Relief Committees" (p. 431) of the 1840's. Thus the play questions the morality of an aesthetics of disinterest. What right have we to be disinterested, even with respect to fictional human misery? Are we not in a sense put to shame by old Baumert's reaction to the absurdly unpoetic Dreissiger-song?

In Hauptmann, as in Shaw, we are offered Must without Can, and it is not unlikely that this logical cornering of the audience has to do with the Nietzschean influence in both cases. But whereas Shaw leaves open a way for us to justify being an audience, as "navigation," Hauptmann simply attacks us for this. What right have we? The traveling salesman, upon seeing Ansorge in Act III of *Die Weber*, says, "Such naturally powerful men are very rare nowadays. We are so steeped in culture" (p. 389); and although there is some satire of the speaker here, there is also some truth. The weavers are more natural, more primitive, thus in a sense more truly human than the other social groups represented; they propagate more quickly, their religious feeling is deeper, they have a primitive love of ritual, especially in their funerals, and their misery places them in a closer relation to the basics of existence.[4] Dreissiger's life, as the play makes clear, is every bit as miserable as the weavers', but his misery lacks natural authenticity; it is concealed from him by convention and manifests itself as a blustering, self-righteous defensiveness by which he only increases it; he is beset by a sense of his own futility, but he has neither an absolute God nor a pressing physical need with which to contend and so steady himself.

And Dreissiger's situation, like the remarks about newspaper articles and weaver-relief committees, is an attack on the audience. We too, by sitting in the theater, by "steeping" ourselves in culture, are living our lives unauthentically, carrying out that unnatural self-concealment by which human misery, our own and others', is necessarily augmented. Hauptmann assaults his audience not by way of their particular prejudices, not by way of anything in their lives outside the theater, but rather by way of their situation here and now as an audience, and this procedure is shared by works that have practically no external resemblance to *Die Weber*. It is by sitting in the theater, for example, by sitting and expecting from the play a meaning, a new and somehow valuable perspective upon our existence, that we of the audience find ourselves in the position of waiting for Godot; and Genêt goes out of his way to make clear at the end that his *Balcony*, together with the street before it (our aimless experience in common) and the rooms behind (our experience as self-closeted individuals), is merely an image of the theater, in which we are sitting to no real purpose, as no real community. Perhaps the middle term between Hauptmann and the French absurdists is represented by Büchner's *Woyzeck*, where the carnival-booth mirrors grotesquely our situation in the theater, while the moral indefensibility of our attitude as spectators is shown by the doctor, since we too, after all, are as it were experimenting with Woyzeck, attempting to learn something from his anguished behavior.[5]

I think it can be argued on general principles that absurd drama, or drama tending in that direction, must necessarily embody an assault upon its audience of the general type I have described. For if the absurdity on stage is meant to reflect an absurdity in existence, then surely the relation of audience to work must partake of this larger absurdity; the work cannot represent the world in a rationally clear manner. What we are confronted with in the first instance, therefore, is a reminder of the absurdity of our situation as a theater audience, and the various changes that can be rung on this idea are clear in the works of Ionesco. Dramatic dialogue, for example, looked at from a certain point of view, is a compoundedly ridiculous affair: words spoken by people who do not really mean them, concerning a situation that does not really exist, in the presence of other people who, come what may, will try to discover in them a significance even beyond the immediate. All Ionesco's dialogue, but especially that in *La cantatrice chauve*, mocks the audience for participating in this absurd game. Or we think of *La leçon* and *Les chaises*, where the audience's desire for some form of edification is mocked. Even *Rhinocéros*, it seems to me, fits into this pattern, despite the allegory to which Ionesco himself calls attention. The rhinoceros is not merely a symbol, but a symbol of symbolic meaning in general, and the spreading of rhinoceritis is a mocking reflection of the reductive mental process by which we normally understand a dramatic work; we are not satisfied until we have reduced all the actual images to mere manifestations of the work's "meaning," namely an idea which does not actually reside in the images any more than rhinoceros inhabit southern France. Even if the spectator sides resolutely with Bérenger and is determined, if necessary, to be the last human in a world of logic, system, and suppressed rancor—even if the spectator is determined *not* to be merely a member of the audience in whose midst he is sitting—still this itself constitutes an interpretation of the images, a participation in the communal game of symbolic reduction, hence a symptom of rhinoceritis. There is no way out; our very sitting in the theater makes us liable to attack.

2

The assault upon the audience—as practiced good-humoredly by Jarry, Apollinaire, Beckett, Ionesco, and with less good humor by Hauptmann or Genêt or perhaps Artaud—is not a general characteristic of the modern theater. Avant-garde stage techniques involve by definition an attack on the audience's conventional expectations, and the content of practically all modern plays implies some sort of attack on what are assumed to be typical conditions or prejudices in society. But the drama of assault, as I wish to define it here, is drama in which the audience is attacked *for being an audience*, not for any particular human or social qualities. A play that seeks to disorient its audience will often be drama of assault—but not always. In *Sei personaggi*, for example, and even more clearly in Pirandello's later "myths," the ultimate aim is not attack, but rather restoration of the audience's being on a higher level. And the case of *Die Weber* proves that not all drama of assault is necessarily disorienting; Hauptmann's audience find themselves all too clearly oriented with respect to the stage, in a relation of hopeless self-understanding and even guilt.

But what does all this have to do with the tradition from German Classicism? Is the drama of assault not simply a modern *Sturm und Drang*? In fact there is a great difference here. Eighteenth-century drama of shock, at least in its most significant manifestations, is meant to liberate its audience; it is based on the vaguely Rousseauistic notion that in every individual, suppressed by convention, there slumbers perhaps not genius itself but at least a personality which is sympathetic to the general aims of genius, and that a society of such personalities, once released from their chrysalides by a sufficient shock, would be a truly free society, a renascence of the human race, a society that would somehow manage to reveal itself as every individual's free act.[6] I think it is not possible, except perhaps among the lesser works of German expressionism, to find cases where a similar notion is important in shaping more recent drama. Modern authors, after the growth of psychology as a discipline in the nineteenth and twentieth centuries—and also those eighteenth-century German authors who outgrew their *Sturm und Drang* phase—tend to be wary of any assumptions concerning the nature of the human self. That the self is conscious of itself is a fact which the dramatist can and perhaps must work with, but any assumptions beyond this are unnecessarily limiting and dangerous. The idea of somehow liberating the audience remains important in the German movement and in modern drama as a whole, but from Classicism onward it is understood that complex ironic techniques are required by this idea, that shock, even assuming it is achievable in the theater, is not enough.

An attempt to liberate the audience is by no means necessarily implied in modern drama of assault. There is no such attempt in either Hauptmann or Genêt, and the liberation that may be aimed at in those absurd dramas which tend more toward either the comic or the mythic is certainly not a *Sturm und Drang* liberation of sovereign individuality. But on what basis, then, can we speak of a drama of assault in the first place? Is there a genuine relation between Hauptmann and absurd drama, or is the idea of "assault" merely a word that happens to cover several distinct phenomena?

Let us return to *Die Weber*. Our situation as a theater audience, again, is contrasted unfavorably with the authenticity and immediacy of the weavers' struggle for existence; we, like Dreissiger, are every bit as miserable and helpless as the weavers, except that our misery is concealed, thus ultimately compounded, by our self-delusion. This contrast, however, does not apply strictly except to the situation of the weavers *as it had been*, as we hear about it; what the play shows is not the weavers' authentic humanity but rather the process of their self-conscious degeneration. Self-consciousness in the weavers has taken on the Hegelianly inevitable character of negation and self-repudiation; the weavers have been made intensely aware of their own situation, so that they, no less than we ourselves, now experience the incongruity between *an sich* and *für sich*. They do not submit to this inevitable process without a struggle; the quietness and timidity of their entrance in Act IV, and the mysterious solemnity with which, according to Hornig, they demolish Dreissiger's (p. 451), are apparently the effects of a powerful striving to preserve the integrity and natural authenticity of their weaver-being. But such striving is futile. The process of self-awareness, once begun, leads inevitably to self-division and chaos; we hear that the destruction of Dietrich's, unlike that of Dreissiger's, had become a drunken spree (p. 465), then the drunken weavers actually appear, and finally old Baumert himself staggers in, brandishing a slaughtered cock. The weavers have lost their very selves and there is now no hope for them, as Baumert appears to recognize when he leaves old Hilse with the request, "If something happens, say a prayer for me too" (p. 475).

The real subject matter of the play, in other words, is self-consciousness, and although Hauptmann is careful not to overload his dialogue with literary or metaphysical allusions, it is significant that in the dedication to his father he compares himself with Hamlet (p. 321), and that we also think of Hamlet when we hear Ansorge say, at the end of Act IV, "Who am I? The weaver Anton Ansorge. Is he crazy, Ansorge? It's true, I'm dizzy as a horse-fly. What's he doing here? What he feels like. Where is he, Ansorge?" (p. 443). Again, *Die Weber* belongs not to a tradition of inflammatory drama from the *Sturm und Drang* but to the tradition of self-conscious tragedy from German Classicism, and specifically to that melancholy tragic mode which is established by *Wallenstein*.

This in turn enables us to understand a bit more about the series of potential heroes discussed earlier, for it is now clear that the play's overall structure is phrenographic, that it represents, as it were, one pulse of self-consciousness in a single huge weaver-mentality which includes the whole stage. The first three hero-figures, Bäcker, Jäger, and Wittig, constitute a movement away from the center of weaver-being, in that Jäger is no longer a weaver and Wittig never has been; that the actual rebellion begins only with Wittig's attack on Kutsche thus suggests, again, that the rebellion is the weavers' taking leave of their own selves. By being

self-conscious, we are self-alienated; there is an unavoidable discrepancy between the self that knows and the self that is known;
an unfamiliar and unaccountable personality creeps into the fabric of our experience, our deeds are done, our very thoughts are
thought, by someone who is not strictly ourselves (as Wittig is not
a weaver). Hauptmann later says:

> Goethe searched for the primal plant. It would make more sense to
> search—in man's psyche—for the primal drama, which is perhaps
> also the earliest thought-process.
>   The origin of everything dramatic, in any case, is the split or
> doubled ego. The first actors were *homo* and *ratio*, or "you" and
> "I." The first stage was unveiled nowhere but in man's head. It
> remains the smallest and the largest that can be built. It denotes the
> world, it comprehends the world, more than those proverbial
> boards.[7]

Given the basic importance of self-consciousness as a theme in
Die Weber, it is clear that the progression Bäcker-Jäger-Wittig, and
the championing of the weavers at the crucial point by a nonweaver, are meant to represent phrenographically this "Ur-
drama," the dramatically fundamental division of the ego from
itself. It is also significant that Wittig is in his way a student of the
French Revolution, and is known as something of a socialist
agitator (pp. 403, 407–9), for his presence thus injects a theoretical
element, a division between *homo* and *ratio*, into what would
otherwise be the weavers' immediate human reaction against intolerable conditions.

The purpose of self-consciousness, however, of metaphysical
speculation, theoretical reason, practical self-criticism, is to unify
the self through knowledge, not to divide it; the striving for self-
unity on a level higher than that of a mere object is precisely what
brings about our conscious self-alienation. This means that we are
no sooner divided from ourselves consciously, or no sooner aware
of this, than we must begin struggling to put ourselves back together again, to regain what now appears to us the lost self-unity
of our past. Therefore the progression Wittig-Kittelhaus-Hilse, a
movement inward, toward the center of weaver-being, follows
naturally upon the outward progression Bäcker-Jäger-Wittig.
Self-consciousness is a kind of psychic pulse, an alternation of
centrifugal and centripetal forces (as in *Egmont* and *Faust*), a

search for ourselves by which we abandon ourselves, or a flight from ourselves by which we seek ourselves.

This abstract-phrenographic structure of *Die Weber* ("abstract" because the human self in general is represented, not a particular self) is worked out with great subtlety and consistency. Kittelhaus and old Hilse, the bearers of the movement inward, are the two most religious men in the play (the apparent etymological relation between *religio* and *religare*, "to bind together again," is noted frequently by nineteenth-century German thinkers), and the two aspects of religion they represent, "duty" (p. 435) and feeling or "certainty" (p. 463), correspond to the two principal aspects of the divided self, *ratio* and *homo*. The self, by being conscious, is divided into an observer and an observed, and it is the self as observer or overseer (duty, *ratio*, Kittelhaus) who first perceives this division and attempts to heal it by asserting a rational order. But this attempt is doomed from the start, for the detached existence of the observer (or allegorically, the fact that Kittelhaus belongs to Dreissiger's social circle, separate from the weavers) is just the problem; and in Act V, accordingly, the stage presents us with a vision of the self in utter chaos. The relatively unified self of the past, in the form of old Hilse, is still treated with respect by Bäcker, who represents the first degree of alienation; but he is threatened brutally by Jäger, and Wittig simply takes no notice of him. The old self, the original object of self-observation (*homo*), is still observable, but the process of self-observation has left that old self an empty shell (does Hilse suggest *Hülse*, as Wittig obviously suggests *wütig?*),[8] its substance dissipated in the anguished self-division of consciousness.

There is no hope, there is no way back for the self that has become conscious of itself; and we in the audience, in that we see this bleak truth, this "primal drama," displayed before us on the stage, are made more self-conscious and so subjected to the truth yet more completely, or, again, we are assaulted. This relentless pessimism, moreover, represents Hauptmann's basic stance as a dramatist; his attempts to uncover another side of the truth in comedies and dramatized visions are never really successful. When, at the end of his life, he turns to the incomparably bleak Atrides tetralogy, he is simply returning to himself.

Once it is understood that Hauptmann's naturalism is in essence a theater of uncontrollable self-consciousness, a vision of

the self's infinite and futile self-complication, the relation between this theater and the theater of the absurd becomes clear. For
the theater of the absurd is also basically a vision of stampeding
self-consciousness. Evidently, as Esslin points out, the growth of
absurdist stage techniques has to do with the idea that in our
modern world the last shreds of any credible universal order have
been blown away; God is dead, therefore existence no longer
makes sense.[9] The recognition that God is dead, however, is a
recognition not so much about the world as about the self; the
death of God is our recognition that God has been merely an
arbitrary idea imposed by ourselves upon existence to the end of
making it livable. Any appearance of objective order in things, if
we look at it too closely—even the seemingly indispensable
categories of space, time, and causality—is revealed as an arbitrary imposition of our own desires and needs upon the gross
matter of perception; and the disintegration of order in the
modern world, the collapse of shared values, the advent of absurdity, is the result of just such a looking-too-closely; our consciousness of the world has revealed itself increasingly as a consciousness of self, and in this form has potentiated itself into
chaos. Thus, in absurd drama, and at least in Hauptmann's brand
of naturalism, the assault upon the audience is in the final
analysis only a revelation of the audience's constant assault on
themselves, a revelation of the tendency of self-consciousness to
undermine the integrity of existence.

3

Modern drama of assault, represented by authors as diverse as
Hauptmann and Ionesco, is a drama which employs the spectator's situation in the theater as a device for revealing the morbid
or chaotic aspect of his self-consciousness. This drama does not
bear an especially close relation to the drama of Sturm und Drang,
either in history or in spirit, for it is not basically a drama of
liberation; it is, rather, a drama of uncontrollable self-consciousness, and so evidently owes a great deal to at least the critical
aspect of German idealist philosophy, the idea that when we
look at the world we do not actually see beyond the operation
of the mind. In the history of drama the obvious forerunners are
German melancholy tragedy, for Hauptmann, and for the absurdists the drama of extreme irony which had been practiced by

Tieck, Grabbe, and to an extent Büchner. The direct influence of the German dramatic movement is much clearer in Hauptmann, whereas in French absurdist drama the influence is almost all indirect, by way of philosophical idealism and its offshoots, by way of Pirandello's Hegelian dramaturgy, by way of Strindberg. But all these influences lead us back eventually to Lessing's crucial question, why there should be such a thing as drama in the first place, especially in post-Enlightenment Europe. And both Hauptmann and the absurdists in a sense answer this question negatively: there is no longer any real justification for drama; the self-conscious erosion of shared values, of communal experience, has progressed too far; drama can exist now only by assaulting us with the knowledge of our cultural inability to realize its essential aim. Perhaps there is a certain covert hope that the experience of the problem of self-consciousness at its extreme will produce, dialectically, a movement toward human reintegration; but the drama may not indulge itself in images of this hope, for otherwise the necessary extremity of the problem will not be achieved.

The idea of a drama of assault can be defended both abstractly and historically. But what kind of category is it? Does it not make more sense to link Hauptmann with Strindberg and speak of a "drama of despair," a drama that plunges its audience as far as possible into the misery of the human condition? Does it not make more sense to link Ionesco and Beckett with Pirandello and speak of a "drama of disorientation"? Despair and disorientation are two ways of responding to self-consciousness considered primarily as a problem (i.e. the *Egmont* problem as opposed to the Egmontian achievement), two developments of the melancholy tragic mode, so that their nature as categories is clear.

The importance of the category of assault is that it cuts across those of despair and disorientation and articulates them. In particular, Strindberg differs from Hauptmann in essentially the same way that Pirandello differs from Ionesco or Beckett. In the later Strindberg, the fundamental misery of existence is resolved into a lucid musical structure to which we are invited to relate ourselves as if it were our own creation; in the very process of being plunged more deeply into our condition, we are also elevated above it, as the authors of our own misery. But no corresponding elevation is aimed at in plays like *Die Weber*. Likewise, in Pirandello the audience is disoriented in order that they be enabled to receive their own being in a higher and better-founded form. But again this sort of elevation is not intended by the merciless disorientation of absurd drama.

If despair and disorientation are *modes of response* to the problem of self-consciousness, let us define dramatic elevation and dramatic assault as *degrees of saturation*. Every drama in the final analysis aims at some sort of elevation for its audience, some improvement in us or for us; otherwise there would be no reason for writing drama in the first place. And every drama must involve at least a mild assault, must begin by at least disturbing its audience; otherwise nothing can be accomplished. But there are obvious differences among plays in this respect. A play can aim to elevate us in a specific way, or it can challenge us to improve ourselves in our own unforeseeable ways; the play can aim at elevating us now, as we sit in the theater, or at a theatrical experience that will lead to our elevation later. In drama that aims at elevating its audience in a specific way as they sit in the theater, I shall speak of *high* saturation; such drama is fully saturated with its meaning; its whole intention is contained in the theatrical experience. In drama that aims at no specific elevation and leaves its audience to accomplish their own improvement, if any, in their own ways, I shall speak of *low* saturation, which usually means drama of assault. In drama that does aim at a specific form of elevation, but does not expect this to be accomplished fully in the theater, I shall speak of *medium* saturation, and the correct term for this sort of drama will usually be drama of enlightenment, that increases our sense of direction in the real world after we leave the theater.

I propose these distinctions as the beginning of a taxonomy of modern drama, a coordinate system by which plays can be classified and related to each other.

	Degrees of Saturation	
Modes of Response	ASSAULT	ELEVATION
DISORIENTATION	Absurd drama	Pirandello
DESPAIR	Hauptmann	Strindberg

This scheme may not be unambiguous or universally applicable. There are obviously more than two possible dramatic modes of response to a modern view of the human condition, and there is no reason why a single dramatic work should not incorporate several modes of response at different levels of saturation. The scale of saturation is a continuum, and the comparison in degree of saturation between works embodying different modes of response will never be more than approximate. Moreover, a play cannot be classified in this scheme except by an extensive and probing interpretation of the sort that is not likely to win general acceptance in all its details. And finally, since I have not (I repeat) set up my own general theory of drama, I have no grounds on which to deny the possible existence of valuable or important works that do not fit anywhere in my categories.

But still, several important functions are carried out by this taxonomy. If the scheme makes sense historically, and if it orders meaningfully at least a significant segment of major modern drama, then we can do a bit of tidying up in the terminology of modern dramatic criticism. On the negative side, both Bentley's idea of "realism" and Brustein's of "revolt," while remaining significant in a general literary context, will be seen to have no direct connection with the idea or history of drama as a genre. And on the positive side, for example, we can make progress in the discussion of "absurd" drama by defining it as drama of disorientation, minimally saturated. This definition will not help us decide exactly which dramas to classify as absurd; we shall still argue about whether disorientation is the principal mode of response in a given work, and about the degree of saturation. But we shall at least know a bit more exactly what is at issue. When critics speak of a certain human sympathy and pathos in *En attendant Godot*, for instance, what they mean is that this play appears somewhat more saturated, appears to make somewhat more specific demands on its audience, than say *La cantatrice chauve*.

One important point can also be made about the evaluation of modern plays, for there is a strong tendency in dramatic criticism to associate high saturation with high quality. Esslin, for example, defends absurd drama on the grounds that it "touches the religious sphere"[10] and in saying this he is quite wrong; only drama of relatively high saturation, which aims at a specific communal experience, can be "religious" in any reasonable sense of the word. But Esslin's defense is also unnecessary, for saturation is not a measure of value. Highly saturated drama can be of very low quality. Purely conventional drama, for example, is by definition highly saturated, since it requires a well-defined reaction from the audience as they sit there, and requires nothing beyond this. Hauptmann's visionary plays, like *Hanneles Himmelfahrt* and *Die versunkene Glocke,* are oversaturated; they lack a solid basis in language and poetic structure for the experience they attempt to impose on us. And of course no drama could be more thoroughly saturated than Wagner's—to which Nietzsche would have responded: saturated in *what?*

On the other hand, drama of low saturation requires an exceptionally delicate touch, as becomes obvious in plays where it is missing. Max Frisch's *Biedermann und die Brandstifter,* for example, is meant to be of low saturation, "ohne Lehre" (without a teaching), and to assault its audience disorientingly by way of their normal theatrical detachment, which is like Biedermann's inactivity. But Frisch (as a dramatist) does not really manage to write without teaching, and the woodenness of this play's unfolding is the best proof of how much genius is needed to produce something like *Rhinocéros,* which is also a social allegory but still succeeds in being genuine drama of assault. Or in the drama of despair we think of *Death of a Salesman,* which sets off Hauptmann's genius in the same way Frisch does Ionesco's. Miller, like Hauptmann the naturalist, aims for low saturation, but his work lacks the complex inner structure of consciousness we have observed in *Die Weber;* it does not mount a genuinely theatrical assault upon the audience.

The idea of low saturation has special significance in the discussion of modern drama, because prior to the late nineteenth century, practically all major drama, except perhaps farce, is at least of medium saturation, at least meant to enlighten its audience in some way. This is true, for example, of German Classical drama, even though the German movement is a major historical factor in the growth of modern unsaturated drama of assault. And it is also true of the *Sturm und Drang.* From a modern point of view, much *Sturm und Drang* drama appears to be of low saturation—which is why it is often thought to have a special affinity with modern drama—but this appearance is delusive, a result of the fact that we no longer take seriously the eighteenth-century message in those plays. What drove Lenz crazy and almost did the same for young Goethe, what quickly drove Goethe, Schiller, and Klinger toward more conservative poetic modes, was the constant thwarting of their hope for a more open society, their hope that their ideas might actually begin to take hold, their hope, in other words, that their works might function on a level of at least medium saturation. Again, several *Sturm und Drang* plays, especially *Götz, Der Hofmeister,* and *Die Räuber,* serve as important models for various modern dramatists; but for this purpose they had to be misinterpreted, and usually in the spirit of the Classical-idealist tradition of intense concentration on the problem of self-consciousness.

4

If the taxonomy of modern drama suggested above is to be useful, it must be expanded. So far we have distinguished two dramatic modes of response to self-consciousness as a *problem;* and in order to remain within the structure of concepts suggested by German Classicism, we must proceed by defining modes of response to self-consciousness as a simple inevitable *fact,* and as a quasi-divine *power,* as the true seat and expression of our highest humanity.

Drama responding to self-consciousness as a fact will tend to be dialectical in a content-oriented sense—as distinct from the sense in which modern drama's form is generally indebted to dialectical thought.[11] Logical disputation will play a considerable part in works belonging to this category, as will the perverse tendency of self-consciousness to transform impressions, feelings, ideas, and even realities into their opposites. Drama of paradox, not drama of absurdity, will appear frequently, and we shall certainly expect to find Wilde, Shaw, Giraudoux, Kaiser, and Dürrenmatt among the authors represented. Works classifiable as tragedy will probably be absent altogether, but tragicomedies (in Guthke's restricted sense), in which the tragic is comic and the comic tragic, will be normal.[12]

In fact, it is possible to define tragicomedy as one of the two principal modes under the general heading of response to self-consciousness as a fact, the other being (for want of a better term) drama of paradox. Drama of paradox can be serious without being tragic; but when it does approach the tragic, when it begins to reveal a single governing metaphysical paradox of being, it tends naturally to become tragicomedy, for otherwise self-consciousness would assume a certain heroic value beyond its factualness. Within the general category of response to self-consciousness as a fact, however, we must not regard tragicness as a measure of value. *Heartbreak House* and *Saint Joan*, which are tragicomedies, may be better plays than, say, *Major Barbara* or *Pygmalion*, but are they better than *Man and Superman*? Is Dürrenmatt's tragicomedy *Der Besuch der alten Dame* even as good as his untragic *Die Physiker*? Or on a lower level of saturation we might compare Kaiser's *Von morgens bis mitternachts* or Sartre's *Huis clos*, both quite clearly tragicomedies, with *The Importance of Being Earnest* or *The Playboy of the Western World*, which are untragic dramas of paradox. Again the distinction is not translatable into an evaluative judgment.

The dramatic modes of response to self-consciousness as a fact, however, become especially interesting when highly saturated. In Shaw and Dürrenmatt, as also in much Giraudoux and Anouilh, we have works at a relatively high level of saturation, but a level which does not exceed "medium." Shaw's audience does live its life more intensely in the theater than on the street, and there is an analogy between the idea of "navigation" and the audience's combined detachment and involvement. But this is only an analogy, not yet fully realized within the theatrical experience; it still needs to be applied in the real world, whereas the Strindbergian experience, for example, does not need to be applied. Nor is Pirandello of any special use to us here. When he discovers (for his purposes) the mode of disorientation, in the "theater" plays, he discovers thereby a means of operating at maximum saturation; but his tragicomedies, like *Il giuoco delle parti*, and his dramas of paradox, like *Così è (se vi pare)*, are not more saturated than those of the other authors mentioned.

In fact it is not easy to see how tragicomedy or drama of paradox *can* achieve a level of saturation comparable with that of the *Sei personaggi* or late Strindberg. Maximum saturation, again, involves the achievement in the theater of the audience's ultimate elevation, the play's final meaning; and how can this happen in the case of an unreservedly dialectical drama, in which everything tends to imply its opposite and no limit is set to this process by any specific valuation or interpretation of self-consciousness? How can any meaning be final? Must the play not of necessity point us out into the real world, where its mechanism of antitheses continues? As far as I know, only one modern author solves the problem of genuine tragicomedy and drama of paradox at maximum saturation, and that is Ibsen.

That Ibsen is a fundamentally dialectical dramatist (again, dialectical in content) has been recognized for some time, even without Johnston's discussion of the realistic "cycle" as a developing Hegelian structure. Brustein, for example, has no difficulty supporting his point that "for Ibsen . . . the ultimate Truth lies only in the perpetual conflict of truths," and on this basis he gives a neatly unified account of Ibsen's career.[13] But this idea does not answer the most crucial question about Ibsen, the question of why, after *Emperor and Galilean*, he has "finished with the messianic drama" (Brustein, p. 65). Why does he not develop the prose realism of the later plays as an extra string to his bow? why does he *change* styles so completely? Is it only a question of "killing his Romantic desire for self-expression for the sake of a selfless seeking after truth" (Brustein, p. 65)? And shall we then postulate a "remorse" for this "killing," in order to account for the strong poetic self-expressiveness of the very last plays?

My contention is that Ibsen's goal, within his favored modes of tragicomedy and drama of paradox, is maximum saturation, and that his uncompromised striving for maximum saturation is what necessitates the shift to prose drama on modern subjects. In the Faustian phase represented by *Brand, Peer Gynt,* and *Emperor and Galilean,* the striving for saturation is obvious; each play is larger than the last, more and more of the world is crammed onto the stage, the theater threatens to eclipse reality altogether, and the "World-Historic Drama" on Julian is apparently meant to generate the world-spirit's own universal "Er-Innerung" in the theater. Yet, *Emperor and Galilean* already abandons the form of verse, and already follows Ibsen's first clearly realistic play, *The League of Youth*. Ibsen is evidently not satisfied with the Faustian style, and in order to understand the reason for this, we must understand exactly how he is aiming for maximum saturation.

Brand and *Peer Gynt,* it seems to me, are Ibsen's *Iliad* and *Odyssey*. They are dialectical national epics, meant at once both to express and to challenge the national spirit represented by their audience, to create that spirit anew as a self-developing force, rather than a system of institutions. As epics, and as social ritual in the theater, they seek to awaken in their audience a sense of communal identity; but in that they are dialectical plays, they address the spectator primarily as a free individual, they are drama of revolt, a complex advocacy of "total resistance to whatever is established" (Brustein, p. 48). In *Emperor and Galilean* this procedure is developed, but not changed essentially. Here the intended communal experience is not "national" but "racial" (letter to Hoffory, 26 February 1888), the experience of belonging to mankind as a whole, an experience which includes even our erring from man's historical destiny, since as man we are "*forced* to err."[14] But again, as in the national epics, the dialectical structure of the play's thought has the effect of placing us in a negative relation to any particular idea of human nature, so that we are also cast forth as lonely, groping individuals.

Ibsen, in other words, is attempting to articulate the experience of his audience into individual and communal components, to the end, ultimately, that these components be fused in a higher unity, not merely muddled with one another as they are in ordinary life. The spectator is meant to experience his individual and his communal nature simultaneously yet separately, as a dialectical tension, and this experience—if Johnston is at all correct about Ibsen's awareness of Hegel—is meant to be an intimation of our true essence as Spirit, that Spirit which seeks its higher self-unity by way of absolute self-division. Ibsen draws the bow tighter than Shaw. What counts in Shaw is primarily the *balance* between individual and communal, between being a revolutionist and getting married, for example, or between being Joan's admirer and being her murderer, whereas what counts in Ibsen is the sheer *separation*, which at its maximum approaches the pure self-negation of Spirit itself. Hegel, in the same way, on the threshold of absolute knowledge, arrives at his distinction between the experience of "Ego=Ego" and the consciousness of the "community."[15]

Shaw's aim is to promote the art of "navigation" in reality, for which the theater is practice, but Ibsen's aim is to awaken *in the theater* something close to a direct experience of man's essence as Spirit; this is the particular form of maximum saturation he is seeking. However, the method employed in the three Faustian plays is highly questionable, and the very form of these plays, their bursting of the theater's walls, their demand for a new kind of theater, is a tacit admission of this. Is the spectator really plunged into the lonely abyss of the Ego, or does he merely conform to theatrical convention by accepting the play's dialectic as a hypothetical artistic structure? Can the idea of the nation or of the human race serve as a focus of communal identity, or does the audience merely receive it as one poetic image among others?

I do not mean to say that Ibsen's Faustian plays are artistically unjustifiable, but Ibsen makes at least one demand of them which they do not satisfy; they do not achieve a strict articulation of the audience's experience into individual and communal components, or at best they achieve this only under special conditions which cannot be assumed. And the importance of this demand is the reason for Ibsen's change of style in his last twelve plays. These "realistic" plays, first of all, are not so much social dramas as domestic dramas with a social dimension; this is true even in *An Enemy of the People,* where the breadth of the social canvas reflects Thomas Stockmann's tragicomic insistence on carrying his family-fatherly ineffectualness into public affairs. Thus the social is revealed mainly by its in part obvious, in part insidious effect on private life; or in other words, one major problem that had thwarted Ibsen in his Faustian phase, that what we think of as our individuality is only a social convention, is now asserted as an integral element of dramatic structure, and asserted in such a way—since the society depicted is contemporary and typical— that the spectator cannot overlook the application to himself. His feeling of individuality, as he sits in the theater, is only a convention, a conditioned reflex; the play positively insists that he recognize this.

But on the other hand, the spectator is not invited to transcend his individuality in favor of a sense of social belonging, for he is shown that the effect of the social in private life is precisely to isolate us. The late plays are mainly about lonely people, whose loneliness is conditioned by the general character of society; and the depiction of contemporary society, by placing the spectator over against his *own* social condition, has the effect of separating him and forcing him into an isolation comparable with the characters', while the characters' isolation in turn helps make him aware of this. Both the specific nature of the fiction and the total theatrical situation, therefore, are calculated to involve the spectator in an uncomfortable paradox; he must experience a disturbing socialness in his individuality and a disturbing isolation in his community membership. And this impairment of both the individual and the communal, in turn, sharpens his awareness of each of these areas of experience, and thereby defines and separates them.

This approach to the problem of maximum saturation is elaborated differently in each of the twelve realistic plays, but some general remarks can be made, especially about Ibsen's way of conceiving his characters. Schiller's Mary functions as a projection of the communal life of the audience, and her death sets the seal upon the community's existence *as* a community; while at the opposite extreme of character-conception, in Hauptmann's naturalistic plays (not only *Die Weber*), the idea of a humanly valuable community is directly denied us, the characters do not embody the social, but rather are oppressed or engulfed by it, and the spectator is thrown back upon his own guilty and sorrowing individuality. Ibsen, however, takes care to remain equidistant from these poles. His characters, in the realistic phase, are never tragically triumphant nor ever utterly crushed; their "destiny," as States has it, is to retain exactly that amount of tragic depth necessary "to crave a Destiny."[16] The audience is thus never allowed either to blossom as a community or to disintegrate utterly into despairing units of loneliness, although both these possibilities (corresponding to the two aspects of the characters' relation with society) are constantly present. Again, the effect is articulation of the spectator's experience into individual and communal components.

Especially important, however, is that Ibsen's "realistic" technique is eminently *theatrical*; it no longer insists Faustianly upon a new theater but rather derives its power directly from the nature of the actual theater in which it is used. By placing us over against an artistic vision of man, the theater in general approaches us as individuals, but our individuality, as we experience it theatrically, is incomplete. It does not include the possibility of action or free choice; it has the nature of a social-artistic convention, even when this is not so strongly emphasized as it is by Ibsen. And yet, we also do not transcend our individuality in the theater. A theatrical performance is undeniably a social event, but as the vehicle for a work of art it also has a certain adversarial or critical tendency with respect to society, which prevents our submergence in a sense of communal belonging; when this critical tendency is entirely absent, we speak of Philistine entertainment, not art at all.

The theater (as we know it) tends of its own accord to articulate our experience. In daily life our individual and our social being are hopelessly confused. When we feel in perfect tune with society, like Consul Bernick or Torvald Helmer, we can suddenly find ourselves out on a limb, vulnerable as individuals. When we feel ourselves heroically at odds with society, we soon discover that our efforts belong to a mechanism that favors society's baser tendencies; thus Helene Alving's fund and Thomas Stockmann's research ultimately promote an unholy coincidence of interests between establishment and opposition (Manders and Engstrand, Peter Stockmann and Hovstad). In the theater, however, our individual and social selves are both aroused, but both are also thwarted in such a way that we experience them as clearly separate from one another; and it is this basic separation that enables the theater to develop with special intensity either our anguished individualness (e.g. Hauptmann) or our triumphant socialness (e.g. Schiller), or to derive special meaning from the balance between them (e.g. Lessing, Shaw). But Ibsen's late prose dramas are aimed at neither the individual nor the social, nor any special combination of detachment and involvement; they seek, rather, to carry as far as possible that simple articulation of our experience which is already inherent in the theater as an institution, in order that this eventually become, in the theater, the experience of Spirit itself. In everyday life the inner opposition of self-consciousness produces confusion, which the theater tends to resolve into a relatively clear tension between opposed modes of experience, and Ibsen's aim is to develop this clarifying tendency to the point of metaphysical self-knowledge for his audience.

The artistic procedure in Ibsen's late plays is so extraordinarily simple that it is hard to talk about; it employs none of those devices which provide the critic with an easy starting point, no strikingly symbolic scenes like Leicester's in the locked room, no obvious interpretive problems like the discrepancy between Egmont's reputation and his behavior, no obtrusive self-interpretation in dialogue, like Maximus' "world-will" (V, 535). Yet there is one significant distinguishing feature in these plays, which is subtle in each by itself but becomes quite obvious in the "cycle" as a whole—the relation between the theme of the thwarted or perverted *project* (e.g. Consul Bernick's joint-stock company, Helmer's model household, Mrs. Alving's orphanage, Thomas Stockmann's crusade) and the idea of *art*. Already the projects of Gregers Werle and Rosmer are philosophical in nature, whereupon in *The Lady from the Sea* the two unsuccessful projects are actual works of art, Ballestad's and Lyngstrand's attempts to develop Ellida's situation as a tragedy; then comes Lövborg's manuscript, and then Solness's Faustianly impure decision to build houses for people as an act of titanic self-magnification, as the self-assertion of "a free builder" (X, 425), which quasi-divine freedom has now degenerated into a kind of paranoia; then Allmers attempts in theory and practice, in his book and his child, to define human responsibility; Borkman's dreams and Foldal's unknown tragedy are pendants to each other; and the climax of the development is Rubek's defiled statue.

The perverted or violated project gradually reveals its relation with the idea of philosophical art, and thus calls our attention to a specific artistic feature of the plays themselves. What interferes with the fulfillment of all those quasi-artistic projects within the fiction is real life, in the form of the particularity, limitedness, weakness of *individuals* (even Ellida's turning out not to be a sea sprite after all, though it may be a good thing, is an individual limitation by contrast with poetic possibility); and this suggests at least a hypothetical parallel with the dramatic work of art we are observing. In all twelve of the cycle plays an obvious symbolic structure communicates to us the presence of an ideal artistic-philosophical intention or "project" behind them, but what the plays actually show, their concentration on real life, appears to interfere with this intention in the same way that real life interferes with the fictional projects; Brustein's perception of an "ambivalence" involving "drama of ideas" and "drama of action" (Brustein, p. 48) refers to this contrast or interference. The parallel between the actual project and the fictional project, however, suggests that this intervention of real life in the ideal artistic intention reflects not any "selfless" objectivity, but precisely the opposite, an *individual limitedness* on the part of both author and spectator; Rubek insists that the expansion of his statue had been dictated by "knowledge of life" (XI, 447), but his inclusion of his own person as "remorse for a forfeited life" (XI, 450) is a tacit admission that this "knowledge" had been only weakness. The contrast between ideal and real in the effect of the plays thus reflects our experience as individuals, that individual limitedness and accidentalness which prevents the author and ourselves from communicating on a strictly ideal plane.

If Ibsen's ultimate aim had been to show the ideal thwarted by the real, the communal by the individual, if he had wished only to show (like Schiller) that the conscious mental faculty by which we form an idea of truth is also the medium by which we inevitably become conscious of ourselves, hence isolated and confused as individuals, the result would have been drama of despair, more or less in the manner of Chekhov—where the ideal is but dimly suggested, like a musical string of which the existence is not perceived except when it breaks, whereas the happenings on stage reveal a consciously self-complicating everydayness in which the clear contours of ideal truth cannot possibly be held fast. But Ibsen's plays are not drama of despair; they are drama of paradox (or tragicomedy, as the case may be),[17] and their paradoxicalness is completed by just that non-Chekhovian element in them which most obviously conflicts with the idea of "realism," namely, their contrivedness, their occasional nearness to the *pièce bien faite*, their coincidences, their overstrained moral summations, like Lona's in *Pillars of Society,* their striking formal *tours de force* like the Rat-Wife in *Little Eyolf* or the perfect temporal continuity of *John Gabriel Borkman* or the quadrangle of "elective affinities" in *When We Dead Awaken*. These devices are meant to be recognized as devices, as an arbitrary but disturbingly familiar theatrical language which reminds us, by its nature as a language, that the theatrical performance is an organized communal event in which we are participating. As real life interferes with the plays' ideality and calls attention to our status as individuals, so an obvious theatricalness interferes with the plays' objectivity and calls attention to the communal conventions we are involved in.

Theme and structure, then, interact as yet a further means of articulating our experience into individual and communal components; again, both our individuality and our socialness, as revealed by these plays, are of questionable value, but what counts is that they are *separated*, that we achieve a basic inner clarity which is the indispensable condition for anything like a "resurrection" of true humanity in the form of Spirit. Once this inner clarity is achieved, moreover, it becomes possible for us to comprehend the plays' ideal intention after all, but again only by way of a paradox, only in that we continue to experience our individuality as an impediment to communication on the ideal plane—for if we cease to experience this, then our inner situation is no longer clearly articulated. Thus comprehension and noncomprehension become identical; we experience yet again the whole fundamental paradox of the Spirit, which achieves birth only in the form of resurrection, which arrives at full self-knowledge only by way of self-negation.

In any case, it is not as a rule very difficult to distinguish between drama of disorientation and the general mode that includes tragicomedy and drama of paradox. Guthke's formulation, if we broaden the terminology a bit, serves the purpose admirably: "The grotesque [drama of disorientation] is the vision of an absurdity . . . which defies all intellectual efforts to clarify and elucidate its possible meaning in terms of human understanding. One of the charms of the tragicomic [and drama of paradox], on the other hand, is the possibility to think through, almost ad infinitum, the complicated mechanism by which the comic and the tragic are intertwined and indeed identified" (Guthke, pp. 73–74). It is true, for example, that we are required to think carefully by *Sei personaggi*, but there comes a point in that play where our thinking reaches a dead end, where the fiction no longer makes any sense and our very being disintegrates in order to be renewed. There is no such point in Shaw or Ibsen. Here, if we cease thinking through the play's implications logically, then either the play has failed or we have; in Shaw we are no longer "navigating," in Ibsen the articulation of our experience, which depends on a certain rational distance from each component, collapses. Even if our logic does not actually profit us, still, like Garcin at the end of *Huis Clos*, we must get on with it anyway. The uniqueness of Ibsen's late plays is that our thinking about them does get us somewhere, does in a sense resurrect us, even without the aid of an ironic or quasi-musical mechanism of transcendence.

5

Let us turn now to our third major category of dramatic response to self-consciousness, the modes of response to self-consciousness as a quasi-divine *power* in man. Self-consciousness, regarded in this way, does not isolate us as individuals but rather pulls us together into a reborn community, and in this general category, therefore, we shall expect to find a rebirth of the two principal traditional modes of communal experience in the theater, the tragic and the comic.

At maximum saturation in both the neo-tragic and the neo-comic, it seems to me that Hugo von Hofmannsthal is practically in a class by himself, and it is not unconnected with this that he is also the one major modern dramatist who understands fully both the dramatic achievement of German Classicism and the dramatic significance of *The Birth of Tragedy*. The category of response to self-consciousness as a power will in fact tend naturally to be represented, especially at high levels of saturation, by authors with a deep sense of tradition, who operate on the basis of a genuine critical understanding of past achievement. Eliot certainly belongs here, at least with *Murder in the Cathedral* and *The Cocktail Party*, and on a somewhat lower level of saturation— which, again, does not imply low quality but in fact, in this case, is the source of a special atmosphere of unstrained poetic communication—so does Yeats.

This category, however, becomes especially interesting at lowest saturation. Lorca, for instance, works quite clearly at lower saturation than Eliot or Yeats, and Maeterlinck, if he had ever fully realized his notion of "static drama," might have approached minimum saturation. But it is still not clear, either from these examples or on general principles, how a true minimum of saturation is even possible in the neo-tragic or neo-comic mode. If self-consciousness, the inward opening-up of our being, "the atmosphere of the soul," is a positive power in us, it is difficult to see how drama, which like all art shows us something of ourselves, can fail to intend some specific increase or improvement of this power.

Or rather, as in the case of Ibsen and drama of paradox at maximum saturation, it would be difficult to see this if it were not for the work of one man, Jean Cocteau. The neo-tragic is not Cocteau's only mode, but at least *Orphée* and *La machine infernale* belong to it, and both these plays represent strictly unsaturated drama. The stage techniques in *Orphée* are close to those of the drama of disorientation, but the effect of the play as a whole is not at all disorienting. Our sense of self is not confused, but rather exercised and indeed flattered by the ebullient mental agility which is not only expended upon us but also evidently credited to us as an audience. In Ionesco and the later absurdists there is always a relentless if uninterpretable logic, and even in Jarry and Apollinaire, correspondingly, there is a kind of relentless illogic;

but the secret of *Orphée* is that it contains nothing whatever that is relentless or inexorable or even indecorously insistent. All its constituent parts, whether mental or physical, are flexible, reversible, rearrangeable in the play of metaphorical associations by which our humanly interiorized world, the potentially chaotic consciousness of the audience, is transfigured. The secret is balance. The images and motifs are never either so nonsensical or so hammering as to lose the air of being mere conventions, yet also never so conventional as to admit of a clear interpretation; we are being spoken to in a language that makes sense, and so reflects us as a cohesive community, but a language of which the sense lies just a step beyond what we can define. Our self-consciousness is suffused with a knowledge of its fundamental and general validity but with no sense of direction, with a feeling of strength but with no notion of any use for its strength; and this, it seems to me, is practically a definition of neo-tragic (or neo-comic) drama at minimum saturation.

La machine infernale is an entirely different sort of play, but its effect is ultimately the same. It is Cocteau's answer to the supposed death of tragedy; it is the myth of Oedipus, hung about with all the incongruous associations that cling to it, like seaweed, when it is dragged up from the depths of the modern mind, but a tragedy nonetheless, and perhaps even more so because of its encumberedness, a celebration of eternal humanity, of the triumph of being "enfin, un homme," in the jaws of more than one implacable "machine." The myth, I mean, by being tortured in the machine of history and consciousness, has become in a sense more perfectly a myth, just as Oedipus becomes more perfectly a man in the machine of fate. This much is clear; but it still leaves open the crucial question of *how* the myth of Oedipus functions as a myth for us, how it reflects and establishes us as a community. The parallel between the tortured man and the tortured myth makes it clear that the myth *must*, somehow, emerge purified from the theatrical proceeding, that we are being addressed, again, in a language which *must* make sense, but which we cannot quite make sense of. The idea of our own subjection to the machine of modern society suggests an allegorical but not a strictly mythical relation between ourselves and the play, and Cocteau's characteristic theatrical legerdemain, again, tends to keep the mind at work and in motion, but not yet secured within a self-stabilizing structure of irony such as characterizes, say, *Murder in the Cathedral* or Hofmannsthal's *Der Turm*, or for that matter *Egmont*. We are hove to but not yet anchored. Our status as a mythically founded community is assured, but without being actually achieved or even satisfactorily envisioned; and this, again, seems to me to define unsaturated neo-tragic drama.

In the case of Cocteau as of Ibsen, then, the system of concepts I have proposed enables us to say something quite specific about what we should otherwise be obliged merely to admire as the author's "originality." I do not mean that Ibsen and Cocteau are not original, but their originality is that of an Einstein, not that of a prize-fight promoter, whose undeniably suspenseful "dramas" are not only original but strictly unpredictable. As the theory of relativity at once creates and solves a problem which then turns out to belong to the structure of the physical universe, so the dramas of Ibsen and Cocteau at once create and solve specific problems which turn out to belong firmly within the evolved structure of drama as a genre; and only this type of argument, I think, can in any sense establish an author's greatness.

6

In the scheme I have suggested, finally, there is one other specially problematic area, besides maximally saturated drama of paradox and minimally saturated neo-tragedy; that is the level of medium saturation in drama of despair or disorientation. If self-consciousness is a self-potentiating problem in our existence, it appears that either we must succumb to it (theater of assault, low saturation) or else the theater, by raising itself up magically to the status of a truly communal art form, must instantly and radically solve it (Strindberg, Pirandello). If a drama of enlightenment is possible, if it is possible for us to find our way in the real world despite the problem of self-consciousness, then this has turned out to be not quite so deep a problem after all, but something more like the simple fact which occupies drama of paradox.

Especially in the drama of despair, however, there is quite a well-developed corpus at intermediate levels of saturation. Perhaps the single really serious mistake in Guthke's book on tragicomedy, in fact, is his failure to recognize this. A number of plays, in particular, cause Guthke some worry—*Juno and the Paycock* and *The Plough and the Stars*, for example, which he calls only "mixed drama" (Guthke, p. 141) but still includes in the history of tragicomedy, and "works like" *König Nicolo,* which he mentions without venturing an opinion on Wedekind's more significant plays.

Let us begin with O'Casey. *Juno and the Paycock* and *The Plough and the Stars,* first of all, are neither tragicomedy nor drama of paradox, for the relation between tragic and comic elements in them is antithetical, not paradoxical. Ireland's struggle for her freedom has the effect of cruelly distorting that basic Irish wit and stamina and instinct for survival which produce the plays' comic moments: Johnny Boyle's inflexible rancor, and Jack Clitheroe's whipping-up of himself to an inflexible "Ireland is greater than a wife," are perhaps necessary, perhaps historically useful, but they are also violations of the Irish spirit, just as the rebellion in Hauptmann is a violation of the weavers' spirit. The Irish, like Hauptmann's weavers, have been made conscious of their need for liberation, and this consciousness disrupts their unity of being, thus at least endangering the very spirit that needs to be freed.

These two plays of O'Casey, then, are drama of despair, focused primarily on the inevitable self-conscious disintegration of human existence. It is even suggested, as in Hauptmann—for instance, by the evident connection between Mary Boyle's fate and her reading of Ibsen—that our situation in the theater exposes us to the same degenerative process experienced by the characters. The major difference from Hauptmann is O'Casey's working out of the comic aspects of his material, but it seems to me that this also has to do with our being a theater audience. Again, the comic and the tragic are not joined by mutual implication as in tragicomedy; the tragic, rather, represents what Irish consciousness (by being conscious, not by being Irish) has inevitably *become,* whereas the comic represents what the Irish people, in spite of this, still basically *are.* The "in spite of this" is all-important, for it corresponds to the fact that in spite of the self-conscious degeneration of our being, which is in progress right now, we are still managing (as a theater audience) to participate in an event we find enjoyable. We are not overcoming or transcending our condition, but we are managing somehow to bear it; we have been maneuvered into the position of teaching ourselves a lesson in how to cope with real life, and the possibility of such coping, even though we are not shown exactly how we must accomplish it, produces medium saturation, certainly a higher saturation than that of *Die Weber*.

A parallel argument applies to Wedekind. The brilliance of Wedekind's most significant works, *Frühlings Erwachen*, *Erdgeist*, *Die Büchse der Pandora*, and *Der Marquis von Keith*, lies in the fact that, despite their highly specific satirical tendency, they remain true drama of despair; they are not ultimately topical plays but rather, in Bentley's fine perception, they are "negatively religious."[18] The problem of generations in *Frühlings Erwachen*, the problem of the sexes in the Lulu plays, and the problem of genius in *Keith* are all aspects of the basic problem of human self-dissociation, the wound of existence, as Büchner's Danton has it. This is relatively clear in the Lulu plays and in Keith's instinctive self-lacerating avoidance of success, because success would deprive him of the very substance of his being, his striving upward. But even in *Frühlings Erwachen*, the specific social problems presented are all hedged about with a hopelessness that reveals their eternal dimension; we are shown, for example, a complete range of parental types, from liberal to conservative, from the highly intelligent to the utterly stupid, and none are capable of even communicating with their children. There is, moreover, a parallel between the play as a whole and Melchior's treatise on sexual intercourse—both are simple objective descriptions of what is usually not discussed—and the implication is that what Wedekind describes is as natural and as unavoidable as what Melchior describes, that objectivity is no help and can in fact be as much an occasion for terminal despair (Moritz) as hypocrisy.

But in Wedekind, as in O'Casey, there is an extravagantly comic tendency which resists despair, and as in O'Casey this tendency is related to our willing and enjoyable situation as a theater audience. The appearance of Life as a masked gentleman at the end of *Frühlings Erwachen* is not a tacked-on moral, but rather an acknowledgment of what we and the author are actually doing, namely living, in spite of our knowledge of how senseless it is. The trick, in both Wedekind and O'Casey, is to develop the antitheses without compromising them, to suggest the idea of coping or surviving, which produces medium saturation, without interfering with the irresistible self-conscious movement of despair;

and the method, in both cases, is to call our attention to two separate aspects of our situation as an audience, our interpreting consciousness and our simple being-alive.

The most important case, however, is Chekhov, whom Guthke, and not only Guthke, assigns unequivocally to the domain of tragicomedy (Guthke, p. 140). I think this is wrong. In drama of despair at medium saturation there is a combination of elements in tension—the movement of despair and the possibility of coping nonetheless—which is easily confused with the combination of tragic and comic in tragicomedy, but must be clearly distinguished from it; and the case of Chekhov, being one of the least obvious, is one of the most crucial for understanding this distinction.

Guthke's own point about the "charm" of tragicomedy, which lies in the infinite logical ponderability of its paradoxes, ought already to make the distinction fairly plain, for Chekhov's plays are quite clearly not meant to offer us food for thought. They are focused not upon logical problems, like the plays of Shaw and even Ibsen, but rather upon unappealable realities, which are contemplated uninterruptedly by both characters and audience and, as a result of this contemplation, become only more real. This is the self-conscious movement of despair, and in The Sea Gull it is reflected by a kind of philosophical allegory. In Act III, Trepleff loses Nina to a successful literary man, and in Act IV he has become a successful literary man himself, but loses Nina yet again; this represents the natural and inevitable process by which the conscious mind remakes itself for the sake of its object, but in doing so necessarily participates in a whole world of change by which the object is also altered, so that desire remains as hopeless as ever. The self-conscious self, by its nature, cannot be what it needs to be or have what it needs to have, and this truth is all the more effective in Uncle Vanya, The Three Sisters, and The Cherry Orchard, where it is embedded more deeply in action and dialogue, thus not blunted for the spectator by his sense of achievement at having deciphered an allegorical pattern in the action.

But in Chekhov, as in Wedekind and O'Casey, the movement of despair is balanced by a countermovement, which is produced via the curious melancholy sociability of the characters. The inexorability of the process of consciousness, the fact that this process must eventually crystallize as an oppressive and unalterable reality, provides human beings with a firm setting in which to talk, or share significant silences, and so achieve genuine if futile communication. Chekhovian dialogue at its most intense is not so much a matter of the characters' speaking to each other as of their listening to each other and themselves, and perceiving through the words (or failure thereof) the overlapping shadows of a universal and a strictly personal unhappiness. Thus genuine communicative openness and imprisonment in the self become identical, and the parallel with our situation as listeners in the theater, though subtle, is deeply effective; we too are keeping ourselves in existence, and more or less in equilibrium, by a futile sociability at the brink of the abyss.

Again, however, the opposed movements in Chekhov do not constitute a paradox of the sort that produces tragicomedy. The effects of the two movements, our loneliness and our togetherness, have become practically identical (this being almost the exact opposite of the separation of individual and communal experience in Ibsen), but the movements themselves are distinct in origin and nature; the self-conscious movement of despair is the *way* we exist, whereas our sociable coping with it is equivalent to the simple fact *that* we exist, that our despair does not instantly destroy us. As in Wedekind and O'Casey, therefore, we have drama of despair on at least the level of medium saturation, and in fact on a relatively high level, since the parallel between sociability on stage and society in the theater makes the envisioned method of coping quite specific and immediate for us as we sit there. But society as we experience it in the theater is not a new and directly elevating phenomenon, like Strindberg's transformation of his audience into the creatively fulfilled authors of their misery; it is, rather, an intimation of the true nature of our existence in general, a signpost, a lesson, as this is characteristic of medium saturation.

This argument more or less completes our scheme, and we can now summarize it in a diagram. The scheme, again, is not meant to be used as a guide to interpretation, but rather it is the summary of a number of partial interpretations of specific works with regard to the evolution of the genre. I have arranged the diagram by authors, but in doing so I mean to refer only to the works I have mentioned; other works by the same authors might easily belong elsewhere. Three names are in parentheses: Schnitzler because I have not defended my placing of him at all, Brecht because he is treated below, and Genêt because it occurs to me that he may well belong somehow between drama of disorientation and drama of despair.

	Saturation		
	Low	*Medium*	*High*
power ⌐ neo-tragic Cocteau	Maeterlinck, Yeats, Lorca, Eliot	Hofmannsthal
∟ neo-comic (Schnitzler)		
fact ⌐ tragicom. Kaiser, Sartre	Shaw, Pirandello, Giraudoux, Anouilh, Dürrenmatt	Ibsen
∟ paradox Wilde, Synge		
problem ⌐ disorien. absurd, etc. (Genêt)	(Brecht)	Pirandello
∟ despair Hauptmann	O'Casey, Wedekind, Chekhov	Strindberg

(Self-consciousness as a . . .)

It should be noted, also, that the distinction of two modes of response in each category corresponds roughly to the distinction between sensitive and energetic style. The lower of each pair (drama of despair or paradox, neo-comic drama) tends toward sensitive style, the upper toward energetic.

In any case, the diagram must not be regarded as more than a heuristic device for exploring modern drama in its particular evolved form. I offer the mere possibility of such an ordering of modern theatrical works as evidence for the historical importance of the German Classical drama of self-consciousness.

10 The Classic Modern: Brecht

From a modern point of view the age of German Classicism appears to have been a relatively settled and comfortable
time in which to live. Next door, in France, social existence was
being shaken to the roots by the Revolution and its consequences,
but although this caused the Germans a great deal of anxiety and a
certain amount of direct humiliation, the actual changes in German life do not appear to have been nearly so sudden or frighten-
ing. Especially in a literary view of history—the view that tends to
be adopted not only by critics but by poets as well—the half
century or so that straddles the year 1800, despite the turmoil
produced by Romanticism and by a growing discontent with
older political and social thought, still appears to repose more or
less comfortably in the shadow of that vigorous but self-disci-
plined old man whose hours, when he was not busy producing
what Germans will probably never cease to regard as their greatest
poetry, were spent in collecting and arranging scientific speci-
mens, passing apodictically on the work of others, and attending
to the affairs of a conservative state. The falsity of this view of the
age of Goethe need not concern us here. What is important is that
such a view exists, that it tends especially to arise in the field of
literature, and that it produces in modern German authors an
urge to go beyond what are imagined as the limits of Classicism.

1

Most modern English authors regard their work as different
from Shakespeare's, not as needing to surpass Shakespeare; the

intellectual assumptions and immediate problems of the Elizabethans, we assume, were widely different from ours. But the
problems of the early post-Enlightenment, or of the age of German
Classicism, are undeniably similar to ours, except (again, we assume) that they have by now been revealed in much greater depth
and difficulty; the age of Goethe, from our point of view, appears
relatively comfortable, whereas our own age appears to us a distinctly uncomfortable one, requiring of our art much more drastic
measures in order to come to grips with it. Therefore the German
classics must be surpassed, Goethe's *Faust,* as Thomas Mann
suggests, must be "unwritten"; the German classics do not belong
to a world different from our own, but rather they appear to represent a direct challenge, a humane, tolerant, poetically sophisticated attempt to ward off precisely the enormous problems we
now still find ourselves grappling with, an attempt, therefore,
which obviously failed and must be replaced by something more
effective. That among major figures in modern German drama,
only Hofmannsthal felt no need to rebel against German Classical
poetics, has to do, I think, with his being a Viennese, thus in a
position to regard himself as belonging to a somewhat different
tradition; he could acknowledge unreservedly the success of
German Classical drama without feeling his own efforts, in consequence, superfluous. With our immediate forebears, as it were our
fathers, we are naturally in competition, but we can freely emulate
uncles like Goethe and Schiller if we are lucky enough to have
them.

   The German classics, then, as seen from a modern German point
of view, must be surpassed. And yet they are also much too valuable to be dismissed, for especially in the field of drama they
constitute the establishment of an unquestionably modern and
useful poetic idiom. What the German Classical authors had
lacked, a solid indigenous poetic tradition, is available to modern
German authors for the asking, and no serious author is likely to
be entirely unaware of the advantages of having and keeping such
a tradition; it provides him with a universe of poetic discourse, a
reasonably reliable basis for communication, a basis that retains
its effectiveness even if he chooses to communicate by ostenta-
tiously flouting its values or conventions. Therefore, in modern
German literature, there is a marked ambivalence with respect to
the works of the Classical age; these works, paradoxically, are at

once both useful and obsolete. And one clear instance of this ambivalence is Brecht.[1]

Before dealing with Brecht in detail, however, let us turn to the question of the general effect upon modern German drama of its ambivalence toward Classicism. First, the need to surpass the classics accounts in large part for the relative dearth of major German works (except from Vienna) in the neo-comic and neo-tragic modes, for these are the modes with which Classicism is associated most naturally. The scheme of modes suggested at the end of Chapter 9 is intended only as a partial description of the evolved form of drama in the late nineteenth and twentieth centuries, and therefore need not be exactly applicable to German drama around 1800. But from a modern point of view neo-tragic and neo-comic appear to characterize at least the works of Goethe, Schiller, and Kleist more closely than any other modes; and even in Lessing—though he in some ways anticipates drama of paradox—there is still the feeling that man is being celebrated as man, that our self-consciousness is a power which, if not itself divine, is capable of producing through wisdom like Nathan's a specially intimate relation with the divine.[2] Thus, for a modern German author, neo-tragic or neo-comic drama would seem a meeting with the classics on their own ground, and from such a meeting no real surpassing of Classicism could be hoped for.

Hence the curious fact that important modern German drama (outside Vienna)—say, Hauptmann, Wedekind, Kaiser, Brecht, and Dürrenmatt, after which group, in my opinion, there is a quantum leap to the next level down—does not markedly favor traditional forms, even though it possesses the most solid and recent dramatic tradition in Europe. Its characteristic modes, rather, are what we might call the unclassical (drama of paradox, tragicomedy) and the anticlassical (drama of despair), for these are the modes that appear to offer the best opportunity of surpassing the classics. Drama of paradox and modern tragicomedy represent the striking out on a new path, for although these modes owe a great deal indirectly to German Classicism, they are actually generated only by the development of dialectic philosophy that followed later. And drama of despair is something more like a direct attack on Classicism, an insistence that the problem of self-consciousness has not been solved after all, despite the apparent pretensions of the Classical authors.

But the other side of the ambivalence also makes itself felt; modern German drama must surpass Classicism, but without dissociating itself entirely. Hauptmann's true genius is shown in the drama of despair at extremely low saturation, but Hauptmann himself was not satisfied with this type of drama, for it removed him too far from the Classical mainstream of German poetry. Hence the oversaturation of his comic and visionary dramas and dramas on the theme of art. Unsaturated drama of despair represents a turning away from Classicism, an insistence upon the impossibility of anything like a Classical communal mastering of the problem of self-consciousness, whereas drama of despair at medium or high saturation (which is what Hauptmann attempts in his comedies and visions) represents an alternative to Classicism, a positive coming to grips with the human condition despite our more advanced knowledge of its hopelessness. I do not think Hauptmann's more saturated plays are successful; the positive elements in them tend to compromise the movement of despair, which is exactly what is not permitted to happen in O'Casey, Wedekind, Chekhov, Strindberg. But this judgment is not a necessary part of the present argument.

I shall probably run into objections, however, when I assert that another symptom of Germany's ambivalence with respect to its own Classical heritage is the almost complete absence of a German drama of disorientation. A number of German playwrights have tried their hand at this mode; Frisch has already been mentioned, Weiss and Handke might be added, and some expressionist plays are probably also intended to be disorienting, although it is not always easy to distinguish between disorientation and the characteristic expressionist attempt to emulate Strindberg in drama of despair at maximum saturation. But I still maintain that, excepting one author, there is no true drama of disorientation in Germany, nothing really comparable to Ionesco and Beckett or Jarry and Apollinaire or the Pirandello of the "theater" plays. German works tending in this direction are either admonitory to the point of schoolmasterliness, or unimaginative, or else they fail to achieve that consistency of logic or illogic which makes the absurd truly disturbing.[3]

I do not mean to suggest that the German mind is too rigid or pedantic to allow itself the freedom of disorientation. It is much more difficult, for example, to achieve genuine disorientation with a reader in his armchair, who determines for himself the pace and rhythm at which he perceives the work, than with a theater audience, who have their pace and rhythm imposed from without; yet the one modern author in whose case I think we can speak unequivocally of disorienting narrative is Franz Kafka. Nor do I mean to suggest that failure in the mode of disorientation is even a serious fault in modern German drama. My point is that drama of disorientation tends by nature to take on at least the appearance of a complete cutting-loose from tradition, and that German dramatists, quite properly, are reluctant to risk this, for their tradition is an important asset even to the most radical among them. Sitting in a theater, for Germans of this century, is not at all an absurd thing to do, but rather, by virtue of the German dramatic movement, it is a culturally better-founded proceeding than anywhere else in Europe. This, again, produces a pull in both directions with respect to the German classics.

Yet drama of disorientation, properly considered, also offers the modern German dramatist a unique opportunity, for disorientation—more than drama of paradox, and certainly more than despair—is itself a deep and important tendency in the works of the Classical period and becomes obvious in certain authors on the fringe of Classicism, say Tieck, Grabbe, the Lenz of *Pandaemonium Germanicum*, and to an extent the Büchner of *Woyzeck* and *Leonce und Lena*. The advantage of German Classicism over the other principal dramatic tendencies of the late eighteenth century is precisely that it neither accommodates its audience (drama of sympathy) nor hopes to remake human existence by main force (drama of shock), but rather, by raising subtle but disturbing questions, attempts to disorient its audience with respect to their normal existence, in order that existence take on for them a metaphysically deepened form. Again, it must be kept in mind that the terminology of the previous chapter is not applicable ad libitum to the drama of different ages; a theater audience in eighteenth-century Germany brought with it a clearer set of conventional expectations—and so does an audience today, when they go to what they know is an eighteenth-century play—than that of the modern audience at a modern play, for modern drama, from the beginning, has been characterized by an often chaotic clash of conventions. Therefore a modern play must go further than an eighteenth-century play in order to be truly disorienting;

in modern drama, we can distinguish clearly between the neo-tragic and the drama of disorientation, between the modes repre-sented by Cocteau and by Ionesco, or between those represented by Hofmannsthal's "theater" play *Ariadne auf Naxos* and by *Sei personaggi*, whereas a careful consideration of *Egmont* or *Maria Stuart* or *Homburg* tends to cloud this distinction. For just this reason, however, a German Classical play can be disorienting without being strictly drama of disorientation.

German Classical drama, then, *mutatis mutandis*, has a ten-dency in the direction of drama of disorientation, and it is thus at least conceivable that a true modern German drama of disorienta-tion could satisfy at a stroke both sides of its ambivalence toward Classicism, could be a carrying forward of the Classical tradition, yet also a clear surpassing of the Classical models, inasmuch as full-fledged drama of disorientation by nature denies the validity of our habitual or traditional ways of thinking. But this hypotheti-cal drama could be of neither high nor low saturation, since thea-ter of the absurd, or something comparable, would relinquish con-tact with the Classical tradition altogether, while in a German context the Pirandellian restoration of our being on a higher plane as we sit in the theater would not be much more than a revival of the Classical achievement. Thus a disorienting drama at medium saturation is required, and herein lies the problem. Medium sat-uration is characterized in general by the teaching of some sort of lesson, by a sharpening of the audience's sense of direction in the real world, and this sort of result seems at first glance to be in-compatible with disorientation as a technique. Indeed, the admon-itory or didactic tendency in some recent German dramatists is just what keeps them from achieving true drama of disorientation.

Brecht, however, whose work positively flaunts its didactic quality, is the exception to this rule, and therefore, along with Hofmannsthal, but at the other end of the scale, he represents a culmination of the German dramatic movement. If Hofmannsthal succeeds in giving German Classical drama itself a truly modern form, then Brecht, against all probability, arrives at a synthesis of the modern tendencies to supersede and to preserve the Classical achievement.

2

I do not mean that disorientation is Brecht's conscious aim throughout his career, nor do I mean that disorientation and "alienation" are the same, or that Brecht himself would have described his works as drama of disorientation. There is a great deal in his theory, especially when he speaks later of "dialectical" drama, as well as a certain amount in his dramatic practice, which tends to associate him with drama of paradox, drama in response to self-consciousness as a fact, and in his historicized dialogue he shares at least one important dialectical theater technique with Giraudoux and Shaw.[4] But disorientation is nevertheless his natural and essential mode. His whole development is governed by the tension between this fact and an equally strong tendency toward didactic or at least mundanely useful drama. In effect—whether or not by intention, or to whatever extent—Brecht achieves an intermediately saturated drama of disorientation which, apart from its other qualities, is of great significance in carrying forward and holding together the German dramatic movement.

The distinction between drama of paradox and drama of disorientation, for the purpose of discussing Brecht, hinges on the distinction between paradox and contradiction. A paradox is an apparent contradiction which ultimately, but not immediately, admits at least the possibility of being resolved; the mutual implication of tragic and comic in tragicomedy is a paradox, for the logicalness by which each arises from the other challenges us intellectually to discover their common source (cf. Guthke on tragicomedy as inexhaustible fuel for thought). But a contradiction is a point at which our thinking is simply thwarted, a problem to which there is no answer, and if Reinhold Grimm is strictly correct when he defines Brechtian alienation "very simply as a *showing of contradictions*,"[5] then Brecht's work cannot properly be reckoned drama of paradox or tragicomedy.

The distinction between paradox and contradiction is not always easy to apply in practice. Some critics would agree that Brecht's conception of his characters involves or at least admits contradiction,[6] but this is an especially difficult area in which to achieve clarity. Nietzsche, who apparently exercised some influence on Brecht's idea of the human ego,[7] differs from Schiller mainly in his insistence that human nature is based on an unresolvable contradiction between the constitutive drives. But even in *The Birth of Tragedy* we should perhaps still speak of paradox rather than contradiction, for at least the idea of a resolution is present in the notion of a "primal contradiction" of which human nature is the image. While it may be true, therefore, that Brecht often gives the impression of contradictoriness in the delineation of his people, this is not yet an argument sufficient to show that his mode is disorientation.

However, we can give a satisfactory answer to one crucial question without further development of our basic concepts, the question of *why* Brecht should have been attracted to drama of disorientation, why he should not have been content, especially in his later years, to transmit to his audience the firm intellectual orientation offered by Communist theory. Let us look first at "Die Ballade vom Wasserrad" which, when it was lifted from *Die Rundköpfe und die Spitzköpfe* (III, 1007–8) and made an independent poem, received an altered final refrain:

> For then the wheel turns no longer
> And the merry game is discontinued,
> When the water, with liberated
> Strength, attends to its own affairs. [III, 1*][8]

The metaphor of the water wheel, in the poem as a whole, is quite exact. "The great ones of this earth" rise and fall in an endless succession of revolutions which they like to regard as their own action and interaction, whereas the real motive power of the process is the fact that the lower classes keep feeding them; their changes of fortune are merely the rotation of a rigid wheel which is driven by the elemental power of the people beneath.

But when this process finally comes to a halt, when the old system collapses, it is interesting that the metaphor collapses too. What can it possibly mean that the water, from now on, will "do its own thing"? As long as the old corrupt system remains in effect, the metaphor makes perfect sense; the flowing of the water suggests the flowing away of life, the passing of time and generations, while the sameness of the wheel denotes the interchangeability of rulers, one being as bad as the next. But the metaphorical vehicle includes no satisfactory parallel for either the demise of the old system or the nature of the system that will replace it. This does not disturb us as long as there is no mention of the coming of a new system; but in the revised version our attention is called forcibly to an important idea which obviously represents the poem's lesson, yet is rendered at least imaginatively unconvincing by its refusal to belong to the basic metaphorical structure. If we recall, in addition, that one of Brecht's favorite images for the triumphant world-shaping human power which socialism encourages is precisely the *controlling* of water, not its freedom (*Kleines Organon*, no. 25; *Der kaukasische Kreidekreis*; cf. *Faust*), then we might be excused for wondering not only why he revised the "Wasserrad" as he did, but why he wrote it in the first place.

And yet, it seems to me that even in its revised version, and even from a doctrinaire socialist point of view, the poem makes sense. Walter Sokel, as far as I know, has gone further than any other critic in clarifying the importance for Brecht of something like an existentialist idea of *decision*: "The actions of the characters must be shown as avoidable and freely chosen, not as decrees of fate or determination by milieu. Alienation-technique serves to divest them of their matter-of-course quality and reveal them as decisions which could have turned out differently."[9] But even Sokel limits his conclusions rather too strongly when he concedes that "as an heir of the Enlightenment, he [Brecht] requires that the existence of the person depicted [i.e. the latter's decisions] be tried and judged in mundane-practical and rational terms with regard to social usefulness and to the doctrine which this implies for the spectator." For Brecht, "doctrine" is not quite so simple. If decision is a crucial element in the idea of man presented on stage, surely the audience, who are also human, are not expected simply to submit to the play's teaching; surely they too must make a decision. I will argue that even under an established socialist regime, in Brecht's view, decisions must be made which can turn out differently, and that this is implied even in *Der kaukasische Kreidekreis*, which appears to glorify socialist unanimity.

But let us return to the "Wasserrad" song. Brecht deliberately creates a metaphorical cul-de-sac in order to make clear that a more humane and rational society will not come about of its own accord, that socialist revolution is not an inevitable result of the order of nature (just as it is not a natural part of the poem's metaphorical order), but rather a true change, depending on the reader's free decision. A kind of lyrical alienation effect is used, which places the reader on his own feet and challenges him to end the poem himself, to "change the world: it needs it!" (II, 651–52). If the world needs to be changed, then our decision to do this must be a true decision, not merely a reaction determined by objective circumstances, for objective circumstances belong by definition to the world that needs to be changed.

This makes clear how it can happen that Brecht is both a Communist and a dramatist of disorientation, for disorientation of some sort is the indispensable precondition of a truly free decision. A man who is well oriented, certain of his place and path in existence, is not in a position even to imagine changing the world. Decision does not take place unless it is accompanied by the full knowledge that one could as easily be wrong as right, unless one is unbending in one's resolve, yet also capable of saying, as the Agitators say to the Young Comrade, "It is possible that we are wrong, and you right" (II, 656). These words, moreover, are deeply significant with respect to *Die Massnahme* as a whole. "We"—the audience, the speaking participants, and even the party—*can be wrong;* and this knowledge alone becomes ever more disorienting the more we understand the importance of *not* being wrong, the more we understand that "courage is nothing; arriving at the goal is everything" (II, 579). It may be true that the classical methods of socialism are "drawn from knowledge of reality" (II, 657), and that "only after learning from reality can we change reality" (II, 663); but reality—again, by defintion—does not provide us with unambiguous teachings, and even the Control Chorus in *Die Massnahme* declines to exclude "rage," "outrage," and "swift intervention" (II, 663) from the catalogue of what is necessary to change the world.

3

The play we shall discuss in detail, however, is *Der kaukasische Kreidekreis,* for not only is this play centered upon a relatively uncontroversial, hence presumably unambiguous lesson about life under socialism, but it is also often regarded as a kind of mellowing in late Brecht, a fundamentally humane work, more effective emotionally than propagandistically.[10] If it can be argued, therefore, that *Der kaukasische Kreidekreis* is still essentially drama of disorientation, and that its use of this mode is socialistic in the sense I have outlined, then the possibility of a similar argument for most of Brecht's other major plays will follow.

Brecht himself insists that the *Kreidekreis* is not a "parable," even though "the introductory scene suggests otherwise, since outwardly, in fact, the whole story is told in order to clear up the issues bearing on possession of the valley" (XVII, 1205); and this may be strictly correct on hindsight. But when the peasant woman announces "a theatrical piece which has to do with our question" (V, 2006), the audience *expects* the play to have parabolic significance with respect to the nature, growth, or implementation of socialist doctrine; and this expectation is used as a means of disorienting us, for if it is not strictly defeated, it is at least confused by the actual story we see. At least seven distinct and sometimes contradictory lessons can be derived from the inner play:

i. The lesson of the play's last words:

> That what exists should belong to those who are good for it, so
> Children to the motherly, that they thrive,
> Conveyances to good drivers, for the sake of good driving,
> And the valley to the water-bringers, that it bring fruit. [V, 2105]

This lesson is perhaps derivable from the first part of the inner play, Grusche's story; but it has little immediate relation to the second part, Azdak's story. Can we, then, take it as *the* lesson of the inner play?

ii. The lesson that the basically senseless cyclical mechanism of capitalist society, as represented by the succession of palace revolution, war and restoration, produces via a kind of dialectical miracle (Azdak's legitimate judgeship) the possibility of a fulfilled life and even a measure of class-consciousness for truly good souls in the lower classes. "My child will have to fear hunger, but not the hungry," says Grusche (V, 2102). This idea (unlike i) accounts for the Azdak-plot, and is socialistic in the sense that it shows the self-contradicting tendency of capitalism. But it is also counter-revolutionary, for it suggests that capitalist society is still somehow humanly tolerable.

iii. Exactly the opposite of ii: namely, that justice and humanity can prevail under capitalism *only* by the most improbable coincidences, which means that that social order must be swept aside. This lesson is revolutionary enough, but it requires (like Schiller's theory of flagellant tragedy) that we adopt a negative attitude toward the whole inner fiction, including Grusche's and Azdak's successes.

iv. The lesson that our emotional life must be cultivated and preserved even under the worst conditions, even when it appears a dangerous "seduction" (V, 2025). It is Grusche's emotional attachment to Michel, after all, that makes her a fit mother. But this lesson calls into question the decision about the disputed valley, which goes against emotion.

v. Again, exactly the opposite of *iv*: that a society in which sentiment is necessary to produce a semblance of order is hopelessly corrupt. The same objection applies here as in *iii*.

And finally, two lessons that have to do with the apparent superfluity of material in the inner play:

vi. That history, as passed down to us, is class propaganda, that unconnected details in the lives of little people are as revealing, historically and socially, as "the famous deeds of lords and generals in our school-books" (XVII, 1053). But this does not explain how the particular details of the inner play are chosen and ordered.

vii. The lesson that superfluity, in the form of poetry, even when it is not directly instructive or useful, is as necessary in our existence as economics, that "the voice of the old poet" must be heard "even in the shadow of Soviet tractors" (V, 2007). But if poetry—as a sign of our more-than-mechanical humanity—must be preserved, why should our equally human sense of home ground and our taste for good goat cheese be sacrificed?

As I say, then, there is a superfluity of material in the inner play, too many possibilities for interpretation. Ordinarily this would not matter. But in the opening frame scene of the *Kreidekreis* it is indicated that the inner play will "clear up" certain points of applied socialist doctrine; and the presence of strictly contradictory meanings (*ii* and *iii*, *iv* and *v*), not merely paradoxes, is therefore distinctly disorienting. At least two of the interpretive possibilities, moreover (*ii*, *iv*, possibly *vii*), can reasonably be regarded as counter-revolutionary.

Let us begin with lesson *vii*, for the idea of poetry evidently has something to do with the play's deeper meaning. At the end of the frame scene the expert from the capital explains to the singer that he has pressing business, and asks whether the inner play cannot be shortened a bit, to which Arkadi Tscheidse replies with one word—a word to which Brecht often attaches great significance—the word "Nein" (V, 2007; cf. II, 629; III, 1186). As the play progresses, however, we soon discover that the inner play *could* be shortened, whole episodes could be removed, without damage to its basic content; and yet the poet arbitrarily refuses even to consider this. Thus, just at the beginning of the inner play, the image of the impatient expert, fretting about indisputably important matters while the poet's story wanders "epically" onward, is impressed on our minds; and this is meant to suggest the question of whether we too are not wasting our time in the theater. There is a contradiction in our status as an audience which is parallel to the contradictions Brecht notes in Grusche's status as a mother (XVII, 1208–10). To the extent that we affirm the play's basic social message, we are compelled to ask whether it is right to spend time enjoying the play in its whole lengthy development, by which the basic message tends to be obscured, intellectually and emotionally. Why should this irrational enjoyment of ours, and of the fictional audience, be privileged above "the love for a particular piece of land" (V, 2004), which even the expert says must be acknowledged? Can the one feeling replace the other or be offered in payment for it? These questions are not fruitfully discussible; they are not a paradox which is intellectually interesting ad infinitum. They are, rather, aspects of a simple unbridgeable gulf which is opened by Arkadi's uncompromising "Nein."

But this gulf of contradiction is not merely a source of anguish. Grusche, as Brecht says, using the English word, is a "sucker" (XVII, 1206), and in that we allow ourselves to be engaged by the doctrinally unnecessary elaboration of the play as a whole, we are suckers too. Yet Grusche demands of Azdak nothing but the opportunity to continue being a sucker, in which demand she is being doubly a sucker, and the result, paradoxically, is that when she wins her case, "she is a 'sucker' no longer." She has now simply become Michel's mother; and while this does not actually relieve the contradictions in her situation—we need only remind ourselves of the real mothers in Brecht—it does integrate those contradictions into a more cohesive and supportable mode of existence. Likewise, by analogy, we in the audience are truly suckers only as long as we resist this, like the expert or like Grusche in the early days of her motherhood. But once we accept our situation in the theater and acknowledge its permanence or repeatableness, once we subscribe to the singer's totally unsupported assertion that "old and new wisdom form an excellent mixture" (V, 2007), the contradiction we suffer becomes an integral part of our life. Why, if the business of socialism is to change the world, should the mixing of old and new wisdom be possible or even desirable? No reason is given. We simply are, at the same time, both an artistically sensitive audience, capable of irrational enjoyment, and also (presumably) a rationally purposeful socialist community.

Thus the play teaches, by way of our situation here and now in the theater, that disorientation (the immediate experience of contradiction) is and must be our unchanging way of life Only by being constantly in a state of disorientation are we constantly capable of making true decisions, decisions that could have turned out otherwise, and only in this way do we (like the Agitators in Die Massnahme) avoid the danger of socialism's becoming a machine that devours us, no longer a human endeavor to change the world. Again, the world cannot change if we feel too much at home in it; and the function of art, or at least art like Der kaukasische Kreidekreis, which is neither slavishly realistic nor mechanically doctrinaire, the function of that art which transforms what it sees according to its own lights—"in a bold and even autocratic way" (XVII, 1210), as Brecht says approvingly of a series of drawings on the Kreidekreis theme—is not to expose existing contradictions, but rather to introduce an element of salutary disorientation into life. Nor does it matter that through art we deliberately maintain a certain disorientedness in society, that even a planning commission for the "redistribution of songs" (V, 2006) is conceivable. Precisely the need for this sort of deliberate self-disorientation ought to make clear to us the risk we take by affirming socialist principles, the risk of de-humanization, which in turn reminds us that socialism itself must constantly be our free decision, always in danger of turning out otherwise. Brecht intended to admonish his Soviet readers specifically that "in the great revolutionary upheaval we are experiencing, it is not merely a question of changing one situation for another, but rather the new age is an age of uninterrupted unheaval" (XVII, 952–53).

Furthermore, once we understand the importance of the idea of art in the Kreidekreis, we can perhaps recognize in the plot a parable after all, or even an allegory. Art, especially in its enjoyable or "culinary" aspect (cf. e.g. XVII, 1006–8), is the natural child of primitive or corrupt social conditions, as Michel is the natural child of Natella Abaschwili; hence the possibility of counter-revolutionary meanings in the play, which remind us of the "natural" ancestry of our own present experience. But under socialism, if artistic enjoyment is insisted upon, art becomes an insoluble problem—it raises the question, for example, of why other irrational claims (like those of the goatherds) must be ruthlessly sacrificed—just as for Grusche, by her insistence on saving him, Michel becomes a source of ineluctable contradictions. By dealing courageously with these contradictions, however, Grusche becomes Michel's true mother, and it can be argued by analogy that the problematic quality of art under socialism makes our relation to it more authentic than under conditions where it is taken for granted. Artistic enjoyment drugs the bourgeois, whereas it braces and challenges the socialist. Even the specific motif of the chalk circle functions in the allegory thus understood, for by declining to drag art over bodily to itself, by declining to reduce it to mere doctrine, by allowing it to retain the irrational enjoyability it had possessed in its bourgeois form, socialism becomes, as it were, art's true mother; we preserve for ourselves the bracingly problematic, truth-bearing quality of art, and so in truth integrate it into our socialist way of life after all.

The story of Azdak, whom Brecht compares to the Shakespearean wise fool (XVII, 1206), is also relevant here, for Azdak is a walking contradiction, a courageous lickspittle who, by an absurd set of coincidences, finds himself in the position of dispensing something which is "almost" justice (V, 2105) under utterly degenerate social conditions. This corresponds to the idea that art is the necessarily but degradingly disguised form (as wise fool) which justice and humanity must take under capitalism, the idea that art is the thwarted expectation of revolution (Azdak is "a disappointed revolutionary" [XVII, 1206]), thus, again, the idea that art fulfills its true destiny under socialism. Art is born naturally of capitalism, as the refuge of an inborn human desire for truth and justice which social conditions force underground, whereas under socialism art could never *originate*, since the same desire receives more direct satisfaction; but the naturalness of that relation is obviously perverted, as is that of the relation between Michel and his natural mother. Only under socialism, by being in a sense unnatural, can art become what it ought to be and claims to be, a source of genuine enjoyment and not merely a symptom of bad conscience, a vehicle of genuine enlightenment concerning our human situation as decision-makers, not merely a flattering self-reflection or a shadow in lieu of substance.

Let us note, however, that in spite of all this, the audience of *Der kaukasische Kreidekreis* does not need absolutely to be an audience of socialists. The point of view we are meant to adopt in order to understand the play is made clear in the frame scene, whatever our actual politics may be—although I suppose neo-Nazis are strictly excluded. We are being shown as it were the blueprints for a radically new utilization of our own artistic homeland, our native valley, and like the peasants of "Galinsk" we are presumably ready at least to listen. Thus, even if our opinions are nonsocialist and remain so at the end, we have still understood that art contains within itself the possibility of a radical transfunctioning without any change in its basic nature; at least this particular work of art, therefore, becomes a problematic and disorienting experience for us; and this in turn *is* the new function envisioned for art under socialism, which means that at least for the time being, we find we have ceded the valley after all. Moreover, the notion of socialism as a free decision that could have turned out otherwise makes it possible even for the nonsocialist, whose decision has turned out otherwise, to regard himself as participating in the same basic mental situation as the socialist audience more directly addressed.

4

Brechtian alienation is in the final analysis not a simplifying but a subtilizing of the relation between audience and stage, and a subtilizing which is similar to that carried out by German Classical drama (whether or not Brecht knew this) insofar as it connects our situation here and now in the theater with our deeper nature as the self-conscious perceivers and shapers of a problematic entity called the "world." In particular, the lesson of Der kaukasische Kreidekreis, or the lesson of lessons, which we both understand and undergo in the theater, is practically identical with the lesson of Schiller's Tell (we have also noted the specific parallel between apple-shot and bridge-crossing), the lesson that we must learn to live affirmatively in a state of strict inner contradiction. "Remain constantly in conflict with yourself! Remain One, but constantly divided!" (II, 786); and the special irony in these obviously ironic words at the end of Die heilige Johanna der Schlachthöfe is that they also contain an important positive truth.

But the relationship of the Kreidekreis to Tell—or also to Nathan, another play that trains us to live in a contradiction, another play about "wisdom" (cf. V, 2007; XVII, 1205)—is by no means unique; for if we review our arguments, we shall find that acceptance of the necessity of living in a contradiction may be regarded as the general lesson of German Classical drama, except that in *Egmont, Maria Stuart,* and *Prinz Friedrich,* the "lesson" aspect as such is not prominent. We must learn a technique of deliberate self-delusion for the sake of truth, like Egmont (or like socialists in the theater); we must follow Mary in transforming our externally conditioned subjection into a free act (as Grusche transforms suckerhood into motherhood); we must recognize, as the Elector must recognize at least twice, that we can truly promote the truth only by arguing in a sense against it, which recognition determines the whole approach of the *Kreidekreis.* And the lesson inherent in the very form of German Classical drama, that we can meet the problem of self-consciousness by intensifying it, but not by circumventing it, corresponds to Brecht's implied teaching in the *Kreidekreis* that our rational remaking of the world confronts us eventually with the necessity of carrying out an irrational and highly questionable self-conscious operation on ourselves by the use of art.

Thus Brecht, whether he will or no, is a direct heir to the German classics, while at the same time his work, both by being drama of disorientation and by being socialist drama, is also a supersession of the Classical modes. In this way he combines more perfectly than anyone else the two opposed tendencies of modern German drama with respect to its heritage, and so in a sense fulfills the destiny of both his chosen form and his native culture.

5

With Nietzsche and Brecht, in their different ways, at least one major phase or pulse of the German dramatic movement reaches a natural term, and so does the present attempt to describe it. One point that perhaps needs stress, however, is that the inexact applicability of the categories of Chapter 9 to German Classical drama does not modify my argument concerning the importance of German Classicism in the historical genesis of modern drama. Although the idea of "saturation" is applicable practically anywhere, the scheme of "modes of response" to self-consciousness, which are enlighteningly differentiable in modern drama, would often be a source of confusion in dealing with German

Classicism. Modern European drama, in other words, is not German Classical drama in disguise. But German Classical drama is still an indispensable precedent (as indeed, though at much greater removes, Greek tragedy and Elizabethan drama also are) without which modern drama would not have arisen in the particular way it has, and German drama assumes this character mainly by keeping alive the question of drama as a genre, especially with regard to the idea of self-consciousness. Thus it is possible for there to be a close relation between German Classicism and the descriptive categories I have applied to modern drama, even though modern plays do not as a rule look like German Classical plays; the descriptive categories arise from the general Classical-idealist concern with self-consciousness, but this need not imply that they be applicable to Classical drama.

In any case, I have attempted to strike a balance between history and theory, in the hope of at least sketching a history that will show modern drama as a single cohesive phenomenon. At this point I am vulnerable; perhaps modern drama is not cohesive. Why should it be? This question can be answered only on the most general plane, and I will conclude, therefore, by presenting for inspection, once more, my axioms: European literature of the late nineteenth and twentieth centuries, by comparison with other ages, shows an extraordinary concentration of genuinely important dramatic works, and vigorous poetic efflorescences of this sort (or of the sort exemplified by the German dramatic movement) do not occur by accident; the geographical and temporal coincidence of the works that compose them cannot fail to reflect some deeper cohesion. At least the only fruitful working assumption is that such cohesion exists; without this assumption the most interesting questions remain unasked. And if the flourishing of a particular genre is distinguishable, then this must have to do both with the nature of the genre and with its quality as an evolving historical phenomenon.

The key concept is that of tradition, and it is, admittedly, a difficult concept. Literature does not happen except in the presence of literary tradition; but all calculations based on this tenet contain an automatic element of uncertainty, which arises from the interaction of literature with the world in general, and from the unquestionable existence—let us not forget our Lessing—of system-confounding genius. What I am attempting, therefore, is to define as exactly as possible the limits of intelligibility in any discussion of the traditional background of modern drama—limits about which our main concern today must still be to reach them, whereupon, once this is done, we can begin to worry about overstepping them.

Notes

Anything like a complete bibliography on the subjects discussed would be too long to be useful, and a selected bibliography would merely reaffirm opinions already expressed in the text and notes. Several works I should have liked to treat in more detail, especially Walter Benjamin, *Ursprung des deutschen Trauerspiels*, and Max Spalter, *Brecht's Tradition*; and a number of works I have not even mentioned, because their very importance would have taken me too far in one direction or the other: Erich Heller, *The Disinherited Mind*, for example, on certain characteristics of literary Germanness, as well as Benno von Wiese, *Die deutsche Tragödie von Lessing bis Hebbel*, and works of Bentley and Brustein other than those I have drawn from explicitly. Most of my own works that grew up with the present work and have a special bearing on it are mentioned in the notes, and I offer them as a second line of defense on points which might need one. The reader may also be interested in an essay which supplements the remarks I have made about *Faust*: "Interrupted Tragedy as the Structure of Goethe's *Faust*," *Mosaic*, XI/1 (Fall, 1977), 37–51.

Introduction

1. Raymond Williams, *The Long Revolution* (New York and London, 1961), p. 264.

2. What I am saying is not far from the idea of "middle distance" in J. P. Stern, *On Realism* (London and Boston, 1973), pp. 113–28.

3. Williams, p. 263.

4. See also my essay "'Tis Sixty Years Since," *GQ*, 45 (1972), 684–702.

5. Robert Boies Sharpe, *Irony in the Drama* (Chapel Hill, 1959); Bert O. States, *Irony and Drama* (Ithaca and London, 1971); John Gassner, *Form and Idea in Modern Theatre* (New York, 1956); J. L. Styan, *The Dark Comedy*, 2d ed. (Cambridge, Eng., 1968); Eric Bentley, *The Playwright as Thinker* (1946; rpt. New York, Harvest Books, n.d.); Francis Fergusson, *The Idea of a Theater* (Princeton, 1949, rpt. 1968); Peter Szondi, *Theorie des modernen Dramas* (1956; rpt. Frankfort/Main, 1966); Karl S. Guthke, *Geschichte und Poetik der deutschen Tragikomödie* (Göttingen, 1961), and *Modern Tragicomedy* (New York, 1966).

Chapter 1 Prinz Friedrich von Homburg

1. Wolfgang Wittkowski, "Weltdialektik und Weltüberwindung: Zur Dramaturgie Kleists," in Reinhold Grimm, ed., *Deutsche Dramentheorien*, 2 vols. (Frankfort/Main, 1971), I, 270, asserts that the important indications of what Kleist thought about drama are found in his essays on the emotions. What Wittkowski discusses is thus not a theory of drama but a theory of feeling, and while he does this well, he does not arrive at any really fruitful conclusions.

2. See Nietzsche on Euripides in Chapter 12 of *Die Geburt der Tragödie*, and Camille on theater in the third scene ("Ein Zimmer") of Act II of *Dantons Tod*. On Goethe see my article "'Vorspiel auf dem Theater': The Ironic Basis of Goethe's *Faust*," *GQ*, 49 (1976), 438–55.

3. Adam Müller, *Kritische, ästhetische und philosophische Schriften*, ed. W. Schroeder and W. Siebert, 2 vols. (Neuwied and Berlin, 1967), I, 276. The argument begins on p. 275. References to this volume are from the lectures "Über die dramatische Kunst" (1806) and are cited as Müller plus page numbers.

4. Grimm's *Wörterbuch* gives no instance of "Rampe" meaning "footlights" before Heine, but the Larousse *Nouveau dictionnaire étymologique et historique* (1964) says that French "rampe" in this meaning occurs from the seventeenth century on. In *Prinz Friedrich* the word occurs in the stage directions preceding lines 1 (twice), 30, 42, 67, 78, 88, 1830, 1840, 1846, 1852, and in dialogue in lines 143, 181, 182. All references to Kleist are found in Heinrich von Kleist, *Sämtliche Werke und Briefe*, ed. Helmut Sembdner, 2 vols., 5th ed. (Munich, 1970). Line numbers in *Prinz Friedrich* are given following the quotations.

5. Müller, p. 244. Heinz Politzer, "Kleists Trauerspiel vom Traum," in his *Hatte Ödipus einen Ödipus-Komplex?* (Munich, 1974), p. 159, is reminded, interestingly, of "die modernen Illusions- und Spiegelkünste Pirandellos," but not in exactly our sense.

6. J. M. Ellis, *Kleist's Prinz Friedrich von Homburg: A Critical Study* (Berkeley, 1970). References are cited as Ellis plus page numbers.

7. Natalie's situation as she herself describes it (591–96) is historically impossible. See Kleist, *Prinz Friedrich von Homburg*, ed. Richard Samuel (Berlin, 1964), pp. 185–86. Still, Kleist's association of Natalie with Netherlandic nobility suggests very clearly the idea of independence.

8. Politzer, pp. 174–75.

9. I think this refutes one limited point in an otherwise good essay by Arnold J. Henschel, "The Primacy of Free-Will in the Mind of Kleist and in the *Prinz von Homburg*," *GL&L*, 17 (1963–64), 102.

10. According to Ellis, p. 106, "the demolition of the 'education' theory of the play" should be credited to Walter Silz, "On the Interpretation of Kleist's *Prinz Friedrich von Homburg*," *JEGP*, 35 (1936), 500–516. Silz, p. 512, does argue that "there is no real evidence for the traditional assumption that the Elector meant from the beginning merely to educate the Prince." However, the assumptions actually countered by Silz's arguments are: (1) that the Elector's ultimate aim is to teach respect for the law, and (2) that he succeeds in this with the Prince (neither of which I make). The basic point of V. C. Hubbs, "Heinrich von Kleist and the Symbol of the Wise Man," *Symposium*, 16 (1962), 173–74, about the Elector's immediate (not ultimate) objective, remains valid.

11. This parallel is noted, for example, by Hans Mayer, "Der 'Prinz von Homburg' als Denkspiel und als Traumspiel," in his *Vereinzelt Niederschläge* (Pfullingen, 1973), p. 263.

12. Samuel's ed., p. 201.

13. Sigurd Burckhardt, "*Egmont* and *Prinz Friedrich von Homburg*: Expostulation and Reply" (orig. 1963), in his *The Drama of Language* (Baltimore and London, 1970), pp. 94–100.

14. For extremely detailed comparisons, see Hanna Hellmann, "Kleists 'Prinz von Homburg' und Shakespeares 'Mass für Mass,'" *GRM*, 11 (1923), 288–96, and Meta Corssen, *Kleist und Shakespeare* (Weimar, 1930), pp. 29, 39–40, 66–67, 71.

15. Compare Hubbs, pp. 173–74.

16. Ernst Cassirer, "Heinrich von Kleist und die Kantische Philosophie," in his *Idee und Gestalt* (1924; rpt. Darmstadt, 1971), p. 196.

17. There is a kind of rhythm in Schiller's aesthetic works relating to these categories. In "Die Schaubühne als eine moralische Anstalt betrachtet" (1784), the ultimate emphasis is upon a human community transcending all national boundaries. Then, in the systematic writings of the 1790's, individual moral freedom is stressed. And in "Über den Gebrauch des Chors in der Tragödie" (1803), there is a kind of synthesis: the aim of art is, "actually to *make* man free," but in order to do this, "the dramatic poet must reopen the palaces, he must bring the courts of justice out under the open sky, he must reestablish the gods"; he must, in other words, re-create man's truly communal existence.

18. Kleist has an early essay on this subject, in *Werke*, II, 301–15.

19. See John Geary, *Heinrich von Kleist: A Study in Tragedy and Anxiety* (Philadelphia, 1968), p. 179.

20. Cf. Schiller and note 17 above.

21. Of course we also think of *Faust*, and the Erdgeist of whom Faust says, "Du stiessest grausam mich zurücke / Ins ungewisse Menschenlos" (ll. 628–29), "you thrust me cruelly back into the uncertain condition of man"; this repulse, like that in *Prinz Friedrich*, later appears as a kind of boon (ll. 3217–18).

22. See the classic and classically simple argument of Percy Lubbock, *The Craft of Fiction* (1921; rpt. New York, 1957), pp. 16–25.

23. *Werke*, II, 342.

24. *Werke*, II, 345.
25. *Werke*, II, 345.

Chapter 2 Lessing and the Problem of Drama

1. Some of the more intellectually interesting works on various aspects of the German tradition are Walter Benjamin, *Ursprung des deutschen Trauerspiels* (1928; rev. ed. Frankfort/Main, 1963); Walter Hinck, *Das deutsche Lustspiel des 17. und 18. Jahrhunderts und die italienische Komödie* (Stuttgart, 1965); Robert R. Heitner, *German Tragedy in the Age of Enlightenment* (Berkeley, 1963); Max Spalter, *Brecht's Tradition* (Baltimore, 1967); Kurt Wölfel, "Moralische Anstalt: Zur Dramaturgie von Gottsched bis Lessing" and Fritz Martini, "Zur Poetik des Dramas im Sturm und Drang," the two last in *Deutsche Dramentheorien* (Frankfort/Main, 1971), I, 45–166.

2. *Hamburgische Dramaturgie*, nos. 79–80, in *Gotthold Ephraim Lessings sämtliche Schriften*, ed. K. Lachmann and F. Muncker, 3d ed., 23 vols. (Stuttgart, 1886–1924), X, 122–23. Lessing quotations are from this edition. Further quotations from the *Hamburgische Dramaturgie* are designated by *HD* plus issue-number ("Stück") plus page number in Lachmann/Muncker, IX (for nos. 1–52), X (for nos. 53–104); quotations from *Laokoon* are designated by *L* plus chapter plus page in Lachmann/Muncker, IX.

3. Lillo's dedication in *The London Merchant* (1731). Alois Wierlacher, *Das bürgerliche Drama* (Munich, 1968), shows that eighteenth-century bourgeois drama is basically sentimental drama. See also Lothar Pikulik, *"Bürgerliches Trauerspiel" und Empfindsamkeit* (Cologne and Graz, 1966).

4. On *Laokoon*, see *Dichtung und Wahrheit*, Books VIII and IX, on the *Dramaturgie*, Book XI; in *Goethes Werke*, "Weimarer Ausgabe," 143 vols. (Weimar, 1887–1918), XXVII, 164, and XXVIII, 78, 84–86 (this edition henceforth abbreviated *WA*).

5. Diderot, *De la poésie dramatique*, esp. X, on the involuntariness of "illusion," and XI, on the nonessentialness of surprise; also XIII, on the avoidance of schematic contrasts in character, and II, on the theater as a place where good and bad men weep together.

6. The second series of notes on "Dramatic Illusion," in Coleridge, *Shakespearean Criticism*, ed. T. M. Raysor, 2d ed., 2 vols. (New York and London, 1960), I, 181–82.

7. Goethe, *Wilhelm Meisters theatralische Sendung*, Book Three, ch. 11, *WA*, LI, 256.

8. Lessing, *Briefe, die neueste Litteratur betreffend*, no. 17, in Lachmann/Muncker, VIII, 42.

9. On Philotas as "der erste glaubwürdige Jüngling des deutschen Dramas," that is, the first typical *Sturm und Drang* figure, see Leonello Vincenti, "Lessings 'Philotas'" (orig. 1937), in G. and S. Bauer, eds., *Gotthold Ephraim Lessing*, Wege der Forschung, vol. 211 (Darmstadt, 1968), p. 202. For Lessing's anticipatory rejection of *Sturm und Drang* prejudices concerning "genius," see *HD* 96 and 101–4, or the remark that "Das Theater soll niemanden, wer es auch sey, Anstoss geben" (*HD* 2, p. 190). On Lessing's dissatisfaction with bourgeois drama, see F. J. Lamport,

"Lessing and the 'Bürgerliches Trauerspiel,'" in *The Discontinuous Tradition* (Stahl Festschrift), ed. P. F. Ganz (Oxford, 1971), pp. 14–28.

10. Lessing's dreaming is done for him by Johann Arnold Ebert, who writes him, on the occasion of *Emilia Galotti*, "o Shakespear-Lessing!" (14 March 1772; Lachmann/Muncker, XX, 151).

11. Moses Mendelssohn, *Gesammelte Schriften*, 16 vols. (Berlin, 1929–; rpt. 1972), II, 147–55. For Marmontel on illusion, see his *Poétique françoise*, 2 vols. (Paris, 1763), II, 112.

12. "Vom bürgerlichen Trauerspiele," in *Neue Erweiterungen der Erkenntnis und des Vergnügens*, 6 vols. (Leipzig, 1755), pp. 3–4, 24; quotations from Wierlacher, p. 33.

13. Aristotle, *Poetics*, xiii, 1452b–53a. The "philanthropic" probably refers to our feeling that something good has happened for mankind in general, which is why it is aroused when a villain is ruined but not when he succeeds. If it were a fellow-feeling with the villain, then his success would not exclude it, which Aristotle says it does; indeed, Lessing himself remarks that we feel a certain desire to see Shakespeare's Richard achieve his aims (*HD* 79, pp. 121–22). On Lessing and Aristotle in general, and on Lessing's bias as a reader, see Max Kommerell, *Lessing und Aristoteles* (Frankfort/Main, 1960).

14. See *HD* 77, Lessing's letter to Nicolai of Nov. 1756, and his letters to Mendelssohn of 28 Nov. and 18 Dec. 1756 and 2 Feb. 1757.

15. See e.g. *HD* 5, 11, 35, 84 (quoting Diderot), 97.

16. *Poetics*, xv, 1454b.

17. Ilse Graham, *Goethe and Lessing* (London, 1973), pp. 3–13.

18. Fred O. Nolte, "Lessing's *Emilia Galotti* in the Light of his *Hamburgische Dramaturgie*," *Harvard Studies and Notes in Philology and Literature*, 19 (1937), pp. 178–79, n., 185 and n.

19. *Poetics*, xiii, 1452b. Cf. *HD* 79, p. 120.

20. For a very deep and thorough treatment of ambiguity and ambivalence in *Emilia*, see Frank G. Ryder, "*Emilia Galotti*," *GQ*, 45 (1972), 329–47, and "*Emilia Galotti* and the Algebra of Ambivalence," in L. T. Frank and E. E. George, eds., *Husbanding the Golden Grain: Studies in Honor of Henry W. Nordmeyer* (Ann Arbor, 1973), pp. 279–94. For a thorough but not very penetrating study of the relation between theory and practice in Lessing, see Reinhart Meyer, "*Hamburgische Dramaturgie*" und "*Emilia Galotti*" (Wiesbaden, 1973). On Lessing's theoretical difficulties in his practice, see my article "The Idea of the Audience in Lessing's Implied Tragic Dramaturgy," in *Lessing Yearbook*, 11 (1979).

Chapter 3   Nathan der Weise

1. The works mentioned in the notes to this chapter do not by any means cover the ground. A good introduction, including bibliography up to its time, is *Nathan der Weise*, ed. Peter Demetz (Frankfort/Main and Berlin, 1966). More recently, the *Lessing Yearbook*, 3 (1971), contains a series of three fine articles on *Nathan* by Ruth K. Angress, Michael J. Böhler, and Paul Hernadi; and Armin Volkmar Wernsing, "Nathan der Spieler," *WW*, 20 (1970), 52–59, makes some very interesting points.

2. F. J. Lamport, "Lessing and the 'Bürgerliches Trauerspiel,'" p. 26, is correct on this point.

3. *Nathan der Weise,* IV.ii.141–47. In Lachmann/Muncker (Chap. 2, n.2), III, the lines in the play are numbered separately for each act, and I give these line numbers for quotations, as well as act and scene. Otherwise the conventions described in Chap. 2, n.2, are followed.

4. *HD* 48. Diderot, *De la poésie dramatique,* XI.

5. Demetz, p. 125, finds fault with the "overcomplicated" past history of the plot, as have other critics before him. This point is not to be taken lightly. See section 5 below.

6. *De la poésie dramatique,* XIII.

7. On the generality of dramatic characters and their instructiveness, see e.g. *HD* 2, pp. 188–89; *HD* 89, pp. 162–64; and the extensive quotations from Hurd in *HD* 92–95, esp. pp. 182, 185–86.

8. Demetz, p. 132. The argument begins on p. 130.

9. Letter to Karl Wilhelm Ramler, 18 Dec. 1778.

10. Some of the following is drawn from my essay, "Reason, Error and the Shape of History: Lessing's Nathan and Lessing's God," *Lessing Yearbook,* 9 (1977), 60–80 (by permission of the Lessing Society).

11. R. K. Angress, "Lessing's Criticism of Cronegk: *Nathan in Ovo?*" *Lessing Yearbook,* 4 (1972), 29.

12. See R. K. Angress, "'Dreams that were more than dreams' in Lessing's *Nathan,*" *Lessing Yearbook,* 3 (1971), 108–27, esp. p. 118, on the Templar's resentment against his father.

13. E.g. Demetz, pp. 146–47.

14. Cf. *Die Erziehung des Menschengeschlechts,* par. 68, where Lessing warns against expressing too much of the truth.

15. It is wrong, as Demetz points out, p. 144, to see Nathan as the "monument to an intellectual attitude which is beyond all conflict." But Demetz is wrong in supposing that the only alternative is to admit that Nathan is educated in the course of the play. Nathan is not educated; he remains the same throughout, but his sameness contains an ineradicable inner conflict, a painful irony. See also Christoph E. Schweitzer, "Die Erziehung Nathans," *Monatshefte,* 53 (1961), 277–84.

Chapter 4 Iphigenie auf Tauris

1. See the conversation of April 1780 reported by Jacobi, in Goethe, *Gedenkausgabe der Werke, Briefe und Gespräche,* ed. Ernst Beutler, 24 vols. (Zurich, 1948–1953), XXII, 129.

2. *Italienische Reise,* I, 10 Jan. 1787, in *WA,* XXX, 247. References to *Iphigenie* are located by line numbers alone in parentheses.

3. Not all references are listed for each point of this type; the reader may consult relevant sections in Hans Gerhard Gräf, *Goethe über seine Dichtungen,* 9 vols. (Frankfort/Main, 1901–1914).

4. See Goethe's diary of 6 and 8 April 1779 and the letters to Knebel, of 14 March 1779, and to Dalberg, of 21 July 1779.

5. See Jakob Baechtold, ed., *Goethes Iphigenie auf Tauris in vierfacher Gestalt* (Freiburg i. B. and Tübingen, 1883).

6. See Willi Flemming, *Goethe und das Theater seiner Zeit* (Stuttgart, 1968), pp. 45–47.

7. *L* i; *HD* 18, pp. 101–4 (Chap. 2, n. 2).

8. Sigurd Burckhardt, "'The voice of truth and of humanity': Goethe's *Iphigenie*" (orig. 1956), in his *Drama of Language* (Baltimore, 1970), pp. 36, 40.

9. *HD* 80.

10. See also Lessing, *Briefe, die neueste Litteratur betreffend*, no. 17; *HD* 73.

11. See *HD* 14, p. 75.

12. For an explicit connection between the "purely human" and "anachronisms" in drama, see Goethe's essay on Manzoni's *Adelchi* in *WA*, XLII, 1, p. 171.

13. The idea of the audience's participation, its necessary contribution to the whole theatrical process, is not often stressed by Goethe, but it is stressed very strongly in early letters concerning *Iphigenie* and in scenes 10 and 16 of the Lauchstädt *Was wir bringen* (1802), in *WA*, XIII, 1, esp. pp. 72–73.

14. On Goethe's idea of truth, and on the idea that truth is realized precisely in that the content of one's utterance conceals it, see my essay on the Faust "Vorspiel" (Ch. 1, n. 2). There is even a certain irony in Orestes' famous use of the word "truth" (1081) when he resolves to reveal his identity.

15. On the conscious wielding of one's own inborn nature, see the conclusion of my "Goethe's Egmont as a Politician," *ECS*, 10 (1977), 351–66. On the possibility of criticizing bourgeois Germanness while in the same breath affirming it, see Frank G. Ryder and Bennett, "The Irony of Goethe's *Hermann und Dorothea*: Its Form and Function," *PMLA*, 90 (1975), 433–46.

16. *HD* 18.

17. In a little essay entitled "Deutsches Theater," Goethe in fact expresses dissatisfaction with Ekhof, Schröder, and Iffland for transforming into a kind of moral doctrine something at least very close to the intended effect of *Iphigenie*, "eine An- und Ausgleichung aller Stände und Beschäftigungen zu einem allgemeinen Menschenwerthe" (*WA*, XL, 177).

18. For the connection between Goethe's essay and Schiller's thinking see Goethe's letter to Schiller of 23 Dec. 1797, in which the essay was enclosed. The idea that an intimation of our moral freedom arises as an analogue to the freedom of our intellect from the artistic illusion which compels our senses, can be found in practically all Schiller's aesthetic writings. For the intellectual range and historical importance of this idea, see my "Nietzsche's Idea of Myth: The Birth of Tragedy from the Spirit of Eighteenth-Century Aesthetics," *PMLA*, May 1979.

Chapter 5 *Egmont* and the Maelstrom of the Self

1. See Jeffrey L. Sammons, "On the Structure of Goethe's *Egmont*," *JEGP*, 62 (1963), 241–51. This essay does not go far enough, but it goes further than anything else I know of. Schiller is the first to speak of a "Salto mortale in eine Opernwelt," in "Über Egmont, Trauerspiel von Goethe," *Schillers Sämtliche Werke*, Säkular-Ausgabe, 16 vols. (Stuttgart and Berlin, 1904), XVI, 190.

2. *WA*, VIII, 219. Further references to *Egmont* are located by page number alone in parentheses.

3. See my essay "Goethe's Egmont as a Politician," *ECS*, 10 (1977), 351–66.

4. There is much secondary literature on this topic, and the reader will quickly recognize my own views as rather old-fashioned, inasmuch as I think that Goethe's discussion of *Egmont* in *Dichtung und Wahrheit* does describe the play's actual intention, and that the word "demonic" does express basically one idea for Goethe, an idea related to the idea of "daimon." Walter Muschg, "Goethes Glaube an das Dämonische," *DVLG*, 32 (1958), 321–43, and Konrad Schaum, "Dämonie und Schicksal in Goethes 'Egmont,'" *GRM*, N.F. 10 (1960), 139–57, and others raise interesting questions but do not refute what I like to think of as my own common-sense approach, i.e. the assumption that Goethe used words more or less consistently and knew how to interpret his own works.

5. Schiller, p. 183.

6. For Goethe's general skepticism about self-knowledge see the conversation with Eckermann of 10 April 1829 and the letter to Lavater of 4 Oct. 1782, as well as the letters on "heautognosis" to Hegel, 17 Aug. 1827, and Varnhagen von Ense, 8 Nov. 1827.

7. On Goethe's idea of "suppliren," the idea that the reader must "supply" an essential part of the meaning of a good book, see e.g. *WA*, pt. 2, III, 118; and on a similar idea applied to the dramatic spectator see "Weimarisches Hoftheater" (*WA*, XL, 78–79), as well as Chap. 4, n. 13 above.

Chapter 6 The Importance of Being Egmont

1. On the phrenographic in *Faust* see my essay "The Two 'Study' Scenes and the Pentagram in Goethe's *Faust*," *ELWIU*, 5 (1978), 223–37. On phrenography in the type of the dream-play, see Walter H. Sokel, *The Writer in Extremis* (Stanford, 1959), esp. p. 41, on the use of light in Sorge's *Der Bettler*. On character-centered drama, see e.g. Jakob Michael Reinhold Lenz, "Anmerkungen übers Theater," in *Werke und Schriften*, ed. B. Titel and H. Haug, 2 vols. (Stuttgart, 1966), I, 342–43.

2. More can be said concerning Hofmannsthal, and I have done so in a forthcoming book-length study.

3. Kleist's direct influence in later literature is documented in Helmut Sembdner, ed., *Heinrich von Kleists Nachruhm* (Bremen, 1967), which includes interesting and unexpected remarks by or about Björnson, Giraudoux, Cocteau, as well as Ionesco's assertion ("Expérience du théâtre," *NRF*, 6 [1958], 252) that apart from the ancients and Shakespeare, Kleist and Büchner are the only dramatic authors he can read receptively. Otto Brahm, both a Kleist-pioneer with his book *Heinrich von Kleist* (Berlin, 1884) and a very influential figure in the development of naturalist drama, is of course important in the transmission of Kleist's indirect influence. On Büchner's exceptionally deep presence in modern German literature (hence, in various ways, also his effect on other literatures), see Dietmar Goltschnigg, *Rezeptions- und Wirkungsgeschichte Georg Büchners* (Kronberg/B., 1975).

4. Georg Büchner, *Sämtliche Werke und Briefe*, ed. Lehmann, 4 vols. (Hamburg, 1967), I, 45–46. Further quotations are located by *DT* plus page number.

5. *WA*, VIII, 223. Further quotations are designated by *Eg.* plus page number.

6. See Goethe's essay "Literarischer Sansculottismus," *WA*, XL, 196–203.

7. Franz Grillparzer, *König Ottokars Glück und Ende*, Act III, ll. 1913–17.

8. Bertolt Brecht, "Verfremdungseffekte in der chinesischen Schauspielkunst," in *Gesammelte Werke*, "Werkausgabe," 20 vols. (Frankfort/Main, 1967), XVI, 622.

9. Brecht, XVI, 674; "Kleines Organon für das Theater," par. 26. Further quotations from this work are designated by *KO* plus paragraph number.

10. Brecht, II, 422.

11. Brecht, II, 484.

12. Ibsen critics, from Brandes on down, tend to be curiously protective of their author's originality—as if, in order to demonstrate originality, one had to show complete independence from tradition. If we consider the amount of time Ibsen spent in Germany, however, plus his debt to Oehlenschlaeger, who was definitively influenced by the Germans, it is hard to see how he can be thought of outside the German dramatic tradition. At any rate, Josef Wihan, *Henrik Ibsen und das deutsche Geistesleben* (Reichenberg i.B., 1925; rpt. 1973), produces dozens of quite obvious echoes of German drama in Ibsen, up to and including the realistic plays.

13. On Goethe's early influence in Russia, see André von Gronicka, *The Russian Image of Goethe* (Philadelphia, 1968); on Schiller's, see Otto P. Peterson, *Schiller in Russland* (New York, 1934), Hans-Bernd Harder, *Schiller in Russland* (Bad Homburg v.d.H.: Gehlen, 1969), Edmund K. Kostka, *Schiller in Russian Literature* (Philadelphia, 1965). I cannot say exactly how much Chekhov, for example, owes to the Germans, though he is known to have been at least impressed by Hauptmann, Ibsen, Strindberg; and of course the German tradition, by way of Hauptmann, Ibsen, and the ducal players of Meiningen, was important for Stanislavsky. I mention Chekhov here (as Ibsen above) because of his effect on later drama.

14. See Alois Wierlacher, *Das bürgerliche Drama* (Munich, 1968), on "der neue Held," pp. 44–85.

15. In the Preface to *The Playboy of the Western World*.

16. Chekhov writes to A. Tikhonov of his intentions as a dramatist, "I wanted to say simply and honestly, 'Look at yourselves, look how badly and boringly you lead your lives!' The most important thing is that people come to recognize this. As soon as they understand it, they will have to live differently and better" (quoted from Siegfried Melchinger, *Anton Chekhov* [New York, 1972], p. 66). Does this mean that he wants to depict real life, or does it also mean that the spectator must look at himself *as a spectator in a theater* and learn something thereby?

17. See Wihan, pp. 66–71; also Michael Meyer, *Henrik Ibsen* (London, 1967), p. 115.

18. Schiller, *SA*, XVI, 124.

19. The ideas of W. G. Moore, "A New Reading of 'Wilhelm Tell,'" *German Studies Presented to Professor H. G. Fiedler* (Oxford, 1938), pp. 278–92, have been developed by W. F. Mainland, ed., *Schiller: Wilhelm Tell* (New York, 1968), pp. xix–lxix; David B. Richards, "Tell in the Dock," *GQ*, 48 (1975), 472–86; and Frank G. Ryder, "Schiller's *Tell* and the Cause of Freedom," *GQ*, 48 (1975), 487–504. See also Ludwig W. Kahn, "Freedom: An Existentialist and an Idealist View," *PMLA*, **44 (1949)**, 5–14, on *Tell* and *Les mouches*.

20. On Brecht's paradoxical debt to Schiller and to German Classicism in general, see Gunter Hartung, "Brecht und Schiller," *Sinn und Form,* 18 (1966), Sonderheft 1, 743–66, and Walter H. Sokel, "Brechts marxistischer Weg zur Klassik," in Grimm/Hermand, ed., *Die Klassik-Legende* (Frankfort/Main, 1971), pp. 176–99, as well as the relevant sections in Hans Mayer, *Bertolt Brecht und die Tradition* (Pfullingen, 1961), and Werner Mittenzwei, *Brechts Verhältnis zur Tradition* (Berlin, 1972). Heinz Ehrig, *Paradoxe und absurde Dichtung* (Munich, 1973), incidentally, sees Schiller as a kind of forerunner even of absurd drama; see also Kahn's essay, as well as Käte Hamburger, "Schiller und Sartre," *JDSG,* 3 (1959), 34–70.

21. Schiller was not likely to express his deepest feelings in a letter to Böttiger, but Böttiger was notorious for trumpeting things abroad, and what Schiller said to him is therefore something he wanted to be public knowledge.

22. One more or less standard answer to this question is that Schiller wished to train himself as a pure tragic artist, without becoming emotionally involved in his material; see Emil Staiger, "Schiller: Agrippina" (orig. 1950), in *Die Kunst der Interpretation* (Zurich, 1955), pp. 132–60; Gerhard Storz, *Der Dichter Friedrich Schiller* (Stuttgart, 1959), pp. 259–63; Benno von Wiese, *Schiller* (Stuttgart, 1959), pp. 633–34. Wolfgang Wittkowski, "Octavio Piccolomini" (orig. 1961), in K. L. Berghahn and R. Grimm, eds., *Schiller,* "Wege der Forschung," vol. 323 (Darmstadt, 1972), pp. 407–65, shows the limits of this thinking and makes some interesting points concerning hero and spectator. Ilse Graham, in various works, especially "The Structure of the Personality in Schiller's Tragic Poetry," in F. Norman, ed., *Schiller: Bicentenary Lectures* (London, 1960), pp. 104–44, bypasses the question by fitting Wallenstein into typical Schillerian character-patterns; but the question does not go away.

23. *Schillers Werke,* National-Ausgabe (Weimar, 1943–), XIII, 41–2. This edition is abbreviated *NA* below.

24. Lenz, e.g. p. 364, does not have much use for *Hamlet* for this reason; see also Goethe on the melancholy influence of English literature in general and *Hamlet* in particular, e.g. *Dichtung und Wahrheit,* Book XIII (*WA,* XXVIII, 212–16).

Chapter 7   Schiller's Theoretical Impasse and *Maria Stuart*

1. *SA,* XII, 198–99.

2. Letter to Wilhelm von Humboldt, 29–30 November 1795. E. L. Stahl, *Friedrich Schiller's Drama* (Oxford, 1954), p. 71—and others—are of the opinion that *Tell* is at least partially a "sentimental idyll."

3. Ilse Graham, *Schiller: A Master of the Tragic Form* (Pittsburgh, 1975), p. 99. The general argument covers pp. 99–109.

4. Ilse Graham, *Schiller's Drama: Talent and Integrity* (London, 1974), pp. 209, 210.

5. Graham, *Master,* p. 101. It is extremely important to understand, as Graham does, that *Person/Zustand* is not simply a parallel distinction to idealist/realist. Our argument concerning Egmont's insistence on the vision of his destined self could be taken as an illustration of the hubris of *Person.*

6. Stahl, p. 58.

7. Klaus L. Berghahn, " 'Das Pathetischerhabene': Schillers Dramentheorie," in *Deutsche Dramentheorien* (Frankfort/Main, 1971), I, 242.

8. On Wallenstein and the prolongation of "Bestimmbarkeit" cf. *SA*, XII, 81 n., Schiller's characterization of men born "zu grossen Rollen." See also Graham, *Master*, p. 127.

9. On Lessing and *Wallenstein* see Graham, *Schiller's Drama*, pp. 245–83.

10. See Chap. 6, n. 22.

11. Käte Hamburger, "Schiller und Sartre," *JDSG*, 3 (1959), 39–40; cf. *SA*, XII, 266.

12. Graham, *Schiller's Drama*, pp. 149–70.

13. Ibid., pp. 167–68.

14. Duke Karl August in fact insisted that the actual communion not be carried out on stage, and an accordingly revised text was used in the first performance.

15. Benno von Wiese, *Schiller* (Stuttgart, 1959), p. 722, makes this point but does not develop it. See also Graham, *Schiller's Drama*, p. 166.

16. Lessing, *Laokoon*, Lachmann/Muncker, IX, 8 (see Chap. 2, n. 2).

17. Johann Gottfried Herder, "Shakespear," in *Herders Sämmtliche Werke*, ed. B. Suphan, 33 vols. (Berlin, 1877–1913), V, 217–18.

18. The secondary literature claims repeatedly that Schiller himself called the scene with Melvil "der unentbehrliche Schlussstein des Ganzen," but I find no direct contemporary evidence for this quotation. Graham, von Wiese, the *SA* and the *NA*—all of whom give detailed references for quotations much less important—simply record the remark without comment.

Chapter 8 Breakthrough in Theory

1. See Reinhold Grimm, "Brecht und Nietzsche," *Istituto Universitario Orientale, Sezione Germanica* (Naples), *Annali*, 17, no. 2 (1974), 5–29.

2. The importance of Nietzsche and Kierkegaard in modern thought is dealt with very simply and interestingly in the introduction to Walter Kaufmann, ed., *Existentialism from Dostoevsky to Sartre* (Cleveland and New York, 1956), pp. 11–51. Kaufmann is not fair to Kierkegaard, but the reader can allow for this.

3. See Walter H. Sokel, *The Writer in Extremis* (Stanford, 1959), pp. 8–23, on Kantian philosophy and the "modern" in general.

4. M. H. Abrams, *Natural Supernaturalism: Tradition and Revolution in Romantic Literature* (New York, 1973), esp. chs. 3–5.

5. Brian Johnston, *The Ibsen Cycle* (Boston, 1975); and Anne Paolucci, *Pirandello's Theater* (Carbondale, 1974), pp. 18–19, also p. 106. The reference about "I-Thou" and "We" in Hegel is from the *Phänomenologie*, in Georg Wilhelm Friedrich Hegel, *Sämtliche Werke*, Jubiläumsausgabe, ed. H. Glockner, 20 vols. (Stuttgart, 1927), II, 147. Paolucci is perhaps a bit too cautious about Pirandello's knowledge of Hegel. Pirandello, after all, not only lived in the same intellectual Italy as Croce, but also studied in Germany.

6. "Memory," "inwardization." Hegel, *Werke*, II, 573, 619. For a fine discussion of the dialectical in Ibsen, see also Robert Brustein, *The Theatre of Revolt* (Boston and Toronto, 1962), pp. 37–83.

7. With regard to the later plays, the so-called "myths," Paolucci, pp. 19–20, 106, *et passim*, suggests that the idea of the theater as institutionalized self-consciousness is not so much superseded as incorporated into more comprehensive configurations.

8. Karl S. Guthke, *Modern Tragicomedy* (New York, 1966), e.g. pp. 19–22. Even in his German book *Deutsche Tragikomödie*, Guthke does not fully appreciate Hegel's centralness. The other quotes are from *Modern Tragicomedy*, pp. 134, 118.

9. David I. Grossvogel, *20th Century French Drama* (New York and London, 1961), orig. in 1958 as *The Self-Conscious Stage in Modern French Drama*. In the case of French drama, the effect of German dialectic philosophy is not easy to pin down, especially since there is a well-documented French "Hegellosigkeit" in the early decades of this century; see Roberto Salvadori, *Hegel in Francia* (Bari, 1974). But there are many avenues of indirect influence: Victor Cousin and nineteenth-century French controversies on psychology and history; the considerable influence of Schopenhauer; and of course a number of dramatists, Kleist, Büchner, Ibsen, Strindberg, Pirandello, who in various ways transmit German dialectical thought. Other critical works that supplement my arguments include Anthony Swerling, *Strindberg's Impact in France 1920–1960* (Cambridge, Eng., 1971), and Thomas Bishop, *Pirandello and the French Theater* (New York, 1960).

10. Thus I include in dialectic philosophy not only the doctrines grouped by Wilhelm Windelband, *A History of Philosophy*, 2 vols. 1892; rpt. New York, Harper Torchbooks, 1958), II, 590–615, under the heading "System of Reason," but also at least Schopenhauer, Nietzsche, Kierkegaard, and, at one interpretive remove, some Marxist and some existentialist thought as well. Critics and historians of literature tend to use the word "dialectic" rather loosely, but in some cases, including my own, this loose usage is justified. My main concern obliges me to touch on an aspect of nineteenth-century German philosophy which is defined not from within but from without, by its relation to dramatic form, and for this purpose the word "dialectic" is especially useful. Another work in which this word is used loosely but (I think) justifiably is Peter Heller, *Dialectics and Nihilism* (Amherst, Mass., 1966).

11. On the history of Socratic culture implied in *The Birth of Tragedy*, see my "Nietzsche's Idea of Myth," *PMLA*, May 1979. On tragedy's "Selbstmord, in Folge eines unlösbaren Conflictes," see *The Birth of Tragedy*, ch. 11, in Nietzsche, *Werke*, ed. G. Colli and M. Montinari, Pt. 3, vol. 1 (Berlin and New York, 1972), p. 71. On the dialectical history of Greek art, see ch. 3, pp. 37–38. Further references to *The Birth of Tragedy* are designated by page and chapter in parentheses.

12. See the introduction to the *Vorlesungen über die Philosophie der Geschichte*, in Hegel, *Werke*, XI, 47–50.

13. The abstract argument is found in no. 15 of the *Briefe*, SA, XII, 54–60.

14. See e.g. Abrams and Sokel, the excellent discussion of German influences in A. G. Lehmann, *The Symbolist Aesthetic in France 1885–1895* (Oxford, 1950), and of course the relevant sections in René Wellek, *A History of Modern Criticism*, 4 vols. (New Haven, 1955–).

15. Nietzsche, *Werke*, Pt. 6, vol. 3 (1969), p. 15. Further quotations from this volume are indicated by page number.

16. Nietzsche, pp. 33, 36, against "Theatrokratie."

17. Brecht, *Werke* (see Chap. 6, n. 8), II, 525–26.

18. Friedrich Dürrenmatt, *Die Physiker* (Zurich, 1962), p. 75.

19. See the "Author's Note" to *A Dream Play*, in *Six Plays of Strindberg*, trans. E. Sprigge (Garden City: Anchor, 1955), p. 193. There is a direct line to Artaud's "theater of cruelty" from here.

20. *Five Plays of Strindberg*, trans. E. Sprigge (Garden City: Anchor, 1960), p. 194; further references are by page numbers.

21. That Strindberg thought of Nietzsche as offering a way to overcome suffering by affirming it is suggested by a quotation in Gunnar Brandell, *Strindberg in Inferno*, trans. Jacobs (Cambridge, 1974), p. 129. As for Schiller, there is no doubt that Strindberg knew him; but V. J. McGill, *August Strindberg: The Bedeviled Viking* (New York, 1965), p. 84, says Strindberg actually translated some of Schiller's theoretical works.

22. *Birth of Tragedy*, 151, xxv.

23. See e.g. Sokel on Strindberg in Germany, Swerling on Strindberg in France.

24. Eric Bentley, *The Playwright as Thinker* (New York: Harvest Books, n.d.). pp. 1–22 *et passim*; and Eric Sellin, *The Dramatic Concepts of Antonin Artaud* (Chicago, 1968). Compare also the broader and falser distinction made by Lionel Abel, *Metatheatre* (New York, 1963), p. 113, between world as "reality" and as "projection of human consciousness."

25. Walter Kaufmann, *Hegel* (Garden City, 1965), pp. 46–58.

26. Hegel, *Vorlesungen über die Ästhetik*, in *Werke*, XIV (*Ästhetik III*), p. 529; cf. p. 485. Further references to this volume are designated by "*Ästh.*" plus page number.

27. *Werke*, II, 558–59, 565–66, 568–69. Further references to this volume are designated by "*Phän.*" plus page number.

28. Maurice Maeterlinck, "Le réveil de l'âme" and "Le tragique quotidien," in *Le trésor des humbles*, 28th ed. (Paris, 1902), pp. 29, 197–98.

29. Obviously action plays no special role in the theory of *The Birth of Tragedy*, and in a footnote to *Der Fall Wagner* (*Werke*, pt. 6, vol. 3, p. 26), Nietzsche makes the point that "drama" has nothing to do etymologically with the idea of action.

30. Kaufmann, pp. 67–70. On the relation between *Die Erziehung des Menschengeschlechts* and drama, see also my "Reason, Error and the Shape of History," *Lessing Yearbook*, 9 (1977), 60–80. On Hegel and Goethe see e.g. Karl Löwith, *From Hegel to Nietzsche*, trans. D. E. Green (Garden City, 1967), pp. 2–28 *et passim*.

31. Peter Szondi, *Poetik und Geschichtsphilosophie I* (Frankfort/Main, 1974), pp. 496–98. Kaufmann's general point about Hegel's resistance to triadic schematizing, pp. 167–68, is well taken, but the triadic scheme in the *Ästhetik* is entirely explicit. One reason for Hegel's lack of interest in the novel may have been the German Romantics' emphasis on the ironic quality of this genre; cf. Hegel on irony in the *Ästhetik*, *Werke*, XII, 100–06. See also Johnston, and J. Loewenberg, *Hegel's Phenomenology: Dialogues on the Life of the Mind* (La Salle, Ill., 1965), on Hegel's system as essentially dramatic.

32. See Sokel on the theme of "Poeta dolorosus," pp. 55–82, esp. pp. 64–65.

33. Bentley, p. 193.

34. See Chap. 2, n. 9.

35. Bernard Shaw, *Collected Plays with Their Prefaces*, 7 vols. (London: Reinhardt, Bodley Head, 1970–1974), II, 527. Further references are designated by volume and page.

36. Francis Fergusson, *The Idea of a Theater* (Princeton, 1968), p. 184.

37. Nietzsche, *Werke*, Pt. 3, vol. 1, p. 302.

38. In "Ibsen Triumphant," from *Our Theatres in the Nineties*, III (22 May 1897), in *The Works of Bernard Shaw*, 33 vols. (London: Constable, 1930–), XXV, 145, Shaw says, "To sit there getting deeper and deeper into the Ekdal home, and getting deeper and deeper into your own life all the time, until you forget that you are in a theatre, . . . to go out, not from a diversion, but from an experience deeper than real life ever brings to most men, or often brings to any man: that is what The Wild Duck was like last Monday at the Globe." The part about forgetting that one is in a theater is something Shaw himself never hoped or tried seriously to achieve, but the rest is what he aimed at.

39. Fergusson, pp. 181–82. Fergusson makes a distinction here with which I do not agree.

40. *Opere di Luigi Pirandello*, 6 vols., 4th ed. (Verona: Mondadori, 1967–1969), IV (*Maschere Nude* I), p. 44; further references are by page numbers.

41. On the general literary importance of this aspect of dialectic philosophy, see Abrams, pp. 172–77 *et passim*.

42. See Sartre on Hegel in *Le Monde*, 14 May 1971, p. 21, and also *L'être et le néant*, esp. Part III, ch. 1, sec. 3. Also A. James Arnold, "Camus' Dionysian Hero: 'Caligula' in 1938," *South Atlantic Bulletin*, 37, no. 4 (Nov., 1973), 45–53.

43. Nietzsche may not be entirely correct on Wagner as a Hegelian (*Werke*, Pt. 6, vol. 3, p. 30), but there is something in what he says. On Wagner in France, see Lehmann, esp. pp. 194–206.

Chapter 9 The Assault upon the Audience

1. The early critical cliché about Hauptmann as a "poet of compassion" is to an extent revived by Leroy R. Shaw, *The Playwright & Historical Change* (Madison, 1970), pp. 20–48. For a carefully balanced criticism of this general view, see Karl S. Guthke/Hans M. Wolff, *Das Leid im Werke Gerhart Hauptmanns* (Berkeley and Los Angeles, 1958).

2. See Hauptmann, *Die Weber*, Dichtung und Wirklichkeit, ed. Hans Schwab-Felisch (Frankfort/Main, 1968), pp. 97–98, 165–66.

3. Hauptmann, *Sämtliche Werke*, Centenar-Ausgabe, ed. H.-E. Hass, 11 vols. (Frankfort/Main: Propyläen, 1962), I, 343–45, 369, 383, 431. Further quotations from *Die Weber* are designated by page number in this volume.

4. See Hauptmann's own description of the Silesian weavers in Schwab-Felisch, pp. 161–65.

5. Hauptmann gave something of a pioneering lecture on Büchner in the society "Durch" in 1885.

6. See Fritz Martini, "Die Einheit der Konzeption in J. M. R. Lenz' 'Anmerkungen übers Theater,'" *JDSG*, 14 (1970), 159–82, as well as *Deutsche Dramentheorien* (Frankfort/Main, 1971). I, 123–66.

7. Hauptmann, *Werke*, VI, 932.

8. That Wittig is *wütig* in disguise is suggested strongly by his own words in dialect, "o du meine Gitte" (p. 403) for "o du meine Güte," and Hilse would be the same dialect variation on *Hülse*. In fact, although not quite so exactly, Kittelhaus may be meant to suggest *Kuttelhof*, "slaughter-yard, shambles, chaos."

9. Martin Esslin, *The Theatre of the Absurd* (Garden City: Anchor, 1961), pp. 290ff.

10. Esslin, p. 312.

11. In other words, I am now speaking of "dialectical drama" more or less in Bert O. States' sense, *Irony and Drama* (Ithaca and London, 1971), pp. 139–70.

12. Karl S. Guthke, *Modern Tragicomedy* (New York, 1966); further references are designated by Guthke and page numbers.

13. Robert Brustein, *The Theatre of Revolt* (Boston and Toronto, 1962), p. 48; further references are designated by Brustein and page numbers.

14. *The Collected Works of Henrik Ibsen,* 13 vols. (New York, 1923), V, 537; further references by volume and page.

15. Hegel, *Sämtliche Werke* (Stuttgart, 1927), II, 598–601, 602ff.

16. States, p. 154.

17. It seems to me that the two types can be differentiated clearly enough in Ibsen, although there may be doubtful or transitional cases. Clearly *The Wild Duck* is a tragicomedy, and the ludicrousness of Hedda Gabler's marriage to Tesman, indeed even of her suicide, which is tragic because it is ludicrous, produces a tragicomic movement. Also, in *The Master Builder* and *When We Dead Awaken,* the motif of insanity makes it possible to interpret every step of the action comically, as mere self-symbolizing overinflatedness in the characters, whereupon precisely this, the indistinguishability of destiny from delusion, becomes a source of the tragic, and yet again of the comic, in a foolish young woman's uncaring reconciledness with existence. *Ghosts* and *Rosmersholm,* on the other hand, represent most clearly Ibsen's nontragic *genre sérieux*.

18. Eric Bentley, *The Playwright as Thinker* (New York: Harvest Books, n.d.), p. 43.

Chapter 10 The Classic Modern: Brecht

1. See Chap. 6, n. 20. Not only Sokel's essay on Brecht but also the other contributions to *Die Klassik-Legende* are of interest in this general connection.

2. On Nathan's wisdom as a kind of *imitatio dei* see my essay "Reason, Error and the Shape of History," *Lessing Yearbook,* 9 (1977), 60–80.

3. Judgments of this sort, incidentally, are possible only on the basis of categories differentiated at least as minutely as those of the preceding chapter. Karl S. Guthke's tendency, for example, in *Modern Tragicomedy* (New York, 1966), pp. 73–74, to equate the absurd and the "grotesque," has the effect of obscuring the necessary distinctions.

4. On Brecht and Shaw, see Reinhold Grimm, *Bertolt Brecht und die Weltliteratur* (Nuremberg, 1961), pp. 16–18, as well as Brecht's "Ovation für Shaw," in *Gesammelte Werke* (Frankfort/Main, 1967), XV, 96–101. Further references to this edition of Brecht are designated by volume and page.

5. Reinhold Grimm, *Bertolt Brecht: Die Struktur seines Werkes*, 4th ed. (Nuremberg, 1965), p. 73.

6. See esp. Walter H. Sokel, "Brecht's Split Characters and His Sense of the Tragic," in *Brecht: A Collection of Critical Essays*, ed. Peter Demetz (Englewood Cliffs, 1962), pp. 127–37, and also Brecht's "Ovation für Shaw."

7. See Reinhold Grimm's essay, "Brecht und Nietzsche," *Istituto Universitario Orientale, Annali*, 17, no. 2 (1974), pp. 22–23.

8. Denn dann dreht das Rad sich nicht mehr weiter
   Und das heitre Spiel, es unterbleibt
   Wenn das Wasser mit befreiter
   Stärke seine eigne Sach betreibt.

9. Walter H. Sokel, "Figur—Handlung—Perspektive: Die Dramentheorie Bertolt Brechts," in *Deutsche Dramentheorien* (Frankfort/Main, 1971), II, 576; the other quotation is from p. 577.

10. See Sokel, "Split Characters," pp. 136–37, as well as well as the excerpt from Ronald Gray's book reprinted in the same collection of essays, pp. 151–56.

Index

MODERN DRAMA AND GERMAN CLASSICISM

Designed by G. T. Whipple, Jr.
Composed by The Composing Room of Michigan, Inc.,
in 10 point VIP Melior, 2 points leaded,
with display lines in Bulmer.
Printed offset by LithoCrafters, Inc.
on Warren's Number 66 text, 50 pound basis.
Bound by LithoCrafters, Inc.
in Holliston book cloth
and stamped in All Purpose foil.

Library of Congress Cataloging in Publication Data
BENNETT, BENJAMIN, 1939–
     Modern drama and German classicism.

     Includes index.
     1. German drama—18th century—History and
criticism.   2. German drama—History and criticism.
3. European drama—History and criticism.
I. Title.
PT636.B4   832'.6'09   79-14644
ISBN   0-8014-1189-0